Storyworlds in Short Narratives

Brill's Series on the Early Middle Ages

Managing Editor

Bonnie Effros (*University of British Columbia*)

Editorial Board

Lisa Bailey (*University of Auckland*)
Deborah Deliyannis (*Indiana University*)
Eduardo Manzano (*CCHS-CSIC Madrid*)
Walter Pohl (*Austrian Academy of Sciences*)
Edward Roberts (*University of Kent*)
Andrea Sterk (*University of Minnesota*)

VOLUME 31

The titles published in this series are listed at *brill.com/bsem*

Storyworlds in Short Narratives

Approaches to Late Antique and Early Byzantine Tales

Edited by

Stavroula Constantinou
Andria Andreou

BRILL

LEIDEN | BOSTON

This is an open access title distributed under the terms of the CC BY-NC-ND 4.0 license, which permits any non-commercial use, distribution, and reproduction in any medium, provided no alterations are made and the original author(s) and source are credited. Further information and the complete license text can be found at https://creativecommons.org/licenses/by-nc-nd/4.0/

The terms of the CC license apply only to the original material. The use of material from other sources (indicated by a reference) such as diagrams, illustrations, photos and text samples may require further permission from the respective copyright holder.

The publication of this volume was made possible thanks to funding from the Cyprus Foundation of Research and Innovation and the A.G. Leventis Foundation.

Cover illustration: Roman or Byzantine mosaic with a peacock and flowers, 3rd–4th century, Metropolitan Museum of Art. Available in the public domain.

The Library of Congress Cataloging-in-Publication Data is available online at https://catalog.loc.gov
LC record available at https://lccn.loc.gov/2024032319

Typeface for the Latin, Greek, and Cyrillic scripts: "Brill". See and download: brill.com/brill-typeface.

ISSN 1878-4879
ISBN 978-90-04-70733-7 (hardback)
ISBN 978-90-04-70735-1 (e-book)
DOI 10.1163/9789004707351

Copyright 2025 by Stavroula Constantinou and Andria Andreou. Published by Koninklijke Brill NV, Leiden, The Netherlands.
Koninklijke Brill BV incorporates the imprints Brill, Brill Nijhoff, Brill Schöningh, Brill Fink, Brill mentis, Brill Wageningen Academic, Vandenhoeck & Ruprecht, Böhlau and V&R unipress.
Koninklijke Brill NV reserves the right to protect this publication against unauthorized use.

This book is printed on acid-free paper and produced in a sustainable manner.

Contents

Preface VII
Notes on Editors and Contributors IX

Introduction 1
 Stavroula Constantinou and Andria Andreou

PART 1
Tale Theory and Poetics

1 The Art of the Short Narrative: Toward a Theory of the Late Antique and Byzantine Tale 13
 Stavroula Constantinou

2 Telling a *thauma* in Hagiography and Paradoxography 40
 Christian Høgel

3 To Render Unbelievable Tales Believable: The Storyworlds of Paradoxography 59
 Ingela Nilsson

PART 2
The Art of Storytelling

4 Didactic Tales in Galen 83
 Sophia Xenophontos

5 Repetition and the Storyteller's Profile in Early Byzantine Tale Collections 107
 Stavroula Constantinou and Andria Andreou

6 Circulation of Hagiographical Tales along the Incense Route: Storytelling as Technology of Enchantment 131
 Nicolò Sassi

PART 3
Tales in Collections

7 Stunning with a List, Dazzling with a Catalogue: The Form of
   Paradoxographical and Christian Miracle Collections Revisited   159
      Julia Doroszewska

8 (Auto)biographical, Marvelous, and Supernatural Stories in Early
   Byzantine Hagiographical Anthologies   192
      Stavroula Constantinou and Andria Andreou

9 Space in Edifying Stories: The Case of Anastasios Sinaites   221
      Markéta Kulhánková

   General Index   239

Preface

This volume emanates from a four-year research project entitled 'Storyworlds in Collections: Toward a Theory of the Ancient and Byzantine Tale (2nd–7th c. CE)' (2019–2022) that was funded by the European Regional Development Fund and the Republic of Cyprus through the Foundation of Research and Innovation (Project: Post-Doc/0718/0021) and the A.G. Leventis Foundation. This project and the present volume have five essential and strongly interconnected objectives: (1) to offer a first systematic approach to the early Greek tale; (2) to provide a theoretical framework for the study of the tale that could be also used for that of short fiction in general; (3) to bring to the fore similarities and differences between ancient and early Byzantine tales and in so doing to highlight the importance of undertaking comparative examinations between ancient and Byzantine literature; (4) to create new and, hopefully, significant knowledge in the fields of Classics, Byzantine Studies, and Literary Studies, which may prove useful for other disciplines, such as Philosophy, Cultural Studies, Folklore Studies, and Cognitive Studies; and finally (5) to use methodologies and approaches that create an interdisciplinary, comparative, connected, and collaborative project and volume.

The volume's chapters were developed from papers delivered in the framework of two scholarly events organized by the editors – a workshop and a conference – at the University of Cyprus in December 2020 and November 2021 respectively. Even though the two events had to adopt a hybrid mode due to the COVID-19 pandemic, they proved fruitful for allowing the contributors to develop their ideas and reach the results that have made this publication possible. As the volume's contents reveal, the tale is a dynamic and complex genre of short fiction inviting a rich array of critical responses. Divided into three parts (tale theory and poetics; stories, storytellers, and storytelling; and tales in collections), the volume's chapters discuss the theory and poetics of tales, the art of storytelling, inherent features of the tale, the arrangement of tales in collections, and the types and characteristics of tales incorporated in collections.

The chapter authors base their theoretical and comparative approaches on a rich variety of texts that are here discussed for the first time in the same volume. These include medical texts, paradoxography, martyr legends, and hagiographical collections and miscellanies including collective biographies, miracle collections, collections of beneficial tales, and *Apophthegmata Patrum*. This is also the first time that many different and often less studied ancient and early Byzantine writers have been brought together. These include Antigonos, Parthenios, Phlegon of Tralles, Galen, Herakleitos the Paradoxographer,

Pseudo-Alexander of Aphrodisias, Timothy of Alexandria, Palladios of Hellenopolis, John Moschos, Sophronios of Jerusalem, and Anastasios of Sinai. We hope that the fresh readings of these texts and authors that the volume provides will initiate more studies that will further illuminate not only the examined corpus, but also the characteristics and the importance of the genre of the tale.

The editors wish to thank all volume contributors. We are grateful to them for both their insightful and creative chapters and their keen response to and support of this project. We would also like to warmly thank Jane Burkowski for her admirable editorial work, Kate Hammond and Petra Stiglmayer at Brill for their guidance and help, and the volume's anonymous reviewers for their helpful and constructive comments. Our thanks go also to our institution, the University of Cyprus, and its Centre for Medieval Arts and Rituals for supporting the project's implementation and for hosting all its events.

Finally, we wish to express once again our sincere thanks and gratitude to the Cyprus Foundation of Research and Innovation and the A.G. Leventis Foundation that made this project possible. We shall also mention that some of the ideas that inform the volume's approach were developed in the framework of the project 'Network for Medieval Arts and Rituals' (NetMAR), which received funding from the European Union's Horizon 2020 research and innovation programme under grant agreement no. 951875. The opinions expressed in this document reflect only the authors' views and in no way reflect the European Commission's opinions. The European Commission is not responsible for any use that may be made of the information it contains.

Stavroula Constantinou and Andria Andreou
Nicosia, January 2024

Notes on Editors and Contributors

Andria Andreou
is a Postdoctoral Researcher at the Centre for Medieval Arts and Rituals of the University of Cyprus. Her research interests lie mainly with Byzantine hagiography, genre, and the orchestration of characters in Byzantine literature. Her current research focuses on the history, the evolution, and the interpretation of early Byzantine tales. Her recent publications explore the construction of the storyteller in Byzantine collections of tales and the history of the early Byzantine tale.

Stavroula Constantinou
is the Founder and Director of the Centre for Medieval Arts and Rituals at the University of Cyprus and the editor-in-chief of the diamond open access journal *Eventum: A Journal of Medieval Arts & Rituals* (https://riviste.unimi.it/index.php/eventum). She has been the coordinator of the European-funded twinning project 'Network for Medieval Arts and Rituals' (Horizon 2020; grant agreement no. 951875) and the principal investigator of two other projects ('Lactating Breasts: Motherhood and Breastfeeding in Antiquity and Byzantium' and 'Storyworlds in Collections: Toward a Theory of the Ancient and Early Byzantine Tale') funded by the European Regional Development Fund and the Republic of Cyprus through the Foundation of Research and Innovation and the University of Cyprus. Currently, she is coordinating the Marie Skłodowska Curie Doctoral Network project 'Storytelling as *Pharmakon* in Premodernity and Beyond: Training the New Generation of Researchers in Health Humanities' (Horizon Europe; grant agreement no. 101169114). She has written widely on hagiography, gender, emotions, and the body. Her recent and forthcoming publications look at tale-theory, the rituals of Byzantine motherhood, and the intersections between artistic expressions and rituals.

Julia Doroszewska
is a Research Fellow at the Faculty of History, University of Warsaw. Her research interests include imperial Greek and Latin prose, as well as late antique hagiography and ancient folklore. In her research on ancient mentalities, she combines literary studies with anthropological approaches (in particular the concept of liminality). She has published on Phlegon of Tralles, to whom she dedicated a monograph, Plutarch, and Apuleius. She is currently conducting two research projects: 'Epiphanies of the Saints in Late Antique Literature' and 'Thinking about Thinking: Conceptual Metaphors of Cognition in the Plutarchan Corpus'.

Christian Høgel

is Professor of Byzantine Literature at the University of Lund. He is also co-editor of the diamond open access journal *Interfaces: A Journal of Medieval Literature*. He has published widely on Byzantine hagiography, specializing in the field of *metaphrasis* (the rewriting of hagiography), but also on the early Greek translation of the Qur'an, and the concept of *humanitas* in ancient and medieval Latin authors. His books include *Symeon Metaphrastes: Rewriting and Canonization* (Copenhagen: 2002) and *The Human and the Humane: Humanitas as Argument from Cicero to Erasmus* (Göttingen: 2015).

Markéta Kulhánková

is a Senior Researcher at the Institute of Slavonic Studies of the Czech Academy of Sciences and Associate Professor in Classical Philology at the Centre for Early Medieval Studies, Masaryk University. Her research focuses mainly on Byzantine narrative, both in verse and in prose. She published a monograph entitled *Das gottgefällige Abenteuer: Eine narratologische Analyse der byzantinischen erbaulichen Erzählungen* (2015). She is also interested in the reception of Byzantium in modern culture and translates Byzantine and Modern Greek literature into Czech.

Ingela Nilsson

is Professor of Greek at Uppsala University specializing in Byzantine Greek literature. She is the principal investigator of a research programme entitled 'Retracing Connections: Byzantine Storyworlds in Greek, Arabic, Georgian, and Old Slavonic (*c.*950–*c.*1100)' (2020–2027). Her research interests concern processes of rewriting, storytelling, and narratology. Her recent publications include *Writer and Occasion in Twelfth-Century Byzantium: The Authorial Voice of Constantine Manasses* (Cambridge: 2021) and (ed. with Julie Hansen) *Critical Storytelling: Experiences of Power Abuse in Academia* (Leiden – Boston: 2022).

Nicolò Sassi

is Assistant Professor of Ancient and Medieval Christianity at Saint Louis University. His research focuses on the histories and literatures of the late ancient and medieval Christian East. To date, his publications have explored mystical texts in Byzantine Greek and Syriac (the *Corpus Areopagiticum* and Pseudo-Hierotheos' *Book of Secrets*), Coptic Gnostic literature from the Nag Hammadi library (*Trimorphic Protennoia*, NHC XIII.1), and medieval Ethiopian hagiography.

NOTES ON EDITORS AND CONTRIBUTORS

Sophia Xenophontos
is Associate Professor of Classics at the Aristotle University of Thessaloniki and Principal Investigator of the project 'The Physician of the Soul: Medicine and Practical Ethics in Galen', funded by the Wellcome Trust (UK). She is the author of *Ethical Education in Plutarch: Moralising Agents and Contexts* (Berlin – Boston: 2016), *Theodore Metochites' On Morals or Concerning Education: Introduction, Translation, and Notes* (Cambridge, MA – London: 2020), *Georgios Pachymeres, Commentary on Aristotle, Nicomachean Ethics: Critical Edition with Introduction and Translation* (with Crystal Addey, Berlin: 2022), *Galen, On Avoiding Distress, On My Own Opinions. Critical Edition and Translation* (with Ioannis Polemis, Berlin: 2023), and *Medicine and Practical Ethics in Galen* (Cambridge: 2024). Her publication record includes also several articles and book chapters on practical ethics, the therapy of the emotions, and the reception of the classsics in Byzantium. Xenophontos is the founder and editor-in-chief of the book series 'Theorising the Greek and Roman Classics' (Routledge, UK) and a member of Academia Europaea.

Introduction

Stavroula Constantinou and Andria Andreou

The tale, a short narrative of oral tradition having divine, human, and animal characters that often encounter marvelous, magical, and miraculous phenomena and objects, has not attracted much interest from classicists and medievalists, even though it was a popular genre in ancient and medieval cultures. Paradoxography, for instance, which is an important source of ancient tales focusing on the marvelous, 'has not been treated kindly by modern critics. The standard literary histories scarcely mention it, and when scholars do have occasion to refer to the genre, they give it poor reviews'.[1] Along similar lines, Graham Anderson has remarked: 'By so much as asking whether the ancient world had a Red Riding Hood [...], we enter an area of cultural history which has been almost entirely forgotten or ignored'.[2] More than twenty years later, Anderson's words are still valid, given that the first collected volume on the cultural history of ancient fairy tales appeared no earlier than 2021. Consequently, it will take some more time before the fairy and other tales of antiquity receive the research attention they deserve.[3]

Compared to ancient paradoxography, its Byzantine counterpart has not been studied at all, a fact that gives the wrong impression that the Byzantines did not appreciate paradoxography or that they did not produce any *mirabilia*.[4] Byzantine frame narrative, on the other hand, has recently received some critical attention.[5] The situation with the medieval Latin tradition, to mention a Western example, is even worse, since the entire literature is marginalized. As Jan Ziolkowski laments, despite its extremely large quantity, its quality, and its

---

1   Hansen W. (trans.), *Phlegon of Tralles' Book of Marvels* (Exeter: 1996) 9.

2   Anderson G., *Fairytale in the Ancient World* (London – New York: 2000) ix.

3   Felton D. (ed.), *A Cultural History of Fairy Tales in Antiquity* (London: 2021).

4   One important admirer of paradoxography was Patriarch Photios (858–867, 877–886), as attested by the considerable space he devotes to the genre in his *Library*. As for Byzantine *mirabilia*, they can be detected in works traditionally treated as hagiography, but also in chronicles and epistolography, among others. For *mirabilia* in hagiographical collections, see Chapter 8.

5   The few existing studies focus on frame narratives; see Toth I., "Fighting with Tales: The Byzantine *Book of Syntipas the Philosopher*", in Cupane C. – Krönung B. (eds.), *Fictional Storytelling in the Medieval Eastern Mediterranean and Beyond*, Brill's Companion to the Byzantine World 1 (Leiden – Boston: 2016) 380–400; Krönung B., "The Wisdom of the Beasts: The Arabic Book of *Kalīla and Dimna* and the Byzantine *Book of Stephanites and Ichnelates*", in Cupane – Krönung, *Fictional Storytelling* 427–460.

© STAVROULA CONSTANTINOU AND ANDRIA ANDREOU, 2025 | DOI:10.1163/9789004707351_002

This is an open access chapter distributed under the terms of the CC BY-NC-ND 4.0 license.

importance, 'medieval Latin in comparison with the medieval vernacular literatures remains unappreciated'.[6] Lastly, medieval Arabic tales, except for those belonging to the tradition of *Arabian Nights* and that of *Kalīla wa Dimna*,[7] are also depreciated in modern Western scholarship.[8]

As for tale sources that have attracted scholarly interest, they have been treated as devoid of aesthetic value. For instance, the *Apophthegmata Patrum*, a popular source of early Christian tales that were circulating in different languages including Greek, Coptic, Syriac, Arabic, and Latin, have been characterized as a 'material' with 'little literary artifice'.[9] Apart from a few exceptions,[10] the Byzantine tale collections *par excellence* – the miracle and edifying story collections – have been mostly treated as sources for the history of pilgrimage and monasticism and not as literary works.[11] Not surprisingly, beneficial stories are rarely studied from a literary perspective, since even specialists treat them in a derogatory manner.[12]

---

6   Ziolkowski J.M., "Towards a History of Medieval Latin Literature", in Mantello F.A.C. – Rigg A.G. (eds.), *Medieval Latin: An Introduction and Biographical Guide* (Washington, DC: 1996) 505–536, at 505. For one of the very few studies on Latin tales, see idem, *Fairy Tales from before Fairy Tales: The Medieval Latin Past of Wonderful Lies* (Ann Arbor: 2007).

7   Chraibi A., *Les mille et une nuits: Histoire de texte et classification des contes* (Paris: 2008); Chraibi A. – Ramirez C., *Les mille et une nuits et le récit oriental en Espagne et en Occident* (Paris: 2009).

8   Monroe J., *The Art of Badīʿ Az-Zamān Al-Hamadhānī as Picaresque Narrative* (Beirut: 1983).

9   Ward B., "Introduction", in Ward B. – Russell N. (eds.), *The Lives of the Desert Fathers*, Cistercian Studies 34 (Kalamazoo, MI: 1980) 1–46, at 3.

10   These exceptions include the following studies: Cain A., *The Greek Historia Monachorum in Aegypto* (Oxford: 2016); Constantinou S., "Grotesque Bodies in Hagiographical Tales: The Monstrous and the Uncanny in Byzantine Collections of Miracle Stories", *Dumbarton Oaks Papers* 64 (2010) 43–54; eadem, "Healing Dreams in Early Byzantine Miracle Collections", in Oberhelman S. (ed.), *Dreams, Healing, and Medicine in Greece: From Antiquity to the Present* (Aldershot: 2013) 189–198; eadem, "The Morphology of Healing Dreams: Dream and Therapy in Byzantine Collections of Miracle Stories", in Angelidi C. – Calofonos G. (eds.), *Dreaming in Byzantium and Beyond* (Aldershot: 2014) 21–34; Johnson S.F., *The Life and Miracles of Thekla: A Literary Study*, Hellenic Studies 13 (Cambridge, MA – London: 2006); Ivanov S. (ed.), *Spiritually Beneficial Tales in Byzantine and Slavic Literature*, Special Issue, *Scripta* 8/9 (2010); Kulhánková, M. *Das gottgefällige Abenteuer: Eine narratologische Analyse der byzantinischen erbaulichen Erzählungen* (Červený Kostelec: 2015).

11   See, for example, Talbot A.-M., "Pilgrimage to Healing Shrines: The Evidence of Miracle Accounts", *Dumbarton Oaks Papers* 56 (2002) 153–173; Krueger D., "Between Monks: Tales of Monastic Companionship in Early Byzantium", *Journal of the History of Sexuality* 20.1 (2011) 28–61.

12   See, Binggeli A., "Collections of Edifying Stories", in Efthymiadis S. (ed.), *The Ashgate Research Companion to Byzantine Hagiography*, vol. 2: *Genres and Contexts* (Farnham: 2014) 143–159, at 143. An exception is a special issue of *Scripta & E-Scripta* 8/9 (2010) on beneficial tales in Byzantine and Slavic literature which was edited by Sergey Ivanov.

INTRODUCTION

Turning to literary studies, we realize that, as for the current state of scholarship on modern and contemporary fiction,[13] the novel is the main source for classical and medieval fiction studies. According to Tim Whitmarsh, the ancient novel has attracted so much interest in the last two or three decades because it 'embodies the spirit of (post-) modernity better than any other ancient form'.[14] A medievalist, Roberta Krueger, who is the editor of *The Cambridge Companion to Medieval Romance*, has similarly remarked that 'medieval romance narratives astound the reader [...]. These fictions continue to intrigue modern audiences [...] by the diversity of their forms and subject matter, the complexity of their narrative strategies and perspectives, and the many critical responses they invite'.[15] But, as the contents of this volume amply demonstrate, such statements are just as valid for ancient and later short fiction. Obviously, the exclusion of the tale from discussions on ancient and medieval fiction is quite problematic, as it creates a false understanding of the narrative forms and characteristics of these fictions.

The situation is not much different for later and modern short fiction. As Sarah Copland emphatically remarks, 'with narrative theory embracing [...] fields as diverse as medicine and law, and at the same time engaging with a much broader corpus of narrative "texts", it has long puzzled me that no work has been published on the relationship between narrative theory and [...] the short story'.[16] The fact that there are no significant narrative theories devoted to the short story becomes even more puzzling when one thinks of the large production of short fiction, on the one hand, and of the short stories written by renowned authors, such as Miguel de Cervantes (1547–1616), Walter Scott (1771–1832), James Joyce (1882–1941), and Jorge Luis Borges (1899–1986), on the other. As the American author George Garrett (1929–2008) has put it, it is 'strange that so many of our best writers coming along, in schools and out, do their best work in the short story form. Strange that the short story has not managed to capture and keep its rightful place'.[17]

In fact, there are a few theoretical works that are based on short fiction: Tzvetan Todorov's study of Boccaccio's *Decameron* and Roland Barthes'

---

13   For the centrality of the novel in contemporary narrative studies and the lack of interest in short fiction, see, e.g., Copland S., "To Be Continued: The Story of the Short Story Theory and Other Narrative Theory", *Narrative* 22.1 (2014) 132–149.

14   Whitmarsh T., "Introduction", in idem (ed.), *The Cambridge Companion to the Greek and Roman Novel* (Cambridge: 2008) 1–14, at 1.

15   Krueger R.L., "Introduction", in eadem (ed.), *The Cambridge Companion to Medieval Romance* (Cambridge: 2000) 1–9, at 1.

16   Copland, "To Be Continued" 132.

17   In May C., *The Short Story: The Reality of an Artifice* (New York: 1995).

analysis of "Sarrasine".[18] One could also mention the works of Vladimir Propp and Claude Bremond on the fairy tale.[19] It must be pointed out, however, that these theorists' use of short fiction has to do either with their structuralist methods' easier applicability or their interest in folklore and not with any intention of developing a short fiction theory. In general, the terms 'narrative' and 'fiction' are reserved for the novel. This is not only because the novel is the dominant narrative genre, but also because most narratologists and theorists do not draw a distinction between the novel and the short story. For them, both short and long stories are narratives with the same features: a beginning, middle, and an end, characters, place, time, and events. Surprisingly, even the narratologists and critics who acknowledge the existence and even the importance of narrative forms other than the novel do not pay any serious attention to them. A case in point is Northop Frye, who, even though he notes that the identification of fiction with the novel is erroneous, does not undertake a systematic analysis of any short literary form.[20]

Short narrative's absence from modern narratology, despite its centrality to understanding fiction, prevents theorists from providing a more sufficient analysis of the workings of different forms of narratives. Based solely on the novel and its elements, narratologists examine the development of the beginning-middle-and-end plot, its characters, their perspectives and actions in time and space, in an attempt to figure out how the sequences of events determine the story's form and structure. Of course, such plot-centered approaches are very useful and offer interesting insights into many novels, but they prove ineffective when it comes to short fiction.

Unlike the novel, short fiction mostly does not follow any integral laws about character, credibility, and plot structure. Anton Chekhov's (1860–1904) short stories and those of his followers, for example, exhibit a randomness, inexplicability, and open-endedness that cancel all narrative rules detected by narratologists.[21] In sum, short fiction cannot be theorized in the same way as long narratives such as the novel and biography that have a mimetic mode of temporal development. It is, therefore, essential to produce a new narratological theory that will be inspired by the particular nature of short fiction and will

---

18 Todorov T., *Grammaire du Décaméron*, Approaches to Semiotics 3 (The Hague: 1969); Barthes R., *S/Z* (Paris: 1970).

19 Propp V., *Morphology of the Folktale*, trans. L. Scott, Indiana University Research Centre in Anthropology, Folklore, and Linguistics 10 (Austin, TX: 1968); Bremond C., *La logique du récit* (Paris: 1973).

20 Frye N., *Anatomy of Criticism: Four Essays* (Princeton: 1957) 303.

21 Shcherbenok A., "'Killing Realism': Insight and Meaning in Anton Chekhov", *Slavic and East European Journal* 54.2 (2010) 297–316.

INTRODUCTION 5

be used alongside the narrative theories deriving from the study of long fictions. A narratological theory emanating from short fiction could provide an invaluable tool for both narratologists and scholars studying short narrative forms, such as the early (Greek) tale (first–seventh century) that is the subject of the present volume.

By examining the early Greek tale, this volume not only provides the first systematic study of an important premodern genre, but also fills a gap in ancient and Byzantine narrative studies. The volume's nine chapters are organized around three interconnected parts – "Tale Theory and Poetics"; "The Art of Storytelling", and "Tales in Collections" – each consisting of three chapters. Part 1 constitutes a first attempt to provide a theoretical framework for the study of the early tale. In Chapter 1, with the title "The Art of Short Narrative: Toward a Theory of the Late Antique and Byzantine Tale", Stavroula Constantinou develops a tale theory which revolves around the three interdependent constituents of the tale that determine its form, meaning, function, and power: the storyteller, (inter)storyness, and story-effect. Even though Constantinou's examples derive mostly from early Byzantine hagiography, her tale theory could be used to analyze both earlier and later tales detected in different types of tale collections and texts.

In Chapter 2, entitled "Telling a *Thauma* in Hagiography and Paradoxography", Christian Høgel deals with an essential characteristic of the early tale's poetics: *thauma*, which in paradoxography is called 'the marvelous' while in hagiography it is named 'the miraculous'. Whether representing the marvelous or the miraculous, *thauma* serves the same purposes: to evoke a sense of wonder due to the transgression of physical laws, the distinction between agent and source, and the suddenness with which it takes place; and to encourage readers and listeners to compare and evaluate its reality as a marvelous (in paradoxography) or miraculous (in hagiography) event.

In Chapter 3 ("To Render Unbelievable Tales Believable: The Storyworlds of Paradoxography"), Ingela Nilsson introduces the term 'storyworld' to refer to the material of the tales included in paradoxography. As Nilsson shows, the tales' storyworlds have the power to make unbelievable phenomena believable. Despite their extreme brevity – or thanks to it – smaller tales incorporated into paradoxographical collections have whole storyworlds in which audiences are immersed. What makes these storyworlds attractive and thus believable is their worldedness – a combination of connections and similarities with the audiences' actual world. It is through their worldedness that storyworlds become what Nilsson calls 'possible worlds', namely worlds that can be treated as acceptable by readers or listeners who share common rules of causality and verisimilitude.

Part 2 focuses on the storytelling act, examining the storyteller's role, art, and impact on a tale's audiences. In Chapter 4, entitled "Didactic Tales in Galen", Sophia Xenophontos analyzes a particular kind of storyteller and his workings: the medical author and practitioner as personified by the most significant and influential author-physician of antiquity, Galen of Pergamum (AD 129–c.216), who was also an important philosopher of his times. Using both his medical and philosophical knowledge, Galen emerges as a unique and highly original storyteller. Galen's didactic tales, which are an integral part of his innumerable writings, are specially designed to achieve two important aims: to strengthen the storyteller's authority in the fields of medicine and practical ethics; and to have a great didactic and emotional impact upon his audiences whose perspectives and expectations are met. Galen's authority as a storyteller and his works' effects are also achieved through a sequence of storytelling strategies, transforming his otherwise technical and scientific texts into influential and appealing works.

In Chapter 5, with the title "Repetition and the Storyteller's Profile in Early Byzantine Tale Collections", Constantinou and Andria Andreou discuss how the use of rhetorical and narrative devices such as repetition may determine the storyteller's profile, thus proving once again the strong interconnection between storytelling and storyness as defined in Chapter 1. Examining tales incorporated into early Byzantine anthologies covering a period from the fifth to the seventh century, the chapter's authors detect three different storytelling profiles that emerge through the employment of triple repetitions, both on a stylistic and a narrative level. These are the holy, the chosen, and the repentant storyteller. Contrary to the general idea that repetition is boring and unoriginal, Constantinou and Andreou show that repetition creates storytellers and tales that are fresh, exciting, and original.

The audience's wonder as the result of the storyteller's art and storyness might also be associated with what Nicolò Sassi calls the 'technology of enchantment' (Chapter 6: "Circulation of Hagiographical Tales along the Incense Route: Storytelling as Technology of Enchantment"). According to Sassi, the technology of enchantment is related to the ways in which hagiographical tales, which travel along the Incense Route, are adapted and readapted to connect the worldly with the otherworldly, inviting their audiences to approach life as a reality inhabited by the sacred. These enchanting – or wonder-ful, we might say – tales transformed the audiences' vision and experience of the world, rendering their daily spaces enchanted. The shrine of Menas and the city of Lydda, for instance, were perceived not as intermediary stops on a traveler's way from one place to another, but as sacred spaces where the inaccessible divine became accessible.

INTRODUCTION

The volume's last part concentrates on tales in collections, as anthologies are the most common and rich sources of early tales. Focusing on the stylistic device of the catalogue in paradoxography and early Byzantine hagiography, Julia Doroszewska, the author of Chapter 7 ("Stunning with a List, Dazzling with a Catalogue: The Form of Paradoxographical and Christian Miracle Collections Revisited"), illustrates the device's imaginative employment and its authorial implications. Doroszewska, whose approach is inspired by Umberto Eco's book *La vertigine della lista* (*The Infinity of Lists*, 2009), shows how paradoxographers and hagiographers use the catalogue to achieve a threefold purpose: to present marvelous and miraculous phenomena; to organize the rich and infinite contents of their collective works; and to bring their audiences closer to the essence of the marvelous and the miraculous. Following Eco, Doroszewska suggests that the dizziness produced by the catalogue and its repeated employment constitutes a symptom of anxiety before innumerable facts that authors are unable to reduce to a common denominator. At the same time, such a plain thing as the catalogue is endowed with an immense and startling power that renders both a collection and its individual tales enchanting.

According to Chapter 8 ("(Auto)biographical, Marvelous, and Supernatural Stories in Early Byzantine Hagiographical Anthologies"), the primary structural unit of the tale is the episode that is initiated and driven forward by the story's agent, who is also responsible for a tale's form and general structure. As Constantinou and Andreou show, three important types of agents include the human, the marvelous, and the supernatural agent. These agents create, in turn, the three corresponding tale categories that are included in early Byzantine collections: the (auto)biographical, the marvelous, and the supernatural tale. Each tale category might have one of the following structures: single-episode, multiple-episode, or frame structure.

As the last chapter of the volume, Chapter 9 ("Space in Edifying Stories: The Case of Anastasios Sinaites"), reminds us, however, there are also other elements that might be important in a particular tale or collection of tales. One such element is space, which, even though it is not expected to play a role in narratives that are short and dense – normally space is essential in long narratives – might have a number of functions, and thus significantly contribute to the overall effect of a tale or tale collection. Markéta Kulhánková unearths the construction and uses of space in Anastasios Sinaites' (*c.*630–701) first collection of tales. She suggests that the uniqueness of this work lies in the ways in which the author manipulates space, both on the micro level of individual tales and on the macro level of the tales' arrangement in the collection.

Far from being exhaustive, this volume nonetheless makes a case for the marginalized genre of the Greek tale, offering significant tools for approaching it. The volume's chapters analyze important elements that exist for the sake of the tale: its origin and circulation through telling and retelling, its forms and characteristics, and its power and impact. By providing a first theoretical framework for the study of the tale and by examining comparatively works that have not been considered (together) before, the volume contributors have created new knowledge in the fields of Classics, Byzantine Studies, and Literary Studies, which may prove useful for other disciplines, such as Philosophy, Cultural Studies, Folklore Studies, and Cognitive Studies.

All in all, this is an interdisciplinary, comparative, connected, and collaborative volume aiming to promote the establishment of the tale as an important literary form that needs to be moved from the margins into the center of ancient and Byzantine literary studies. In fact, more critical approaches to the early tale will allow a holistic understanding of ancient and Byzantine narrative literature, which now is only partial, as thus far scholars have almost exclusively studied the long narrative forms. Hopefully, the volume will initiate a number of other studies through which the importance of the old tale will be further established. Such projects concern the study of the later Byzantine tale and that of other medieval traditions (e.g., Latin, Arabic, Jewish, Slavic, and Western vernacular literary production) that could also be comparatively examined. The establishment of the cultural and critical history of the premodern tale will prove useful also for scholars of contemporary short fictions – particularly short story scholars who consider Edgar Allan Poe (1809–1849) as the originator of the genre.[22]

Bibliography

Anderson G., *Fairytale in the Ancient World* (London – New York: 2000).

Barthes R., *S/Z* (Paris: 1970).

Binggeli A., "Collections of Edifying Stories", in Efthymiadis S. (ed.), *The Ashgate Research Companion to Byzantine Hagiography*, vol. 2: *Genres and Contexts* (Farnham: 2014) 143–159.

Bremond C., *La logique du récit* (Paris: 1973).

Cain A., *The Greek Historia Monachorum in Aegypto* (Oxford: 2016).

Chraibi A., *Les mille et une nuits: Histoire de texte et classification des contes* (Paris: 2008).

---

22 Lohafer S., "Short Story", in Herman D. – Jahn M. – Ryan M.-L. (eds.), *Routledge Encyclopedia of Narrative Theory* (New York – London: 2005) 528–530.

Chraibi A. – Ramirez C., *Les mille et une nuits et le récit oriental en Espagne et en Occident* (Paris: 2009).

Constantinou S., "Grotesque Bodies in Hagiographical Tales: The Monstrous and the Uncanny in Byzantine Collections of Miracle Stories", *Dumbarton Oaks Papers* 64 (2010) 43–54.

Constantinou S., "Healing Dreams in Early Byzantine Miracle Collections", in Oberhelman S. (ed.), *Dreams, Healing, and Medicine in Greece: From Antiquity to the Present* (Aldershot: 2013) 189–197.

Constantinou S., "The Morphology of Healing Dreams: Dream and Therapy in Byzantine Collections of Miracle Stories", in Angelidi C. – Calofonos G. (eds.), *Dreaming in Byzantium and Beyond* (Aldershot: 2014) 21–34.

Copland S., "To Be Continued: The Story of the Short Story Theory and Other Narrative Theory", *Narrative* 22.1 (2014) 132–149.

Felton D. (ed.), *A Cultural History of Fairy Tales in Antiquity* (London: 2021).

Frye N., *Anatomy of Criticism: Four Essays* (Princeton: 1957).

Hansen W. (trans.), *Phlegon of Tralles' Book of Marvels* (Exeter: 1996).

Ivanov S. (ed.), *Spiritually Beneficial Tales in Byzantine and Slavic Literature*, Special Issue, *Scripta* 8/9 (2010).

Johnson S.F., *The Life and Miracles of Thekla: A Literary Study*, Hellenic Studies 13 (Cambridge, MA – London: 2006).

Krönung B., "The Wisdom of the Beasts: The Arabic Book of *Kalīla and Dimna* and the Byzantine *Book of Stephanites and Ichnelates*", in Cupane C. – Krönung B. (eds.), *Fictional Storytelling in the Medieval Eastern Mediterranean and Beyond*, Brill's Companion to the Byzantine World 1 (Leiden – Boston: 2016) 427–460.

Krueger D., "Between Monks: Tales of Monastic Companionship in Early Byzantium", *Journal of the History of Sexuality* 20.1 (2011) 28–61.

Krueger R.L., "Introduction", in Krueger R.L. (ed.), *The Cambridge Companion to Medieval Romance* (Cambridge: 2000) 1–9.

Kulhánková M., *Das gottgefällige Abenteuer: Eine narratologische Analyse der byzantinischen erbaulichen Erzählungen* (Červený Kostelec: 2015).

Lohafer S., "Short Story", in Herman D. – Jahn M. – Ryan M.-L. (eds.), *Routledge Encyclopedia of Narrative Theory* (New York – London: 2005) 528–530.

May C., *The Short Story: The Reality of an Artifice* (New York: 1995).

Monroe J., *The Art of Badīʿ Az-Zamān Al-Hamadhānī as Picaresque Narrative* (Beirut: 1983).

Propp V., *Morphology of the Folktale*, trans. L. Scott, Indiana University Research Centre in Anthropology, Folklore, and Linguistics 10 (Austin, TX: 1968).

Shcherbenok A., "'Killing Realism': Insight and Meaning in Anton Chekhov", *Slavic and East European Journal* 54.2 (2010) 297–316.

Talbot A.-M., "Pilgrimage to Healing Shrines: The Evidence of Miracle Accounts", *Dumbarton Oaks Papers* 56 (2002) 153–173.

Todorov T., *Grammaire du Décaméron*, Approaches to Semiotics 3 (The Hague: 1969).

Toth I., "Fighting with Tales: The Byzantine *Book of Syntipas the Philosopher*", in Cupane C. – Krönung B. (eds.), *Fictional Storytelling in the Medieval Eastern Mediterranean and Beyond*, Brill's Companion to the Byzantine World 1 (Leiden – Boston: 2016) 380–400.

Ward B., "Introduction", in Ward B. – Russell N. (eds.), *The Lives of the Desert Fathers*, Cistercian Studies 34 (Kalamazoo, MI: 1980) 1–46.

Whitmarsh T., "Introduction", in Whitmarsh T. (ed.), *The Cambridge Companion to the Greek and Roman Novel* (Cambridge: 2008) 1–14.

Ziolkowski J.M., "Towards a History of Medieval Latin Literature", in Mantello F.A.C. – Rigg A.G. (eds.), *Medieval Latin: An Introduction and Bibliographical Guide* (Washington, DC: 1996) 505–536.

Ziolkowski J.M., *Fairy Tales from before Fairy Tales: The Medieval Latin Past of Wonderful Lies* (Ann Arbor: 2007).

PART 1

Tale Theory and Poetics

∴

CHAPTER 1

The Art of the Short Narrative: Toward a Theory of the Late Antique and Byzantine Tale

Stavroula Constantinou

As C.S. Lewis (1898–1963) has noted in his essay "On Stories" (1960), in the novel the story 'exists merely as a means to something else', whereas in short fiction it is 'everything else [that] is there for the sake of the story'.[1] Although a number of short story scholars and later critics have agreed with Lewis about the story's significance for short fiction, with the exceptions of Susan Lohafer's work on storyness and that of John Gerlach, which focuses on preclosure and closure,[2] there are no other book-length studies dealing with any aspects of the story.[3] In other words, there is a need to produce a theoretical work on short fiction that will be the equivalent of that on long fiction. For instance, the short fiction theoretical counterpart of Peter Brooks' famous book *Reading for the Plot* (1984) could have been titled *Reading for the Story*.

As the title of his book suggests, Brooks is interested in plot, the novel's essence, which 'develops its propositions only through temporal sequence and progression'.[4] Obviously, the narrative theory suggested here is at odds with that of Brooks, who looks at 'the temporal dynamics that shape narratives in our reading of them, the play of desire and time that makes us turn the pages

---

1 Lewis C.S., "On Stories", in idem (ed.), *Essays Presented to Charles Williams* (Grand Rapids, MI: 1966) 90–105, at 90.
   The research for this chapter was co-funded by the European Regional Development Fund and the Republic of Cyprus through the Foundation of Research and Innovation (Project: Post-Doc/0718/0021), as well as by the A.G. Leventis Foundation. Some of the ideas that inform the chapter's arguments were developed in the framework of the project 'Network for Medieval Arts and Rituals' (NetMAR), which received funding from the European Union's Horizon 2020 research and innovation programme under grant agreement no. 951875. The opinions expressed in this document reflect only the author's view and in no way reflect the European Commission's opinions. The European Commission is not responsible for any use that may be made of the information it contains.

2 Lohafer S., *Coming to Terms with the Short Story* (Baton Rouge – London: 1983) and eadem, *Reading for Storyness: Preclosure Theory, Empirical Poetics and Culture in the Short Story* (Baltimore: 2003); Gerlach J., *Toward the End: Closure and Structure in the American Short Story* (Tuscaloosa: 1985).

3 Lohafer's notion of storyness is further discussed below.

4 Brooks P., *Reading for the Plot: Design and Intention in Narrative* (Cambridge, MA: 1984) xi.

© STAVROULA CONSTANTINOU, 2025 | DOI:10.1163/9789004707351_003

This is an open access chapter distributed under the terms of the CC BY-NC-ND 4.0 license.

and strive toward narrative ends'.[5] He is searching for 'the motor forces that drive the text forward, of the desires that connect narrative ends and beginnings and make of the textual middle a highly charged field of force'.[6] In tales, in contrast, time and the causal processes of events are annihilated. While reading a tale, readers have the desire not to turn the page, but rather to pause to absorb the tale's strangeness, ambiguity, and incomprehensibility, as well as to fill in the numerous lacunae that result from its shortness. The readers or listeners of tales are invited to reflect on the 'single bizarre occurrence of epiphany and terror' and to decode their allegories so that they can understand their significance.[7]

In an attempt to approach the (early) tale, one should take into account the three essential elements determining its circulation, form, meaning, function, and power: the storyteller, storyness, and story-effect. As the terms themselves suggest, the storyteller is the individual transmitting a tale, the *addresser* in Roman Jakobson's communication model. Storyness concerns what makes the tale a tale, namely its integral devices that create the form and meaning of the *addresser's message* in the Jakobsonian model – being supplemented by *context* (the setting or the reason for the *message*'s communication), *contact* (the connection between *addresser* and *addressee*), and *code* (the use of common language).[8] Finally, story-effect refers to the tale's impacts on its different audiences, the Jakobsonian *addressees* of the *message*.[9]

This chapter is thus organized according to this tripartite tale theory. It is divided into three parts according to the constituent on which each lays its focus: the storyteller, storyness, and story-effect. It should be pointed out, however, that the unavoidable interdependency of the tale's three components is so strong that it is impossible to talk about one without taking into consideration the others. Furthermore, the lines between the three tale ingredients are not always clear. As the following discussion will show, the fictional storyteller and audience can sometimes be seen as parts of storyness, particularly in cases when the storyteller and story-listener are also heroes of the tale. Elements of

---

5 Ibidem, xiii.

6 Ibidem, xiii–xiv.

7 Eagleton T., *Heathcliff and the Great Hunger: Studies in Irish Culture* (London – New York: 1995) 150.

8 Even though the *context, contact,* and *code* of the Jakobsonian model cannot be much discussed here, they are essential for achieving a better understanding of the cultural history of the early Greek tale. A discussion about the cultural work and codes of tales circulating along the Incense Route is found in Chapter 6 of this volume.

9 Jakobson R., "Closing Statement: Linguistics and Poetics", in Sebeok T.A. (ed.), *Style in Language* (Cambridge, MA: 1960) 350–449.

THE ART OF THE SHORT NARRATIVE 15

storyness, such as repetition and humor, on the other hand, are at times used for the construction of the storyteller's and the story-listener's profile.

1   Storyteller

With its roots firmly based in orality, the tale cannot exist without the storyteller, the person who passes it on to others. The storyteller, who is generally a man, might tell a story of personal experience or circulate a tale that he has heard from someone else. When presenting the story of the miraculous cure he receives from saints Kyros and John, Sophronios of Jerusalem (634–638), for example, assumes his storytelling role thus:

> I become a grateful promulgator of the saints and I am going to add to what I have told so far what has happened to me. [...] I am also going to give my name, city, homeland, and the monastic community where I have been nurtured and formed up according to God's will. [I am going to talk] about my eye disease and the divine visit of the saints.
>
> γιγνόμεθα ἁγίων εὐγνώμονες κήρυκες, καὶ τὰ καθ' ἑαυτοὺς τοῖς προλεχθεῖσιν ἐπάγωμεν· [...] λέξωμεν δὲ καὶ ὄνομα, καὶ πόλιν, καὶ πατρίδα, καὶ φροντιστή-ριον, ὅθεν τε ἔφυμεν καὶ ὅπη Θεοῦ βουληθέντος ἐτάχθημεν, καὶ ἐπὶ τούτοις ὀφθαλμῶν τὴν ἀσθένειαν, καὶ τὴν θείαν τῶν ἁγίων ἐπίσκεψιν.[10]

Like Sophronios, most storytellers sharing an autobiographical tale or the story of someone they have met before do provide some information about themselves. They give their name, origin, profession, or religious vocation. They might also describe their bodily and emotional situation, especially when they suffer from some incurable disease, as is the case with Sophronios, or when they find themselves in difficult situations, like Thekla's hagiographer who is excommunicated by a local bishop, as shown in Chapter 8.

The storytellers telling stories which appear to have a long-term oral circulation, in contrast, are mostly anonymous and give no personal information. With such storytellers anyone who undertakes to tell these stories to

---

10   Sophronios of Jerusalem, *Miracles of Kyros and John* (BHG 477–479), ch. 70, 23–28, ed. N.F. Marcos, *Los 'Thaumata' de Sofronio: Contribución al estudio de la 'incubatio' cristiana* (Madrid: 1975). Unless otherwise indicated, translations are my own. For a commentary on the text see also the translation by J. Gascou, *Miracles des saints Cyr et Jean* (BHG 477–479) (Paris: 2006).

different audiences throughout the centuries may identify. Unidentified storytellers populate, for instance, the anonymous collection of the *Apophthegmata Patrum* that includes stories which are committed to writing after decades or even centuries of oral transmission, and as a result of this long process the first storyteller's identity is forgotten, while no subsequent storytellers consider it necessary to talk about themselves. In many stories of the anonymous *Apophthegmata Patrum*, the storyteller is introduced with the following stereotypical phrase: 'someone recounted that [...]' (Διηγήσατό τις ὅτι [...]), suggesting that this someone might be anyone undertaking to retell the tale that follows.[11]

The storytellers, who are also authors producing tale collections to save important stories from oblivion and to benefit wider audiences, both contemporary and later, might have to undertake long and tiring journeys to find material for their works. This material is provided by other storytellers whom the storyteller-authors consider pious and trustworthy sources of tales. As Palladios (363–431) writes, for instance, in his *Lausiac History* (c.419), 'I would make a journey of thirty days, or twice that, and covered on foot, God help me, the whole land of the Romans, and I accepted the hardship of travel gladly in order to meet a man full of the love of God and to gain what I lacked' (ἀλλὰ καὶ τριάκοντα ἡμερῶν καὶ δὶς τοσούτων ὁδὸν ἐξανύσας, ὡς ἐπὶ θεοῦ πεζῇ τῇ πορείᾳ πατήσας πᾶσαν τὴν γῆν ῥωμαίων, ἠσμένισα τὴν κακουχίαν τῆς ὁδοιπορίας ἐπὶ συντυχίᾳ ἀνδρὸς φιλοθέου, ἵνα κερδήσω ὅπερ οὐκ εἶχον).[12] Storytellers, as is the case with Palladios, might also find some of their stories in written sources that they consider equally valid and reliable.[13]

The storyteller has attracted some interest from narratologists, who have been influenced by cognitive linguistics and discourse analysis. Monika Fludernik, for instance, has focused on conversational storytelling as a remarkable form of narrative in and of itself and as an archetype of all narration.[14] However, she is interested in narrative structures as they have developed from oral storytelling to the realistic novel and beyond, and not in storytelling as an inherent feature of short fiction. In fact, like most narratologists, Fludernik

---

11   *Sayings of the Desert Fathers* (*Apophthegmata Patrum*; Anonymous Collection) ch. 37, ed. and trans. J. Wortley, *The Anonymous Sayings of the Desert Fathers: A Select Edition and Complete English Translation* (Cambridge: 2013) 31.

12   Palladios of Hellenopolis, *Lausiac History*, Prologue, p. 11.5–10, ed. D.C. Butler, *The Lausiac History of Palladius*, vol. 2: *Introduction and Text* (Cambridge: 1904) 1–169; trans. R.T. Meyer, *Palladius: The Lausiac History, Translated and Annotated*, Ancient Christian Writers 34 (New York: 1964) 24.

13   Meyer, *Palladius* 7.

14   Fludernik M., *Towards a 'Natural' Narratology* (London – New York: 1996).

THE ART OF THE SHORT NARRATIVE   17

does not draw a distinction between the narrative qualities of long and short fiction. She sees both as canonical literary narratives with the same features, which, as she suggests, should be approached in the context of the narrative properties of oral non-literary genres.

A theoretical approach to the storyteller and the nature of storytelling that is relevant here is that of the German philosopher Walter Benjamin, as described in his famous essay "Der Erzähler: Betrachtungen zum Werk Nikolai Lesskows" (1936/7).[15] Benjamin presents the storyteller as the man who tells and retells stories that he collects from traveling and local lore. The storyteller talks from experience, both his own and that of others, and turns this very experience into that of his listeners. In short, the storyteller, who might be the hero, listener, or reader of the stories he shares, is a teacher and sage who advises and edifies others. Storytelling is thus an act of generosity, and as such it appears eminently suitable for Christian storytellers – most of the storytellers examined here – for whom philanthropy is a major virtue.

In his attempt to share various remarkable experiences, the ancient and Byzantine storyteller instills the story with his presence from the outset. Often the storyteller starts by explaining how he has gained access to the tale he is about to tell, adding some information about his storytelling sources. For example, John Moschos (d. 619) introduces a tale in his *Spiritual Meadow* by saying: 'Abba Gregory, a former member of the Imperial Guard, told us of a brother of the Community of Choziba who [...]' ('Ὁ ἀββᾶς Γρηγόριος ὁ ἀπὸ Σχολαρίων, ἔλεγεν ἡμῖν ὅτι ἦν τις ἀδελφὸς ἐν τῷ κοινοβίῳ τοῦ Χουζιβᾶ, ὃς [...]).[16] The source of Moschos' tale having as its hero a nameless monk at the Choziba monastery in Palestine is the abbot of the monastery, Gregory, who used to be an imperial official and who at some point, as the storytelling voice of Moschos informs us a bit later, became bishop in Caesarea in Palestine. It is, therefore, more important to name the tale's source rather than the tale's hero, as it is the authority of the source (an abbot and bishop famous for his exemplarity) that guarantees the truthfulness and the didactic character of the story.

---

15   Benjamin W., "The Storyteller: Reflections on the Works of Nikolai Leskov", in idem, *Illuminations: Essays and Reflections*, ed. H. Arendt, trans. H. Zohn (New York: 1969) 83–109.

16   John Moschos, *Spiritual Meadow* (BHG 1440f–1442z), ed. in *Patrologia Graeca* (PG) 87.3:2852–3112, ch. 25.2869; trans. J. Wortley, *John Moschus: The Spiritual Meadow*, Cistercian Studies 139 (Kalamazoo, MI: 1992) 17. See also the translation by R. Maisano, *Il Prato Giovanni Mosco: Presentazione, traduzione e commento* (Naples: 1982) and by V. Déroche – C. Bouchet – M.H. Congourdeau, *Fioretti des moines d' Orient: Jean Moschos*, Le pré spirituel, Les Pères dans la foi 94–95 (Paris: 2006).

There are also cases in which the storyteller presents himself as the chosen individual of a deity or saint who is asked to circulate a sacred story or to produce a collection of texts including tales. In Hermas' *Shepherd* (second century), for instance, an angel appears to the author in the guise of a shepherd (Vision 5),[17] ordering him to write down a collection of mandates (commandments) and similitudes (parables) for both his own spiritual improvement and that of the wider Christian community.[18] In his *Sacred Tales*, a collection of divine, mostly healing, dreams composed some decades after the *Shepherd*, Aelios Aristides (117–180) reports that the god Asklepios instructs him to keep a record of their interchanges and the godly healings he receives through the medium of dreams.[19]

Like Hermas' work, which has a title directly linked to one of his visions' divine figures (the angel as shepherd), the title of *Sacred Tales* is also divinely ordained. In a dream appearance to Aristides' foster father, Asklepios provides the title of Aristides' work: 'The Sacred Tales' ('Ιεροὶ λόγοι).[20] Like the anonymous hagiographer of Thekla's miracle collection (fifth century) discussed in Chapters 5, 7, and 8 of this volume, who portrays himself as the saint's beneficiary and her chosen storyteller and orator, Aristides presents himself as the special protégé and orator of Asklepios, who, as is the case with Thekla, both saves his devotee from grave illness and fosters his text productivity.[21]

---

17   Hermas, *Shepherd*, ed. M. Whittaker, *Die apostolischen Väter I: Der Hirt des Hermas*, Die griechischen christlichen Shriftsteller 48, 2nd ed. (Berlin: 1967) 1–98, ch. 25.

18   For Hermas' role as a chosen transmitter of divine revelations and for his transformation throughout this process, see, for example, Cox Miller P., *Dreams in Late Antiquity: Studies in the Imagination of a Culture* (Princeton: 1994) 131–147; Tarvahauta U., "A Just Man or Just a Man: The Ideal Man in the Visions of Hermas", *Patristica Nordica Annuaria* 35 (2020) 69–97; Young S., "Being a Man: The Pursuit of Manliness in *The Shepherd of Hermas*", *Journal of Early Christian Studies* 2.3 (1994) 237–255.

19   Aelios Aristides, *Sacred Tales*, ed. C.A. Behr, *P. Aelii Aristidis Opera quae exstant omnia* (Leiden: 1976) 2.2.

20   *Sacred Tales* 2.9; trans. C.A. Behr, *P. Aelius Aristides, The Complete Works*, vol. 2: *Orations XVII–LIII* (Leiden: 1981) 293.

21   The intertextual relationships between the *Sacred Tales* and the *Miracle Collection of Thekla* are beyond the scope of this chapter, but I intend to explore them in a future publication. For Aristides' status as Asklepios' chosen dreamer and orator, see, for instance, Cox Miller P., "'All the Words Were Frightful': Salvation by Dreams in the Shepherd of Hermas", *Vigiliae Christianae* 42 (1988) 327–338; eadem, *Dreams in Late Antiquity* 184–204; Petridou G., "'One Has to Be So Terribly Religious to Be an Artist': Divine Inspiration and *Theophilia* in Aelius Aristides' *Hieroi logoi*", *Archiv für Religionsgeschichte* 20.1 (2018) 257–271. For Aristides' use of dream tales as a means of self-representation, see Downie J., "Dream Hermeneutics in Aelius Aristides' *Ieroi logoi*", in Oberhelman S. (ed.), *Dreams, Healing, and Medicine in Greece: From Antiquity to the Present* (Aldershot: 2013) 109–128.

THE ART OF THE SHORT NARRATIVE

In addition to the chosen storytellers, there are those who, having themselves benefited as the listeners of other storytellers' tales, feel that it is their duty to retell these tales and thus pass the knowledge and edification to others. A case in point is the author-storyteller of the *History of the Monks in Egypt* who writes in this work's prologue:

> For I have truly seen the treasure of God hidden in human vessels. I did not wish to keep this to myself and conceal something which would benefit many. [...] Accordingly, since I have derived much benefit from these monks, I have undertaken this work to provide a paradigm and a testimony for the perfect, and to edify and benefit those who are only beginners in the ascetic life.

> Εἶδον γὰρ ἀληθῶς τὸν τοῦ θεοῦ θησαυρὸν ⟨ἐν ἀνθρωπίνοις κεκρυμμένον σκεύεσι· ὃν οὐκ ἐβουλόμην κρύπτειν καλύψας⟩ τὴν τῶν πολλῶν ὠφέλειαν. [...] Ὅθεν πολλὴν ὠφέλειαν ἐξ αὐτῶν πορισάμενος ἐπὶ τὴν ἐξήγησιν ταύτην ἐχώρησα, πρὸς ζῆλον μὲν καὶ ὑπόμνησιν τῶν τελείων, πρὸς οἰκοδομὴν δὲ καὶ ὠφέλειαν τῶν ἀρχομένων ἀσκεῖν.[22]

In contrast to Benjamin's understanding of the storyteller as a canonical force possessing the same characteristics in every single tale, the storytellers discussed so far display different features. There are, for example, personal and impersonal storytellers, authoritative and less authoritative storytellers, storytellers who are ordered by a divinity to tell and write down one or more tales, and storytellers who assume their role because they cannot keep just for themselves the tales they know. As Stavroula Constantinou and Andria Andreou have amply demonstrated in a recent article drawing significantly from Benjamin's discussion of the storyteller and Monica Fludernik's work on conversational storytelling, there are at least three types of storytellers in early Byzantine tales as far as storytelling voice is concerned: the single omnipresent storyteller, the chain storyteller, and the combined storyteller.[23]

The single omnipresent storyteller is identified with the author of a work including tales – a literary miscellany (e.g. paradoxography and *Apophthegmata*

---

22 *History of the Monks in Egypt* (ВHG 1333–1334), Prologue, 22–24, 73–75, ed. A.J. Festugière, *Historia monachorum in Aegypto*, Subsidia hagiographica 34 (Brussels: 1961); trans. N. Russell, "The Lives of the Desert Fathers", in Ward B. – Russell N. (eds.), *The Lives of the Desert Fathers*, Cistercian Studies 34 (Kalamazoo, MI: 1981) 47–119, at 49, 50–51.

23 Constantinou S. – Andreou A., "The Voices of the Tale: The Storyteller in Early Byzantine Collective Biographies, Miracle Collections, and Collections of Edifying Tales", *Byzantine and Modern Greek Studies* 46.1 (2021) 24–40, DOI: 10.1017/byz.2021.31.

Patrum), a collection (e.g. miracle collections and collective biographies), or a frame narrative (e.g. *History of the Monks in Egypt*). Chain storytelling refers to the mode in which a particular tale is transmitted through a sequence of storytellers. In this case, a storyteller shares a tale with someone who retells it to another individual, who, in turn, transmits it to a third potential storyteller, and so on, reflecting the infinite transmission of a tale through generations and centuries. Finally, combined storytelling has characteristics of both single-voice and chain storytelling. This third storytelling mode is detectable in tale collections in which there are tales told by an omnipresent storyteller, the collection's author, and tales that reach the author-storyteller through a chain of storytellers.

In addition to the storytelling types presented so far, Chapter 5, which focuses on the storyteller, for example, brings to the fore some more categories of storytellers, suggesting that there are as many different kinds of storytellers as there are different types of tales. Of course, many more studies are needed to achieve a good understanding of the multifarious storytelling figures that are incorporated into ancient and early Byzantine tales. For example, what about storytellers transmitting other types of tales, such as mythological, ethnographical, and animal tales? Do these storytellers behave differently depending on the type of texts in which such tales are included? In other words, is the storyteller of a collection of animal tales different from the storyteller who tells animal tales in the framework of a letter or a homily? What about the differences between storytellers of animal tales and those of hagiographical tales? How does a tale's purpose – religious, healing, didactic, satirical, or entertaining – determine the storyteller's profile? In what ways does a storyteller's social and bodily situation influence a tale's storyness and effect? But let us move on to the second constituent of the tale, storyness.

2   Storyness

As implied above, storyness is not used here in the cognitive approach sense adopted by short fiction theorists. According to Lohafer, who has introduced the concept to short fiction studies, storyness concerns reading experience and not the art and craft of storytelling and story-writing that interest us now. Borrowing from textual linguistics, discourse analysis, and cognitive science that 'anatomizes' the production of narratives to explain behavior and to study how the human mind processes literature,[24] Lohafer has argued that when

---

24   Lohafer, *Reading for Storyness* 133.

THE ART OF THE SHORT NARRATIVE

processing a short narrative, readers not only arrive at final closure, but also identify a series of what she has termed 'preclosure points' at which the story might have finished but has not. In other words,[25] the mind tends to 'chunk' a story into several discrete parts of preclosure or closure.[26] Thus readers, as proposed by Lohafer, read a story for its ending.

Despite its usefulness – particularly for drawing attention to 'every single word of an unfolding story',[27] Lohafer's storyness suggests that a short narrative is in its entirety a kind of ending. If there is no closure, then there is no story. Yet what about open-ended stories like the Chekhov type of story mentioned in the Introduction? Should such texts be dismissed as non-stories because they have no closure? And what happens with stories that have an ending, but in which this ending does not have an impact on its readers, as it does not have the characteristics they are expecting for a closure? Do they still count as stories? In sum, Lohafer's approach cancels the very creation of stories which are meant to be read or heard in themselves and not exclusively for their ending. In fact, the art of short fiction lies in the different combinations of all its inherent parts having certain effects on the readers or listeners. But before discussing story-effect, let's explain how the concept of storyness is used in the tale-theory approach undertaken here and how it applies to ancient and early Byzantine tales.

For our purposes, as suggested earlier, storyness stands for the tale's form and structure and for its storytelling devices, namely for all those elements that are responsible for the tale's artistry, which according to Charles May lies in 'those magical episodes, lyrical and dramatic, in which we confront the Thou moments in which we are torn away to "dangerous extremes"'.[28] In other words, what are those structures and devices that create short fiction – the tale in our case – which May has described as 'the most paradoxical [...] of all art forms, for it gives us reality and unreality at once, gives us both the familiar and the unfamiliar, the universal and the particular, tells us both at the same time that we are separate and that we are unified'?[29]

The storytelling devices of the ancient and early Byzantine tale can be divided into two major groups: stylistic and narrative devices. The most prevalent stylistic devices include metaphor, imagery, allegory, repetition, and the catalogue. The dominant narrative devices, on the other hand, are the

---

25   Ibidem, 38.
26   Ibidem, 33.
27   Ibidem, 131.
28   May C., 'I Am Your Brother': Short Story Studies (online publication: 2013) 63.
29   Ibidem, 64.

following: epiphany, dream or vision, and the monstrous and the grotesque, but also allegory and repetition, which might be used as both stylistic and narrative devices.[30] These devices, the stylistic and the narrative, are employed by our authors in various combinations which create the supernatural or marvelous worlds of their tales that are determined by the nature of the tales' characters and objects. Supernatural tales involve deities, saints, demons, and objects with exceptional powers. Marvelous tales unfold around strange and bizarre phenomena and objects that lie at the limits of knowledge and rationality.

Turning now to the most frequent narrative devices of early tales, epiphany appears to have four essential features. First, it is a rapid hearing, tactile, or olfactory experience that frequently entails an intensification of sensory stimuli and of emotional involvement. Second, it is a mysterious revelation whose meaningfulness exceeds its observable characteristics. Third, it constitutes an instance of poetic art that is characterized by forceful rhetoric and intensity. Fourth, it is a literary moment exhibiting repeated patterns. Depending on the type of otherworldly figure that manifests itself into the human world, our epiphanies might be divided into three large categories: theophany, *hagiophany*, and *demonophany* – the last two terms being created as parallels to theophany. Theophany signifies a manifestation of one or more gods. Hagiophany denotes the appearance of one or more saints, while demonophany stands for the presence of Satan and his demons.

The tales of epiphany *par excellence* are the miracle stories whose protagonists actively seek divine help. In Christian miracles, to which I now turn, epiphany takes mostly the form of hagiophany. The tale protagonists may see the miraculous saints as themselves or in disguise; they may hear the saints' bodiless voices; they may touch the saints' bodies; they may smell the saints or some other intense smell without seeing or hearing the saintly figures; and finally, they may feel the saints without seeing, hearing, or smelling them. Hagiophany may also take different forms depending on the types of miracles performed: cult, healing, punishment, war miracles, and miraculous control over animals and extreme natural phenomena.

For reasons of space, in what follows I will briefly discuss a hagiophany that effects a climate transformation for the comfort of a pregnant woman. The woman in question, who is named Bassiane, is the heroine of a tale from the *Miracle Collection of Thekla*. During the final months of her pregnancy,

---

30   For example, allegory is an essential narrative device of Hermas' visionary tales; see Tagliabue A., "Learning from Allegorical Images in the *Book of Visions* of *The Shepherd of Hermas*", *Arethusa* 50.2 (2017) 221–255. As for the use of repetition as a narrative device, see Chapter 5 in this volume.

THE ART OF THE SHORT NARRATIVE

Bassiane has a visionary experience of Thekla, whom she sees in person. Bassiane's hagiophany takes place after a bodily crisis. The storyteller presents in detail the reasons for the crisis:

> One summer day, when the sun was blazing fiercely, Bassiane was spending time in the martyr's shrine [...]. As night came on the heat intensified [...]. She began to be distressed, since she was unaccustomed to the heat: she did not know what to do; She was having trouble breathing, and she was drenched in sweat. At one instant, she would toss on her bed, trying to restore and refresh her weary body, and she repeated this numerous times. At the next instant, she would bound up from her bed, when she was already quite soaked, and lean against the marble revetment, which was certainly cooler and could refresh her. In the end she was defeated by the terrible heat – [...] the weight of her belly, swollen because she was with child, oppressed her. [...] – She rushed to one of the cisterns lying nearby.

> Αὔτη ποτὲ ἐν ὥρᾳ θέρους, καὶ ἡνίκα μάλιστα ἑαυτοῦ φλογωδέστερός ἐστιν ὁ ἥλιος, ἐνδιέτριβε μὲν τῷ νεῷ τῆς μάρτυρος [...]. Νυκτὸς δὲ ἐπιλαβούσης καὶ τῆς φλογὸς ἐπιταθείσης, ἤσχαλλε μὲν τὴν ἀρχήν, ὡς ἂν καὶ ἀσυνήθης, καὶ διηπορεῖτο, καὶ ἄσθματος ἐπληροῦτο, καὶ ἱδρῶτι κατερρεῖτο, καὶ ποτὲ μὲν κατὰ τὰ χαμεύνια αὐτὰ περιεστρέφετο, ἀεὶ τὸ κάμνον τοῦ σώματος θεραπεύουσα καὶ ἀναψύχουσα, καὶ τοῦτο ποιοῦσα συχνότερον, ποτὲ δὲ καὶ ἀναπηδῶσα τῆς κοίτης, ἡνίκα διάβροχός τε ἦν ἤδη λοιπόν, καὶ τοῖς μαρμάροις ἑαυτὴν προσήρειδεν, ὡς ψυχροτέροις τε οὖσι μᾶλλον καὶ ἀναψύξαι δυναμένοις αὐτήν. Τέλος δε, ὡς ἐνικᾶτο τῷ κακῷ – [...] γαστρὸς ὄγκος αὐτὴν ἐπὶ παιδὶ κυρτουμένης συνεῖχε [...] – ὥρμησε μὲν ἐπὶ τί ποτε τῶν παρακειμένων φρεάτων.[31]

Being unable to bear this difficult situation any longer, Bassiane rushes to a nearby cistern to enter into its deep waters with the intention of finding some comfort. This was, however, a dangerous endeavor, since, as the storyteller points out, 'death was going to be the result of her poor condition in any case' (ἀποπνιγῆναι. τοῦτο γὰρ ἦν τὸ πάντως ἐσόμενον τοῦ κακοῦ πέρας).[32] It is at this critical moment that Thekla appears as *deus ex machina*:

---

31   *Miracles of Thekla*, ch. 19.9–22 (BHG 1718); ed. G. Dagron, *Vie et miracles de sainte Thècle: Texte grec, traduction et commentaire*, Subsidia hagiographica 62 (Brussels: 1978) 285–412; trans. S.F. Johnson, "The Miracles of Thekla", in Talbot A.M. – Johnson S.F. (trans.), *Miracle Tales from Byzantium*, Dumbarton Oaks Medieval Library 12 (Cambridge, MA – London: 2012) 1–201, at 83.

32   *Miracles of Thekla*, ch. 19.25–26; trans. Johnson, "The Miracles of Thekla" 85.

The martyr appeared and, seizing her *himation*, stopped the woman's headlong rush ⟨for the cistern⟩ and rebuked her for her recklessness. [...] This most gentle of women ⟨Thekla⟩ dipped her finger into [a basin full of water]. [...] She then applied it [...] to Bassiane's forehead and to each of her shoulders, and then went away leaving only the sweet west wind blowing on her.

Παραφανεῖσα δὲ ἡ μάρτυς καὶ τοῦ ἱματίου αὐτῆς λαβομένη, τῆς μὲν ὁρμῆς ἔπαυσε, πολλὰ λοιδορησαμένη τῆς τόλμης αὐτήν [...]· καὶ τὸν αὐτῆς ἡ πραο-τάτη καθιμήσασα δάκτυλον [...], ἐπαλείφει τὸ μέτωπον τούτῳ καὶ τῶν κατα-κλείδων ἑκατέραν, καὶ ἀπῆλθε, ζέφυρον [...] αὐτῇ μόνον λιγυρὸν ἐπιπνέοντα καταλείψασα.[33]

The saint's appearance and disappearance are sudden. Thekla gives directions and acts, providing the scene with a certain realism. First, Thekla seizes Bassiane abruptly by her clothing to put a halt to her flight to the cistern, while at the same time she explains the risks of such a move by reproaching the pregnant woman. The saint's relatively violent, yet caring, movement is soon turned into the gentle touch of a caregiver.[34] With her finger, Thekla applies to Bassiane's body some fresh water that she receives from the woman's female servant. The mysteriousness of the martyr's hagiophany becomes perceptible through the suddenness of her departure, which is associated with the transformation of the fierce heat into a 'sweet west wind' (ζέφυρον λιγυρόν) which is felt only by Bassiane, who spends the rest of the summer feeling 'as if she were enjoying springtime in the wooded, breezy suburb of Daphne' (αὐτὴ μόνη ὡς ἐν ἦρι καὶ ὡς ἐν Δάφνῃ τῷ πολυδένδρῳ καὶ πολυανέμῳ χωρίῳ διάγουσα).[35]

The tale of Bassiane has a tripartite structure that has hagiophany at its very center. First, the hagiographer prepares Thekla's hagiophany. Second, the actual hagiophany takes place, and finally the effects of the hagiophany on the heroine are presented. But how is the hagiophany prepared for? This is fulfilled through the following steps. Firstly, the character (Bassiane) is introduced into the narrative and her piety is described: she is a follower of Thekla who every day spends time in the martyr's shrine. Then follows a detailed description of the extreme weather conditions and of how these affect the heroine: she is heavily pregnant and oppressed by the unusual and unbearable heat. She finds

---

33   *Miracles of Thekla*, ch. 19.26–34; trans. Johnson, "The Miracles of Thekla" 85.

34   Cf. other hagiophanies of Thekla in which the martyr exhibits the same behavior (miracle 12) that are analyzed in Chapter 7.

35   *Miracles of Thekla*, ch. 19.35–36; trans. Johnson, "The Miracles of Thekla" 85.

THE ART OF THE SHORT NARRATIVE   25

herself in such a desperate situation that she attempts to comfort herself in a
dangerous manner: by entering the deep waters of a nearby cistern.

The hagiophany itself constitutes an independent unit within the miracle
story, having its own beginning, middle, and end. It opens with the martyr's
sudden introduction into the narrative when the latter reaches its climax. As
suggested by her movements, words, and bodily acts, Thekla's intervention
in Bassiane's life at that very moment is fleshy. The hagiophany ends through
Thekla's sudden disappearance, which is associated with an abrupt change in
the weather. The last part of the tale is concerned with the aftermath of the
martyr's hagiophany. Bassiane is the only person who experiences a springtime
amidst the fierce heat of the summer. She has an easy labor through which she
is liberated from both pregnancy and captivity.

The narrative closes with the storyteller's explanation of how Bassiane's
story is turned into the tale that he includes in his work: 'And a witness to this
is the child born from the woman, the very famous Modestos, who is still alive
and adorns the city that is called 'peace', and he recounts this miracle with
every possible grace. He is a kind man and filled with fine artistic sense' (Καὶ
μάρτυς ὁ ἐκ ταύτης τότε γενόμενος παῖς, Μόδεστος δὲ ἦν οὗτος ὁ πάνυ, ἔτι τε καὶ νῦν
ἐν ζῶσι τελῶν, καὶ τὴν εἰρήνης, ἐπώνυμον πόλιν κοσμῶν, καὶ τὸ θαῦμα τοῦτο μετὰ
πολλῶν καὶ ὅσων τῶν χαρίτων διηγούμενος· εὔθυμος δὲ ὁ ἀνήρ, καὶ πολλῆς γέμων
τῆς εὐμουσίας).[36] The transformation of Bassiane's hagiophany and her subsequent delivery into a narrative is firstly performed by the heroine herself, who
shares her experience with her own son, who is also a beneficiary of the saint.
Modestos is not just a trustworthy and sympathetic storyteller, but also an art-
ful storyteller. It is thanks to his artistry that the tale is widely circulated, reaching the hagiographer's ears too. We thus have a storytelling chain consisting
of three authoritative storytellers (Bassiane, Modestos, and the hagiographer),
each of them initiating a different transmission process of the tale. Bassiane's
narrativization and first storytelling act brings the tale into the transmission
circle. Modestos publicizes the story to other potential storytellers of his times.
Lastly, by committing the tale to writing, the hagiographer ensures its endur-
ance throughout the centuries.

By using as a case study the hagiophanic experience of a pregnant woman
featuring in the miracle collection of Thekla, I have shown that hagiophany
is a central element of the tale's storyness. It is introduced into the narrative
at a crucial point, preventing Bassiane's drowning. At the same time, it is a
transformative experience and a powerful instance of dynamism, intensity,
and mysteriousness. While it has its own unity, the actual scene of hagiophany

---

36   *Miracles of Thekla*, ch. 19. 36–41; trans. Johnson, "The Miracles of Thekla" 85.

becomes an integral part of the examined tale's tripartite structure, contributing to its closure. Hagiophany is also an essential element of the poetics of the tale that is endowed 'with fine artistic sense' (γέμων τῆς εὐμουσίας), to use the author-storyteller's words. Of course, Bassiane's story provides just one instance of hagiophany. Thekla's miracle collection, which abounds with hagiophanies, includes a rich variety of this type of epiphany. Evidently, a systematic examination not only of hagiophany, but also of theophany and demonophany, will shed light on their different characteristics and uses, their narrative and aesthetic dimensions, their effects, and their continuities and transformations from ancient to early Byzantine literature.[37]

Compared to epiphany, there are more publications examining the narrative devices of dream and vision in ancient and early Byzantine tales.[38] As far as ancient tales are concerned, the dreams and visions in the tales of Hermas and those of Aristides, for example, have attracted good scholarly interest.[39] For our purposes here, Patricia Cox Miller's analysis is remarkably enlightening. She describes how the dreams and visions of Hermas and Aristides emerge 'in the midst of everyday earthly reality', a characteristic that as indicated above is an important feature of storyness.[40] Furthermore, Cox Miller discusses the elaborate character and complex structure of Hermas' dream tales, which further reveal their artistry. The *Shepherd*'s tales include framing dreams having dreams-within-dreams-within-dreams. Often, as Cox Miller has pointed out, it

---

37 When available, the results of Doroszewska's current project entitled 'Epiphanies of the Saints in Late Antique Greek Literature' (http://historia.uw.edu.pl/en/research-project/epiphanies-of-the-saints-in-late-antique-greek-literature/) are expected to contribute to a better understanding of late antique epiphanies and to initiate further studies on the subject. For epiphanies in Aristides' *Sacred Tales*, see Tagliabue A., "An Embodied Reading of Epiphanies in Aelius Aristides' Sacred Tales", *Ramus* 45 (2016) 213–230.

38 See, for example, Bronwen N. – Costache D. – Wagner K., *Dreams, Virtue and Divine Knowledge in Early Christian Egypt* (Cambridge: 2019) 179–184; Constantinou S., "Healing Dreams in Early Byzantine Miracle Collections" in Oberhelman, *Dreams, Healing and Medicine* 189–197; Csepregi I., "Changes in Dream Patterns between Antiquity and Byzantium: The Impact of Medical Learning on Dream Healing", in Csepregi I. – Burnett C. (eds.), *Ritual Healing: Magic, Ritual and Medical Therapy from Antiquity until the Early Modern Period* (Florence: 2012) 131–146; Zeppezauer D., "Warum wirken Wunder?: Die Sprache der Ärzte im Traum", *Zeitschrift für Antikes Christentum* 17.1 (2013) 143–159.

39 See, for example, Cox Miller, "'All the Words Were Frightful'"; eadem, *Dreams in Late Antiquity* 131–147, 184–204; Harkins A.K., "Looking at the *Shepherd of Hermas* through the Experience of Lived Religion", in Gasparini V. – Patzelt M. – Raja R. – Rieger A.K. – Rüpke J. – Urciuoli E. (eds.), *Lived Religion in the Ancient Mediterranean World: Approaching Religious Transformations from Archaeology, History and Classics* (Berlin – Boston: 2020) 49–70; Tarvahauta, "A Just Man or Just a Man"; Downie, "Dream Hermeneutics in Aelius Aristides' *Ieroi logoi*".

40 Cox Miller, *Dreams in Late Antiquity* 133.

THE ART OF THE SHORT NARRATIVE   27

is hard to distinguish between the frame and the dreams. As she herself has formulated it, 'inner and outer change place and are multiplied, as though multiple consciousness is what these nested dreams are leading the dreamer into'.[41]

In a previous study, I have also tried to analyze the structure, but also the types, forms, and narrative functions of healing dreams and visions in tales that are incorporated into Byzantine miracle collections.[42] As I have shown, dreams and visions are independent narrative units within a tale, having their own morphology. Yet, like epiphanies, dreams and visions interact with the rest of the narrative. In sum, dreams and visions achieve the following: they set the story in motion; they determine its unfolding; they change its direction; they slow down or accelerate its closure; and finally, they contribute to the tale's attractiveness by creating the effects of suspense and surprise. Similarly with the device of epiphany, dreams and visions, even though they have been more systematically studied, still remain largely unexplored. The same is valid also for the monstrous and the grotesque, the last important devices of storyness discussed here, which are the least examined devices.

There are only a couple of articles investigating the monstrous and the grotesque in ancient and early Byzantine tales. The first examines the monstrous in Phlegon of Tralles' *Mirabilia*, while the second focuses on the monstrous and the grotesque in miracle tales.[43] Interestingly, both articles concern the body, suggesting that the most prevalent form of the monstrous and the grotesque in our corpus is directly related to the human body. Focusing on the hermaphrodite bodies of *Mirabilia*, Julia Doroszewska concludes that it is a dynamic narrative device activating a whole series of other bizarre actions and phenomena which take place 'in an irrational chain of causation' and thus endow the text with mystery and fascination.[44] Employing Mikhail Bakhtin's theory of the grotesque body, the second article investigates the revolting imagery of the sickly, punished, and suffering body in miracle collections. Beyond its religious significance, as the article shows, the monstrous and grotesque body is

---

41   Eadem, "'All the Words Were Frightful'" 332.

42   Constantinou S., "The Morphology of Healing Dreams: Dream and Therapy in Byzantine Collections of Miracle Stories", in Angelidi C. – Calofonos G. (eds.), *Dreaming in Byzantium and Beyond* (Aldershot: 2014) 21–34.

43   Doroszewska J., "Between the Monstrous and the Divine: Hermaphrodites in Phlegon of Tralles' *Mirabilia*", *Acta antiqua Academiae scientiarum Hungaricae* 53 (2013) 379–392, DOI: 10.1556/AAnt.53.2013.4.4; Constantinou S., "Grotesque Bodies in Hagiographical Tales: The Monstrous and the Uncanny in Byzantine Collections of Miracle Stories", *Dumbarton Oaks Papers* 64 (2010) 43–54.

44   Doroszewska, "Between the Monstrous and the Divine" 389.

not only the kernel around which the miracle tale develops, but a device of great aesthetic and entertainment value.

Another important aspect of storyness that is not sufficiently discussed in this volume is intertextuality – or what I would call 'inter-storyness'. The story-ness of the tale, which comes into being through a chain of storytellers, both textual and extra-textual, who tell and retell it and thus adjust it to fit new circumstances and the expectations of different audiences, is unavoidably a construct of inter-storyness. Inter-storyness also concerns the dialogue and interrelations between different tales or tale collections and previous texts. A systematic examination of the inter-storyness of ancient and Byzantine tales, such as those of Aristides and the hagiographer of Thekla mentioned above, will not only illuminate the latter's literary techniques, but will also reveal hidden aspects of the first, thus providing a better understanding of both works.

3   Story-Effect

Tales, like any other literary form, are addressed to different audiences. The complex and multifaceted audiences of ancient and early Byzantine tales may be divided into four large categories: the embedded audience, the implied audience, the intended audience, and the real audience. The embedded or inscribed audience is part of the storytelling situations that are created within the tales reflecting their oral transmission, which is revived each time they are read. The embedded audience consists of three types of inscribed listeners: storytellers, a group of mostly anonymous auditors, and characters who listen to stories-within-the-story. Each of these types has its own internal categories and characteristics that prove the dynamic and sophisticated nature of the tale.

To the group of the storyteller-listeners belong the authors of the texts and the storytellers of a storytelling chain or a frame tale. The authors of tale collections or other texts including tales appear as listeners of stories, as suggested, for example, by the said tale from the *Spiritual Meadow* where Moschos presents himself as the reteller of a tale he has heard from Gregory, the abbot of Choziba monastery and later Bishop of Caesarea. With the exception of autobiographical stories and stories reporting their personal experiences with other protagonists, authors renounce the authorship of their works' tales, highlighting instead their roles as listeners and compilers. They continuously remark that they retell, collect, and pass on in a written form what they have heard from others. Moschos writes, for instance, in the prologue of the *Spiritual Meadow*: 'as I have put together a copious and accurate collection, so I

THE ART OF THE SHORT NARRATIVE   29

have emulated the most wise bee, gathering up the spiritually beneficial deeds of the fathers' (ὡς πολλὴν καὶ ἀληθῆ συλλογὴν ἐποιησάμην· ὡς ἐπὶ τῆς σοφωτάτης μελίττης τὰ ψυχωφελῆ τῶν Πατέρων ἀρυσάμενος κατορθώματα).[45] Using the conventional topos of the bee simile, Moschos presents in the most graphical way his roles as a selective listener of ascetics' stories and as an accurate compilator who creates a collection of these stories by remaining faithful to their original forms and contents.

The storyteller-listeners of a storytelling chain or a frame tale are mainly pious pilgrims and monastics, both eponymous and anonymous, who pass on the stories they hear from each other until these stories reach the author-storyteller-listener – the last participant in the chain or the one who closes the initial frame. As is mostly the case with the author-storyteller-listener,[46] the chain and frame storyteller-listeners are commonly embedded in the tale at the outset. Thus we read, for instance, at the beginning of the third tale of the *Lausiac History*: 'the aforementioned blessed Isidore had met Antony of sacred memory and told me of an incident well worth recording which he had heard from him' (Ὁ μακάριος οὗτος Ἰσίδωρος συντετυχηκὼς Ἀντωνίῳ τῷ μακαρίτῃ γραφῆς ἄξιον διηγήσατό μοι πρᾶγμα, ἀκηκοὼς παρ' αὐτοῦ).[47] In this storytelling chain, there are two listeners: Isidore and Palladios, the author, who listen to the same story at different points in time.

The first listener that is of interest here, Isidore, is also the protagonist of the *Lausiac History*'s first tale (ch. 1). Isidore is the first holy man whom Palladios meets when he goes for the first time to Alexandria, that is during the emperorship of Theodosios I (379–395). In the first tale, Palladios describes Isidore as a 'wonderful man' and as a man 'with completely beautiful character and knowledge' (ἀνδρὶ θαυμασίῳ παντόθεν κεκοσμημένῳ ἔν τε ἤθει καὶ γνώσει).[48] In other words, Isidore has all the qualities of an exemplary storyteller-listener. Impressed by Isidore's holiness, Palladios asks him to become his ascetic instructor. Even though Isidore refuses to undertake this role and sends Palladios to another ascetic – Dorotheos, the protagonist of the next tale (ch. 2) – he teaches the author through his storytelling acts. He tells Palladios tales he has heard from other equally pious storytellers, such as Antony the Great, who is the first storyteller of the third tale.

---

45   *Spiritual Meadow*, Prologue, 2852; trans. Wortley, *John Moschus* 4.
46   One exception, an author-storyteller-listener inscribed not at the beginning, but at the end of the tale, is provided in the hagiophany tale from the miracle collection of Thekla discussed above.
47   *Lausiac History*, ch. 3, p. 18.12–14; trans. Meyer, *Palladius* 34.
48   *Lausiac History*, ch. 1, p. 15.8–9; trans. Meyer, *Palladius* 31, with modifications.

This exchange between Isidore and Palladios seems to last for fifteen years: from the first time the two men meet – at that point Isidore is seventy years old – until the time of Isidore's death that takes place when he is eighty-five years old. In fact, Isidore proves an exemplary storyteller-listener not only for Palladios, but also for his other distinguished visitors. In the tenth tale, we are informed that Melania the Elder (350–c.410) hears stories from Isidore about another ascetic, Pambo, who is the protagonist of this tale. Melania, in turn, the only female storyteller of the collection, is another frequent chain storyteller-listener. She appears listening to and telling stories in at least four different tales (chs. 5, 9, 10, 46).

The groups of chiefly nameless auditors that are inscribed in the examined tales are either small and private or large and public. An ascetic's visitors seem to form small groups not larger than ten people. For example, in the *Spiritual Meadow* it is reported that when visiting ascetics' cells and monasteries Moschos is accompanied by his friend, the aforementioned Sophronios who later becomes Patriarch of Jerusalem and writes another tale collection, the *Miracles of Kyros and John*. The author of the *History of the Monks in Egypt*, to mention a second example, belongs to a group of seven individuals, possibly also monks, meeting Egyptian monastics. These small groups are homogeneous: they consist of religious men, co-travelers who desire to be edified through encountering exemplary ascetics and listening to their stories.

As for the large and public groups of listeners, these are mainly mixed audiences, yet homogeneous to a great extent. They might be the inhabitants of a whole city, such as Thessalonike, participating in a liturgical assembly celebrating the holiness of Saint Demetrios and listening to his miracle accounts (*Miracles of Demetrios*). They might be the patients populating a shrine that listen to the stories of other people's miraculous healings while waiting to receive their own cures (e.g. *Miracles of Kosmas and Damian*). Finally, they might be the members of a monastic community listening to their abbot's tales (e.g. Anastasios of Sinai's *Edifying Tales*).

As for the characters who listen to stories-within-the-story, they can be either eponymous or anonymous men who might be related to the protagonist and storyteller. To my knowledge, these characters form two antithetical types of listeners: the nosy and eager listener and the incredulous and bored listener that offer a humorous version of the practice of story-listening.[49] The nosy and eager listener is mostly exemplified in the *Narrations* of Daniel of Sketis. This listener is always embodied by the same character, Daniel's nameless disciple,

---

49   A more systematic examination of these characters might reveal also other types of listeners.

THE ART OF THE SHORT NARRATIVE   31

who is present in almost all eight tales edited together by Britt Dahlman.[50] This disciple is not only Daniel's most devoted follower, but also the most dedicated listener of his stories, also asking for information that might not initially be provided by Daniel. The tale in which the disciple's curiosity and desire for a particular story reach their highest point, however, is that of Eulogios (ch. 6), where Daniel, contrary to his common custom, does not behave as an eager storyteller because, as he insists, this is a confidential story that must remain untold.[51]

The disciple, however, takes Daniel's reluctance to share Eulogios' story personally and thus becomes so angry that he stops speaking with his master. He even refrains from preparing Daniel's daily meal as was customary. The hungry master then goes to the disciple's cell asking for explanations. During this meeting, which takes the form of an exchange between a father and a son, the disciple informs Daniel that he no longer does consider him a father, suggesting that he will stop being his follower. Taking the disciple's words at face value, Daniel is about to leave. He is, however, prevented by the disciple, who states that he will not let him go unless he reveals Eulogios' story.

The disciple's final act and words provide the scene with a humorous dimension, as it is clearly manifested that his 'anger' and avenging stance are playacted. The disciple uses them as tricks to push Daniel to satisfy his curiosity by telling the tale of Eulogios. In fact, the disciple would never renounce his beloved master. As the author-storyteller remarks, 'the brother could not bear seeing the elder afflicted at any time, for he loved him very much' (οὐκ ἠδύνατο γὰρ ὁ ἀδελφὸς ἰδεῖν τὸν γέροντα θλιβόμενόν ποτε· ἠγάπα γὰρ αὐτὸν πάνυ).[52] Daniel, in turn, prolongs the amusement of the scene by agreeing to tell Eulogios' tale provided that the disciple prepares his meal. Eventually, both men return to their usual roles that are designed for each other: the storyteller and the story-listener.

An instance of the bored and incredulous listener can be found in the *History of the Monks in Egypt* – in the frame tale that involves Kopres (ch. 10), a monastic who is another great listener and teller of tales.[53] While Kopres tells one of his long stories, one of the listeners that belongs to the author-storyteller's

---

50   Daniel of Sketis, *Narrations* (BHG 2099z–2102f, 79–80, 121–122, 618, 2255, 2453), ed. B. Dahlman, *Saint Daniel of Sketis: A Group of Hagiographic Texts*, Studia Byzantina Upsaliensia 10 (Uppsala: 2007) 108–187.

51   Daniel's behavior as a storyteller in this particular tale is discussed in Chapter 5.

52   Daniel of Sketis, *Narrations*, ch. 6, 49–51; trans. Dahlman, *Saint Daniel* 151.

53   For Kopres' storytelling role, see Constantinou – Andreou, "The Voices of the Tale" 32–34 and Chapter 8 in this volume.

group is 'overcome with incredulity' (ἀπιστίᾳ) and falls asleep.[54] The incredulous listener then receives a divine dream which recreates the scene of the actual hearing of Kopres' stories. In the dream, he sees himself and the others listening to Kopres, who reads from a magnificent book with gold letters. The scene also includes an otherworldly figure saying to the dreamer in a frightening way 'are you dozing instead of listening attentively to the reading?' (Οὐκ ἀκούεις προσεχῶς τοῦ ἀναγνώσματος, ἀλλὰ νυστάζεις;).[55] At these words, the man wakes up and becomes a storyteller in his turn, sharing his supernatural experience, which becomes a lesson on the act of story-listening. It teaches how to become an exemplary listener for one's spiritual benefit.

The implied audiences of the tales under discussion are their ideal listeners or readers. Like the embedded audiences, implied audiences are also constructed within the texts through the storytellers' words and behavior. First, storytellers directly address their implied audiences by using cajoling words and phrases, such as 'most faithful' (πιστότατοι),[56] 'lovers of Christ' (φιλόχριστοι),[57] 'your fondness for listening' (ὑμετέρα φιληκοΐα),[58] and 'God-loving and dear brothers' (φιλόθεοι καὶ ἀγαπητοὶ ἀδελφοί).[59] This flattering rhetoric is found in the prologues of tale collections and miscellanies and in different parts of individual tales: at the beginning of a tale, where they function as *captatio benevolentiae*; at various points during storytelling to direct the audience's attention to particular parts of the tale, thus guiding its perception; and at the end of the tale, to point to the tale's moral message.

The ideal audiences are those behaving like the exemplary embedded audiences that find the storyteller's tales true, admirable, inspiring, edifying, and imitable. In addition to flattering their audiences, storytellers declare how they work to find tales with these characteristics. The author-storyteller of Thekla's miracle tales, for instance, writes in the prologue of the collection: 'I have made mention of people, places, and names, so that the audience has **no doubts** about these events, but rather can consider them from close up and **examine the truth** of what I have said' (Διὰ τοῦτο δὲ προσώπων καὶ τόπων καὶ

---

54 *History of the Monks in Egypt*, ch. 10, 160, trans. Russell, "The Lives of the Desert Fathers" 85.

55 *History of the Monks in Egypt*, ch. 10, 163–164; trans. Russell, "The Lives of the Desert Fathers" 85–86.

56 *Miracles of Kosmas and Damian* (BHG 385–391) p. 130.58, ed. L. Deubner, *Kosmas und Damian: Texte und Einleitung* (Leipzig – Berlin: 1907) 193–206.

57 Ibidem, p. 109.22–35.

58 Ibidem, p. 117.75–79.

59 E.g. John, Archbishop of Thessalonike, *Miracles of Demetrios* (BHG 499–523), ch. 2, 27, ed. P. Lemerle, *Les plus anciens recueils des Miracles de Saint Démétrius*, vol. 1: *Le texte* (Paris: 1979) 4–165; trans. mine.

THE ART OF THE SHORT NARRATIVE   33

ὀνομάτων ἐμνημονεύσαμεν, ὥστε μηδὲ περὶ αὐτῶν τοὺς ἐντυγχάνοντας ἀμφιβάλλειν, ἀλλ᾽ ἐγγύθεν ἔχειν καὶ ποιεῖσθαι τὴν περὶ ὧν εἰρήκαμεν ἐξέτασιν τῆς ἀληθείας).[60] Even though, as the hagiographer remarks a little earlier, he has collected great numbers of Thekla's miracles, he chooses to include in the collection only those miracles whose beneficiaries are contemporary or lived recently. All the miracles of the anthology derive from exclusively truthful sources which, as also manifested in Modestos, the source of Bassiane's story analyzed above, he names and locates so that his audiences can at any time prove their veracity. As well as in prologues, the tales' truthfulness is a recurrent theme also in individual tales and particularly in those that might seem too strange to be true.[61]

Concerning the tales' admirable, imitable, and edifying character, we read in the prologue of the alphabetical collection of the *Apophthegmata Patrum*:

> In this book, the virtuous asceticism and the **admirable** way of life and words of the holy and blessed fathers are written. They are meant to **inspire** and **teach** the ones who wish to **imitate** their heavenly conduct, so that they may make progress on the way leading to the kingdom of heaven.

> Ἐν τῇδε τῇ βίβλῳ ἀναγέγραπται ἐνάρετος ἄσκησις καὶ θαυμαστὴ βίου διαγωγὴ καὶ ῥήσεις ἁγίων καὶ μακαρίων πατέρων πρὸς ζῆλον καὶ παιδείαν καὶ μίμησιν τῶν τὴν οὐράνιον πολιτείαν ἐθελόντων κατορθοῦν καὶ τὴν εἰς βασιλείαν οὐρανῶν βουλομένων ὁδεύειν ὁδόν.[62]

As the criterion for choosing the miscellany's contents – the virtuous ascetic lives and words of the holy desert fathers – their ability to provoke admiration is proclaimed. The implied audiences are prospective or current ascetics that through reading or listening to the book's admirable, and therefore attractive, contents will acquire the needed knowledge and human examples leading them to the acquisition of their own holiness. As is the case with the tales' veracity, so also their admirability and didacticism are repeatedly mentioned within individual tales of the examined corpus.[63]

In contrast to the previous two audience categories (embedded and implied audiences), the intended audience is discernible in the prologues and epilogues

---

60 *Miracles of Thekla*, Prologue, 18–21; trans. Johnson "The Miracles of Thekla" 3; emphasis added.

61 See, for example, *Miracles of Thekla*, chs. 18, 20–21; 33, 62–64; 38, 37–40; 39, 15–17.

62 *Sayings of the Desert Fathers* (*Apophthegmata Patrum*; Alphabetical collection), Prologue, 72, ed. in PG 65:72–440; emphasis added.

63 See, for example, *Apophthegmata Patrum* (Anonymous Collection), chs. 410 (p. 262) and 761 (p. 620) (admirability); 618 (p. 464) and 725 (p. 574) (didacticism).

of collections and miscellanies and not in individual tales. The intended audience might be the same as the implied audience, as suggested in the aforementioned prologue of the alphabetical collection of the *Apophthegmata Patrum*. In that case, groups of ascetics are both the implied and the intended audience of the text – they might, in fact, also be part of the work's actual audiences, which are described in some detail below. As well as a group of persons (i.e. monastic communities, pilgrims, inhabitants of a city, sufferers seeking miraculous cures), the intended audience of a tale collection might be represented by just one individual, the person that inspires its creation, to whom the author devotes his work. A case in point is Moschos' *Spiritual Meadow*, which is written for and devoted to the author's most beloved friend and co-traveler Sophronios:[64]

> Think of the present work in the same way [as someone entering a meadow in spring] Sophronios, my sacred and faithful child. For in it, you will discover the virtues of holy men who have distinguished themselves in our own times [...]. From among these I have plucked the finest flowers of the unmown meadow and worked them into a crown which I now offer to you, most faithful child; and through you, to all its readers and listeners. I have called this work *meadow* on account of the delight, the fragrance and the benefit which it will afford those who come across it [...]. So I have striven to complete this composition to inform your love, oh child.

> Τοιοῦτον δὲ καὶ τὸ παρὸν πόνημα ὑπολάμβανε, ἱερὸν καὶ πιστὸν τέκνον Σωφρόνιε. Εὑρήσεις γὰρ ἐν αὐτῷ ἀρετὰς ἁγίων ἀνδρῶν ἐν τοῖς χρόνοις ἡμῶν διαλαμψάντων· [...] ἐξ ὧν τὰ καλὰ δρεψάμενος ἄνθη πλεκτὸν στέφανον ἀκηράτου λειμῶνος λαβών, προσφέρω σοι, τέκνον πιστότατον, καὶ διὰ σοῦ τοῖς πᾶσι. Διὸ καὶ τὸ παρὸν τοῦτο τὸ πόνημα Λειμῶνα ἀπεκαλέσαμεν, διὰ τὴν ἐν αὐτῷ τέρψιν τε καὶ εὐωδίαν, καὶ ὠφέλειαν τοῖς ἐντυγχάνουσιν [...]. Διὸ πρὸς τὸ παρὸν ἐλήλακα σύνταγμα, πληροφορῶν τὴν ὑμετέραν, τέκνον, ἀγάπην.[65]

As suggested by the encomiastic phrases that Moschos uses to address Sophronios ('my sacred and faithful child' and 'most faithful child'), the author considers the latter as both the ideal and the intended reader of his work, which he himself names *leimōn* ('meadow'). Moschos uses the image of the

---

64   For the two men's friendship, see Chadwick H., "John Moschus and His Friend Sophronius the Sophist", *Journal of Theological Studies* 25.1 (1974) 41–74.

65   *Spiritual Meadow*, Prologue, 2852; trans. Wortley, *John Moschus* 3–4, with modifications.

THE ART OF THE SHORT NARRATIVE 35

meadow that flourishes in spring to achieve a triple purpose: to present his work method; to describe the nature of his text; and to explain its use. Moschos sees himself as a gardener entering a spring meadow that has beauties arresting the eyes and nostrils and charming the senses. Being an experienced gardener, Moschos can tell the flowers with the finest quality, which he plucks and turns into the most dazzling flower garland.

The creation of the floral crown (ἄνθη πλεκτὸν στέφανον) functions as a meta-poetic image of the anthologist's workshop. The word 'anthology', deriving from the Greek work *anthologia* (ἀνθολογία), literally means flower-gathering. Just as the garland is created by flowers that are the best of the best, the collection consists of tales that are the best of the best. Moschos undertook this pleasant, yet difficult, task because he wanted to produce the most valuable work that he could offer as a powerful gift of love and friendship to Sophronios and through his friend to wider audiences. What is thus originally designed as a gift of friendship turns into a gift of philanthropy aspiring to provide delight and edification to the world at large. The fact that the *Spiritual Meadow* has been such a popular text throughout the ages constitutes the strongest indication of its use as both an entertaining and edifying text.[66]

One important role of the first three audiences (fictional, implied, and intended) is to influence the perceptions of the final audience, that is, the actual (real) audience, either contemporary (primary) or posterior (secondary). Like the previous audiences, the actual reader or listener of the discussed works is also invited to find the tales similarly true, admirable, imitable, and edifying. As the preceding discussion has made clear, the tales appear as performances that are designed to have positive and edifying effects on all their audiences – inscribed, implied, intended, and real – that at times coexist, at times correspond, and at other times are inconsistent. It should be pointed out, however, that the three textually constructed audiences (inscribed, implied, and intended) cannot be taken as witnesses of actual audiences' behaviors, since an author's audience, to use the title of Walter Ong's often-cited article, 'is always a fiction'.[67] Being fictions, these audiences, as mentioned earlier, could be examined also from the point of view of storyness. Yet their possible impact on the texts' actual audiences renders them inseparable from story-effect.

Through the storyteller and storyness all audiences are meant to be directed, while their thoughts and emotions are expected to be evoked and transformed. The audiences' mental and emotive responses are particularly important, as

---

66   For the *Spiritual Meadow*'s popularity and relevant bibliography, see Chapter 9.
67   Ong W.J., "The Writer's Audience Is Always a Fiction", *Modern Language Association* 90.1 (1975) 9–21.

they effect their immersion in the texts' storyworlds, by means of which they may appreciate the stories as true or believable, admirable, inspiring, edifying, and even imitable.

Being used to describe the work of special people (e.g. monastics, pious laypeople), *mirabilia* (products of magic and oddities of nature and culture) and *miracula* (events of divine origin), as well as the feeling they evoke, it is not surprising that the word 'wonder', as both verb and noun, and its various derivatives and synonyms (e.g. *thaumazō, thauma, thaumastos, thaumasios, thaumasmos, thaumasiourgēma, thaumasiourgia; paradoxos; semeion; teras; dynamis*), are the most repeated words in early tales. People's deeds are wonder-ful because they are beyond bodily pleasure and desire. Marvels are wonder-ful because they exceed human knowledge and expectations about nature and culture. Lastly, miracles are wonder-ful because they are produced by divine power and attest to its presence in the human world.

The tripartite tale theory (storyteller, storyness, and story-effect) that has been outlined here provides medievalists, short story scholars, and narratologists with a useful theoretical model, as it includes all the elements that exist for the sake of the story: its origin and circulation through retelling (storyteller and listeners who appear as potential storytellers), its form and characteristics (storyness and its relationship with that of other texts), and its power and impact on both intra-textual and extra-textual audiences (story-effect, both emotional and intellectual).

Bibliography

Primary Sources

Aelios Aristides, *Sacred Tales*. In ed. C.A. Behr, *P. Aelii Aristidis Opera quae exstant omnia* (Leiden: 1976).

Daniel of Sketis, *Narrations* (BHG 2099z–2102f, 79–80, 121–122, 618, 2255, 2453). In ed. B. Dahlman, *Saint Daniel of Sketis: A Group of Hagiographic Texts*, Studia Byzantina Upsaliensia 10 (Uppsala: 2007) 108–187.

Hermas, *Shepherd*. In ed. M. Whittaker, *Die apostolischen Väter 1: Der Hirt des Hermas*, Die griechischen christlichen Shriftsteller 48, 2nd ed. (Berlin: 1967) 1–98.

History of the Monks in Egypt (BHG 1333–1334). In ed. A.J. Festugière, *Historia monachorum in Aegypto*, Subsidia hagiographica 34 (Brussels: 1961).

John, Archbishop of Thessalonike, *Miracles of Demetrios* (BHG 499–523). In ed. P. Lemerle, *Les plus anciens recueils des Miracles de Saint Démétrius*, vol. 1: *Le texte* (Paris: 1979) 4–165.

John Moschos, *Spiritual Meadow* (*Leimonarion*) (BHG 1440f–1442z). In *Patrologia Graeca* 87.3:2852–3112.

Miracles of Thekla (BHG 1718). In ed. G. Dagron, *Vie et miracles de sainte Thècle: Texte grec, traduction et commentaire*, Subsidia hagiographica 62 (Brussels: 1978) 285–412.

Miracles of Kosmas and Damian (BHG 385–391). In (partial) ed. L. Deubner, *Kosmas und Damian: Texte und Einleitung* (Leipzig – Berlin: 1907) 193–206.

Palladios of Hellenopolis, *Lausiac History*. In ed. D.C. Butler, *The Lausiac History of Palladius*, vol. 2: *Introduction and Text* (Cambridge: 1904) 1–169.

Sayings of the Desert Fathers (*Apophthegmata Patrum*), Alphabetical Collection. In *Patrologia Graeca* 65:72–440.

Sayings of the Desert Fathers (*Apophthegmata Patrum*), Anonymous Collection. In ed. J. Wortley, *The Anonymous Sayings of the Desert Fathers: A Select Edition and Complete English Translation* (Cambridge: 2013).

Sophronios of Jerusalem, *Miracles of Kyros and John* (BHG 477–479). In ed. N.F. Marcos, *Los 'Thaumata' de Sofronio: Contribución al estudio de la 'incubatio' cristiana* (Madrid: 1975).

Secondary Works

Behr C.A. (trans.), *P. Aelius Aristides, The Complete Works*, vol. 2: *Orations XVII–LIII* (Leiden: 1981).

Benjamin W., "The Storyteller: Reflections on the Works of Nikolai Leskov", in Benjamin W., *Illuminations: Essays and Reflections*, ed. H. Arendt, trans. H. Zohn (New York: 1969) 83–109.

Bronwen N. – Costache D. – Wagner K., *Dreams, Virtue and Divine Knowledge in Early Christian Egypt* (Cambridge: 2019).

Brooks P., *Reading for the Plot: Design and Intention in Narrative* (Cambridge, MA: 1984).

Chadwick H., "John Moschus and His Friend Sophronius the Sophist", *Journal of Theological Studies* 25.1 (1974) 41–74.

Constantinou S., "Grotesque Bodies in Hagiographical Tales: The Monstrous and the Uncanny in Byzantine Collections of Miracle Stories", *Dumbarton Oaks Papers* 64 (2010) 43–54.

Constantinou S., "Healing Dreams in Early Byzantine Miracle Collections", in Oberhelman S. (ed.), *Dreams, Healing, and Medicine in Greece: From Antiquity to the Present* (Aldershot: 2013) 189–197.

Constantinou S., "The Morphology of Healing Dreams: Dream and Therapy in Byzantine Collections of Miracle Stories", in Angelidi C. – Calofonos G. (eds.), *Dreaming in Byzantium and Beyond* (Aldershot: 2014) 21–34.

Constantinou S. – Andreou A., "The Voices of the Tale: The Storyteller in Early Byzantine Collective Biographies, Miracle Collections, and Collections of Edifying Tales", *Byzantine and Modern Greek Studies* 46.1 (2021) 24–40, DOI: 10.1017/byz.2021.31.

Cox Miller P., "'All the Words were Frightful': Salvation by Dreams in the Shepherd of Hermas", *Vigiliae Christianae* 42 (1988) 327–338.

Cox Miller P., *Dreams in Late Antiquity: Studies in the Imagination of a Culture* (Princeton: 1994).

Csepregi I., "Changes in Dream Patterns between Antiquity and Byzantium: The Impact of Medical Learning on Dream Healing", in Csepregi I. – Burnett C. (eds.), *Ritual Healing: Magic, Ritual and Medical Therapy from Antiquity until the Early Modern Period* (Florence: 2012) 131–146.

Dahlman B. (trans.), *Saint Daniel of Sketis: A Group of Hagiographic Texts*, Studia Byzantina Upsaliensia 10 (Uppsala: 2007).

Déroche V. – Bouchet C. – Congourdeau M.H. (trans.), *Fioretti des moines d'Orient: Jean Moschos*, Le pré spirituel, Les Pères dans la foi 94–95 (Paris: 2006).

Doroszewska J., "Between the Monstrous and the Divine: Hermaphrodites in Phlegon of Tralles' *Mirabilia*", *Acta antiqua Academiae scientiarum Hungaricae* 53 (2013) 379–392, DOI: 10.1556/AAnt.53.2013.4.4.

Downie J., "Dream Hermeneutics in Aelius Aristides' *Ieroi logoi*", in Oberhelman S. (ed.), *Dreams, Healing, and Medicine in Greece: From Antiquity to the Present* (Aldershot: 2013) 109–128.

Eagleton T., *Heathcliff and the Great Hunger: Studies in Irish Culture* (London – New York: 1995).

Fludernik M., *Towards a 'Natural' Narratology* (London – New York: 1996).

Gascou, J. (trans.), *Miracles de saints Cyr et Jean* (*BHG 477–479*) (Paris: 2006).

Gerlach J., *Toward the End: Closure and Structure in the American Short Story* (Tuscaloosa: 1985).

Harkins A.K., "Looking at the *Shepherd of Hermas* through the Experience of Lived Religion", in Gasparini V. – Patzelt M. – Raja R. – Rieger A.K. – Rüpke J. – Urciuoli E. (eds.), *Lived Religion in the Ancient Mediterranean World: Approaching Religious Transformations from Archaeology, History and Classics* (Berlin – Boston: 2020) 49–70.

Jakobson R., "Closing Statement: Linguistics and Poetics", in Sebeok T.A. (ed.), *Style in Language* (Cambridge, MA: 1960) 350–449.

Johnson S.F. (trans.), "The Miracles of Thekla", in Talbot A.M. – Johnson S.F. (trans.), *Miracle Tales from Byzantium*, Dumbarton Oaks Medieval Library 12 (Cambridge, MA – London: 2012) 1–201.

Lewis C.S., "On Stories", in Lewis C.S. (ed.), *Essays Presented to Charles Williams* (Grand Rapids, MI: 1966) 90–105.

Lohafer S., *Coming to Terms with the Short Story* (Baton Rouge – London: 1983).

Lohafer S., *Reading for Storyness: Preclosure Theory, Empirical Poetics and Culture in the Short Story* (Baltimore: 2003).

Maisano R. (trans.), *Il Prato Giovanni Mosco: Presentazione, traduzione e commento* (Naples: 1982).

May C., 'I Am Your Brother': Short Story Studies (online publication: 2013).

Meyer R.T. (trans.), *Palladius: The Lausiac History, Translated and Annotated*, Ancient Christian Writers 34 (New York: 1964).

Ong W.J., "The Writer's Audience Is Always a Fiction", *Modern Language Association* 90.1 (1975) 9–21.

Petridou G., "'One Has to be So Terribly Religious To Be An Artist': Divine Inspiration and *Theophilia* in Aelius Aristides' *Hieroi logoi*", *Archiv für Religionsgeschichte* 20.1 (2018) 257–271.

Russell N. (trans.), "The Lives of the Desert Fathers", in Ward B. – Russell N. (eds.), *The Lives of the Desert Fathers*, Cistercian Studies 34 (Kalamazoo, MI: 1981) 47–119.

Tagliabue A., "An Embodied Reading of Epiphanies in Aelius Aristides' Sacred Tales", *Ramus* 45 (2016) 213–230.

Tagliabue, A. "Learning from Allegorical Images in the *Book of Visions* of *The Shepherd of Hermas*", *Arethusa* 50.2 (2017) 221–255.

Tarvahauta U., "A Just Man or Just a Man: The Ideal Man in the Visions of Hermas", *Patristica Nordica Annuaria* 35 (2020) 69–97.

Wortley J. (trans.), *John Moschus: The Spiritual Meadow*, Cistercian Studies 139 (Kalamazoo, MI: 1992).

Wortley J. (trans.), *The Anonymous Sayings of the Desert Fathers: A Select Edition and Complete English Translation* (Cambridge: 2013).

Young S., "Being a Man: The Pursuit of Manliness in *The Shepherd of Hermas*", *Journal of Early Christian Studies* 2.3 (1994) 237–255.

Zeppezauer D., "Warum wirken Wunder?: Die Sprache der Ärzte im Traum", *Zeitschrift für Antikes Christentum* 17.1 (2013) 143–159.

CHAPTER 2

Telling a *thauma* in Hagiography and Paradoxography

Christian Høgel

1   Introduction

It is a common thing to tell a story about what goes against expectations. In many such cases, expectations will depend on common notions of what is possible and probable, and when stories go beyond this, storytellers will be taking their audiences into what goes under the label of the wondrous or even miraculous: what in Greek is often referred to as *thauma*. A *thauma* (and cognate terms such as the adjectives *thaumasios* and *paradoxos*) may reflect many experiences and notions about the world and how we live in it, but as found in Greek paradoxography and hagiography, natural or physical laws, as experienced through everyday life, take up a central importance in almost all cases. The author-storyteller and their public know what is normally possible, and the story points out an instance of something transgressing this experience. Whether it is a bird, a river, or a person performing the *thauma*, they all do what birds, rivers, and persons normally are not, or are not thought of as, capable of doing, namely act beyond what we will here call the laws of nature. This is, in the examples we shall be dealing with, what the term *thauma* singles out.[1]

This use of *thauma* is slightly different from that very often found in much Homeric and classical literature (with numerous later imitators), where *thauma* refers to the impression that persons, buildings, or works of art may

---

1   On literary analysis of miracles in (Byzantine Greek) hagiography, see Constantinou S., "The Morphology of Healing Dreams: Dream and Therapy in Byzantine Collections of Miracle Stories", in Angelidi C. – Calofonos G. (eds.), *Dreaming in Byzantium and Beyond* (Aldershot: 2014) 21–34. On the social or even anthropological aspects of miracles, see Brown P., "The Rise and Function of the Holy Man in Late Antiquity", *Journal of Roman Studies* 61 (1971) 80–101; Kee H.C., *Miracles in the Early Christian World* (New Haven: 1983), and Flusin B., *Miracle et histoire dans l'œuvre de Cyrille de Scythopolis* (Paris: 1983), see esp. 157 on the use of the compound *paradoxon thauma*; Grant R.M., *Miracle and Natural Law in Graeco-Roman and Early Christian Thought* (Amsterdam: 1952) was unfortunately not available to me. The very idea of anything transgressing nature requires a notion of nature; on this see Lloyd G.E.R., "Greek Antiquity: The Invention of Nature", in Torrance J.R. (ed.), *The Concept of Nature* (Oxford: 1992) 1–24.

© CHRISTIAN HØGEL, 2025 | DOI:10.1163/9789004707351_004

This is an open access chapter distributed under the terms of the CC BY-NC-ND 4.0 license.

cause upon a person in the story (an impression that is normally thought of as passing on to the audience).[2] These instances hardly point beyond any laws of nature, though the emotional response in the recipient may be of a similar kind. The wonder of beauty, grandeur, physical or mental strength, etc. may be startling, and this idea of wonder also has an enormous position within Greek (and other) reflections on the power of art and artistic performance. Nevertheless, what becomes singled out in what may be called the short tale genres of paradoxography and hagiography is mostly the *thauma* involving actual transgression of physical/natural laws, evidencing what we could not or would not foresee since our daily life experience would in physical/natural terms exclude the very possibility. Such instances are often referred to collectively as miracles or wonders (in those days and today), but the semantic fields of these notions need to be further defined, since they involve numerous associations both old and modern.

'Miracle' – from Latin *miraculum* – to a large degree mirrors the Greek *thauma*, but will here only be taken in its performative sense, i.e. a miracle caused by someone or something. Or, to put it in more active terms, in all cases discussed here there will be an agent performing the miracle. This agent may in many cases not be the ultimate source or cause; often we are meant to understand that God, a god, 'nature', or some larger power or system is behind, enabling this exception to the common possible.[3] Often this will point to whole systems of (religious) belief and (philosophical) knowledge, but what interests us here is the notion of a causality, something operating behind or in support of the agent.

'Wonder' is another term that often covers what lies in the *thauma*, especially in paradoxography, and the Greek *paradoxon* (both as adjective 'wondrous' and as noun 'wonder') also comes close to reflecting modern perceptions of the term 'wonder'. The sources of wonders are many (including the aesthetic/moral ones excluded above), but one that should be highlighted from the start is distance (from the place of the narration), which is often of

---

2 On *thauma* in ancient literature, see esp. Lightfoot J., *Wonder and the Marvellous from Homer to the Hellenistic World* (Cambridge: 2021), and the chapter "Cataloguing the Marvellous: Herodotus and Paradoxography", in Priestley J. (ed.), *Herodotus and Hellenistic Culture* (Oxford: 2014) 75–87; also the online site on paradoxography constructed by Hardiman R., "Paradoxography", https://sites.google.com/site/paradoxography/ (last visited May 29, 2022).

3 The use of the concept of 'miracle' has come under hard debate lately; see e.g. Bersee T., *On the Meaning of 'Miracle' in Christianity: An Evaluation of the Current Miracle Debate and a Proposal of a Balanced Hermeneutical Approach* (Leuven: 2021). In the present text, the basis will in the first place be the occurrence of *thauma, paradoxon,* and related words.

importance in accounting for things observed.[4] The wondrous, according to such thinking, is found in distant places. This could suggest that physical/natural laws are perhaps not quite so universal after all. As we shall see, wonder in this meaning of exception through distance goes into paradoxographical tales but never to the degree of constructing a clear notion of a beyond with other physical/natural laws.

With this basis in the common use of the concept of *thauma* in paradoxography and hagiography, I will argue that the *thauma* tale is a specific type of narration in (classical and late classical/Byzantine) Greek literature, with its specific genre features and narrative modes.[5] More specifically, I will argue that the two types of *thauma* tale share (in general), firstly, a reference to physical laws as a basis; secondly, a distinction between the agent and the source of the *thauma*; and thirdly, a degree of suddenness in the description of the *thauma*, an issue that will be further analyzed below.

An important support for our suggesting the existence of a generically discernable *thauma* tale (found frequently in one of two types, i.e. paradoxographical or hagiographic) is the very fact that they were often compiled in collections. Paradoxographical collections, with varying titles and words announcing the miraculous nature of the narration, show that a specific interest went into gathering and reading about natural *thaumata*, inviting readers and listeners to compare and evaluate.[6] Some collections focused on specific natural phenomena, for example on water, but since its early stages writers of paradoxography were particularly keen on identifying the geography and particular places for each *thauma*, in some cases even making place the organizing principle of a collection.[7] Compilers of such collections would also often make references to where a story had appeared in earlier writing, reminding readers and listeners that such stories were common in historiography, geography, and other genres based on knowledge/research. But when appearing in a collection, these stories took on a life of their own and became a genre

---

4   See the seminal Wittkower R., "Marvels of the East: A Study in the History of Monsters", *Journal of the Warburg and the Courtauld Institutes* 5 (1942) 159–197.

5   Not much scholarship is concerned with the literary similarities and interplay between paradoxography and hagiography, but see Johnson S.F., *The Life and Miracles of Thekla: A Literary Study*, Hellenic Studies 13 (Cambridge, MA – London: 2006), esp. the chapter "Greek Wonders: Classical Models for Christian Miracle Collections" 172–220. See also Chapter 7 in the present volume.

6   See e.g. Geus K. – King C.G., "Paradoxography", in Keyser P. – Scarborough J. (eds.), *Oxford Handbook of Science and Medicine in the Classical World* (Oxford: 2018) 431–444.

7   See section 3 on "The Topological and Geographical Principles of Organization" in Geus – King, "Paradoxography" 436–438.

of its own. The same goes for miracle tales within hagiography.[8] From early on, saints would – as a sort of *imitatio Christi* – perform miracles, and soon it would be obvious, at least to Christian audiences, that tales of persons performing miracles would be narrating the performances of a saintly person. Some hagiographical collections were closely tied to specific locations and in that sense also included a topography as unifying theme.[9] Collections of stories of miraculous healings make up an important segment of Christian *thaumata*, with doctor saints becoming central figures of Greek hagiography.[10] But across these variations, as with the paradoxographical tales, the (Christian) hagiographical miracle tale also has quite a clear generic status, being found in collections as well as commonly embedded in larger tales within hagiography, historiography, and other genres.

To establish an overview of the generic specificities of this *thauma* tale (in both paradoxography and hagiography), we need to look at other types of tales that existed, not least others that were also included in collections. The label edifying or *beneficial* tale is found in hagiography, in rhetorical handbooks, historiography, etc. and singles out tales with a fitting moral, normally in guidance of individual human conduct.[11] Collections of beneficial tales abound, and such collections may group tales according to virtues, but many other systematizations are found (topography, biography, etc.). The beneficial tale is thus a generic type of short tale that parallels that of the *thauma* tale very well. And as with the *thauma* tales, beneficial tales also enter larger narrations or are, conversely, excerpted into collections stringing such tales into a type of their own. Yet the beneficial tale, normally, does not include a *thauma* or any transgression of the laws of nature. Examples of tales that overlap these distinctions (beneficial/miraculous) do of course exist – no generic classification system is tight – but the very existence of the distinct collection types supports

---

8   On hagiographical collections (of miracle tales), see Efthymiadis S., "Collections of Miracles (Fifth–Fifteenth Centuries)", in idem (ed.), *The Ashgate Research Companion to Byzantine Hagiography*, vol. 2: *Genres and Contexts* (Farnham: 2014) 103–142. Healing stories make up a large proportion of Christian miracle tales, but the genre includes miracles of many types. Scholarship, nevertheless, tends to define the genre almost uniquely on the basis of the healing feature; see ibidem, 104 and Johnson, *The Life and Miracles of Thekla* 175–176.

9   On the importance of space and place in hagiography, see Veikou M., *Spatial Paths to Holiness: Literary 'Lived Spaces' in Eleventh-Century Byzantine Saints' Lives*, Studia Byzantina Upsaliensia 22 (Uppsala: 2023).

10   Høgel C., "Money and Sainthood: Doctor Saints as Christian Heroes", forthcoming.

11   Binggeli A., "Collections of Edifying Stories", in Efthymiadis, *The Ashgate Research Companion* 2:143–159.

our speaking of the *thauma* tale as a generic category contemporaneous with the tales.

2 The Metaphysics of the *thauma* Tale: the Distinction Between Agent and Source

Having thus singled out the *thauma* tale within hagiography and paradoxography as jointly dependent upon a transgression of natural/physical laws, a metaphysical aspect necessarily enters the discourse. If they are not performed or caused within the normal parameters of daily life, a reader or listener will soon ask or wonder who or what then is behind the surprising powers or abilities of the agent. This power may in some cases seem harder to single out, but the following is an attempt to highlight this question of source as different from the explicit agent in the story (with exceptions that we will also discuss). Whereas the agent – the person, animal, or other entity performing the miracle – is normally obvious in the tale, the ultimate source of this power is, especially in paradoxography, less so. Still, I will here argue that it is a common feature of the *thauma* tale that there is (almost always) a non-human framing of the story. Something beyond human capacity is responsible for the *thauma* taking place or being possible. This is in contrast to many *beneficial* tales, where the person(s) involved can to a larger degree be the cause of their beneficial action or attitude. Certain virtues may, in a Platonic or other spirit, rise to the importance of ultimate cause, and Christian saints are clearly perceived as deriving much, if not all, of their spiritual force and exemplary nature from their faith, but we are usually not meant to take their virtues as part of their miraculous performance. Virtuous behavior normally comes with fully complying with normative rules, and this lies within the scope of any person. But the distinction between agent and source also differentiates our *thauma* tale from many other tales where divine intervention is the cause of miraculous change, e.g. in many pagan accounts of gods entering the scene of action and deciding or redirecting the outcome. Below, we shall see an example of the exceptional instances where Greek hagiography and paradoxography employ this mode of narration. Furthermore, we should also note that the distinction between agent and source, important also for our discussion of Greek hagiography, is not directly taken from the New Testament pattern of Christ's miracles. For in those cases of performed miracles, the agent and source are perceived as one, namely Christ himself. But in hagiography, as in paradoxography, there is a division between source and agent, and since the source is (almost) always the same ('nature' in paradoxography, and God in hagiography), one reason

TELLING A THAUMA IN HAGIOGRAPHY AND PARADOXOGRAPHY 45

for not mentioning the source may be the simple problem of repetition, which could end up sounding redundant.

Let us look at some examples from both paradoxography and hagiography to see the dynamics of agent and source at work. So let us repeat: The agent is the person, animal, or other that performs the miracle; the source is whatever force behind is either mentioned, intended, or adumbrated through the narration. The three following examples from the paradoxographical collection of Antigonos, entitled *Collection of Paradoxical Stories*, may serve as a starting point:

> 30 When wild goats in Crete are hit by an arrow, they seek out dittany. For this drives out the arrows.
>
> 40 Cranes fly high in order to see far away, and if they see dark clouds or a sudden storm, they seek out a resting place. They also have a leader. So, when the others have gone to sleep with their head below their wing, the leader keeps his wing free and his head high up, and if he observes any danger, he informs the others by a loud sound.
>
> 46 Aristotle says that when the eagle grows old, its beak grows bigger and curvier, and in the end, it dies of starvation. Also, according to him, the vulture takes hold of those chicks that the eagle casts out and brings them up. And that the eagle forces the young, while they are still small, to look towards the sun, and kills those that get running eyes or are unwilling to face the sun.

> 30 Τὰς δ' ἐν Κρήτῃ αἶγας τὰς ἀγρίας, ὅταν τοξευθῶσι, ζητεῖν τὴν δίκταμνον· δοκεῖ γὰρ ἐκβλητικὸν εἶναι τῶν βελῶν.
>
> 40 Τὰς δὲ γεράνους εἰς ὕψος πέτεσθαι, ἵνα καθορῶσιν μακράν, κἂν ἴδωσι νέφη καὶ συστροφὴν ἡσυχάζειν· ἔχειν δὲ καὶ ἡγεμόνα· τὰς μὲν οὖν ἄλλας καθεύδειν ὑπὸ τὴν πτέρυγα τὰς κεφαλὰς θείσας, τὸν ἡγεμόνα γυμνὴν ἔχειν προορώμενον, κἂν αἴσθηταί [τι] σημαίνειν ταῖς ἄλλαις βοῶντα.
>
> 46 Ὁ δὲ Ἀριστοτέλης φησίν, τῷ ἀετῷ γηράσκοντι τὸ ῥύγχος αὐξάνεσθαι καὶ γαμψοῦσθαι καὶ τέλος ἀποθνήσκειν λιμῷ. τὴν φήνην δὲ τοὺς ἐκβληθέντας τῶν νεοττῶν ὑπὸ τοῦ ἀετοῦ λαμβάνειν καὶ ἐκτρέφειν. τὸν δὲ ἀετὸν ἐπαναγκάζειν τὰ τέκνα ἔτι ψιλὰ ὄντα πρὸς τὸν ἥλιον βλέπειν, τὸ δὲ δακρύον αὐτῶν καὶ μὴ θέλον ἀντοφθαλμεῖν ἀποκτείνειν.[12]

---

12 Antigonos, *Collection of Paradoxical Stories* [Ἱστορίων παραδόξων συναγωγή], ed. A. Giannini, *Paradoxographorum Graecorum reliquiae* (Milan: 1966) 31–109, at 48 and 52; my translation.

In all these three small tales from Antigonos' collection, we hear of the surprising ways of animals. In the first case (30), goats can cure themselves; in the second (40), cranes have organized their society in a specific way; and in the third (46), Aristotle is quoted for information on how eagles raise their young. The wonder that these tales may produce (as was presumably expected by Antigonos) clearly stems from the surprising similarity – or dissimilarity – that the tales establish between human and animal habits. The clash between the agents (i.e. the animals) and their performance (the more or less human-like behavior) comes through already in the first line of every tale, since the animals need no further introduction. Furthermore, common to all these stories is the lack of indication of why what is told is a *thauma*. The reader or listener is expected to gather that on their own. Also, there is no indication of how these surprising features have come to be, no mythological tale, as would be common in aetiological accounts.[13]

It is only references to places, like Crete in our first story, or to names, like Aristotle in the last story, that point to the empiric nature of the tales. Whenever found, such geographical pinpoints or scientific cross-references underline that this has been observed, by someone, and now credited with (at least a degree of) belief. Lastly, in these examples from Antigonos' collection, all information is given as reported. The use of the accusative with infinitive in the first two stories assures that the reader knows that this is a reported account. In the last tale, a φησί ('says', with Aristotle as subject) governs the clause, whereas many other tales in such paradoxographical collections are introduced with a more impersonal φασί ('they say'). But the result is the same. Antigonos is telling us that somebody, the name of whom is only given in some instances, is giving us this information; he himself is just reporting. This perhaps leaves open the question of ultimate dependability, but it also underlines that nothing is invented, but asserted on the authority of others, implying a basic level of scientific approach, common to most paradoxography.

In hagiography, a *thauma* is often presented in quite a similar way. Let us take an example from an early saint's Life, namely Gregory of Nyssa's *Life of Gregory Thaumatourgos*. This saint became known as a performer of miracles, as is evident in his name extension, but his Life actually gives an account of his whole life, recounting only relatively few miracles. One of these takes place in his youth, when he is falsely accused by a prostitute, who nevertheless receives her pay:

---

13   See Wessels A. – Klooster J. (eds.), *Inventing Origins? Aetiological Thinking in Greek and Roman Antiquity* (Leiden: 2021).

For as she received the money in her hands she was racked by a demonic spirit, wailed in a loud, inhuman, animal cry and fell face down in the midst of the gathering; an awful and fearful sight to those present, her hair wildly disheveled and torn out by her own hands, her eyes rolled back into her head, and her mouth dribbling foam. And the demon which was choking her did not cease till that Great One had called upon God and interceded for her. Such are the stories they tell of the Great One's youth, worthy preludes to those things that he experienced subsequently in his life.

ὁμοῦ γὰρ τῷ ὑποδέξασθαι τῇ χειρὶ τὸ ἀργύριον πνεύματι δαιμονίῳ στρεβλω-
θεῖσα καὶ βρυχηθμῷ θηριώδει παρὰ τὴν ἀνθρωπίνην φωνὴν ἀνοιμώξασα πίπτει
πρηνὴς κατὰ τὸ μέσον τῶν συνειλεγμένων θέαμα φρικτόν τε καὶ φοβερὸν τοῖς
παροῦσιν ἀθρόως γεγενημένη τῶν τριχῶν τε διερριμμένων καὶ ταῖς ἰδίαις χερσὶ
σπαρασσομένων καὶ τῶν ὀφθαλμῶν ἀνεστραμμένων καὶ τοῦ στόματος τὸν
ἀφρὸν παραπτύοντος. καὶ οὐ πρότερον ἀνῆκε καταπνῖγον αὐτὴν τὸ δαιμόνιον
πρὶν ἢ τὸν μέγαν ἐκεῖνον ἐπικαλέσασθαι τὸν θεὸν καὶ ὑπὲρ αὐτῆς ἱλεώσασθαι.
Τοιαῦτα τῆς νεότητος τοῦ μεγάλου τὰ διηγήματα ἄξια τῶν μετὰ ταῦτα βεβιω-
μένων αὐτῷ τὰ προοίμια.[14]

Also here, the events are reported to our author ('such are the stories ...'), and the scene only includes human and demonic characters, of whom we may expect such things as deceit and moral steadfastness, with the demon further-more having the powers to produce the violent attacks that the woman experiences. She is, however, saved from her seizure, and the agent of this is human, namely our Gregory, here called 'the Great One' (capitalization from Slusser's translation). He calls upon God and intercedes for the woman. But through this, we also get to know the ultimate source of Gregory's powers. It is God who provides him with these. Hagiography has numerous ways of indicating this dependency on divine powers: prologues and final prayers; biblical quotations offered as parallels or even covering the actual narration; quoted prayers of the saintly person or authorial explanations; etc. And yet, as we shall see, one may also argue that hagiography shares some of the characteristic reticence of paradoxography on this point. Miracles often happen without any direct reference to the ultimate divine source. Also, we are not told what is wondrous

---

14   Gregory of Nyssa, *Life of Gregory Thaumatourgos* (BHG 715), ed. G. Heil, *Gregorii Nysseni sermones*, Gregorii Nysseni opera 10.1, 3 vols. (Leiden: 1990) 2:11; trans. M. Slusser, *St Gregory Thaumaturgus: Life and Works*, Fathers of the Church 98 (Washington, DC: 1998) 17–18, with adjustments.

or miraculous in the story of Gregory and the prostitute, only that it points to later events in the life of the saint. The miraculous nature of the scene is, however, hardly to be doubted, for the saint is able through invocation to stop the seizure that has caught the woman. Though we would like it to be so, this is not normally within the power of human beings.

Searching further for common features between the two types of *thauma* tales, we see that hetero-diegetic narrators are common in both, i.e. narrators who are not themselves taking active part in the narration. Gregory of Nyssa (*c.*335–395) never met Gregory Thaumatourgos (*c.*213–270), who died more than sixty years before the birth of his biographer. He therefore makes no appearance in the life of his biographee. But Athanasios, the author of the *Life of Antony the Great*, did meet the protagonist of his saintly biography, though only one scene shows them together.[15] Some hagiographers were even closer connected to the location of the saint, e.g. Theodoret of Cyrrhus (*c.*393–466), who functioned as a sort of priestly attendant for Symeon Stylites and wrote about his life within Symeon's lifetime.[16] Kyrillos of Skythopolis wrote his sequence of lives about the Palestinian desert fathers on the basis of accounts passed on to him from the latest representatives of these fathers, also depicted in his oeuvre. But even in these most authorial writings, the action of the hagiographers has minimal impact on the stories. Their main task is to observe. Most other hagiographers do only this, in most cases through the eyes of others.[17] That paradoxographers are equally removed from the action of their texts is perhaps more obvious, since animals and natural phenomena do most of the performing. Furthermore, many paradoxographers are compilers, and as such removed even from the role of direct observer. But persons do appear – just not the author.

What we therefore get in most cases is the voice of a distant storyteller telling stories staging agents of wonder that rely on or conform to a specific source

---

15 Hägg T., "The Life of St Antony between Biography and Hagiography", in Efthymiadis S., *The Ashgate Research Companion to Byzantine Hagiography*, vol. 1: *Periods and Places* (Farnham: 2011) 17–34.

16 On Theodoret's *Life of Symeon Stylites*, see the introduction in Doran R., *The Lives of Simeon Stylites: Translated with Introduction* (Kalamazoo, MI: 1992). On autobiographical stories in collections of miracle tales, see Constantinou S. – Andreou A., "The Voices of the Tale: The Storyteller in Early Byzantine Collective Biographies, Miracle Collections, and Collections of Edifying Tales", *Byzantine and Modern Greek Studies* 46.1 (2021) 24–40, DOI: 10.1017/byz.2021.31., esp. 29–30.

17 According to Constantinou – Andreou, "The Voices of the Tale", collections of miracle tales tend to have 'single-voice storytelling' (as opposed to the 'chain storytelling' that characterizes collective biographies), whereas collections of edifying tales normally have a combination of these.

TELLING A THAUMA IN HAGIOGRAPHY AND PARADOXOGRAPHY

of power. Hagiography has a more explicit manner of presenting this combination of agent and source, based on dogma and biblical quotations, whereas paradoxography may, through piling up cases including wondrous agents, make the reader/listener begin searching for an ultimate source. This source in paradoxographical tales can hardly be anyone or anything but nature, or even Nature, the object of investigation in Greek science.[18] In both types of *thauma* tale, the reader/listener will therefore continuously be invited to accept the actual powers of this source – or have a complicated time questioning it. We may think that hagiography, given its more dogmatic stance, relies on complying readers, but self-assurance is not always the proof of a benign public. We may just as well assume that the self-assurance of early Greek hagiography, not least martyr accounts, lived on as a rhetorical choice in much hagiography, expecting this traditional approach to be able to convince also the skeptical.

3   *Thauma* Tales with Acting Source

Until now, our scope has been looking at the commonly restricted presence of the source in both paradoxography and hagiography. In both cases, the ultimate source of the miracle is normally implied or is to be understood from indirect references. Furthermore, the source normally plays no active role in the scene. To underline this recurrent feature, we will here discuss two exceptional scenes that work contrary to this, first in hagiography and then in paradoxography.

The *Martyrdom of Akindynos, Pegasios, and Anempodistos* tells the story of three men who were martyred under the Persian king Shapur II (309–379). Torture takes up large parts of the text, and in one scene the martyrs start praying, while being burned:

---

18   I fully agree with Lightfoot, *Wonder and the Marvellous* 45–46 that 'to berate these texts for their failure to conform to supposed standards of ancient historiography or scientific and technical treatises is to miss the point entirely', but would insist that their aim to produce wonder, highlighted by Lightfoot, is deeply intertwined with a scientific (or, to some, pseudo-scientific) curiosity. On the importance of paradoxography for a development of the 'factual' and scientific approach in general, see King C.G., "The Creation and Development of an Ancient Scientific 'Fact': Paradoxography in the Peripatos", in Geus K. – Thiering M. (eds.), *Common Sense Geography and Mental Modelling*, Max-Planck-Institut für Wissenschaftsgeschichte Preprints 426 (Berlin: 2012) 139–144, who stresses in particular the opposition between *endoxa* and *paradoxa* (140–143). Also, Geus – King, "Paradoxography" 2 and 13, who underline the importance of the categories of *idion* ('singular') and *adoxon* ('unbelievable').

'Also now, Lord, lover of mankind, see our humility and show pity in this our plight, saving us from the evil-planning mind of this tyrant, and may they all learn that in you we have our God in heaven and our Father without beginning, and the Holy Spirit, worthy of worship, for all time. Amen.' When they had prayed in this manner, the Lord appeared to them, in our common human form, to be seen in white clothing, loosening their fetters and extinguishing the flames with dew, as he had once done appearing to the three young boys. In this manner the destroyers of falsehood were presented, sound and unscathed, to the king.

ʽκαὶ τὰ νῦν, δέσποτα φιλάνθρωπε, ἔπιδε ἐπὶ τὴν ταπείνωσιν ἡμῶν καὶ δεῖξόν σου τοὺς οἰκτιρμοὺς ἐπὶ τῇ κακώσει ἡμῶν ταύτῃ, ἐξαιρούμενος ἡμᾶς τῆς τοῦ τυράννου τούτου κακοτέχνου ψυχῆς, καὶ διδαχθήτωσαν πάντες ὅτι σε ἔχομεν Θεὸν ἐν οὐρανοῖς καὶ τὸν ἄναρχόν σου Πατέρα καὶ τὸ προσκυνητὸν καὶ πανάγιόν σου Πνεῦμα εἰς τοὺς αἰῶνας. Ἀμήν.ʼ Ταῦτα δὲ αὐτῶν εὐξαμένων, ἐφάνη αὐτοῖς ὁ Κύριος ἐν τῇ καθ' ἡμᾶς ἀνθρωπίνῃ μορφῇ, ὡς ἐν ἐσθῆτι λευκῇ ὁρώμενος, καὶ λύων μὲν τὰ δεσμά, τὴν δὲ φλόγα δροσίζων καθά ποτε τοῖς τρισὶ νεανίαις ἐπιφαινόμενοις ἔδρασκε. Διὸ καὶ εὑρέθησαν οἱ τοῦ ψεύδους ἀνταγωνισταὶ κατενώπιον τοῦ βασιλέως σῶοί τε καὶ ἀβλαβεῖς ἱστάμενοι.[19]

The martyrs pray and are saved, but in this scene, the source of salvation is made more explicit than in many other scenes of miraculous saving in martyrdom accounts. It is the Lord himself who arrives, in disguise, and does the loosening and extinguishing. We may even question how much agency remains to the martyrs, though the miracle clearly depended on their prayer. The divine source is furthermore made explicit through the reference to the three young (Hebrew) martyrs from the Old Testament (Daniel, 3:8–30). This parallel also underlines the disguise feature of the divine apparition, aligning this scene with a feature known in Greek literature since Homer. And though the transformation into a human shape, clad in white, takes up less space than normal dressing scenes in the Homeric epics, the listener/reader will also, in the scene involving the three martyrs, understand that a metamorphosis has taken place, that God is now making an appearance in form and clothes fitting for the occasion. But as indicated above, this is not common; the vast majority of miracle scenes in hagiography do not include such a direct presence of God.

Similarly, in paradoxography, we find exceptions to the rule that the source of the miraculous/wondrous is not actively involved in the action. This is in a

---

19   *Passion of Akindynos, Pegasios and Anempodistos* (BHG 21), ed. in *Acta Sanctorum* Nov. 1:461–490, at 463–464; my translation.

TELLING A THAUMA IN HAGIOGRAPHY AND PARADOXOGRAPHY

sense more obvious in paradoxography, if we accept the idea that the source in paradoxography is the broad notion of 'nature', as opposed to the purportedly universal Christian God of Greek hagiography. God is often thought of, as we have seen, as an anthropomorphic acting force, not least in the Old Testament, whereas 'nature' is hardly ever individualized in the same manner. But sometimes certain (rural) pagan divinities come close to representing what we would call the forces of nature, as e.g. in the following paradoxographical account:

> In the city of Orchomenos in Boiotia they say that a fox showed up, which pursued by dog sought refuge in an underground passage, and that the dog then followed it in there and barking made a loud noise, as if finding itself in a large hollow. The hunters suspected some divine meaning behind and widened out the entrance and forced their way in as well. Being able to see, due to the light coming in through some holes, they managed to get a full view of the scene and could afterwards go and report it all to the magistrates.

> Ἐν τῇ τῶν Ὀρχομενίων πόλει τῇ ἐν Βοιωτίᾳ φανῆναί φασιν ἀλώπεκα, ἣν κυνὸς διώκοντος εἰσδῦναι εἴς τινα ὑπόνομον, καὶ τὸν κύνα συνεισδῦναι αὐτῇ καὶ ὑλακτοῦντα ἦχον μέγαν ποεῖν, ὡσανεὶ εὐρυχωρίας τινὸς ὑπαρχούσης αὐτῷ· τοὺς δὲ κυνηγέτας ἔννοιαν λαβόντας δαιμονίαν, ἀναρρήξαντας τὴν εἴσδυσιν συνῶσαι καὶ αὐτούς· ἰδόντας δὲ διά τινων ὀπῶν εἰσερχόμενον ἔσω τὸ φῶς, εὐσυνόπτως τὰ λοιπὰ θεάσασθαι καὶ ἐλθόντας ἀπαγγεῖλαι τοῖς ἄρχουσιν.[20]

Here we hear of a natural wonder, a cave, discovered by chance by hunting dogs. The compiler, Pseudo-Aristotle, tells us his story in the common reported style and with clear indication of place, and the idea that something divine (or 'daemonic', depending on how we understand *daimonian*) is involved derives solely from the reaction of the hunters, who have followed their dog into the cave (just as the dog followed the fox). The compiler or his source expresses no opinion on the matter, but in reporting this aspect of the story as well, Pseudo-Aristotle is suggesting both a degree of wonder, which after all underpins the title of the collection, and a possible source. Some power, benevolent or not, divine or of a lower register, might be involved, and even if less supported than hagiographical *thaumata*, with their biblical parallels, prayers, etc., the involved hunters do help us catch where the wonder in the story lies.

---

20 Pseudo-Aristotle, *On Wondrous Reports* [Περὶ θαυμασίων ἀκουσμάτων] 99, ed. Giannini, *Paradoxographorum Graecorum* 221–314, at 266; my translation.

52 HØGEL

In fact, the paradoxographical stories that operate with humans, either as spectators or more involved, are the ones that come closest to adumbrating that there is a source for the wonder. This may also be expressed negatively, as in this other account from the collection of Pseudo-Aristotle:

> They say that in the ocean, outside the pillars of Hercules, the Carthaginians have found a deserted island, filled with all sorts of wood, navigable rivers, and wonderfully rich in all fruits, several days of sailing away. And since the Carthaginians often engage with this place because of its richness and some even have been living there, the leaders of Carthage have decreed that they will punish with death anyone who sails to the island, and that they will destroy anyone who settles there, so that no information seeps out and a collected crowd does not arrive and become lord of the island and steal the richness from the Carthaginians.

> Ἐν τῇ θαλάσσῃ τῇ ἔξω Ἡρακλείων στηλῶν φασὶν ὑπὸ Καρχηδονίων νῆσον εὑρεθῆναι ἐρήμην, ἔχουσαν ὕλην τε παντοδαπὴν καὶ ποταμοὺς πλουτοὺς καὶ τοῖς λοιποῖς καρποῖς θαυμαστήν, ἀπέχουσαν δὲ πλειόνων ἡμέρων πλοῦν. ἐν ᾗ ἐπιμισγομένων τῶν Καρχηδονίων πολλάκις διὰ τὴν εὐδαιμονίαν, ἐνίων γε μὴν καὶ οἰκούντων, τοὺς προεστῶτας τῶν Καρχηδονίων ἀπείπασθαι θανάτῳ ζημιοῦν τοὺς εἰς αὐτὴν πλευσομένους, καὶ τοὺς ἐνοικοῦντας πάντας ἀφανίσαι, ἵνα μὴ διαγγέλλωσι, μηδὲ πλῆθος συστραφὲν ἀπαντῶν ἐπὶ τὴν νῆσον κυρίας τύχῃ καὶ τὴν τῶν Καρχηδονίων εὐδαιμονίαν ἀφέληται.[21]

In this short paradoxographical account, a wondrous island (deserted, full of wood, with navigable rivers and plenty of fruits) becomes even more wondrous because Carthaginian leaders have blocked any information on the island from reaching the rest of the world. So the natural source of wonder here blends with human impact, though the most important part of the originating source remains nature itself, here also in combination with the distant setting of the story (somewhere in the Atlantic region). In fact, the human influence on the *thauma* in paradoxography may be set in parallel with the importance of animals in some hagiographical texts. Lions are common in the hagiographical Lives told by Kyrillos of Skythopolis, but only as minor characters or minor agents of *thauma*.[22]

---

21   Pseudo-Aristotle, *On Wondrous Reports*, 84; ed. Giannini, *Paradoxographorum Graecorum* 258; my translation with minor corrections.

22   Høgel C., "St. Sabas among the Lions: The Wild and the Completely Wild in the Writings of Kyrillos of Skythopolis", *Ephemerides Theologicae Lovanienses* 97.3 (2021) 449–468.

TELLING A THAUMA IN HAGIOGRAPHY AND PARADOXOGRAPHY

4   Suddenness as Narrative Climax

All in all, what becomes one of the most pervasive features of the *thauma* tale is the compact storytelling that makes expansion of the climax almost impossible.[23] Since the (metaphysical) source of the *thauma* hardly ever enters the scene, little if any narrative time is spent on this, and we proceed directly to the result, the miracle or wonder. But narrative climaxes can in many cases be expanded – in other genres, recognition scenes do, for example, involve confirming dialogues and duels between enemies. The wonder or miracle of hagiography and paradoxography, however, seems to appear before our eyes with a certain suddenness, with little expansion and only sometimes with a small coda of transition. It is as if once the narration is there, the narrator needs to stop and move on. The best parallel to this is probably the comic story, as analyzed by Alenka Zupančič.[24] In her analysis, the comic depends on a bridging or juxtaposing of (or even pointing to a break between) the universal and the concrete or material. It is through a sudden joining of these that the comic effect is produced. The (truly) comic involves relief, by making something universal make its appearance through or in the concrete or material. In the following analysis the miraculous will be read as a non-comic relief, with further parallels.

Let us take a paradoxographical tale as example, the very first story from the collection of Antigonos:

> Timarios, who wrote about Sicilian history, tells that a river called Alexos separates the Locrians from the people of Rhegion, and that the cicadas in the area of Locri sing, while those in the area of Rhegion are silent. But something even more fanciful is told: once citharists from these places came to Delphi, Ariston from the city of Rhegion and Eunomos from Locri. Having drawn lots and about to compete with each other, Ariston said he could not lose, since Rhegion was a colony from Delphi and its god, but Eunomos replied that those who lived in a country of silent cicadas could not possibly sing to a cithara. In the end, Locrian Eunomos won over the singer from Rhegion in the following way: while he was singing a cicada landed on his lyre and joined his song, and then the crowd shouted at what happened and gave him the prize.

---

23   On the use of the concept of climax in connection with paradoxography, see Calcante C.M., "Le climax della natura: Paradossografia e scienza nelle *Notti atiche* di Gellio", *Rivista di cultura classica e medioevale* 35 (1993) 245–263.

24   Zupančič A., *The Odd One In* (Cambridge, MA: 2008), see esp. the section entitled "Physics of the Infinite against Metaphysics of the Finite", 42–60.

Τίμαιος ὁ τὰς Σικελικὰς ἱστορίας συγγεγραφὼς ἐν Ῥηγίῳ φησὶ τοὺς Λοκροὺς καὶ τοὺς Ῥηγίνους ὁρίζοντος Ἄληκος καλουμένου ποταμοῦ τῶν τεττίγων τοὺς μὲν ἐν τῇ Λοκρικῇ ᾄδειν, τοὺς δὲ ἐν τῇ Ῥηγίνων ἀφώνους εἶναι. Λέγεται δέ τι τούτου μυθωδέστερον· ἀφικομένων γὰρ εἰς Δελφοὺς κιθαρῳδῶν Ἀρίστωνος μὲν ἐκ Ῥηγίου, παρὰ δὲ Λοκρῶν Εὐνόμου, καὶ περὶ τοῦ κλήρου πρὸς ἑαυτοὺς εἰς ἀντιλογίαν ἐλθόντων, ὁ μὲν οὐκ ᾤετο δεῖν ἐλαττοῦσθαι, τῆς ὅλης Ῥηγίνων ἀποικίας ἐκ Δελφῶν καὶ παρὰ τοῦ θεοῦ γεγενημένης, ὁ δὲ κατέτρεχεν, ὅτι τὸ παράπαν οὐδὲ καθαρῳδεῖν καθήκει, παρ' οἷς οὐδ' οἱ τέττιγες ᾄδουσιν. εὐημερήσαντος γοῦν τοῦ Ῥηγίνου ἐν τῷ ἀγῶνι ἐνίκησεν Εὔνομος ὁ Λοκρὸς παρὰ τοιαύτην αἰτίαν· ᾄδοντος αὐτοῦ μεταξὺ τέττιξ ἐπὶ τὴν λύραν ἐπιπτὰς ᾖδεν, ἡ δὲ πανήγυρις ἀνεβόησεν ἐπὶ τῷ γεγονότι καὶ ἐκέλευσεν ἐᾶν.[25]

It is probably safe to suppose that this story would have been taken to be funny or at least reflect some humor, but regardless of whether we are able to form such an opinion about the reception of the story in former times, we see that the story, called 'fanciful' (μυθωδέστερον), carefully sets a scene of two opposing arguments that each support the local claims to victory from either singer. One singer bases his claim on the divine origins of their cities, the other on the cicadas actually singing in his country but being silent in the land of the other. One could say (and I believe the story supports this) that the first singer has a lofty argument, whereas the second seems to have a simpler claim. The surprise effect, the climax, of the story comes when a singing cicada arrives and accompanies the second singer. This not only seems to support his claims, but also outdoes the other's lofty claim of divine origin through a tiny cicada – which now suddenly seems to operate on a level comparable to divinities, since the cicada arriving in support apparently has the agency to intervene (like a god) and decide the outcome.

But not least because it is found in a collection of natural paradoxes, we are to think of the cicada as acting on the instigation of nature itself or some similar notion, not as being a divinity. And it is this sudden equation of the single and tiny cicada with a larger system of nature that creates the climactic, and possibly also comic, effect, and makes the story deserve its place as starting point in Antigonos' collection. This is 'fanciful' because we know from daily life experience that cicadas – or any animal – will not take such initiatives and help humans in human competitions, and it is precisely the possible notional borders of such experience that paradoxography is trying out, with comic or non-comic relief as a central feature. And just as with the comic or the joke, in

---

25 Antigonos, *Collection of Paradoxical Stories*; ed. Giannini, *Paradoxographorum Graecorum* 32; my translation.

TELLING A THAUMA IN HAGIOGRAPHY AND PARADOXOGRAPHY

the analysis of Zupančić, the paradoxographical tale too, at least when extending beyond the brief form we discussed above, will work with the same kind of relief and the same kind of sudden equation (or juxtaposition) of a universal force (in paradoxography mostly 'nature') with the unsuspected materialization of this force (in this story, the cicada).

In martyr acts, a similar climax is often sought, though the narrative will often, through recurring repetitions of torture, interrogation, and unsuccessful (non-dialogical) dialogue – interrupted by imprisonment – continuously postpone the moment of relief, making it happen all of a sudden.[26] In the *Passion of Catherine*, these repetitive scenes take up almost the whole text (chs. 1–23), with numerous miracles of survival (of the saint) and conversion (among the spectators). But once we reach the final scene of execution outside the city, it is a divine voice that responds to the prayer of Catherine, calling her up to the heavens and thereby offering the final and climactic miracle. This, however, is seemingly not experienced by the audience; no reactions from them let us think that anyone but the saint has heard the voice. Her final words to the spectators and her executioners follow directly upon the heavenly call, here quoting from the end of the heavenly response:

> 'And as for the grace that you sought after, I will give all those that commemorate you hundredfold in return.' And once this announcement was made, the blessed woman said to the executor, 'Well then, do what the emperor commanded you to do.' The executor approached and cut off her head, and instantly, instead of blood, milk gushed upon the ground. And four angels came and took up her body and placed it on Mount Sinai. And many praised God.

> Περὶ δὲ τῆς χάριτος ἧς ἠτήσω, δώσω πᾶσιν τοῖς μνημονεύουσίν σου ἑκατονταπλασίονα.' Καὶ ταύτης τῆς φωνῆς δοθείσης εἶπεν ἡ μακαρία τῷ σπεκουλατόρι: 'Δεῦρο, ποίει τὸ κελευσθέν σοι ὑπὸ τοῦ βασιλέως.' Προσελθὼν δὲ ὁ σπεκουλάτωρ ἀπέτεμεν αὐτῆς τὴν κεφάλην, καὶ εὐθέως ἀντὶ τοῦ αἵματος γάλα ἔρυσεν ἐπὶ τῆς γῆς. Καὶ κατῆλθον ἄγγελοι τέσσαρες καὶ ἐπῆραν τὸ σῶμα αὐτῆς καὶ ἐπέθεντο ἐν τῷ ὄρει τῷ Σινᾶ. Καὶ πολλοὶ ἐδόξαζον τὸν θεόν.[27]

---

26   On the issue of imprisonment, and of other narrative features in Greek martyrdom accounts, see Papavarnavas C., *Gefängnis als Schwellenraum in der byzantinischen Hagiographie: Eine Untersuchung früh- und mittelbyzantinischer Märtyrerakten*, Millennium Studies 90 (Berlin – Boston: 2021).

27   *Passion of Catherine* (BHG 31), chs. 24–25; ed. J. Viteau, *Passions de ss. Écaterine et Pierre d'Alexandrie, Barbara et Anysia, publiées d'après les manuscrits grecs de Paris et Rome* (Paris: 1897) 4–65; my translation.

Unlike the many prior scenes of violence and spectator reactions, the final and in many ways climactic scene is kept to a minimum: the divine voice is now directed to an audience beyond the scene, addressing the recipients of the story – the later readers and listeners. They are the ones to receive hundredfold. Furthermore, the otherwise eloquent Catherine now speaks in a completely direct and short style to her executor, even heading her instructions with the prosaic δεῦρο ('Well then').[28] Careful preparation thus assures that we see the miracle of this story, announced by εὐθέως ἀντὶ τοῦ αἵματος ('instantly instead of blood'). Milk here becomes the conveyor of the universal – the divine – materializing in a material substance. Four angels do come and transport the body of the saint to her dwelling-place, to the praise of 'many'. But we are not even sure whether these many are the spectators outside the city, some witnesses at Mount Sinai or, in fact, some of us readers and listeners who were addressed earlier. The miracle of milk has become the focal point of the scene, the (here certainly non-comical) relief bridging or juxtaposing the universal and the material, establishing the missing link. It is the (sudden) instance of the universal in action, in the model of Zupančić. In the scene from the *Passion of Catherine*, the suddenness of this is even spelled out in the εὐθέως ('instantly').

5   Conclusions

The aim of this chapter was to show the effects of and commonalities between tales found in Greek paradoxography and hagiography, claiming that shared features and concepts (not least the term *thauma*) allow for the idea of a generic *thauma* tale, which, despite differing metaphysical framings (nature and God, respectively in the two types), works according to a shared scheme: a division between agent and source (of miracle/wonder), a minimal use (or no use) of the source as present participant in the scene of action, and the comic-like (and sudden) appearance of a material substance acting as link between the metaphysical source and the scene of action. The material used in the present chapter for this argument has been selective and small, and the existing examples – not least in hagiography – are legion. Further studies may help in disentangling further similarities and differences, but it is the hope that the present study will be a starting point for seeing commonalities across genres that have mostly been treated as quite separate entities.

---

28   For a discussion of Catherine's eloquence, see Constantinou S., "The Authoritative Voice of St. Catherine of Alexandria", *Acta Byzantina Fennica* 2 (2003–2004) 19–38.

Bibliography

Primary Sources

Antigonos, *Collection of Paradoxical Stories* [Ἱστορίων παραδόξων συναγωγή]. In ed. A. Giannini, *Paradoxographorum Graecorum reliquiae* (Milan: 1966), 31–109.

Gregory of Nyssa, *Life of Gregory Thaumatourgos* (BHG 715). In ed. G. Heil, *Gregorii Nysseni sermones*, Gregorii Nysseni opera 10.1, 3 vols. (Leiden: 1990) 2.

Passion of Akindynos, Pegasios and Anempodistos (BHG 21). In *Acta Sanctorum* Nov. 1:461–490.

Pseudo-Aristotle, *On Wondrous Reports* [Περὶ θαυμασίων ἀκουσμάτων]. In ed. A. Giannini, *Paradoxographorum Graecorum reliquiae* (Milan: 1966) 221–314.

Passion of Catherine (BHG 31). In. ed. J. Viteau, *Passions de ss. Écaterine et Pierre d'Alexandrie, Barbara et Anysia, publiées d'après les manuscrits grecs de Paris et Rome* (Paris: 1897) 4–65.

Secondary Works

Bersee T., *On the Meaning of 'Miracle' in Christianity: An Evaluation of the Current Miracle Debate and a Proposal of a Balanced Hermeneutical Approach* (Leuven: 2021).

Binggeli A., "Collections of Edifying Stories", in Efthymiadis S. (ed.), *The Ashgate Research Companion to Byzantine Hagiography*, vol. 2: *Genres and Contexts* (Farnham: 2014) 143–159.

Brown P., "The Rise and Function of the Holy Man in Late Antiquity", *Journal of Roman Studies* 61 (1971) 80–101.

Calcante C.M., "Le climax della natura: Paradossografia e scienza nelle *Notti atiche* di Gellio", *Rivista di cultura classica e medioevale* 35 (1993) 245–263.

Constantinou S., "The Authoritative Voice of St. Catherine of Alexandria", *Acta Byzantina Fennica* 2 (2003–2004) 19–38.

Constantinou S., "The Morphology of Healing Dreams: Dream and Therapy in Byzantine Collections of Miracle Stories", in Angelidi C. – Calofonos G. (eds.), *Dreaming in Byzantium and Beyond* (Aldershot: 2014) 21–34.

Constantinou S. – Andreou A., "The Voices of the Tale: The Storyteller in Early Byzantine Collective Biographies, Miracle Collections, and Collections of Edifying Tales", *Byzantine and Modern Greek Studies* 46.1 (2021) 24–40, DOI: 10.1017/byz.2021.31.

Doran R., *The Lives of Simeon Stylites: Translated with Introduction* (Kalamazoo: 1992).

Efthymiadis S., "Collections of Miracles (Fifth-Fifteenth Centuries)", in Efthymiadis S. (ed.), *The Ashgate Research Companion to Byzantine Hagiography*, vol. 2: *Genres and Contexts* (Farnham: 2014) 103–142.

Flusin B., *Miracle et histoire dans l'œuvre de Cyrille de Scythopolis* (Paris: 1983).

Geus K. – King C.G., "Paradoxography", in Keyser P. – Scarborough J. (eds.), *Oxford Handbook of Science and Medicine in the Classical World* (Oxford: 2018) 431–444.

Grant R.M., *Miracle and Natural Law in Graeco-Roman and Early Christian Thought* (Amsterdam: 1952).

Hägg T., "The Life of St Antony between Biography and Hagiography", in Efthymiadis S. (ed.), *The Ashgate Research Companion to Byzantine Hagiography*, vol. 1: *Periods and Places* (Farnham: 2011) 17–34.

Hardiman R., "Paradoxography", https://sites.google.com/site/paradoxography/ (last visited May 29, 2022).

Høgel C., "St. Sabas among the Lions: The Wild and the Completely Wild in the Writings of Kyrillos of Skythopolis", *Ephemerides Theologicae Lovanienses* 97.3 (2021) 449–468.

Høgel C., "Money and Sainthood: Doctor Saints as Christian Heroes" (forthcoming).

Johnson S.F., *The Life and Miracles of Thekla: A Literary Study*, Hellenic Studies 13 (Cambridge, MA – London: 2006).

Kee H.C., *Miracles in the Early Christian World* (New Haven: 1983).

King C.G., "The Creation and Development of an Ancient Scientific 'Fact': Paradoxography in the Peripatos", in Geus K. – Thiering M. (eds.), *Common Sense Geography and Mental Modelling*, Max-Planck-Institut für Wissenschaftsgeschichte Preprints 426 (Berlin: 2012) 139–144.

Lightfoot J., *Wonder and the Marvellous from Homer to the Hellenistic World* (Cambridge: 2021).

Lloyd G.E.R., "Greek Antiquity: The Invention of Nature", in Torrance J.R. (ed.), *The Concept of Nature* (Oxford: 1992) 1–24.

Papavarnavas C., *Gefängnis als Schwellenraum in der byzantinischen Hagiographie: Eine Untersuchung früh- und mittelbyzantinischer Märtyrerakten*, Millennium Studies 90 (Berlin – Boston: 2021).

Priestley J. (ed.), *Herodotus and Hellenistic Culture* (Oxford: 2014).

Slusser M. (trans.), *St Gregory Thaumaturgus: Life and Works*, Fathers of the Church 98 (Washington, DC: 1998).

Veikou M., *Spatial Paths to Holiness: Literary 'Lived Spaces' in Eleventh-Century Byzantine Saints' Lives*, Studia Byzantina Upsaliensia 22 (Uppsala: 2023).

Wessels A. – Klooster J. (eds.), *Inventing Origins? Aetiological Thinking in Greek and Roman Antiquity* (Leiden: 2021).

Wittkower R., "Marvels of the East: A Study in the History of Monsters", *Journal of the Warburg and the Courtauld Institutes* 5 (1942) 159–197.

Zupančič A., *The Odd One In* (Cambridge, MA: 2008).

CHAPTER 3

To Render Unbelievable Tales Believable: The Storyworlds of Paradoxography

Ingela Nilsson

1 Introduction

In the second-century novel by Achilles Tatius, *Leukippe and Kleitophon*, the hero-narrator tells a series of tales about sexual attraction in the natural world. There are stones, waters, and snakes desiring each other, but also trees: the male palm tree desires the female, stoops in her direction, and needs to have a shoot from her grafted into his 'heart' (εἰς τὴν τοῦ ἄρρενος καρδίαν). If he does, he revives and stands erect – this is their 'plant marriage' (γάμος φυτῶν), or rather sexual intercourse.[1] The story is well known from a whole series of Greek and Roman authors, from Herodotus and Pliny to Philostratos and Ammianus Marcellinus, and even to twelfth-century novelists Eumathios Makrembolites and Niketas Eugenianos.[2] This is a good example of how so-called paradox-ographical passages found their way into various literary genres throughout the centuries, displaying a wide intertextual network that covered all kinds of texts. In the case of the palm tree in Achilles Tatius, Helen Morales has convincingly argued that the phoenix can be seen as a figure of Leukippe and that 'its extraordinary exhibitionism plays a major role in the dynamics of desire and the visual strategies of the narrative'.[3] Such an interpretation shows

---

1   Achilles Tatius, *Leukippe and Kleitophon* 1.17–18, ed. J.-P. Garnaud, *Achille Tatius: Le roman de Leucippé et Clitophon* (Paris: 2002); the palm tree tale at 1.17.3.
    The writing of this article has been undertaken within the frame of the research programme 'Retracing Connections' (https://retracingconnections.org/), financed by Riksbankens Jubileumsfond (M19–0430:1).
2   For the ancient and late antique tradition, see Hilton J. – Wright W.C., "Erotic Date-Palms in Ammianus Marcellinus (*Res gestae*, XXIV, 3, 12–13)", *Listy filologické/Folia philologica* 138.3/4 (2015) 213–229. For the Byzantine novels, see Eumathios Makrembolites, *Hysmine and Hysminias*, 10.3, ed. M. Marcovich, *Eustathius Macrembolites: De Hysmines et Hysminiae amoribus libri XI* (Munich: 2001), and Niketas Eugenianos, *Drosilla and Charikles*, 4.142–144, ed. F. Conca, *Nicetas Eugenianus de Drosillae et Chariclis amoribus* (Amsterdam: 1990); both probably draw on Tatius, but might well have been aware of the wider popularity of the story.
3   Morales H., "The Taming of the View: Natural Curiosities in *Leukippe and Kleitophon*", in Hofmann H. (ed.), *Groningen Colloquia of the Novel* 6 (1995) 39–50, at 41.

© INGELA NILSSON, 2025 | DOI:10.1163/9789004707351_005

This is an open access chapter distributed under the terms of the CC BY-NC-ND 4.0 license.

how paradoxographical material is not merely a digressive page-filler drawn from some of the many collections at hand, as has sometimes been argued or implied, but serves important didactic, entertaining, and – perhaps most importantly – narrative purposes.

What interests me here is primarily how such curious and unbelievable phenomena are believable within the storyworld in which they are placed: not only how they may serve as symbols or metaphors, as in the example cited above, but how they offer a conceptual space where the unbelievable becomes the norm. Within the basically 'realistic' storyworld of the Greek novel, the inclusion of, for example, a virginity test – a miraculous event that cannot be explained in rational terms – makes sense because of its narrative function, but it also creates a portal to the parallel or meta-textual world of paradoxography.[4] In order to better understand the functions of paradoxography, my analysis will be informed by postclassical narratological ideas of literary worlds as mental models and possible worlds. This approach may open new ways of dealing with the issues of genre and fiction, which often mark the discussion of paradoxography. My focus will be on short tales preserved in collections rather than embedded in longer narratives, and the way in which they contain, imply, and project possible worlds and entire storyworlds despite – or sometimes even thanks to – their brevity.

2　　Paradoxography

Paradoxography is notably difficult to define.[5] There was no unifying term when the material was first composed and collected, which most likely has contributed to the subsequent confusion. John Tzetzes, writer and intellectual

---

4　On virginity tests in the Greek novels, see ibidem, 46–47; Ormand K., "Testing Virginity in Achilles Tatius and Heliodorus", *Ramus* 39.2 (2010) 160–197 with further references. More recently, Bird R., *Sophrosune in the Greek Novel: Reading Reactions to Desire* (London: 2020) 112–115.

5　Standard studies on ancient paradoxography include Ziegler K., "Paradoxographoi", *Paulys Realencyclopädie der classischen Altertumswissenschaft* 18 (1949) 1137–1166; Giannini A., "Studi sulla paradossografia greca I. Da Omero a Callimaco: Motive e forme del meraviglioso", *Istituto Lombardo (Rendiconti di Lettere)* 97 (1963) 247–266, and idem, "Studi sulla paradossografia greca II. Da Callimaco all'età imperiale: La lettura paradossografica", *Acme* 17 (1964) 99–140; Schepens G. – Delcroix K., "Ancient Paradoxography: Origin, Evolution, Production and Reception", in Pecere O. – Stramaglia A. (eds.), *La letteratura di consumo nel mondo greco-latino: Atti del Convegno Internazionale, Cassino, 14–17 settembre 1994* (Cassino: 1996) 375–460. See also the edition by Giannini A., *Paradoxographorum Graecorum reliquae*, Classici Greci e Latini 3 (Milan: 1966).

TO RENDER UNBELIEVABLE TALES BELIEVABLE

in twelfth-century Constantinople, coined the term *paradoxographer* (παρα-δοξογράφος) for Anthemios of Tralles, placed in a series of authors we would see rather as scientists, such as Archimedes.[6] Needless to say, Tzetzes did not invent the word out of nothing: the telling of strange and incredible things and events is well attested in the early Greek tradition (παράδοξα, παραδοξολογέω), but to call it a genre might be rather unhelpful.[7] While it could be understood as 'a sub-genre of history-writing' in the tradition and style of Herodotus,[8] it is also a number of other things: various incredible reports of a medical, scientific, spiritual, philosophical, or generally exotic character. Paradoxographical writings might therefore be better described as a loosely connected group of texts that could be catalogued in different ways depending on the interests of the collector and then drawn on and used by authors of numerous literary genres, such as novels, chronicles, miracles, and saints' Lives.[9]

Key concepts here are θαυμάσιος, ἄπιστος, and παράδοξος – we are dealing with marvelous, incredible, and perplexing things, but somehow they all exist and make sense, since paradoxography constructs a conceptual space where the fantastic and unbelievable themselves become the norm. In this space, the marvels are all 'true' and often drawn from certain 'authorities', which means that paradoxographical literature appears in relation to a body of 'real' knowledge of the human and natural worlds, based on empirical observation. Here we may note again Herodotus and his journalistically documented experiences of a world filled with incredible things and paradoxical behavior, later defamed by historians such as Thucydides focusing on political history and 'truth'. But paradoxographical literature relates also to rational analysis of the kind that was a central feature of the Hellenistic period, and which in turn stemmed from the work of Aristotle and his school in the field of the natural and physical sciences. Emilio Gabba has approached this apparent contradiction of

---

6 John Tzetzes, *Chiliades* 2.154, ed. P.A.M. Leone, *John Tzetzes: Historiae* (Naples: 1968). Note that Anthemios is not included in the section on paradoxography in *Chiliades* 7.144, on which see Jouanno C., "Tzetzès et la paradoxographie", *Revue des études byzantines* 78 (2020) 143–192.

7 Cf. e.g. *Oxford Dictionary of Byzantium*, s.v. "Paradoxography" 1583: 'The genre of mirabilia existed in antiquity', and note the useful comments of Shannon-Henderson K., "Constructing a New Imperial Paradoxography: Phlegon of Tralles and His Sources", in König A. (ed.), *Literature and Culture in the Roman Empire* (Cambridge: 2020) 159–178, at 161, citing Hardie P., *Paradox and the Marvellous in Augustan Literature and Culture* (Oxford: 2009) 14–15 on the function of paradoxography.

8 Johnson S.F., *The Life and Miracles of Thekla: A Literary Study*, Hellenic Studies 13 (Cambridge, MA – London: 2006) 174. See also 175–197 for a very useful overview of paradoxography as 'literary tradition'.

9 See ibidem, 196–197.

paradoxography by arguing that the semblance of rationality may have created an emotional response of credulity in the reader: this kind of text created an experience of what the world would be like if such things were true.[10]

The material itself usually consisted of brief statements or embryonic tales, gathered in collections of various shapes and lengths. As aptly put by Scott Fitzgerald Johnson,

> Paradoxography in its Hellenistic form is, therefore, a system of organization and one with its skeleton exposed: it provides immediate and easily referenced access to otherwise hidden, or effectively lost, knowledge and it offers a textual site for extension, epitomization, and reorganization by its eschewing of the fixed boundaries of traditional narrative.[11]

While much paradoxographical material thus existed beyond traditional narrative boundaries, it could be inserted in all kinds of texts and even, as in Lucian's *True Histories*, be parodied and narrativized. Lucian took such narrativization to the extreme, but paradoxographical material has great potential also in its short, indeed fragmentary form. As noted in a well-known passage in Aulus Gellius' *Attic Nights*, paradoxographical collections were useful in particular for the 'culling' of material to be used in one's own writings.[12] This process marked the entire Greco-Roman tradition and not least novels and miracle tales.[13] The narrative affinity between paradoxographical and novelistic writings is indicated also by readers in the later Greco-Roman tradition. Photios, in his ninth-century account of books he had read, grouped Damaskios – author of the now lost *Logoi paradoxoi* – alongside Lucian, Achilles Tatius, and Heliodorus. As noted by Johnson, 'It is a significant comment on taste that the cross-fertilization of the novel and paradoxography in the Hellenistic and Roman periods, evident in the very "Second Sophistic" writers cited by Photios, continued to be felt in ninth century Byzantium'.[14] It should be noted that the inherent narrative potential of paradoxography is very much present in the

---

10   Gabba E., "True History and False History in Classical Antiquity", *Journal of Roman Studies* 71 (1981) 50–62. Cf. Shannon-Henderson, "Constructing a New Imperial Paradoxography" 161–162.

11   Johnson, *The Life and Miracles of Thekla* 177.

12   Aulus Gellius, *Attic Nights* 9.4, on which see Johnson, *The Life and Miracles of Thekla* 183; more recently Shannon-Henderson, "Constructing a New Imperial Paradoxography" 160–161.

13   On paradoxography and miracles, see Chapters 2 and 7 in this volume.

14   Photios, *Library*, ed. R. Henry, *Photius: Bibliothèque*, 8 vols. (Paris: 1959–77) 4: cod. 130; Johnson, *The Life and Miracles of Thekla* 179.

short forms preserved in collections, despite their fragmented impression; that narrativity can partly explain the popularity of such material in longer narratives, offering authors narrative cues to develop and explore.

Paradoxographical material often goes under the name 'problems' or 'questions', behind which almost anything can hide, including physics, metaphysics, psychology, or mythology. From a modern perspective, science and mythology are often taken to belong to different categories, so that explanations of mythology are treated as euhemerism or allegory, while explanations that relate to nature or the human body are seen as something quite different; such a clear division is, however, rather tenuous. Julia Doroszewska, in a recent article on the paradoxographical collection of Phlegon of Tralles, points out how paradoxography and medicine interact in unexpected but significant ways. Doroszewska reads the 'medical curiosities' described by Phlegon through the lens of contemporary medicine, considering them as case studies subject to scientific explanation rather than curious wonders.[15] In a similar manner, paradoxographical problems and questions often also concern divine providence and other spiritual issues, interacting with mythological and religious concerns. All of this is marked by the use of both literary and non-literary sources and reflects, in the words of Kelly Shannon-Henderson, 'a contemporary dialogue between the textual and the extratextual'.[16] This is an apt way of describing not only the method of Phlegon, but of most texts we now read as paradoxographical or mythographical.

Such an inclusive and methodological way of understanding paradoxography is indicated also by Byzantine readers such as Tzetzes, who – as noted above – coined the term in reference to Anthemios of Tralles, known primarily as an architect and the designer of Hagia Sophia.[17] When Eustathios of Thessalonike, in the same century, discussed interpretations of myths by Palaephatus, author of the rationalizing *On Unbelievable Tales* (Περὶ ἀπίστων), and Herakleitos (the Paradoxographer), author of a similar treatise, he did not place them in any strict category of allegory – as modern scholars might prefer – but simply referred to Herakleitos as the one who makes 'unbelievable tales believable' (ὁ τοῖς ἀπίστοις προθέμενος ἐμφῆναι πίστιν), supposedly

---

15 Doroszewska J., "Beyond the Limits of the Human Body: Phlegon of Tralles' Medical Curiosities", in Kazantzidis G. (ed.), *Medicine and Paradoxography in the Ancient World* (Berlin – Boston: 2019) 117–140. On Phlegon, see also Shannon-Henderson, "Constructing a New Imperial Paradoxography".

16 Shannon-Henderson, "Constructing a New Imperial Paradoxography" 162.

17 See above, n. 7.

by turning fiction or 'lies' into history.[18] While it might be tempting to call Herakleitos a mythographer rather than a paradoxographer, as Jacob Stern suggests, it does not really solve any problem.[19] The numerous fragments, preserved in collections under titles and names that do not always reflect the original version, should be allowed to maintain their heterogeneous and confusing character as preserved in the tradition. The Linnaean organizational practices of modern editors, as in the nineteenth-century *Scriptores rerum mirabilium Graeci*, hides the problem by constructing genres where there were none. If we turn instead to the medieval manuscripts, it is clear that different kinds of texts can be mixed rather freely, and collections can include all kinds of material.[20]

To conclude, paradoxography is not a genre; it is a conceptual space that can cross genres and encompass several worlds, textual and extra-textual. In the following, such worlds will be explored from various textual and cognitive perspectives.

3   Storyworlds and Possible Worlds

Let me start with a basic distinction between two kinds of 'literary worlds', just to avoid confusion. On the one hand, we have the world in which literature is produced and read, and accordingly affected by various political and social conditions: this is the world investigated by, among others, Pascale Casanova in her famous *La république mondiale de lettres* (*The World Republic of Letters*).[21] In the context of paradoxography, it would be the world in which the ancient and late antique texts were written, but also that of Byzantine readers who copied, compiled, and adapted the ancient material for new purposes, sometimes rejecting it in favor of Christian piety. On the other hand, we have the

---

18   Eustathios of Thessalonike, *Commentary on the Odyssey*, ed. G. Stallbaum, *Eustathii, Archiepiscopi Thessalonicensis commentarii ad Homeri Odysseam*, 2 vols. (Leipzig: 1825) 1, at 1:176, line 31; trans. J. Stern, "Heraclitus the Paradoxographer: Περὶ ἀπίστων, *On Unbelievable Tales*", *Transactions of the American Philological Association* 133 (2003) 51–97, at 52.

19   Stern, "Heraclitus the Paradoxographer" 52.

20   Westermann A., *Scriptores rerum mirabilium Graeci* (London: 1839). Cf. Messis C., "Aux marges de la philosophie, au cœur de la curiosité: Le Manuscrit d'Heidelberg Pal. Gr. 398", in Bianconi D. – Ronconi P. (eds.), *La 'Collection philosophique' face à l'histoire: Péripéties et tradition* (Spoleto: 2020) 209–238. Note also Jouanno, "Tzetzès et la paradoxographie" 150–153 on Tzetzes' list of rather disparate authors.

21   Casanova P., *La république mondiale de lettres* (Paris: 1999), trans. M.B. DeBevoise, *The World Republic of Letters* (Cambridge, MA – London: 2004); see also Casanova P., "Literature as a World", *New Left Review* 31 (2005) 71–90.

TO RENDER UNBELIEVABLE TALES BELIEVABLE 65

world in the story: it is all that comes with a narrative, 'the world of the world of art',[22] and that is what in the following will be referred to as the storyworld.

In its most basic sense, the storyworld is the literary world in which characters and their actions are set within one or several works. While this world can be, and often is, defined in relation to the authorial or historical setting of the stories' composition,[23] postclassical narratology has placed emphasis on the cognitive aspects of storyworlds. Readers, in the words of David Herman, 'use textual cues to build up representations of the worlds evoked by stories, or *storyworlds*'.[24] In this sense, storyworlds can be seen as 'mental models': a 'worldmaking practice' according to which the reader maps and works to comprehend a narrative.[25] A storyworld is accordingly the cognitive result of the reading process during which the reader's comprehension is at work. As aptly put by AnnaLinden Weller, writing under her pseudonym as science fiction novelist Arkady Martin, 'A storyworld is thus a co-created world between author and audience, bound by mutually held-in-common rules of causality and verisimilitude'.[26]

This means that a storyworld, even if we understand it as a literary construction, cannot be entirely disconnected from the real world, because readers exist in an experienced reality that affects their ability to imagine and construct the storyworld.[27] In the words of Eric Hayot,

> Aesthetic worlds, no matter how they form themselves, are, among other things, always relations to and theories of the lived world, whether as largely unconscious normative constructs, as rearticulations, or even as active refusals of the world-norms of their age. In this sense they

---

22 Hayot E., "On Literary Worlds", *Modern Language Quarterly* 72.2 (2011) 129–161, at 135.
23 Cf. ibidem, 135–136, on 'the general social and historical space in which an author lived and worked'.
24 Herman D., *Basic Elements of Narrative* (Chichester: 2009) 106.
25 Ibidem, 106; cf. idem, *Story Logic: Problems and Possibilities of Narrative* (Lincoln, NE – London: 2002) 5: 'mental models of who did what to and with whom, when, where, why and in what fashion in the world in which recipients relocate [...] as they work to comprehend a narrative'.
26 Martine A., "The Mysterious Discipline of Narratologists: Why We Need Stories to Make Sense", *Tor.com: Science Fiction, Fantasy, and Related Subjects* (January 29, 2019), https://www.tor.com/2019/01/29/the-mysterious-discipline-of-narratologists/ (last visited November 20, 2020).
27 This works in both ways, because the world of a narrative can also function as an approach to the actual world, 'heightening one's awareness of certain real-world features'; Hayot, "On Literary Worlds" 136.

are also always social and conceptual constructs, as well as formal and affective ones.[28]

This connection between the literary world and the actual world is sometimes termed 'worldedness', which here will be used as a complement in understanding how storyworlds function.

Literary scholars like Casanova and Hayot have argued that the concept of 'world' can help in rethinking traditional paradigms of literary history; while their primary interest is in modern world literature, the model seems useful also for those of us who work on premodern and pre-national literatures. Hayot defines worldedness as 'the world-oriented force of any given work of art', arguing that it is 'an aesthetic effect that merges only at certain scales of the work itself (and hence of the analysis of the work)'.[29] Again, this is something that happens between the work and the reader, and in that sense it is related to the more sociologically oriented idea that all literature is 'entangled' with reality. According to such an approach, literature is seen as a sphere in which human existence can be imagined and negotiated, offering an important tool for commenting on and relating to 'reality'.[30] Worldedness thus offers a useful complement to the storyworld concept: storyworlds need an element of worldedness, because otherwise they would not make sense to people living in the actual world. What is important to remember is that the literary world never can be equated with the actual world in which the author or contemporary reader lived: a storyworld is no mirror, only a reflection that is distorted to various degrees and in very different ways.

This brings me to the third concept that is closely related to and partly overlaps with that of storyworld: the idea of possible worlds. Possible worlds are just what they sound like: the possible world-making that takes place in a literary work (or in a song or a film), creating what could also be termed belief-worlds shared by members of a group. The key here is what I mentioned above in the definition of storyworlds: *mutually held-in-common rules of causality and verisimilitude*. Because a possible world is dominated by its own logic: it does not need to adhere to rules of the actual world (at least not beyond what makes it

---

28   Ibidem, 137.

29   Ibidem, 139.

30   Jusdanis G., *Fiction Agonistes: In Defense of Literature* (Stanford, CA: 2010) 5: 'the role of literature [...] is to highlight itself as a separate realm of human practice wherein we can imagine alternative possibilities of human relationships and political institutions'. Cf. Hayot, "On Literary Worlds" 141: 'World-creation happens most frequently in the ideological unconsciousness of the work, as an expression not of what it does not know but of what it knows most deeply, and thus mentions last'.

comprehensible for actual-world readers), but it has to make sense as a world. Common examples are drawn from fairy tales or superhero comics: such stories suspend belief in the common sense of the word, but they are perfectly logical as long as the characters and their actions are understood and accepted within their own storyworlds and thus by the reader.[31] Even if we, as human beings, are deeply rooted in the notion that there is one world in which we live and through which we think, we can clearly handle the idea of multiple worlds in the form of aesthetic constructions, if not necessarily in physical reality.[32] And this is certainly not a modern thing, but something that ancient literature and art also indicate.

I would like to close these theoretical considerations by underlining that storyworlds can encompass different categories of texts and, at the same time, the same genre can project very different worlds. All stories project worlds, whether historiography or novels, and as noted by Marie-Laure Ryan, 'works such as the *Canterbury Tales*, *Decameron*, or *Arabian Nights* are not worlds with many stories, but rather texts with many worlds. These texts feature a framing story and many embedded ones, told by the characters of the framing story'.[33] This is an important observation for my analysis of the storyworlds of paradoxography, taking us far beyond any clear boundaries of genre as well as fiction.

In the following I will look at three kinds of paradoxographical texts, and I will focus on worlds that relate to sexual attraction or desire (*erōs*). The storyworlds belong in different kinds of discourse, from the scientific and medical to the mythographical and novelistic, written by Pseudo-Alexander of Aphrodisias, Herakleitos the Paradoxographer, and Parthenios. The texts under discussion are known for not offering narratives proper, but rather fragments; their writers 'organized their stories into individual segments with no collective thesis or unifying narrative'.[34] 'All this information, but hardly a narrative', as a colleague put it. But I wish to show how the apparent lack of a unifying narrative is well compensated for by the storyworlds contained in the

---

31 For a detailed overview of the concept's history and use, see Ryan M.-L., "Possible Worlds in Recent Literary Theory", *Style* 26.4 (1992) 528–553.

32 Kukkonen K., "Navigating Infinite Earths: Readers, Mental Models, and the Multiverse of Superhero Comics", *Storyworlds: A Journal of Narrative Studies* 2 (2010) 39–58, esp. 39–40, discussing and arguing against Ryan M.-L., "From Parallel Universes to Possible Worlds: Ontological Pluralism in Physics, Narratology, and Narrative", *Poetics Today* 27.4 (2006) 633–674.

33 Ryan, M.-L., "The Aesthetics of Proliferation", in Boni M. (ed.), *World Building* (Amsterdam: 2017) 31–46, at 37.

34 Johnson, *The Life and Miracles of Thekla* 176.

68   NILSSON

narremes offered in the collections, always depending on the readers' immersion in well-known worlds of possible and mostly unhappy love stories.

4   Pseudo-Alexander of Aphrodisias

Among the writings attributed to Alexander of Aphrodisias is a collection of *Medical Puzzles and Natural Problems* (Ἰατρικὰ ἀπορήματα καὶ φυσικὰ προβλήματα), most often considered to be spurious. Best known for his extensive commentaries on Aristotle, Alexander probably worked at the end of the second or in the early third century. As for the *Medical Puzzles*, we cannot be sure about the dating, but to judge from the content of this particular text, it may well belong in the imperial period.[35] The collection consists of two books, containing 152 and 76 problems respectively and each opening with a preface. The problem that interests me here is 1.87: 'Why do the extremities of people who are struck by desire sometimes go cold, sometimes hot?' (Διὰ τί τῶν ἐρώντων τὰ ἄκρα ποτὲ μὲν ψυχρά, ποτὲ δὲ θερμὰ γίνεται;). The answer is somewhat lengthy, so I will offer a paraphrase rather than cite it in its entirety.

Those who desire someone but have no hope of getting what they desire go cold, pale, and sullen, because the heat remains hidden deep inside, and their extremities go cold. Those who nurture hope, on the other hand, go hot, and their skin turns red. That is why desire is sometimes represented by artists as sullen, sometimes as smiling; sometimes it is represented as a well-fed child (παῖδα δὲ εὐτραφῆ), because desire does not last forever. Only feelings between genuine friends, a father's for a child, or that of a woman for a man, are lasting and sincere. Desire is mostly directed toward strangers, vehement, and crazy. Therefore, it is represented as winged and with a torch, because the souls of lovers are volatile and because their hearts are set aflame; it is represented with an arrow in the right hand and a quiver with arrows in the left, because desire is first accomplished by one ray from the eyes, then followed by many rays in a constant. Finally, desire is represented as naked because passions appear in the open. There are many kinds of desire, 'just as the divine Plato says that Eros is a many-headed beast (πολυκέφαλον θηρίον)'. Quite a few men desire in

---

35   Cf. Sharples R.W., "Implications of the New Alexander of Aphrodisias Inscription", *Bulletin of the Institute of Classical Studies* 48 (2005) 47–56, who argues that the author of the *Medical Puzzles* might have been Alexander's father, also named Alexander. See now Meeusen M., "An Interpretation of the Preface to *Medical Puzzles and Natural Problems* 1 by Pseudo-Alexander of Aphrodisias in Light of Medical Education", in Bouras-Vallianatos P. – Xenophontos S. (eds.), *Greek Medical Literature and Its Readers from Hippocrates to Islam and Byzantium* (London: 2018) 94–109, at 94–96 on the author and context.

TO RENDER UNBELIEVABLE TALES BELIEVABLE 69

unlawful and impious ways, which Alexander has discussed, so he says, in the second book of his *Allegories*, 'turning the fiction of gods into believable stories' (τῶν εἰς θεοὺς ἀναπλαττομένων πιθανῶν ἱστοριῶν).[36]

Like much paradoxography, this text is very difficult to classify. Hidden in the middle of a treatise that is defined as (more or less) medical, it has never been read as anything else, but the interest of the author clearly goes well beyond that – or perhaps our understanding of medicine does not encompass Pseudo-Alexander's sense of what should be included. Only the first few lines treat the human body, in stating why limbs can go cold or hot in a person who is caught by desire. What then follows is something else. To some readers, it is probably simply a list of characteristics. But this text takes us into the story-world of Eros, of desire: a mental model shared by author and audience, created by textual and here also iconographical cues, transgressing the generic boundaries of poetry, fiction, philosophy, medicine – and art! The fact that the final line takes us to allegory shows how the scientific aspects of paradoxography cannot be clearly distinguished from their allegorical or religious connotations. This is underlined also in the preface to Pseudo-Alexander's *Medical Puzzles*: some problems are presented as completely unsolvable (ἄλυτα) and comprehensible only to God (θεῷ μόνῳ γνώριμα) – they cannot be grasped by human intelligence, even with the help of science.[37]

The storyworld of desire seems a good example of such unsolvable problems, for which you need not only rationalistic and medical, but also metaphorical and allegorical explanations. This storyworld is very much present in several narratives of the Greco-Roman tradition, both in novelistic and hagiographical tales – it is indeed the storyworld in which the opening example of the palm tree 'in love' exists and makes sense. I will now move on to another, different world in which sexual attraction plays a crucial narrative role: that of mythology.

5   Herakleitos the Paradoxographer

A series of 'unbelievable tales' (Περὶ ἀπίστων) attributed to Herakleitos (in modern scholarship referred to as 'the Paradoxographer') has come down to

---

36   My paraphrase is based on a new edition in preparation by Carl-Gustaf Lindqvist (Gothenburg University); the old edition goes back to 1841: J.L. Ideler, *Physici et medici Graeci minores*, 2 vols. (Berlin: 1841) 1. I am grateful to Lindqvist for sharing his text with me and also for drawing my attention to this text.

37   Meeusen, "An Interpretation of the Preface" 99.

us in a single thirteenth-century manuscript (Vatican 305).[38] The collection of Herakleitos probably dates to the late first or the second century and contains thirty-nine *lemmata* in which a known myth is briefly told and then explained in terms of rationalism, euhemerism, allegory, or etymology. The manuscript contains various collections of allegories, problems, and marvelous tales, witnessing the unclear boundary between such kinds of texts noted above.[39] The same confusion of category is notable if we try to define the kind of collection that we are dealing with: Herakleitos' *On Unbelievable Tales* (Περὶ ἀπίστων) is similar to, but not the same as the *On Unbelievable Tales* (Περὶ ἀπίστων) of Palaephatus (myths subject to rationalistic explanation), the *Constellations* (Καταστερισμοί) of Pseudo-Eratosthenes (a collection of myths in which characters are transformed into constellations), the *Metamorphoses* of Antoninus Liberalis (a collection of borrowed metamorphosis tales), or the *Sufferings in Love* (Ἐρωτικὰ παθήματα) of Parthenios (a collection of short love stories, some of which are known from other sources on mythology, others not).[40] The most common way of approaching these collections seems to be the kind of interpretation they offer, but here I will focus rather on the narrative construction and believability of the story within the frame of a coherent world.

Several of the tales explained by Herakleitos are about mythological women and how they, in fact, had no magic powers but were simply prostitutes. There is accordingly an interesting shift of gendered agency that I will consider along with the changes in the storyworld constructions. Let us begin with the very first tale of the collection, the true story of Medusa.

> 1. Medusa.
> They say that Medusa turned anyone who looked at her to stone and that when Perseus cut off her head a winged horse emerged.
>
> But here is how it was. Medusa was a beautiful prostitute. Any man who saw her was amazed – turned to stone, so to speak. We ourselves say, 'He saw her and was turned to stone.'
>
> But when Perseus arrived, Medusa fell in love with him: she squandered her possessions on him and ruined the prime of her life. And when she had lost these – her youth and her possessions – she suffered a 'horse'

---

38   Herakleitos the Paradoxographer, *On Unbelievable Tales*, ed. N. Festa, *Mythographi Graeci*, vol. 3.2: *Palaephati Peri apistōn; Heracliti qui fertur libellus Peri apistōn; Excerpta vaticana: Vulgo anonymus De incredibilibus* (Leipzig: 1902).

39   Translation and commentary in Stern, "Heraclitus the Paradoxographer" 73–92. On the ms., the dating, and the author, see ibidem, 51–54 with further references.

40   I shall return to the latter text below.

TO RENDER UNBELIEVABLE TALES BELIEVABLE 71

old age. For the head is the flowering crown of youth – which is what
Perseus took from her.

(1) Περὶ Μεδούσης.
Φασὶ ταύτην ἀπολιθοῦν τοὺς θεασαμένους αὐτήν, καὶ Περσέως ἀποτεμόντος
αὐτῆς τὴν κεφαλήν, ἐξελθεῖν ἵππον πτερωτόν. ἔχει δὲ οὕτω. αὕτη ἑταίρα καλὴ
ἐγένετο ὡς τὸν ἰδόντα αὐτὴν ἔκπληκτον γενόμενον οἷον ἀπολιθοῦσθαι. λέγομεν
δὲ καὶ ἡμεῖς ἰδὼν αὐτὴν ἀπελιθώθη. παραγενομένου δὲ Περσέως ἐν ἔρωτι γενο-
μένη τά τε ὑπάρχοντα κατέφαγε καὶ τὴν ἑαυτῆς ἡλικίαν κατέφθειρεν· ἀπολέ-
σασα δὲ τὴν ἡλικίαν καὶ τὰ ὑπάρχοντα ἵππου γήρας ἐγήρασεν. ἡ γὰρ κεφαλὴ τὸ
τῆς ἡλικίας ἄνθος ἐστίν, ὃ ἀφεῖλεν αὐτῆς ὁ Περσεύς.[41]

This is a rationalistic, not an allegorical, explanation: the interpreter, Herakleitos
(whoever he is), indicates that these are historical events that were somehow
misunderstood and now are 'deconstructed and cured' by him: the methods
are ἀνασκευή and θεραπεία, as the subtitle or brief preface of the collections
indicates.[42] But there is more at play here than those standard models of interpretation, because the rationalistic explanation does not simply replace the
myth. Instead, a new story is uncovered through the interpretation: the storyworld of ancient myth is subverted and replaced by a supposedly more believable reality in which beautiful women are prostitutes who fall in love, waste
their money on a man, and become old. Rationalism does not put an end to,
but engenders new storytelling: history, as Eustathios put it.[43] And this is not
unique, but something that appears also in other tales of the collection, for
instance in the story of Circe:

16. Circe
The myth has been handed down that Circe transformed men with a
potion.
Circe, however, was a prostitute who bewitched her clients at first with
every sort of willingness to please and led them on to be well-disposed
toward her. But when their passion for her grew, she controlled them
through their lust, as they were mindlessly carried along in their pleasures.
Odysseus got the better of her also.

---

41   Stern, "Heraclitus the Paradoxographer" 73.
42   Ibidem, 62–64 and 73 with n. 59.
43   See above, n. 18.

(16) Περὶ Κίρκης.

Ταύτην ὁ μῦθος παρ⟨αδ⟩έδωκε ποτῷ μεταμορφοῦσαν ἀνθρώπους. ἦν δὲ ἑταίρα, καὶ κατακηλοῦσα τοὺς ξένους τὸ πρῶτον ἀρεσκείᾳ παντοδαπῇ ἐπεσπᾶτο πρὸς εὔνοιαν, γενομένους δὲ ἐν προσπαθείᾳ κατεῖχε ταῖς ἐπιθυμίαις ἀλογίστως φερομένους πρὸς τὰς ἡδονάς. ἥττησε δὲ καὶ ταύτην Ὀδυσσεύς.[44]

This, too, is a rationalistic interpretation, explaining how yet another prostitute used men's desire to her advantage.[45]

In the deconstructed stories of Medusa and Circe, the known world of Homeric epics and Greek mythology are subverted through rationalistic explanations: they never existed, this was just history. But at the same time, part of the mythological storyworld is maintained, because Perseus and Odysseus are not dismissed as mythological characters; it is only the women they encounter who were not who the myths said they were: no power, no magic, only prostitution and the abuse of male desire. But in both cases, the men defeat these bad women – the interpreter is careful to point this out: Perseus took away Medusa's youth and beauty, and Odysseus got the better of Circe. Exactly how this happened is left out, which means that the reader is left to their memory of the epic myth, which is placed in the mythological storyworld the interpreter is trying to deconstruct and erase.

Moreover, something very interesting is happening in Herakleitos' fragmentary stories on the level of character: the female power that is possible within the mythological storyworld of ancient Greece is rationalized in order to be replaced with the patriarchal storyworld of the interpreter – one in which all strong women are prostitutes. At the same time, as already noted, the names of the characters remain: they are translated into the new narrative frame, which means that, in a way, part of the mythological universe sneaks in and affects this new story created by the interpreter.[46] Most importantly: the myth that he is trying to deconstruct and replace somehow turns into a new kind of storytelling, or even a new myth: that of men being haunted by vile women trying to seduce them. This myth seems to be 'worlded' in light of the interpreter's contemporary issues with female agency.

---

44   Stern, "Heraclitus the Paradoxographer" 80; see also 69.

45   For the other mythological women 'deconstructed' by Herakleitos as prostitutes, see Scylla (2), the Harpies (8), and the Sirens (14).

46   On the translation of voice and character, see Slater C., "Location, Location, Translation: Mapping Voice in Translated Storyworlds", *Storyworlds: A Journal of Narrative Studies* 3 (2011) 93–116.

TO RENDER UNBELIEVABLE TALES BELIEVABLE 73

6 Parthenios

We have looked at two examples of fragmentary tales from paradoxographical collections, offering portals to storyworlds presumably known by the reader from myth and literature. I would now like to look at one more example of such very short stories, partly overlapping with Pseudo-Alexander and Herakleitos, but yet very different: the *Sufferings in Love* (Ἐρωτικὰ παθήματα) of Parthenios. According to legend, Parthenios was a Greek poet, taken captive by the Romans and eventually becoming Virgil's tutor in Greek. The *Sufferings in Love* is his only preserved work, dedicated to the Roman poet and orator Cornelius Gallus (*c.*70–26 BC). Preserved in a single manuscript (Palatinus Heidelbergensis graecus 398), together with various texts of geographical, paradoxographical, and mythological nature, its transmission resembles that of the texts already discussed above.[47]

The collection contains thirty-six love stories, mostly unhappy ones, drawn from ancient myth and literature. The dedicatory preface explains their use and value:

> Thinking, Cornelius Gallus, that the collection of sufferings in love was very appropriate to you, I have selected them and sent them to you in as brief a form as possible. For those among the present collection that occur in certain poets where they are not narrated in their own right, you will find out for the most part from what follows. You, too, will be able to render the most suitable of them into hexameters and elegiacs. Think none the worse of them because they lack that quality of refined elaboration which you pursue. For I have collected them after the fashion of a little notebook, and they will, I trust, serve you in the same way.

> Μάλιστα σοὶ δοκῶν ἁρμόττειν, Κορνήλιε Γάλλε, τὴν ἄθροισιν τῶν ἐρωτικῶν παθημάτων, ἀναλεξάμενος ὡς ὅτι μάλιστα ἐν βραχυτάτοις ἀπέσταλκα. τὰ γὰρ παρά τισι τῶν ποιητῶν κείμενα τούτων, μὴ αὐτοτελῶς λελεγμένα, κατανοήσεις ἐκ τῶνδε τὰ πλεῖστα· αὐτῷ τέ σοι παρέσται εἰς ἔπη καὶ ἐλεγείας ἀνάγειν τὰ μάλιστα ἐξ αὐτῶν ἁρμόδια. ⟨μηδὲ⟩ διὰ τὸ μὴ παρεῖναι τὸ περιττὸν αὐτοῖς, ὃ δὴ σὺ μετέρχῃ, χεῖρον περὶ αὐτῶν ἐννοηθῇς· οἱονεὶ γὰρ ὑπομνηματίων τρόπον αὐτὰ συνελεξάμεθα, καὶ σοὶ νυνὶ τὴν χρῆσιν ὁμοίαν, ὡς ἔοικε, παρέξεται.[48]

---

47   Parthenios, *The Sufferings of Love*, ed. and trans. J. Lightfoot, *Parthenius of Nicaea: The Poetical Fragments and the* Ἐρωτικὰ παθήματα (Oxford: 1999) 304.

48   Ibidem, 308–309; on this epistolary preface, see 222–224.

Contrary to the ideologically tainted interpretations at the core of both Pseudo-Alexander's and Herakleitos' collections, the aim here is to present story skeletons as brief and clean as possible (ἐν βραχυτάτοις). The addressee, Cornelius Gallus, will be able to develop them as he sees fit, much like Aulus Gellius with the books he found and could cull from in his own writing.[49]

Because of their erotic theme, the stories of Parthenios have often been understood as related to the Greek novels; they have been edited and translated together with the novels, and the first English translation even calls them 'The Love Romances of Parthenios', printed after Longus' *Daphnis and Chloe* in the Loeb Classical Library.[50] But a significant difference between the novels and the *Sufferings in Love* is that the former are fully fledged developments of the kind of skeleton stories you find in the latter. Occasionally they even coincide or overlap, which may have been a reason for early editors and translators to associate them with each other: the story of Daphne (Parthenios 15), the young maiden pursued by Apollo and metamorphosed into a bay tree in order to escape, is included in *Leukippe and Kleitophon* (1.5.5); however, the versions of the story could hardly be more different, and the mythological-allegorical world that it opens in the narrative context of the novel is more or less absent in Parthenios' short version. When Circe appears in the story of Kalchos (Parthenios 12), her magic qualities are intact and there are no moral judgments whatsoever in the narrative, only the bare details of 'what happened'.

Some stories are very short, others rather long, but they are all marked by this indifference to the moral of the characters and the tales. Most tell of heterosexual desire, but there are also homoerotic tales (e.g. Parthenios 7) and even incestuous stories (Parthenios 17), consistently without moralizing comments. Some present different versions of the same story in different authors, in poetry or prose (e.g. Parthenios 11 and 14), others present narratives that stretch across different chapters and could be seen as continuations (e.g. Parthenios 2 and 3, 4 and 34). While a number of characters and events are known from mythology or literature, several stories are known only in these versions, and their original sources, to which Parthenios most often carefully refers, have been lost. Despite the lack of comparative material, the collection offers an exciting example of the plasticity of storytelling in antiquity: the way in which the same tale could be stripped of its personalized characteristics

---

49   See above, n. 12.

50   Ed. G. Thornley, *Daphnis and Chloe by Longus with the English Translation of George Thornley, Revised and Augmented by J.M. Edmonds, The Love Romances of Parthenius and Other Fragments with an English Translation by S. Gaselee* (London – Cambridge, MA: 1955 [1916]).

TO RENDER UNBELIEVABLE TALES BELIEVABLE 75

and presented as narremes for others to use, translated and rewritten in an endless series of tales. This is also the direction in which the manuscript transmission points: while modern readers have associated the *Sufferings in Love* with the novels, due to rather tenuous narrative similarities, the sole manuscript indicates its belonging in a paradoxographical-mythographical context of storyworlds open for culling according to individual taste: to deconstruct, reconstruct, and translate in whatever way seemed best.

7   Transfictionality and the Translation of Storyworlds

Let us return to the definition of and workings of a storyworld; in the words of Marie-Laure Ryan, 'a storyworld is an imagined totality that evolves according to the events told in the story. To follow a story means to simulate mentally the changes that take place in the storyworld, using the cues provided by the text'.[51] In the case of Medusa and Circe, we find ourselves involved with more than one world, implied by one and the same text: the mythological storyworld and its deconstructed, 'actual' history, implying new details that are not part of the original and well-known mythological universe. The reader is challenged to imagine both. The reader is also expected to imagine a storyworld that transgresses boundaries of myth and reality, namely that storyworld of desire depicted by Pseudo-Alexander. This is a mental model that requires the audience's acceptance of Eros as a physical and metaphysical force, impossible to quite understand and part of a mystery that has religious undertones. It straddles what can be verified and what can only be accepted as ἄλυτα.

In the collections of both Pseudo-Alexander and Herakleitos, desire is gendered. In Herakleitos' short stories based on myths, desire is a force exerted by women as a way of having power over men, who ultimately escape it by somehow outwitting their objects of desire. In Pseudo-Alexander's text, desire is gendered as a male emotion, violent and short-lived; only women are capable of long-lasting emotions. Agency accordingly shifts, depending on the context of the storyworld and its degree of worldedness. By contrast, in the ideologically and morally disengaged stories of Parthenios desire is not clearly gendered – the skeletons offered by the author-compiler are open to personal development and translation according to whatever direction that author-poet wishes to take. In some cases, the storyworlds known by the reader from other

---

51   Ryan M.-L., "From Possible Worlds to Storyworlds: On the Worldness of Narrative Representation", in Bell A. – Ryan M.-L. (eds.), *Possible Worlds Theory and Contemporary Narratology* (Lincoln, NE: 2019) 62–87, at 70.

versions may entail indications that affect their own mental simulations and thus the way in which they retell the stories.

The strategy used by Herakleitos and Parthenios could be seen in light of some basic narrative operations of so-called transfictionality, that is, 'the sharing of elements, mostly characters, but also imaginary locations, events, and entire fictional worlds, by two or more works of fiction'.[52] I would prefer to see this not as a primarily fictional strategy, but rather as a transtextual feature that occurs between any kind of texts.[53] According to Ryan, transfictionality

> relies on a number of basic operations: 1) extension, which adds new stories to the [fictional] world while respecting the facts established in the original; 2) modification, which changes the plot of the original narrative, for instance, by giving it a different ending; and 3) transposition, which transports a plot into a different temporal or spatial setting.[54]

All three operations are at play in Herakleitos: the original myth is transposed into a different temporal setting (which is probably also spatial, but there are no textual cues about that); the original plot is modified, especially in terms of characters; and new stories are implicitly added to or grafted upon the facts of the original. Parthenios offers examples of almost reversed processes, in that he deconstructs the known stories and presents them as bare skeletons to be developed by the same means: extension, modification, and transposition. Pseudo-Alexander does something similar, yet different, by summarizing a storyworld known from various literary and artistic contexts, challenging the reader to both recall and construct mental models of desire.

8   Conclusions

It is safe to say that the kind of material investigated here, often despised or at least overlooked by philologists because of its rather curious content

---

52   Ibidem.

53   See also the concept of 'storyness' or 'inter-storyness' in Lohafer S., *Reading for Storyness: Preclosure Theory, Empirical Poetics and Culture in the Short Story* (Baltimore: 2003), that is, the relationship between a tale's *phantasia* and that of previous or contemporary literature. Cf. Ryan M.-L., "Story/Worlds/Media: Tuning the Instruments of a Media-Conscious Narratology", in Ryan M.-L. – Thon J.-N. (eds.), *Storyworlds across Media: Toward a Media-Conscious Narratology* (Lincoln, NE: 2014) 24–38, at 32: 'While texts may project many different storyworlds, a given storyworld may also unfold in many different texts. This situation occurs mostly in oral cultures, when bards tell stories that are familiar to the audience'. For inter-storyness, see also Chapter 1, at 28.

54   Ryan, "From Possible Worlds to Storyworlds" 70.

TO RENDER UNBELIEVABLE TALES BELIEVABLE 77

and transmission in miscellaneous manuscripts, played an important role for Greco-Roman literature in a *longue durée* perspective. Mythological and poetic worlds were constantly drawn on, de- and reconstructed for different purposes, characters were shapeshifters that could be translated freely, and unbelievable or unnatural things could become true within the context of a certain story. Paradoxography thus implies storyworlds of various and overlapping kinds: the textual cues of these storyworlds need to be comprehended and constructed by the reader in order for them to make sense. Most of them have some element of worldedness, but they are, above all, possible worlds. They make sense and are 'true' within the frame of the stories. Boundaries of both genre and fiction become, I would argue, less interesting. The lovemaking of palm trees in the novel by Achilles Tatius belongs as firmly in that world as it does in Pliny's *Natural History*; the blurring of myth, medicine, and science is deliberate in several texts – it was the modern need to classify everything in neat categories that closed some of the windows or indeed portals between fictional, mythological, and transtextual worlds to which ancient and medieval readers had access. In the end, this is all about the power of discourse to construct realities, or, in the words of Eustathios, to render unbelievable tales believable.

Bibliography

Primary Sources

Achilles Tatius, *Leukippe and Kleitophon*. In ed. J.-P. Garnaud, *Achille Tatius: Le roman de Leucippé et Clitophon* (Paris: 2002).

Eumathios Makrembolites, *Hysmine and Hysminias*. In ed. M. Marcovich, *Eustathius Macrembolites: De Hysmines et Hysminiae amoribus libri XI* (Munich: 2001).

Eustathios, Archbishop of Thessalonike, *Commentary on the Odyssey*, ed. G. Stallbaum, *Eustathii, Archiepiscopi Thessalonicensis commentarii ad Homeri Odysseam*, 2 vols. (Leipzig: 1825).

Herakleitos the Paradoxographer, *On Unbelievable Tales*, ed. N. Festa, *Mythographi Graeci*, vol. 3.2: *Palaephati Peri apistōn; Heracliti qui fertur libellus Peri apistōn; Excerpta vaticana: Vulgo anonymus De incredibilibus* (Leipzig: 1902).

John Tzetzes, *Chiliades*. In ed. P.A.M. Leone, *John Tzetzes: Historiae* (Naples: 1968).

Longus, *Daphnis and Chloe*. In ed. G. Thornley, *Daphnis and Chloe by Longus with the English Translation of George Thornley, Revised and Augmented by J.M. Edmonds, The Love Romances of Parthenius and Other Fragments with an English translation by S. Gaselee* (London – Cambridge, MA: 1955 [1916]).

Niketas Eugenianos, *Drosilla and Charikles*. In ed. F. Conca, *Nicetas Eugenianus de Drosillae et Chariclis amoribus* (Amsterdam: 1990).

Parthenios, *The Sufferings of Love*. In ed. J.L. Lightfoot, *Parthenius of Nicaea: The Poetical Fragments and the Ἐρωτικὰ παθήματα* (Oxford: 1999).

Photios, *Library*. In ed. R. Henry, *Photius: Bibliothèque*, 8 vols. (Paris: 1959–77) 4.

Pseudo-Alexander of Aphrodisias, *Medical Puzzles and Natural Problems*. In ed. C.-G. Lindqvist (Gothenburg: forthcoming); J.L. Ideler, *Physici et medici Graeci minores*, 2 vols. (Berlin: 1841) 1.

Secondary Works

Bird R., *Sophrosune in the Greek Novel: Reading Reactions to Desire* (London: 2020).

Casanova P., *La république mondiale de lettres* (Paris: 1999).

Casanova P., "Literature as a World", *New Left Review* 31 (2005) 71–90.

Casanova P., *The World Republic of Letters*, trans. M.B. DeBevoise (Cambridge, MA – London: 2004).

Doroszewska J., "Beyond the Limits of the Human Body: Phlegon of Tralles' Medical Curiosities", in Kazantzidis G. (ed.), *Medicine and Paradoxography in the Ancient World* (Berlin – Boston: 2019) 117–140.

Gabba E., "True History and False History in Classical Antiquity", *Journal of Roman Studies* 71 (1981) 50–62.

Giannini A. (ed.), *Paradoxographorum Graecorum reliquae*, Classici Greci e Latini 3 (Milan: 1966).

Giannini A., "Studi sulla paradossografia greca I. Da Omero a Callimaco: Motive e forme del meraviglioso", *Istituto Lombardo* (*Rendiconti di Lettere*) 97 (1963) 247–266.

Giannini A., "Studi sulla paradossografia greca II. Da Callimaco all'età imperiale: La lettura paradossografica", *Acme* 17 (1964) 99–140.

Hardie P., *Paradox and the Marvellous in Augustan Literature and Culture* (Oxford: 2009).

Hayot E., "On Literary Worlds", *Modern Language Quarterly* 72.2 (2011) 129–161.

Herman D., *Basic Elements of Narrative* (Chichester: 2009).

Herman D., *Story Logic: Problems and Possibilities of Narrative* (Lincoln, NE – London: 2002).

Hilton J. – Wright W.C., "Erotic Date-Palms in Ammianus Marcellinus (*Res gestae*, XXIV, 3, 12–13)", *Listy filologické/Folia philologica* 138.3/4 (2015) 213–229.

Johnson S.F., *The Life and Miracles of Thekla: A Literary Study*, Hellenic Studies 13 (Cambridge, MA – London: 2006).

Jouanno C., "Tzetzès et la paradoxographie", *Revue des études byzantines* 78 (2020) 143–192.

Jusdanis G., *Fiction Agonistes: In Defense of Literature* (Stanford, CA: 2010).

Kukkonen K., "Navigating Infinite Earths: Readers, Mental Models, and the Multiverse of Superhero Comics", *Storyworlds: A Journal of Narrative Studies* 2 (2010) 39–58.

Lightfoot J. (ed. and trans.), *Parthenius of Nicaea: The Poetical Fragments and the Ἐρωτικὰ παθήματα* (Oxford: 1999).

Lohafer S., *Reading for Storyness: Preclosure Theory, Empirical Poetics and Culture in the Short Story* (Baltimore: 2003).

Martine A., "The Mysterious Discipline of Narratologists: Why We Need Stories to Make Sense", *Tor.com: Science Fiction, Fantasy, and Related Subjects* (January 29, 2019), https://www.tor.com/2019/01/29/the-mysterious-discipline-of-narratologists/ (last visited November 20, 2020).

Meeusen M., "An Interpretation of the Preface to *Medical Puzzles and Natural Problems* 1 by Pseudo-Alexander of Aphrodisias in Light of Medical Education", in Bouras Vallianatos P. – Xenophontos S. (eds.), *Greek Medical Literature and Its Readers from Hippocrates to Islam and Byzantium* (London: 2018) 94–109.

Messis C., "Aux marges de la philosophie, au cœur de la curiosité: Le Manuscrit d'Heidelberg Pal. Gr. 398", in Bianconi D. – Ronconi P. (eds.), *La 'Collection philosophique' face à l'histoire: Péripéties et tradition* (Spoleto: 2020) 209–238.

Morales H., "The Taming of the View: Natural Curiosities in *Leukippe and Kleitophon*", in Hofmann H. (ed.), *Groningen Colloquia of the Novel* 6 (1995) 39–50.

Ormand K., "Testing Virginity in Achilles Tatius and Heliodorus", *Ramus* 39.2 (2010) 160–197.

Ryan M.-L., "The Aesthetics of Proliferation", in Boni M. (ed.), *World Building* (Amsterdam: 2017) 31–46.

Ryan M.-L., "From Parallel Universes to Possible Worlds: Ontological Pluralism in Physics, Narratology, and Narrative", *Poetics Today* 27.4 (2006) 633–674.

Ryan M.-L., "From Possible Worlds to Storyworlds: On the Worldness of Narrative Representation", in Bell A. – Ryan M.-L. (eds.), *Possible Worlds Theory and Contemporary Narratology* (Lincoln, NE: 2019) 62–87.

Ryan M.-L., "Possible Worlds in Recent Literary Theory", *Style* 26.4 (1992) 528–553.

Ryan M.-L., "Story/Worlds/Media: Tuning the Instruments of a Media-Conscious Narratology", in Ryan M.-L. – Thon J.-N. (eds.), *Storyworlds across Media: Toward a Media-Conscious Narratology* (Lincoln, NE: 2014) 24–38.

Schepens G. – Delcroix K., "Ancient Paradoxography: Origin, Evolution, Production and Reception", in Pecere O. – Stramaglia A. (eds.), *La letteratura di consumo nel mondo greco-latino: Atti del Convegno Internazionale, Cassino, 14–17 settembre 1994* (Cassino: 1996) 375–460.

Shannon-Henderson K., "Constructing a New Imperial Paradoxography: Phlegon of Tralles and His Sources", in König A. (ed.), *Literature and Culture in the Roman Empire* (Cambridge: 2020) 159–178.

Sharples R.W., "Implications of the New Alexander of Aphrodisias Inscription", *Bulletin of the Institute of Classical Studies* 48 (2005) 47–56.

Slater C., "Location, Location, Translation: Mapping Voice in Translated Storyworlds", *Storyworlds: A Journal of Narrative Studies* 3 (2011) 93–116.

Stern J. (trans.), "Heraclitus the Paradoxographer: Περὶ ἀπίστων, *On Unbelievable Tales*", *Transactions of the American Philological Association* 133 (2003) 51–97.

Westermann A. (ed.), *Scriptores rerum mirabilium Graeci* (London: 1839).

Ziegler K., "Paradoxographoi", *Paulys Realencyclopädie der classischen Altertumswissenschaft* 18 (1949) 1137–1116.

PART 2

The Art of Storytelling

CHAPTER 4

Didactic Tales in Galen

Sophia Xenophontos

1 Introduction: Didactic Tales in Works of Practical Ethics

The powerful role of the tale in social life, communication, and the construction of collective identity is virtually incontestable through the ages.[1] From the anecdote and the myth to the fable, the dream, and even the simple personal experience, these types of storytelling are still pervasive in present-day educational practice, the psychology of marketing, political leadership, and public performance as a whole, thus confirming what the tale discourse of antiquity and the medieval period has always shown: namely that the brief story is a dynamic means of passing on intended meanings and, for that matter, affecting the recipients' decision-making.

The aim of this chapter is to focus specifically on the moral-didactic effect of the ancient tale by looking at its function in the context of practical ethics, a popular philosophical product in the Roman imperial period.[2] As its name suggests, practical ethics involved the composition of relatively short works intended to help people reform their behavior, attain good habits, and eventually reach a stage of internal equilibrium that would guarantee their successful role in society, statesmanship, and other professional activities. An alternative label for practical ethics is 'popular philosophy', pointing to the wider elite readership to which the above-mentioned works were addressed

---

1 Ronald Barthes, for example, famously referred to the universality of narrative and the countless forms of narrative that exist in the world. See Barthes R., "An Introduction to the Structural Analysis of Narrative", *New Literary History* 6.2 (1975) 237–272, at 237.

2 See e.g. Gill C., "The School in the Roman Imperial Period", in Inwood B. (ed.), *The Cambridge Companion to the Stoics* (Cambridge: 2003) 33–58, at 40–44. For a definition and description of the independent discipline of practical ethics, see Van Hoof L., "Practical Ethics", in Beck M. (ed.), *A Companion to Plutarch* (Chichester: 2014) 135–148; cf. Schofield M., "Stoic Ethics", in Inwood, *The Cambridge Companion* 233–256, and Van der Stockt L., "*Semper duo, numquam tres?* Plutarch's *Popularphilosophie* on Friendship and Virtue in *On Having Many Friends*", in Roskam G. – Van der Stockt L. (eds.), *Virtues for the People: Aspects of Plutarchan Ethics* (Leuven: 2011) 19–39, at 19–21.

© SOPHIA XENOPHONTOS, 2025 | DOI:10.1163/9789004707351_006

This is an open access chapter distributed under the terms of the CC BY-NC-ND 4.0 license.

84 XENOPHONTOS

in the ancient world, i.e. practically any thinking person concerned with their self-management and character development.[3]

Some preliminary examples from Plutarch of Chaeronea (*c.45–c.120*), the key moralist of the Roman imperial period, will help us get to grips with the main features of the didactic tale in ancient ethical writings. In one of Plutarch's moral essays, entitled *On Talkativeness*, the philosopher seeks to outline the downsides of over-talking in order to encourage more moderate use of speech. Thus, at one point he provides the following story involving the Roman orator Pupius Piso to advise against prolixity in a more tangible manner:

> If anyone will but review and recollect constantly these and similar instances, he may conceivably stop taking pleasure in foolish chatter. **But as for me, that famous case of the slave puts me utterly to shame when I reflect what immense importance it is to pay attention to what is said and to be master of our purpose.** Pupius Piso, the orator, not wishing to be troubled, ordered his slaves to speak only in answer to questions and not a word more. Subsequently, wishing to pay honor to Clodius when he was a magistrate, Piso gave orders that he be invited to dinner and prepared what was, we may suppose, a sumptuous banquet. When the hour came, the other guests were present, but Clodius was still expected, and Piso repeatedly sent the slave who regularly carried invitations to see if Clodius was approaching. And when evening came and he was finally despaired of, Piso said to the slave, 'See here, did you give him the invitation?' 'I did', said the slave. 'Why hasn't he come then?' 'Because he

---

3 *Popularphilosophie* ('popular philosophy') or *Die popularphilosophisch-ethischen Schriften* ('the popular philosophical-ethical writings') are terms coined by Ziegler K., "Plutarchos von Chaironeia", *Paulys Realencyclopädie der classischen Altertumswissenschaft* 41 (1951) 636–962, at 637, 702, with reference to Plutarch's works on practical ethics. The term *praktische Seelenheilungsschriften* ('practical psychotherapeutic writings') was also deployed by Ingenkamp H.G., *Plutarchs Schriften über die Heilung der Seele* (Göttingen: 1971) for his analysis of Plutarch's *On the Control of Anger, On Talkativeness, On Curiosity, On Compliance*, and *On Praising Oneself Inoffensively*; while 'broadcasting ethics' has been recently devised by Roskam G. – Van der Stockt L., "Efficiency and Effectiveness of Plutarch's Broadcasting Ethics", in Roskam – Van der Stockt (eds.), *Virtues for the People: Aspects of Plutarchan Ethics* (Leuven: 2011) 7–16 for the same purposes. The alternative label 'educated ethics' has also been proposed; see Pelling C.B.R., "What Is Popular about Plutarch's 'Popular Philosophy'?", in Roskam – Van der Stockt, *Virtues for the People* 41–58, at 55–58. On the meaning of 'popular' as 'less- or non-doctrinaire', 'commonsensical', in popular philosophy and ethics in the imperial period, see Morgan T., *Popular Morality in the Early Roman Empire* (Cambridge: 2007) 1–5 and Van Hoof L., *Plutarch's Practical Ethics: The Social Dynamics of Philosophy* (Oxford: 2010) 6–7.

DIDACTIC TALES IN GALEN

declined.' 'Then why didn't you tell me at once?' 'Because you didn't ask me that'.

εἰ δὴ ταῦτα καὶ τὰ τοιαῦτα συνεχῶς τις ἐπίοι καὶ ἀναλαμβάνοι, παύσαιτ' ἂν ἴσως ἡδόμενος τῷ φλυαρεῖν. ἐμὲ δὲ **κἀκεῖνος ὁ οἰκέτης εὖ μάλα δυσωπεῖ, τὸ προσέχειν τῷ λόγῳ καὶ κρατεῖν προαιρέσεως ἡλίκον ἐστὶν ἐνθυμούμενον.** Πούπιος Πείσων ὁ ῥήτωρ μὴ βουλόμενος ἐνοχλεῖσθαι προσέταξε τοῖς οἰκέταις πρὸς τὰ ἐρωτώμενα λαλεῖν καὶ μηδὲν πλέον. εἶτα Κλώδιον ἄρχοντα δεξιώσασθαι βουλόμενος ἐκέλευσε κληθῆναι καὶ παρεσκευάσατο λαμπρὰν ὡς εἰκὸς ἑστίασιν. ἐνστάσης δὲ τῆς ὥρας οἱ μὲν ἄλλοι παρῆσαν ὁ δὲ Κλώδιος προσεδοκᾶτο· καὶ πολλάκις ἔπεμπε τὸν εἰωθότα καλεῖν οἰκέτην ἐποψόμενον εἰ πρόσεισιν. ὡς δ' ἦν ἑσπέρα καὶ ἀπέγνωστο 'τί δ';' ἔφη πρὸς τὸν οἰκέτην 'ἐκάλεσας αὐτόν;' 'ἔγωγ'' εἶπε. 'διὰ τί οὖν οὐκ ἀφῖκται;' κἀκεῖνος 'ὅτι ἠρνήσατο.' 'πῶς οὖν οὐκ εὐθὺς ἔφρασας;' 'ὅτι τοῦτό μ' οὐκ ἠρώτησας'.[4]

The story concerning Pupius Piso is prefaced by a brief remark (marked in bold), which delves into the storyteller's inner world and elucidates his emotional reaction to prattling: he tells us that he feels utter shame (δυσωπεῖ) at the story he is about to narrate. This strategy predisposes the audience to approach the story in a state of critical alertness even before they actually read or hear it. It should be noted that it is not usual for Plutarch to expose his personal views in the writings that make up his *Moralia*. So, in this case, his personal evaluation of talkativeness serves to stress the story's message, especially as there are no concluding remarks here to sum up the moral of the story.

In another illuminating example from the *Moralia*, an incident from Plutarch's own life is used to pass on the intended ethical message, with the author himself, not some other, historical person, being the protagonist of the story. This case describes how the young Plutarch's father taught him to respect his fellow men, unlike the Roman general and statesman Scipio Africanus, who was criticized by the Romans for being utterly non-collegial:

> At any rate Scipio was criticized in Rome because, when he entertained his friends at the dedication of the temple of Hercules, he did not include his colleague Mummius; for even if in general the two men did not consider themselves friends, on such occasions they usually thought it proper to show honour and friendliness to each other on account of their office. *Inasmuch, therefore, as the omission of so slight an act of courtesy*

---

4 Plutarch, *On Talkativeness*, 511D–E, ed. M. Pohlenz, trans. W.C. Helmbold, 447–449, emphasis added.

brought a reputation for haughtiness to Scipio, a man in other respects admirable, how can anyone be considered honourable and fair-minded who detracts from the dignity of a colleague in office, or maliciously flouts him by actions which reveal ambitious rivalry, or is so self-willed that he arrogates and annexes to himself everything, in short, at the expense of his colleague? I recollect that when I was still a young man I was sent with another as envoy to the proconsul; the other man was somehow left behind. I alone met the proconsul and accomplished the business. Now when I came back and was to make the report of our mission, my father left his seat and told me in private not to say 'I went', but 'we went', not 'I said', but 'we said', and in all other ways to associate my colleague in a joint report. **For that sort of thing is not only honourable and kind, but it also takes the sting out of any envy of our reputation.**

ὁ γοῦν Σκιπίων ἤκουσεν ἐν Ῥώμῃ κακῶς, ὅτι φίλους ἑστιῶν ἐπὶ τῇ καθιερώ-σει τοῦ Ἡρακλείου τὸν συνάρχοντα Μόμμιον οὐ παρέλαβε· καὶ γάρ, εἰ τἆλλα μὴ φίλους ἐνόμιζον ἑαυτούς, ἐν τοῖς γε τοιούτοις ἠξίουν τιμᾶν καὶ φιλοφρονεῖ-σθαι διὰ τὴν ἀρχήν. ὅπου τοίνυν ἀνδρὶ τἆλλα θαυμασίῳ τῷ Σκιπίωνι μικρὸν οὕτω φιλανθρώπευμα παραλειφθὲν ὑπεροψίας ἤνεγκε δόξαν, ἦπου κολούων ἄν τις ἀξί-ωμα συνάρχοντος ἢ πράξεσιν ἐχούσαις φιλοτιμίαν ἐπηρεάζων ἢ πάντα συλλήβδην ἀνατιθεὶς ἅμα καὶ περιάγων ὑπ' αὐθαδείας εἰς ἑαυτὸν ἐκείνου δ' ἀφαιρούμενος, ἐπιεικὴς ἂν φανείη καὶ μέτριος; μέμνημαι νέον ἐμαυτὸν ἔτι πρεσβευτὴν μεθ' ἑτέ-ρου πεμφθέντα πρὸς ἀνθύπατον, ἀπολειφθέντος δέ πως ἐκείνου, μόνον ἐντυχό-ντα καὶ διαπραξάμενον· ὡς οὖν ἔμελλον ἐπανελθὼν ἀποπρεσβεύειν, ἀναστὰς ὁ πατὴρ κατ' ἰδίαν ἐκέλευσε μὴ λέγειν 'ᾠχόμην' ἀλλ' 'ᾠχόμεθα', μηδ' 'εἶπον' ἀλλ' 'εἴπομεν', καὶ τἆλλα συνεφαπτόμενον οὕτω καὶ κοινούμενον ἀπαγγέλλειν. **οὐ γὰρ μόνον ἐπιεικὲς τὸ τοιοῦτον καὶ φιλάνθρωπόν ἐστιν, ἀλλὰ καὶ τὸ λυποῦν τὸν φθόνον ἀφαιρεῖ τῆς δόξης.**[5]

Plutarch's personal story has a twofold function here: on the one hand, it decries Scipio's egotism through ethical problematizing, since the long rhetorical question marked in italics warns that competitiveness is no match for the ethical profile of a virtuous man; on the other hand, the story also encourages love of humankind (φιλάνθρωπον), the moralizing gist of the story, which appears at the end of the quoted section (in bold). The two Plutarchan case studies show that imperial-period popular philosophical works tended to employ didactic stories to promote righteous behavior. Whether these stories involved the author himself or another person, the author seems to have been

---

5 Plutarch, *Political Precepts*, 816C–E, ed. and trans. H.N. Fowler, *Plutarch's Moralia*, vol. 10: *771E–854D: With an English Translation* (Cambridge, MA: 1936) 251–253, emphasis added.

DIDACTIC TALES IN GALEN

inclined to take an active part in the narrative through his response to the narrated events, which is explicit and to the point, so as to direct the audience's future conduct in similar situations.

2   Didactic Stories in Galen

With the above in mind, we now turn to the author who is the focus of this chapter, i.e. Galen of Pergamum (129–c.216), antiquity's most important medical author and practicing physician, who was also an important philosopher of the Roman imperial period.[6] Scholarship to date has explored Galen's achievements in a variety of areas, e.g. physiology, anatomy, therapeutic and prognostic theory and practice, logic, psychology, etc. However, his contribution as a practical moralist remains a big unknown. In a monograph devoted to this topic, I give prominence to the social dynamics of Galen's moralism and its interplay with his medical theory and practice, thereby offering a new framework in which we can comprehend his role as a highly original exponent of moral philosophy in the first centuries of the common era.[7] In this chapter, I try to shed some light on a part of his input to the ethical discipline by examining his use of moralizing tales in particular.

Before embarking on the main part of the analysis, it may be useful to stress that Galen is generally fond of using short stories throughout his writings mainly in order to guide, persuade, enhance his authority, and connect with his readers. I will take just two relevant examples. The first one comes from *On My Own Opinions*, Galen's last work, in which he provides a summary of his main views regarding the creation of the world and the function of the human body and soul. This work is introduced by an interesting anecdote involving the celebrated grammarian and poet of the first century BC Parthenios of Nicaea:

> Something seems to have happened to me similar to what they say once befell the poet Parthenius. For while the man was still alive, his poems slipped into the hands of many people from different places. So as he was travelling through a city at one point, he ran into two grammarians

---

6   Basic studies include, for example: Hankinson R.J., "Galen on the Limitations of Knowledge", in Gill C. – Whitmarsh T. – Wilkins J. (eds.), *Galen and the World of Knowledge* (Cambridge: 2009) 206–242 (epistemology), Tieleman T., "Galen's Psychology", in Barnes J. – Jouanna J. (eds.), *Galien et la philosophie: Huit exposés suivis de discussions* (Geneva: 2003) 131–169 (psychology), Van der Eijk P., "Galen on the Nature of Human Beings", in Adamson P. – Hansberger R. – Wilberding J. (eds.), *Philosophical Themes in Galen* (London: 2014) 89–134 (natural philosophy).

7   Xenophontos S., *Medicine and Practical Ethics in Galen* (Cambridge: 2024).

in a school arguing about a poetic line he had written. One of them was interpreting its meaning just as Parthenius had intended it when he had composed [the poem], the other in a contrary sense. Parthenius himself attempted to persuade the latter person by demonstrating that the line had been expressed in a different sense, not as he thought, but the grammarian accepted anything other than being persuaded. 'In fact', [Parthenius] said, 'I have heard the line from Parthenius himself in exactly the sense I am proposing.' Since the man was not persuaded despite these words, [Parthenius] said: 'Well, I risk going crazy; I consider myself the author of these lines, so that I will need to use these servants of mine as witnesses for me to you, so that you will be convinced that I am identical with the Parthenius who wrote these lines.' Something comparable seems to be happening to me just now because of the prevailing failure in relation to [the study of] medicine and philosophy, in which those who acquired no education in the presence of a grammarian or an orator, but acquainted themselves briefly with the arts, misinterpret the works not only of the ancients, who are indeed repeatedly obscure, but also my own, which seem quite lucid to everyone who has received the fundamental education. The difference between my situation and that of Parthenius lies in the matter of witnesses. For Parthenius was in need of servants to testify that he was indeed Parthenius, whereas I provide as witnesses my written views, regarding which I declared that I have secure knowledge or at least a plausible one, just as I also say about [other] matters that I know nothing certain of, due to having no scientific acquaintance with them.

Παραπλήσιόν τι μοι συμβεβηκέναι δοκεῖ τῷ γενομένῳ πόθ', ὥς φασι, Παρθενίῳ τῷ ποιητῇ. Ζῶντος γὰρ ἔτι τἀνδρός, ἐξέπεσεν εἰς πολλὰ τῶν ἐθνῶν τὰ ποιήματα αὐτοῦ. Καί ποτε διερχόμενος πόλιν, ἐπέστη δυσὶ γραμματικοῖς ἐπὶ διδασκαλείῳ διαφερομένοις περί τινος ἔπους τῶν ὑπ' αὐτοῦ γεγραμμένων. Ἐξηγεῖτο δὲ ὁ μὲν ἕτερος αὐτῶν οὕτως τὴν κατ' αὐτὸ λέξιν ὡς ὁ Παρθένιος ἐννοήσας ἐποίησεν, ὁ δὲ ἕτερος ἐναντίως. Ὅν δὴ καὶ πείθειν αὐτὸς ὁ Παρθένιος ἐνεχείρει, καθ' ἑτέραν διάνοιαν ἐπιδεικνὺς εἰρῆσθαι τὸ ἔπος, οὐχ ὡς ἐκεῖνος ᾤετο, ὁ δὲ πάντα μᾶλλον ἢ πεισθῆναι βουλόμενος. 'Καὶ μήν', ἔφη, 'παρ' αὐτοῦ τοῦ Παρθενίου κατὰ ταύτην τὴν ἔννοιαν ἀκήκοα τὸν στίχον, ἣν ἐγὼ διηγοῦμαι.' Ὡς δ' οὐδὲ τοῦτο εἰπόντος ἐπείθετο, 'κινδυνεύω τοίνυν', ἔφη, 'παραπαίειν, νομίζων [ἐ]μαυτὸν εἶναι τὸν ταῦτα γράψαντα, ὥστ' ἐμοὶ μαρτύρων δεήσειν πρὸς σὲ τουτωνὶ τῶν ἐμῶν οἰκετῶν, ὅπως πιστεύσῃς αὐτὸν ἐκεῖνον εἶναί με τὸν Παρθένιον, ὃς ταῦτα ἔγραψε.' Τοιοῦτον δή τι κἀμοὶ νῦν ἔοικε συμβαίνειν διὰ τὴν κατέχουσαν ἀτυχίαν ἰατρικήν τε καὶ φιλοσοφίαν, ἐφ' αἷς οἱ μήτε παρὰ γραμματικῷ μήτε ῥητορικῷ διδασκαλίαν παιδευθέντες, ἀλλ' ἐξαίφνης ἀφικνούμενοι πρὸς τέχνας,

DIDACTIC TALES IN GALEN

παρακούουσι τῶν γεγραμμένων οὐ μόνον τοῖς παλαιοῖς ἔχουσιν ὄντως ἀσαφῶς τε πολλάκις, ἀλλὰ καὶ τῶν ὑφ' ἡμῶν αὐτῶν, ἃ δοκεῖ σαφέστατα πᾶσιν εἶναι τοῖς τὴν πρώτην παιδείαν παιδευθεῖσιν. Διαφέρει δὲ τοὐμὸν τοῦτο πρᾶγμα τοῦ κατὰ Παρθένιον ἐν τῇ τῶν μαρτύρων ὕλῃ. Τῷ μὲν γὰρ ἐδέησε τῶν δούλων μαρτύρων ὡς ὄντως αὐτὸς ὁ Παρθένιος εἴη, ἐγὼ δὲ τὰ γεγραμμένα μαρτυροῦντά μοι παρέχομαι, περὶ ὧν ἀπεφηνάμην ὡς βεβαίως ἐπιστάμενος ἢ κατὰ μόνον τὸ πιθανόν, ὥσπερ καὶ περὶ ὧν οὐδόλως ἐπίστασθαί φημι βεβαίως διὰ τὸ μηδεμίαν ἔχειν αὐτῶν ἐπιστημονικὴν γνῶσιν.[8]

Galen highlights his personal quandary at the time of composition: his contemporaries, especially those lacking training, tend to misconstrue his writings. To substantiate this, he cites an anecdote concerning the poet Parthenios, who suffered from similar misinterpretation in his career. As the passage cited above shows, however, Galen's shared experience with Parthenios also presents some points of divergence, one of which is that, unlike Parthenios, who had to rely on unreliable witnesses to his works, Galen's books act as a thundering validation of his place in the world of medicine and philosophy.

As well as reinforcing Galen's authority, the brief story is also used by Galen to help him make or clinch a point, so as to construct a more robust argument. The following passage from the *Exhortation to the Study of Medicine* makes this clear:

> **This might be a good moment to mention the story of Phryne.** This woman was at a drinking party once; and they started playing one of those games where everyone takes it in turn to give a command to his drinking companions. Phryne had noticed that there were women present who had made themselves up with alkanet, white lead, and seaweed. She ordered water to be brought; the women had to take some in their hands and dip their faces in it once, then immediately wipe them with a napkin. Phryne herself went first. The other women's faces were of course covered with slime, and they looked perfectly monstrous. But Phryne looked better than before: she alone had used no makeup, but relied on her natural beauty, without recourse to cosmetic tricks. **Of true beauty, then, one can only make an accurate test when it is seen as it is, stripped clear of all extrinsic adornments. It is the same with athletics: you can only reasonably examine its worth by seeing whether it is**

---

8 Galen, *On My Own Opinions*, ch. 1, eds. I. Polemis – S. Xenophontos, *Galen, On Avoiding Distress and On My Own Opinions. Critical Edition by I. Polemis and S. Xenophontos; trans. S. Xenophontos* (Berlin: 2023) 96.1–23; trans. Xenophontos, *Galen* 97–99.

of any benefit to the state as a whole or to the private individuals who practise it.

ὅθεν οὐδὲ τὸ τῆς Φρύνης ἄκαιρον ἤδη μοι διηγήσασθαι. αὕτη ποτ' ἐν συμπο-
σίῳ, παιδιᾶς τοιαύτης γενομένης ὡς ἕκαστον ἐν μέρει προστάξαι τοῖς συμπό-
ταις ὃ βούλοιτο, θεασαμένη παρούσας γυναῖκας ἀγχούσῃ τε καὶ ψιμυθίῳ καὶ
φύκει κεκαλλωπισμένας ἐκέλευσεν ὕδατος κομισθέντος ἀρυσαμένας ταῖς χερσὶ
προσενεγκεῖν ἅπαξ αὐτὸ τῷ προσώπῳ καὶ μετὰ τοῦτο εὐθέως ἀπομάξασθαι
σινδονίῳ, καὶ αὐτὴ πρώτη τοῦτ' ἔπραξε. ταῖς μὲν οὖν ἄλλαις ἁπάσαις σπί-
λου τὰ πρόσωπα ἐπληρώθη, καὶ ἦν ὁμοιότατα ἰδεῖν τοῖς μορμολυκείοις, αὐτὴ
δὲ ⟨καὶ⟩ καλλίων ἐφάνη· μόνη γὰρ ἦν ἀκαλλώπιστός τε καὶ αὐτοφυῶς καλή,
μηδεμιᾶς πανουργίας κομμωτικῆς δεομένη. ὥσπερ οὖν τὸ ἀληθινὸν κάλλος
ἀκριβῶς ἐξετάζεται μόνον αὐτὸ καθ' ἑαυτὸ τῶν ἔξωθεν αὐτῷ προσόντων ἁπά-
ντων γυμνωθέν, οὕτω καὶ τὴν ἀθλητικὴν ἐπιτήδευσιν ἐξετάζεσθαι προσήκει
μόνην, εἴ τι φαίνοιτ' ἔχειν χρήσιμον ἢ κοινῇ ταῖς πόλεσιν ἢ ἰδίᾳ τοῖς μεταχειρι-
ζομένοις αὐτήν.[9]

The Galenic narrator announces the opportune reference to the story about Phryne (in bold: 'This might be a good moment to mention the story of Phryne') according to the demands of his exposition, and after amplifying the story itself, he inserts its essential didactic message at the end (also in bold) by comparing the concept of genuine beauty advocated by Phryne with the concept of the authentic value of athletics that concerns Galen in the treatise in question. In doing so, he helps his readers make better sense of his main point.

Finally, in using didactic tales specifically in his works on practical ethics, Galen seeks to endow himself with moral authority so as to support his claim to emotional resilience. The recently discovered essay *On Avoiding Distress* seeks to show that Galen did not feel grieved by the destruction of his books and medical instruments in the Great Fire of 192, while providing readers with hands-on tips on how to maintain comparable tranquility amidst the adversities of life. To that end, Galen introduces a series of anecdotes concerning disciplined philosophers such as Aristippos, Crates, and Diogenes with the following remark (in bold):

I will give you a double reply to this. As for the first, you must recall that you have heard ⟨me⟩ many times recounting such stories, of which

---

9 Galen, *Exhortation to the Study of Medicine*, ch. 10, ed. K.G. Kühn, *Claudii Galeni Opera omnia*, 20 vols. in 22 (Leipzig: 1821–1833) 1:25.25–26.16 = ed. V. Boudon, *Galien, Exhortation à l'étude de la médecine* (Paris: 2000) 105.4–22; trans. P.N. Singer, *Galen: Selected Works* (Oxford: 1997) 46, emphasis added.

DIDACTIC TALES IN GALEN   91

I will now again begin to remind you. The lavish Aristippus was not satisfied with a frugal regimen, but rather participated every day in luxurious meals and constantly offered abundant money to the most fervent of the companions who surrounded him. Although that man still lacked many things, when he was once returning from Piraeus (⟨for⟩ he always used to walk, not only on such short trips but also on the long ones) and saw that his slave was unable to keep up with him, he ordered him to shed as much of his load (this consisted of a bag full of gold coins) as would render the rest easily carried [...]. It was accordingly not a great matter for me to be not at all distressed by the loss of my property, for what was left was always much more than enough.

Ἐγὼ δέ σοι διττὴν ἀπόκρισιν πρὸς τοῦτο ποιήσομαι, τὴν μὲν ἑτέραν, ὑπὲρ ἧς ἀναμνησθῆναί σε χρὴ πολλάκις ⟨ἐμοῦ⟩ ἀκηκοότα διερχομένου τοιούτους λόγους, ὧν καὶ νῦν ἄρξομαι τῆς ἀναμνήσεως. Φιλότιμος Ἀρίστιππος, οὐκ ἀρκούμενος διαίτῃ εὐτελεῖ, ἀλλὰ καὶ ⟨ἐν⟩ πολυτελείαις ὄψων ὢν ἑκάστης ἡμέρας διδοὺς ἀργύριον ἑκάστοτε δαψιλὲς τοῖς θερμοτέροις τῶν κατ' αὐτὸν ἑταίρων, ὅμως καὶ ἔτι πολλῶν δεόμενος ὁ ἀνὴρ ἐκεῖνος, ἀνιών ποτε ἐκ Πειραιῶς (εἰώθει ⟨γὰρ⟩ ἀεὶ βαδίζειν οὐ μόνον τὰς οὕτω βραχείας ὁδούς, ἀλλὰ καὶ τὰς μακράς), ἐπειδὴ ἐθεάσατο τὸν οἰκέτην μὴ δυνάμενον ἔπεσθαι, τοῦ φορτίου (φασκώλιον δὲ ἦν τοῦτο χρυσίων μεστόν), ἐκέλευσεν ἀποχέαι τοσοῦτον, ὡς τὸ λοιπὸν εὔφορον αὐτῷ γενέσθαι [...]. Οὔκουν ἐμοί τι πρᾶγμα μέγα μηδόλως ἀνιαθέντι διὰ χρημάτων ἀπώλειαν (ἦν γὰρ ἀεὶ τὰ λειπόμενα πολὺ πλέω τῶν ἱκανῶν).[10]

The stories about the philosophers delineate Galen as an authority in the field of practical ethics, both because they present him as knowing the stories well enough to narrate and explicate and because they show how he himself practiced the self-discipline that the stories endorse. The basic traits and functions of the short didactic tales we have just surveyed feature in other Galenic writings in different forms and at different levels of sophistication depending on their specific context, aims, and target audience.

In the remainder of this chapter, I will explore Galen's use of moralizing tales using 'tale theory' as a hermeneutic approach. In the first section, I will be discussing two stand-alone stories taken from two different Galenic medical writings, in light of the theoretical framework that has been set up in this volume's first chapter, namely storyness, storyteller, and story-effect. In the

---

10   Galen, *On Avoiding Distress*, ch. 9–11, eds. Polemis – Xenophontos, *Galen* 72.9–76.2; trans. Xenophontos, *Galen* 73–77; emphasis added.

second section, I will be using the same tools to explore a group of interconnected tales that Galen employs cumulatively in one of his moral essays, thus forming a macro-tale, so to speak. Both cases, that of the single, independent tale and that of the macro-tale, comprising smaller stories, will show that tales in Galen are excellent sources of lessons in morality in line with the main conclusion about tales in practical ethics more generally, as seen in the introductory section above.

2.1 Stand-Alone Tales in Galen

The first case study under the category of stand-alone tales comes from Galen's medical work entitled *Elements According to Hippocrates*. More specifically, it is part of a section dealing with Galen's disagreement with the physician Athenaeus of Attalia (fl. end of the first century BC) over the latter's paradoxical view that the elements of medicine were hot, cold, dry, and wet, whereas Galen was adamant that they were fire, water, air, and earth. So he goes on to attribute Athenaeus' mistaken opinion to his defective use of logic; and, in order to prevent other colleagues from committing the same methodological mistakes, he adduces a didactic story from his personal experience, about how as a youth he succumbed to similar fallacies and ended up developing arguments based on unsound premises. Just before relating this story, Galen adds a brief introductory comment, which reads as follows: 'I swear by the gods to tell what happened to me just as it occurred; in fact, I shall try to narrate it' (τὰ γοῦν ἐμοὶ συμβάντα θεοὺς ἐπομνύμενος ἦ μὴν οὕτως ἐρεῖν ὡς ἐγένετο καὶ δὴ πειράσομαι διηγήσασθαι).[11]

On a primary level, this statement helps establish the Platonic origins of the ensuing dialogue, since the punchy locution 'I shall try to narrate it' (πειράσομαι διηγήσασθαι) occurs verbatim twice in the *Phaedo* (59c–d), once in the *Symposium* (174a), and one more time in the *Euthydemus* (272d), all works that Galen was profoundly aware of, particularly in the context of his extensive knowledge of the Platonic corpus.[12] On a secondary level, the same statement may be seen as a meta-narrative signifier of the type of discourse that the author will provide: Galen feels the need to clarify that he will not simply say (ἐρεῖν) what happened. Rather, he will make a serious attempt at narrating it (διηγήσασθαι), suggesting that he will entangle the events with 'storyness', a series of focused strategies that will transform his account into a persuasive

---

11   Galen, *Elements According to Hippocrates*, 1.6, ed. Kühn, *Opera omnia* 1:460.13–15 = ed. P. De Lacy, *Galeni De elementis ex Hippocratis sententia*, Corpus Medicorum Graecorum 5.1.2 (Berlin: 1996) 105.23–24; trans. De Lacy, *Galeni De elementis* 105, slightly modified.

12   See De Lacy P., "Galen's Platonism", *American Journal of Philology* 93.1 (1972) 27–39, at 30.

and attractive construction, aimed at achieving a specific effect, as we will see in a moment.

The authorial intention to use 'storyness' may have been supported, and indeed supplemented, by a similar intention to build up the profile of the storyteller too.[13] The brief prelude to the story emphasises Galen's credentials as a successful omniscient narrator: when he swears by the gods to relate the story with accuracy, he is not interested so much in guaranteeing the veracity of his report as in appearing reliable and respectable to his readers by building an intimate relationship with them, based on honesty and trust.

In the light of the above, let us now turn to the story itself, which is quite extensive, taking up fifty-one printed lines in the standard edition by Phillip De Lacy. It describes the lively exchange between the young Galen and a senior teacher concerning the elements of medical art. Oftentimes, the sequence of chunks in direct speech is interpolated with short remarks in reported speech, provided by the Galenic narrator to inform us about a change of speaker or the overall development of the discussion. Interestingly, there is a third kind of interjected commentary too, namely when the Galenic narrator notifies us of how Galen the character, through his use of sophisms, increasingly infuriated the instructor. In Figure 4.1 we can see exactly how the narrative heralds a series of escalated feelings, leading up to the tutor's emotional outburst.

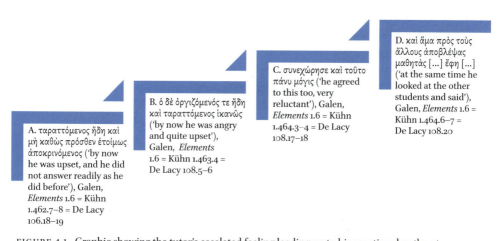

FIGURE 4.1   Graphic showing the tutor's escalated feeling leading up to his emotional outburst

---

13   See, e.g., Constantinou S. – Andreou A., "The Voices of the Tale: The Storyteller in Early Byzantine Collective Biographies, Miracle Collections, and Collections of Edifying Stories", *Byzantine and Modern Greek Studies* 46.1 (2021) 24–40, DOI: 10.1017/byz.2021.31, esp. 31–35.

94   XENOPHONTOS

At first, the tutor was disgruntled and reluctant to answer (A), then he became quite irritated and angry (B). At some point he relented, but with much effort and pain (C), which eventually reignited his exasperation (D) and made him utter the following words:

> 'This fellow', he said, 'who was reared in dialectic and was infected by the itch' – that was the very word he used – 'that it [i.e. the dialectic] causes, turns everything around and twists and muddles everything, playing the sophist with us, in order to display his logical skill [...]. But we', he said, 'have not been taught to resolve sophisms. As he devised it, let him resolve it himself!'

> 'οὗτος', ἔφη, 'τραφεὶς ἐν διαλεκτικῇ καὶ τῆς ἐκεῖθεν ἀναπλησθεὶς ψώρας' – οὕτω γὰρ δὴ καὶ ὠνόμασεν αὐτός – 'ἀναστρέφει πάντα καὶ διαστρέφει καὶ κυκᾷ σοφιζόμενος ἡμᾶς, ἵν' ἐπιδείξηται τὴν λογικὴν παρασκευήν [...]. ἀλλ' ἡμεῖς', ἔφη, 'σοφίσματα λύειν οὐκ ἐμάθομεν. αὐτὸς τοίνυν, ὡς ἔπλεξεν, οὕτως καὶ λυέτω'.[14]

Such strong signposting of Galen's infuriating attitude would no doubt have incentivized the audience to take the part of the instructor, who so unjustly suffers Galen's vain sophistry. In fact, the accusation against Galen put into the teacher's mouth is meant to accentuate the repulsion provoked by Galen's arrogant behavior, if one considers the teacher's negative characterization of Galen's sophistic activity as an 'itch he had to scratch', which the Galenic narrator underscores with the shrewd aside 'that was the very word he used'. All this shows that the Galenic narrator is orchestrating the discussion in such a way as to deter readers from acquiring tendencies like those embraced by the young Galen.

The edifying story-effect manifests itself most clearly in the closing comment, with which the Galenic narrator rounds off this story: 'This happened to me in my nineteenth year; and from then on I kept quiet for the most part, in order not to appear captious' (ταῦτα μὲν ἐμοὶ συνέπεσεν ἔτος ἐννεακαιδέκατον ἄγοντι καὶ τοῦ λοιποῦ τα πλείω μὲν ἐσιώπων ὑπὲρ τοῦ μὴ δοκεῖν ἐρίζειν).[15] This is a critical moment in the plot, a moment of self-confession, since Galen openly admits to his ill-advised juvenile enthusiasm for sophistic showing-off, a practice that he despised later on, in his adult life, both as a medic and a

---

14   Galen, *Elements*, 1.6; ed. Kühn, *Opera omnia* 1:464.5–465.1 = De Lacy, *De elementis* 108.19–110.7; trans. De Lacy, *De elementis* 109–111, slightly revised.

15   Galen, *Elements*, 1.6; Kühn, *Opera omnia* 1:465.1–3 = De Lacy, *De elementis* 110.8–9; trans. De Lacy, *De elementis* 111.

DIDACTIC TALES IN GALEN 95

philosopher. Galen is here self-presented as prudent enough to learn from his mistakes and amend his behavior. In particular, his opting for silence rather than quibbling points to an informed resolution to exercise self-control, rejecting sophistic talkativeness altogether. This case study shows that Galen teaches moral virtue and professional integrity by narrating formidable instances of his own personal failings.

Notwithstanding certain variations, examples such as this can be adduced many times over. There is a similar episode in the work *The Different Kinds of Pulse*,[16] which, alongside the case study from *Elements According to Hippocrates* explored above, allows us to validate the main features of Galen's didactic narration in terms of storyness, storyteller, and story-effect. As far as storyness goes, once again, a lengthy embedded episode (this time six pages long in the printed edition), with Galen as the protagonist, breaks up the technical account, staging a dialogue between him and several other figures, including a sophist and a senior philosopher. The dialogue in direct speech is interpolated with the omniscient narrator's comments, which all stress that Galen the character is so scathing that he gradually annoys his interlocutors. In this particular case, the narrative is injected with strong dashes of humor and irony.[17] For instance, the philosopher's bafflement at Galen's harassment of him is described in the text with the humorous expression 'he was already moving his ears like a donkey',[18] whereas a touch of irony is noticeable when Galen pretends to be slow both in taking in what was said and in formulating answers to questions.[19] Both rhetorical techniques, that of humor and that of irony, facilitate Galen's self-denigration, his intentional undermining of his character that makes him come across as a humane storyteller, with ordinary weaknesses that his audience could easily relate to. This, in turn, as in the previous example from *Elements According to Hippocrates*, helps Galen put across his message more effectively, given that he will have already won the sympathy of his audience and thus made them more receptive to the material presented to them.

On the other hand, the brief narrative introductions and conclusions in which the storyteller frames his personal stories normally emphasize that a critical issue has arisen in life and science, and thus the motivation behind the story he will narrate is an ardent need to rectify people's manners and foster healthy methodological practices. In this specific case from *The Different Kinds*

---

16   Galen, *The Different Kinds of Pulse*, 2.3, ed. Kühn, *Opera omnia* 8:571.6–576.6.

17   There is some sense of humor in the previous case study too, especially in Galen's structured attempts to irritate his interlocutor.

18   ἐπὶ τούτοις ὁ μὲν γέρων ὥσπερ ὄνος ἔσειεν ἤδη τὰ ὦτα, Galen, *The Different Kinds of Pulse*, 2.3, ed. Kühn, *Opera omnia* 8:573.15–16.

19   E.g. Galen, *The Different Kinds of Pulse*, 2.3, ed. Kühn, *Opera omnia* 8:572.14–18.

of Pulse, Galen considers it his duty to promote the use of clear language in scientific discourse and banish the conceptual ambiguity that is often caused by over-talkativeness and argumentative acrobatics. The story-effect, as in the previous example, is to attract the audience's attention, spark their imagination and critical abilities, and eventually lead them to customize the message of this specific story to their own reality, depending on their individual circumstances. These stories would have made readers wonder: 'if the great Galen has bitterly regretted his arrogance and contentiousness both times, why should I ever want to adopt such vices?'

2.2   *Macro-Tales in Galen*

In the previous section of this chapter, we looked at two self-standing cases of storyness in Galen, which, though coming from different works, share common characteristics, thus attesting a sort of patterned poetics for Galen's didactic storytelling. In this section, we will explore how Galen, in the framework of a single treatise, employs a cluster of shorter tales, one after another, again to offer robust ethical recommendations. The treatise in question is entitled *On the Affections and Errors of the Soul* and is Galen's most extensive surviving moral essay. The context where the tales start to appear negotiates the theme of the soul's good condition, which in Galen, as in other ethical philosophers, amounts to the mastery of destructive passions, notably anger. For convenience's sake, I have divided the macro-tale into four moralizing units, which I will discuss in turn. All the tales are narrated in indirect speech by the omniscient narrator, who now takes on the role of an authoritative, paradigmatic moral teacher who has done everything right; he is not the repentant moral transgressor of the first two tales examined in the previous section (from *Elements According to Hippocrates* and *The Different Kinds of Pulse*).

The first tale adumbrates an incident to which the narrator was an eyewitness: that of a man who, unable to open a door, started destroying everything around him, in the grip of extreme rage:

> **In my youth – when I had already engaged in this training –** *I once saw a person hurrying to open a door and, when the operation did not proceed as required, biting the key, kicking the door, cursing the gods; rolling his eyes wildly as madmen do, and all but frothing at the mouth like a boar.* I hated this rage so much that I would never be seen thus disfigured by it. And this, indeed, will be sufficient, at least to begin with: *that you do not curse the gods, do not kick or bite objects of stone or wood, do not take on the appearance of a wild man; but hold back and conceal the anger within yourself.* For one cannot become free from anger immediately, in the same moment that one wishes it; but one can control the ugly manifestation of

DIDACTIC TALES IN GALEN

the affection. And if one does so frequently, one will at some point notice that one is becoming less angry than previously, so that one no longer becomes enraged over either small or great things to a great degree, but only over great ones – to a small degree. Thus, some time later, one will manage to get angry only to a small degree over the greatest things; and then, perhaps – something that I have kept to throughout my life, since imposing it on myself in my youth – never to strike any household servant with my own hand.

ἐγὼ δὲ μειράκιον ὢν ἔτι ταῦτ' ἀσκήσας, ἐπιδὼν ἄνθρωπον ἀνοῖξαι θύραν σπεύδοντα, μὴ προχωρούσης εἰς τὸ δέον αὐτῷ τῆς πράξεως δάκνοντα τὴν κλεῖν καὶ λακτίζοντα τὴν θύραν καὶ λοιδορούμενον τοῖς θεοῖς ἠγριωμένον τε τοὺς ὀφθαλμοὺς ὥσπερ οἱ μαινόμενοι καὶ μικροῦ δεῖν αὐτὸν ἀφρὸν ὡς οἱ κάπροι προϊέμενον ἐκ τοῦ στόματος ἐμίσησα τὸν θυμὸν οὕτως, ὥστε μηκέτ' ὀφθῆναι δι' αὐτὸν ἀσχημονοῦντά με. ἀρκέσει δὲ καὶ τοῦτο τήν γε πρώτην, ὡς μήτε θεοῖς λοιδορεῖσθαί σε μήτε λακτίζειν μήτε δάκνειν τοὺς λίθους καὶ τὰ ξύλα, [καὶ] μήτ' ἄγριον ἐμβλέπειν, ἀλλ' ἐν σαυτῷ κατέχειν τε καὶ κρύπτειν τὴν ὀργήν. ἀόργητος μὲν γὰρ εὐθέως ἅμα τῷ βουληθῆναι γενέσθαι ⟨τις⟩ οὐ δύναται, κατασχεῖν δὲ τὸ τοῦ πάθους ἀσχημον δύναται. τοῦτο δ' ἂν πολλάκις ποιήσῃ, γνωριεῖ ποτε καὶ αὐτὸς ἑαυτὸν ἧττον νῦν ⟨ἢ⟩ πρόσθεν ὀργιζόμενον, ὡς μήτ' ἐπὶ σμικροῖς μήτ' ἐπὶ μέσοις θυμοῦσθαι ἀλλ' ἐπὶ μόνοις τοῖς μεγάλοις μικρόν. οὕτως γὰρ ὑπάρξει ποθ' ὕστερον αὐτὸν καὶ ἐπὶ τοῖς μεγίστοις ὀργίζεσθαι μικρόν, ἤν τις ὅπερ ἐγὼ προστάξας αὐτῷ μειράκιον ὢν ἔτι διὰ παντὸς ἐφύλαξα τοῦ βίου, ⟨φυλάξῃ⟩ τὸ μηδέποτε τυπτῆσαι τῇ χειρί μου μηδένα τῶν οἰκετῶν.[20]

Two points are worth discussing regarding the story-effect here. First, the Galenic narrator's response to the spectacle: 'I hated this rage so much that I would never be seen thus disfigured by it'. This reflective evaluation flags up the negative perception of anger in Galen's society and hence directs the audience to avoid or at least manage this passion. This can also be deduced from the accompanying advice provided in the passage that follows, which mainly advises controlling one's anger through habitual practice. Second, the spectacularized description of the enraged man's behavior enhances the impact of the image on the audience and therefore renders the mastery of rage even

---

20   Galen, *On the Affections and Errors of the Soul*, ch. 4, ed. Kühn, *Opera omnia* 5:16.3–17.6 = 12.11–13.3, ed. W. De Boer, *Galeni De propriorum animi cuiuslibet affectuum dignotione et curatione; De animi cuiuslibet peccatorum dignotione et curatione; De atra bile*, Corpus Medicorum Graecorum 4.1.1 (Leipzig – Berlin: 1937), emphasis added; trans. P.N. Singer, *Galen: Psychological Writings: Avoiding Distress, Character Traits, The Diagnosis and Treatment of the Affections and Errors Peculiar to Each Person's Soul, The Capacities of the Soul Depend on the Mixtures of the Body* (Cambridge: 2013) 252–253.

more pressing, acting on the reader in the manner of 'aversion therapy'.[21] Note that the powerful visualization of the event is enhanced in the text by another rhetorical technique, namely the repetition of the angry man's reactions (see the italic sections), with which Galen warns readers against similar exhibitions of anger.

The second type of tale is an exemplum involving Galen's father, who reprimanded other people for having actually bitten their servants when in a state of uncontrollable rage:

> This was cultivated by my father, too, who indeed berated many of his friends who had bruised a nerve in the act of hitting servants in the teeth. He used to say that they deserved to suffer convulsions and die from the inflammation that they had sustained. For they could perfectly well have waited just a little and applied the number of blows that they wished, with a cane or a strap, carrying out the task in accordance with their judgement.

> ὅπερ ἤσκητό μου καὶ τῷ πατρί· καὶ πολλοῖς ἐπετίμησε τῶν φίλων περιθλάσασι νεῦρον ἐν τῷ πατάξαι κατὰ τῶν ὀδόντων οἰκέτας, ἀξίους εἶναι λέγων ἐπὶ τῇ γενομένῃ φλεγμονῇ καὶ σπασθῆναι καὶ ἀποθανεῖν, ὅπου γ᾽ ἐξῆν αὐτοῖς καὶ νάρθηκι καὶ ἱμάντι μικρὸν ὕστερον ἐμφορῆσαι πληγάς, ὅσαις ἠβούλοντο τῇ βουλῇ τὸ τοιοῦτον ἔργον ἐπιτελεῖν. [22]

On the one hand, the exemplum concerning Galen's father recalls the similar role of the paternal model in a son's formation as seen in Plutarch's story that was discussed in the chapter's introduction. However, Galen's passage is much more equivocal as to the message that his father wished to pass on to his irascible friends, chiefly, it seems, because it is imbued with irony. When Galen has his father say that his friends ought to have postponed their anger and beaten their servants with a cane or a strap instead of damaging their own hands, this could hardly be taken literally, given the general moralizing context here. In

---

21   Alexander L.C.A., "The Passions in Galen and the Novels of Chariton and Xenophon", in Fitzgerald J.T. (ed.), *Passions and Moral Progress in Greco-Roman Thought* (London – New York: 2008) 175–197, at 176 defines 'aversion therapy' as 'a way of displaying the full awfulness of uncontrolled passion and the depths to which sufferers will sink under its sway'.

22   Galen, *On the Affections and Errors of the Soul*, ch. 4; ed. Kühn, *Opera omnia* 5:17.6–12 = ed. De Boer, *De* [...] *animi* [...] *dignotione et curatione* 13.4–12; trans. Singer, *Psychological Writings* 253.

DIDACTIC TALES IN GALEN 99

any case, the exemplum raises the question of the physical maltreatment of slaves and its moral implications,[23] which segues into the third type of tale, the edifying anecdote foregrounding the emperor Hadrian's irascibility:

> The emperor Hadrian, it is said, once struck one of his household servants in the eye with a pencil; and when he realized that the blow had caused him the loss of one eye, Hadrian summoned the servant and allowed him to request a gift from him in recompense for what he had suffered. When the injured party remained silent, Hadrian again encouraged the man not to be shy, but to ask for whatever he wished. At which the servant replied that he had no other request – only an eye. For what gift could compensate for the loss of an eye?

> Ἀδριανὸς δ' αὐτοκράτωρ, ὥς φασι, γραφείῳ πατάξας εἰς τὸν ὀφθαλμὸν ἕνα τῶν ὑπηρετῶν, ἐπειδὴ διὰ τὴν πληγὴν ταύτην ἔγνω γενόμενον ἑτερόφθαλμον, ἐκάλεσέ τε καὶ συνεχώρησεν ἀντὶ τοῦ πάθους αἰτεῖν παρ' αὐτοῦ δῶρον. ἐπεὶ δὲ διεσιώπησεν ὁ πεπονθώς, αὖθις ἠξίωσεν ὁ Ἀδριανὸς αἰτεῖν, ὅτι βούλοιτο, θαρροῦντα· τὸν δ' ἄλλων μὲν οὐδέν, ὀφθαλμὸν ⟨δ'⟩ αἰτῆσαι. τί γὰρ ἂν καὶ γένοιτο δῶρον ἀντάξιον ἀπωλείας ὀφθαλμοῦ;[24]

Galen possibly fictionalized this anecdote, as it is not found in any other surviving source.[25] It warns readers against falling victim to damaging psychological conditions[26] and leads Galen to narrate a similar episode involving

---

23   In the post-Hellenistic ethical-philosophical legacy, the relation between master and servant became a *Leitmotiv* when proposing the control of anger; Trapp M., *Philosophy in the Roman Empire: Ethics, Politics and Society* (London: 2007) 208–210. See e.g. Epictetus, *Discourses*, 1.13; Seneca, *On the Control of Anger*, 1.15, 2.25, 3.12; cf. Seneca, *Letter* 47 'On Master and Slave'. See also Plutarch, *Avoidance of Anger*, 453B–F, 455B, 455E–456E, 458D.

24   Galen, *On the Affection and Errors of the Soul*, ch. 4; ed. Kühn, *Opera omnia* 5:17.16–18.4 = ed. De Boer, *De [...] animi [...] dignotione et curatione* 13.12–18; trans. Singer, *Psychological Writings* 253–254.

25   Hadrian's wrath in this context possibly reflects the hagiographical convention which often presents the Roman torturers of Christian martyrs as uncontrollably angry, as opposed to the calm and almost passionless martyrs. See Constantinou S., *Female Corporeal Performances: Reading the Body in Byzantine Passions and Lives of Holy Women*, Studia Byzantina Upsaliensia 9 (Uppsala: 2005) 19–53, esp. 28–29 and 40–46.

26   For several interpretations of this anecdote, see Schlange-Schöningen H., "Herrschaftskritik bei Galen", in Holmes B. – Fischer K.-D. (eds.), *The Frontiers of Ancient Science: Essays in Honor of Heinrich von Staden* (Berlin: 2015) 655–673, at 657–658 and especially Schlange-Schöningen's own view that this anecdote betokens Galen's opposition to Hadrian's monarchic rule.

a friend from Crete who was also hot-tempered, thus suggesting that anger is a universal trait of human behavior, irrespective of ethnic identity and socio-political standing:

> I should also like to remind you of something that once happened to me, even though I have spoken about it many times. On a journey home from Rome I was travelling in the company of a friend from Gortyn, in Crete, who was in other respects quite an admirable man – straightforward, friendly, kind, liberal in his daily expenditure – but who was so irascible that he regularly used his hands on his servants, and sometimes his legs too; more frequently, though, it would be a leather strap, or any piece of wood that came to hand. When we reached Corinth, we decided to embark all his luggage and his servants – all but two – at Kenchrea and send them to Athens by sea, while he hired a carriage and proceeded by land, via Megara. We went through Eleusis to Thriasion; there he asked the servants who were accompanying him about a certain item of luggage – and they could not tell him anything about it. And so he flew into a rage, and as he had nothing else with which to strike the boys, seized a great knife which was lying there in its sheath, and brought it down, sheath and all, on the heads of both of them, not striking them with the flat of the knife – which would not have been so disastrous – but with the edge. The blade cut right through the sheath, and both servants suffered two very serious wounds – he had hit each of them twice – to the head. When he saw the enormous quantity of blood that was flowing, he left us, making for Athens with great speed, to avoid the possibility of one of the servants dying in his presence. Well, the servants we saved and brought to Athens; but my Cretan friend was utterly disgusted with himself. He took me by the hand, led me into a house somewhere, offered me a strap, stripped, and told me to flog him for what he had done under the compulsion of his accursed rage – these were the words he himself used. I responded, naturally enough, with laughter; but at this he fell to his knees and begged me to do exactly as he had asked. And so, quite evidently, the more earnest his entreaties to be flogged, the more he made me laugh. So, after a fair amount of time had passed in this manner, I promised to give him the blows, if only he would in turn grant me one very small favor – whatever I asked. He agreed, and I commanded him to submit his ears to an argument that I would expound: this would be his punishment. He promised to do so, and I discoursed at some length, explaining what sort of schooling is appropriate for the spirit of rage in us – that of the word, of course; I gave him his flogging – but of a different kind! And with this schooling I left him.

DIDACTIC TALES IN GALEN

βούλομαι δέ σε καὶ τῶν ἐμοί ποτε συμβάντων ἑνὸς ἀναμνῆσαι καίτοι γ᾽ ἤδη πολλάκις ὑπὲρ αὐτοῦ εἰρηκώς· ἀπονοστήσας γὰρ ἐκ Ῥώμης συνωδοιπόρησά τινι
φίλῳ τῶν ἐκ Γόρτυνος τῆς Κρήτης ἀνδρί, τὰ μὲν ἄλλα λόγου τινὸς ἄξιος (καὶ γὰρ
ἁπλοῦς ἦν καὶ φιλικὸς καὶ χρηστὸς ἐλευθέριός τε περὶ τὰς ἐφ᾽ ἡμέρας δαπάνας),
ἦν δ᾽ ὀργίλος οὕτως, ὡς ταῖς ἑαυτοῦ χερσὶ χρῆσθαι κατὰ τῶν οἰκετῶν, ἔστι δ᾽ ὅτε
καὶ τοῖς σκέλεσι, πολὺ δὲ μᾶλλον ἱμάντι καὶ ξύλῳ τῷ παρατυχόντι. γενομένοις
οὖν ἡμῖν ἐν Κορίνθῳ πάντα μὲν ἔδοξε τὰ σκεύη καὶ τοὺς οἰκέτας ἀπὸ Κεγχρεῶν
εἰς Ἀθήνας ἐκπέμψαι κατὰ πλοῦν ἐκτὸς δυεῖν, αὐτὸν δ᾽ ὄχημα μισθωσάμενον
πεζῇ διὰ Μεγάρων πορεύεσθαι. καὶ δὴ διελθόντων ἡμῶν Ἐλευσῖνα καὶ κατὰ
τὸ Θριάσιον ὄντων ᾔρετο τοὺς ἑπομένους οἰκέτας αὐτῷ περί τινος σκεύους· οἱ
δ᾽ οὐκ εἶχον ἀποκρίνασθαι. θυμωθεὶς οὖν, ἐπεὶ μηδὲν ἄλλο εἶχε, δι᾽ οὗ πατάξειε
τοὺς νεανίσκους, ἐν θήκῃ περιεχομένην μάχαιραν μεγάλην ἀνελόμενος, ἅμα
τῇ θήκῃ καταφέρει τῆς κεφαλῆς ἀμφοτέρων, οὐ πλατεῖαν ἐπενεγκών (οὐδὲν
γὰρ ⟨ἂν⟩ οὕτως εἴργαστο δεινόν), ἀλλὰ κατὰ τὸ τέμνον τοῦ ξίφους. ἤ τ᾽ οὖν θήκη
διετμήθη παραχρῆμα καὶ τραῦμα μέγιστον ἐπὶ τῆς κεφαλῆς διττὸν ἀμφοτέροις
εἰργάσατο· δὶς γὰρ ἑκάτερον αὐτῶν ἐπάταξεν. ὡς δὲ πλεῖστον ⟨καὶ⟩ ἄμετρον
αἷμα χεόμενον ἐθεάσατο, καταλιπὼν ἡμᾶς εἰς Ἀθήνας ἀπῄει βαδίζων ὠκέως
ἕνεκα τοῦ ⟨μὴ⟩ διαφθαρῆναί τινα τῶν οἰκετῶν ἔτι παρόντος αὐτοῦ. ἐκείνους
μὲν οὖν ἡμεῖς ἐσώσαμεν εἰς τὰς Ἀθήνας. ὁ δὲ φίλος ὁ Κρὴς ἑαυτοῦ καταγνοὺς
μεγάλως εἰσάγει με λαβόμενος τῆς χειρὸς εἰς οἶκόν τινα, καὶ προσδοὺς ἱμάντα
καὶ ἀποδυσάμενος ἐκέλευσε μαστιγοῦν αὐτὸν ἐφ᾽ οἷς ἔπραξεν ὑπὸ τοῦ κατα-
ράτου θυμοῦ βιασθείς· αὐτὸς γὰρ οὕτως ὠνόμασεν. ἐμοῦ δ᾽ ὡς εἰκὸς γελῶντος
ἐδεῖτο προσπίπτων τοῖς γόνασι, μὴ ἄλλως ποιεῖν. εὔδηλον οὖν, ὅτι μᾶλλον ἐποίει
με γελᾶν, ὅσῳ μᾶλλον ἐνέκειτο μαστιγωθῆναι δεόμενος. ἐπειδὴ ⟨δὲ⟩ ταῦτα ποι-
ούντων ἡμῶν ἱκανὸς ἐτρίβετο χρόνος, ὑπεσχόμην αὐτῷ δώσειν πληγάς, εἴ μοι
παράσχοι καὶ αὐτός ἕν, ὃ ἂν αἰτήσω, σμικρὸν πάνυ. ὡς δ᾽ ὑπέσχετο, παρεκάλουν
παρασχεῖν μοι τὰ ὦτα λόγον τινὰ διερχομένῳ, καὶ τοῦτ᾽ ἔφην εἶναι τὸ αἴτημα.
τοῦ δ᾽ ὑποσχομένου πράξειν οὕτως, πλέον αὐτῷ διελέχθην ὑποτιθέμενος, ὅπως
χρὴ παιδαγωγῆσαι τὸ ἐν ἡμῖν θυμοειδές, [τ]ῷ λόγῳ δῆλον ὅτι καὶ διαμαστιγῶν
ἀλλ᾽ ἑτέρῳ τρόπῳ, παιδαγωγήσας ἀπῆλθον.[27]

This moralizing tale may be seen as an 'ethical case history'. This is a term
I have coined in my book to refer to narratives about curing disturbing emotions, which Galen constructs in imitation of his medical case histories, i.e.
his clinical encounters aimed at treating the body.[28] A couple of examples
will make the connection clearer. First, at the very beginning of the passage

---

27 Galen, *On the Affections and Errors of the Soul*, ch. 4; ed. Kühn, *Opera omnia* 5:18.4–20.9 = ed.
    De Boer, *De* [...] *animi* [...] *dignotione et curatione* 13.19–15.5; trans. Singer, *Psychological
    Writings* 254–255.
28 Xenophontos, *Medicine and Practical Ethics in Galen* 150–152.

concerned, we get information on the patient's condition before Galen's intervention: we learn that despite being friendly and kind, the patient was also hot-tempered, and as a result often inflicted corporal punishment on his servants. This is very close to the traditional description of the patient's background in the medical case histories, which includes the symptomatology and overall circumstances affecting the patient prior to his therapy.[29] Second, the patient's background is typically followed by the causes of his disease. Just as in this ethical case history we learn that there was a specific event that sparked the patient's anger, namely the loss of a piece of luggage. Third, a constituent element of clinical encounters with patients is the recovery from the illness. In the ethical case history, there is a similar focus on Galen's therapeutic enterprise, which includes a lengthy discussion between Galen and the patient, aimed at clarifying to the latter how the spirited part of the soul is schooled not through flogging, but through verbal communication that helps foster commendable moral habits. This is also known as the 'therapy of the word'[30] in ancient ethics. Finally, the last stage of a typical clinical case is the prognostication of the disease, namely an estimation of how the disease will progress in the future on the basis of a concrete time-plan, just like the one found immediately after the quoted section.[31]

---

29   The formal and structural criteria of Galen's medical case histories are analyzed by Mattern S., *Galen and the Rhetoric of Healing* (Baltimore: 2008) 41–46, 65–66.

30   E.g. Singer P.N., "Galen's Pathological Soul: Diagnosis and Therapy in Ethical and Medical Texts and Contexts", in Thumiger C. – Singer P.N. (eds.), *Mental Illness in Ancient Medicine: From Celsus to Paul of Aegina* (Leiden: 2018) 381–420, at 394–395; García Ballester L., "Soul and Body, Disease of the Soul and Disease of the Body in Galen's Medical Thought", in Manuli P. – Vegetti M. (eds.), *Le opere psicologiche di Galeno* (Naples: 1988) 117–152, at 144–145. On the therapy of the word in classical antiquity, see Laín Entralgo P., *The Therapy of the Word in Classical Antiquity*, ed. and trans. L.J. Rather – J.M. Sharp (New Haven: 1970). Verbal interaction with the patient was also suggested by doctors such as Celsus and Caelius Aurelianus; see Gill C., "Ancient Psychotherapy", *Journal of the History of Ideas* 46 (1985) 307–325, at 318–319.

31   'Well, this person, by taking care over himself, improved greatly in the space of a year. In your case, even if you are not capable of a great improvement, you should be satisfied even with some quite small progress in the right direction in the first year. If you continue to withstand the affection, and to soften your rage, you will make more substantial progress in the second year. And if you continue to take care over yourself, in the third, and then in the fourth and fifth year, and beyond, you will be even more conscious of the great improvement in the direction of dignity of life' (ἐκεῖνος μὲν οὖν ⟨ἐν⟩ ἐνιαυτῷ προνοησάμενος ἑαυτοῦ πολὺ βελτίων ἐγένετο. Σὺ δ᾽ εἰ καὶ μὴ πολὺ γένοιο βελτίων, ἀρκεσθήσῃ γε καὶ μικρῷ τινι κατὰ τὸν πρῶτον ἐνιαυτὸν ἐπιδοῦναι πρὸς τὸ κρεῖττον. ἐὰν γὰρ ἐπιμείνῃς τῷ πάθει ⟨τ᾽⟩ ἀντέχων καὶ πραΰνων τὸν θυμόν, ἀξιολογώτερον ἐπιδώσεις κατὰ τὸ δεύτερον ἔτος. Εἶτ᾽ ἐὰν ἔτι διαμείνῃς ἑαυτοῦ προνοούμενος καὶ μᾶλλον ἐν τῷ τρίτῳ καὶ μετ᾽ αὐτὸν ἐν τῷ τετάρτῳ καὶ πέμπτῳ καὶ τοῖς ἑξῆς, αἰσθήσῃ μεγάλης αὐξήσεως εἰς βίου σεμνότητα). Galen, *On the Affection and Errors of*

3 Conclusions

The way Galen narrativizes his personal tales may be associated with the so-called 'healing power of narrating', as explored by Tilmann Habermas in his 2018 book *Emotion and Narrative: Perspectives in Autobiographical Storytelling*. This theory from social psychology postulates that there is a strong social dimension in sharing our personal experiences with other people. It also argues that when we narrate emotionally loaded incidents from our daily lives, we transform them to suit our listeners' perspectives or expectations, and that the typical reasons that drive us to share our emotional experiences in the first place are to vent emotions, elicit empathy or attention, inform or warn others, and most importantly, strengthen shared convictions and world views. All the above correlate strongly with the psychotherapeutic impact and social outlook of Galen's didactic tales, which whether short or long, independent or part of a larger narrative, are, as we have seen, translated into suggested approaches to social and professional life for the consumers of Galen's work. The American poet Muriel Rukeyser famously said that 'the universe is made of stories, not of atoms'.[32] When it comes to Galen's moral universe, there is no doubt that it was made of stories.

Bibliography

Primary Sources

Galen, *Elements According to Hippocrates*. In ed. K.G. Kühn, *Claudii Galeni Opera omnia*, 20 vols. in 22 (Leipzig: 1821–1833) 1 = ed. P. De Lacy, *Galeni De elementis ex Hippocratis sententia*, Corpus Medicorum Graecorum 5.1.2 (Berlin: 1996).

Galen, *The Different Kinds of Pulse*. In ed. K.G. Kühn, *Claudii Galeni Opera omnia*, 20 vols. in 22 (Leipzig: 1821–1833) 8.

Galen, *Exhortation to the Study of Medicine*. In ed. K.G. Kühn, *Claudii Galeni Opera omnia*, 20 vols. in 22 (Leipzig: 1821–1833) 1 = ed. V. Boudon, *Galien, Exhortation à l'étude de la médecine*, Belles Lettres (Paris: 2000).

Galen, *On Avoiding Distress*. In eds. I. Polemis – S. Xenophontos, *Galen, On Avoiding Distress and On My Own Opinions. Critical edition by I. Polemis and S. Xenophontos. Trans. S. Xenophontos*, Trends in Classics Supplementary Volume 151 (Berlin: 2023).

---

the Soul, ch. 4; ed. Kühn, *Opera omnia* 5:20.9–21.5 = ed. De Boer, *De [...] animi [...] dignotione et curatione* 15.6–15; trans. Singer, *Psychological Writings* 255.

32 Rukeyser M., *The Speed of Darkness* (London: 1968) 111.

Galen, *On My Own Opinions*. In eds. I. Polemis – S. Xenophontos, *Galen, On Avoiding Distress and On My Own Opinions. Critical edition by I. Polemis and S. Xenophontos. Trans. S. Xenophontos*, Trends in Classics Supplementary Volume 151 (Berlin: 2023).

Galen, *On the Affections and Errors of the Soul*. In ed. K.G. Kühn, *Claudii Galeni Opera omnia*, 20 vols. in 22 (Leipzig: 1821–1833) 5 = ed. W. De Boer, *Galeni De propriorum animi cuiuslibet affectuum dignotione et curatione; De animi cuiuslibet peccatorum dignotione et curatione; De atra bile*, Corpus Medicorum Graecorum 4.1.1 (Leipzig – Berlin: 1937).

Plutarch, *On Talkativeness*. In ed. M. Pohlenz, *Plutarchi Moralia*, 3 vols. (Leipzig: 1929; repr. 1972).

Plutarch, *Political Precepts*. In ed. H.N. Fowler, Plutarch's *Moralia*, vol. 10: *771E–854D: With an English Translation* (Cambridge, MA: 1936).

Secondary Works

Alexander L.C.A., "The Passions in Galen and the Novels of Chariton and Xenophon", in Fitzgerald J.T. (ed.), *Passions and Moral Progress in Greco-Roman Thought* (London – New York: 2008) 175–197.

Barthes R., "An Introduction to the Structural Analysis of Narrative", *New Literary History* 6.2 (1975) 237–272.

Constantinou S., *Female Corporeal Performances: Reading the Body in Byzantine Passions and Lives of Holy Women*, Studia Byzantina Upsaliensia 9 (Uppsala: 2005).

Constantinou S. – Andreou A., "The Voices of the Tale: The Storyteller in Early Byzantine Collective Biographies, Miracle Collections, and Collections of Edifying Stories", *Byzantine and Modern Greek Studies* 46.1 (2021) 24–40, DOI: 10.1017/byz.2021.31.

De Lacy P. (ed. and trans.), *Galeni De elementis ex Hippocratis sententia*, Corpus Medicorum Graecorum 5.1.2 (Berlin: 1996).

De Lacy P., "Galen's Platonism", *American Journal of Philology* 93.1 (1972) 27–39.

Fowler H.N. (trans.), Plutarch's *Moralia*, vol. 10: *771E–854D: With an English Translation* (Cambridge, MA: 1936).

García Ballester L., "Soul and Body, Disease of the Soul and Disease of the Body in Galen's Medical Thought", in Manuli P. – Vegetti M. (eds.), *Le opere psicologiche di Galeno* (Naples: 1988) 117–152.

Gill C., "Ancient Psychotherapy", *Journal of the History of Ideas* 46 (1985) 307–325.

Gill C., "The School in the Roman Imperial Period", in Inwood B. (ed.), *The Cambridge Companion to the Stoics* (Cambridge: 2003) 33–58.

Habermas T., *Emotion and Narrative: Perspectives in Autobiographical Storytelling* (Cambridge: 2018).

Hankinson R.J., "Galen on the Limitations of Knowledge", in Gill C. – Whitmarsh T. – Wilkins J. (eds.), *Galen and the World of Knowledge* (Cambridge: 2009) 206–242.

Helmbold W.C. (trans.), *Plutarch's Moralia*, vol. 6: *439A–523B: With an English Translation* (London: 1939).

Ingenkamp H.G., *Plutarchs Schriften über die Heilung der Seele* (Göttingen: 1971).

Laín Entralgo P., *The Therapy of the Word in Classical Antiquity*, ed. and trans. L.J. Rather – J.M. Sharp (New Haven: 1970).

Mattern S., *Galen and the Rhetoric of Healing* (Baltimore: 2008).

Morgan T., *Popular Morality in the Early Roman Empire* (Cambridge: 2007).

Pelling C.B.R., "What Is Popular about Plutarch's 'Popular Philosophy'?", in Roskam G. – Van der Stockt L. (eds.), *Virtues for the People: Aspects of Plutarchan Ethics* (Leuven: 2011) 41–58.

Polemis I – Xenophontos S. (eds. and trans.), *Galen, On Avoiding Distress and On My Own Opinions. Critical edition by I. Polemis and S. Xenophontos. Trans. S.* Xenophontos, Trends in Classics Supplementary Volume 151 (Berlin: 2023).

Roskam G. – Van der Stockt L., "Efficiency and Effectiveness of Plutarch's Broadcasting Ethics", in Roskam G. – Van der Stockt L. (eds.), *Virtues for the People: Aspects of Plutarchan Ethics* (Leuven: 2011) 7–16.

Rukeyser M., *The Speed of Darkness* (London: 1968).

Schlange-Schöningen H., "Herrschaftskritik bei Galen", in Holmes B. – Fischer K.-D. (eds.), *The Frontiers of Ancient Science: Essays in Honor of Heinrich von Staden* (Berlin: 2015) 655–673.

Schofield, M., "Stoic Ethics", in Inwood B. (ed.), *The Cambridge Companion to the Stoics* (Cambridge: 2003) 233–256.

Singer P.N. (trans.), *Galen: Psychological Writings: Avoiding Distress, Character Traits, The Diagnosis and Treatment of the Affections and Errors Peculiar to Each Person's Soul, The Capacities of the Soul Depend on the Mixtures of the Body* (Cambridge: 2013).

Singer P.N. (trans.), *Galen: Selected Works* (Oxford: 1997).

Singer P.N., "Galen's Pathological Soul: Diagnosis and Therapy in Ethical and Medical Texts and Contexts", in Thumiger C. – Singer P.N. (eds.), *Mental Illness in Ancient Medicine: From Celsus to Paul of Aegina* (Leiden: 2018) 381–420.

Tieleman T., "Galen's Psychology", in Barnes J. – Jouanna J. (eds.), *Galien et la philosophie: Huit exposés suivis de discussions* (Geneva: 2003) 131–169.

Trapp M., *Philosophy in the Roman Empire: Ethics, Politics and Society* (London: 2007).

Van der Eijk P., "Galen on the Nature of Human Beings", in Adamson P. – Hansberger R. – Wilberding J. (eds.), *Philosophical Themes in Galen* (London: 2014) 89–134.

Van der Stockt L., "*Semper duo, numquam tres?* Plutarch's *Popularphilosophie* on Friendship and Virtue in *On Having Many Friends*", in Roskam G. – Van der Stockt L. (eds.), *Virtues for the People: Aspects of Plutarchan Ethics* (Leuven: 2011) 19–39.

Van Hoof L., "Practical Ethics", in Beck M. (ed.), *A Companion to Plutarch* (Chichester: 2014) 135–148.

Van Hoof L., *Plutarch's Practical Ethics: The Social Dynamics of Philosophy* (Oxford: 2010).

Xenophontos S., *Medicine and Practical Ethics in Galen* (Cambridge: 2024).

Ziegler K., "Plutarchos von Chaironeia", *Paulys Realencyclopädie der classischen Altertumswissenschaft* 41 (1951) 636–962.

CHAPTER 5

Repetition and the Storyteller's Profile in Early Byzantine Tale Collections

Stavroula Constantinou and Andria Andreou

1 Introduction

In our attempt to examine the device of repetition in early Byzantine tale collections and its relation to the profile of the examined works' storyteller(s), we inevitably ask Michael Toolan's question: 'How can something as dull as repetition bear at all directly on what is fresh, exciting and original in literary narratives?'[1] As Toolan goes on to remark, 'we criticize things as "boring and repetitive" (never as "boring and unrepetitive") and we seem never to celebrate anything as "interesting and repetitive". Indeed, boring and repetitive is almost a tautology, a boring repetition'.[2] Yet our tendency to treat repetition and tediousness as synonyms prevents us from approaching and appreciating repetition in works where it plays a central role and becomes an essential element of their poetics.

Early Byzantine tale collections favor repetition on both a stylistic and a narrative level. Stylistic repetition involves repetition of vocabulary (e.g. stereotypical words and phrases),[3] themes (e.g. the miraculous

---

1 Toolan M., *Making Sense of Narrative Text: Situation, Repetition, and Picturing in the Reading of Short Stories*, Routledge Studies in Rhetoric and Stylistics (New York – London: 2016) 23.

The research for this chapter was co-funded by the European Regional Development Fund and the Republic of Cyprus through the Foundation of Research and Innovation (Project: Post-Doc/0718/0021), as well as by the A.G. Leventis Foundation. Some of the ideas that inform the chapter's arguments were developed in the framework of the project 'Network for Medieval Arts and Rituals' (NetMAR), which received funding from the European Union's Horizon 2020 research and innovation programme under grant agreement no. 951875. The opinions expressed in this document reflect only the authors' view and in no way reflect the European Commission's opinions. The European Commission is not responsible for any use that may be made of the information it contains.

2 Toolan, *Making Sense of Narrative Text* 24.

3 See, e.g., the repetition of the introductory phrase 'narrated to us' (διηγήσατο ἡμῖν) + name of the ascetic + geographical location in a large number of tales in John Moschos' *Spiritual Meadow* (BHG 1440f–1442z), ed. in *Patrologia Graeca* 87.3:2852–3112, for instance at 2865, ch. 18, 5. For the ideology surrounding repetition in Byzantium see also Chitoiu D., "Repetition

---

© STAVROULA CONSTANTINOU AND ANDRIA ANDREOU, 2025 | DOI:10.1163/9789004707351_007

This is an open access chapter distributed under the terms of the CC BY-NC-ND 4.0 license.

cure),[4] and rhetorical devices (e.g. irony).[5] Narrative repetition includes the recurrent use of the same narrative elements (e.g. type of characters),[6] devices (e.g. the healing dream),[7] and structures (e.g. the linear healing narrative).[8] The striking repetitive character of early Byzantine tale collections is probably one of the reasons why these texts have been largely neglected by previous scholars who considered them monotonous, tiresome, and devoid of any literary merit.[9]

This chapter aims to bring to the fore some of the ways in which early Byzantine authors employ the device of repetition to create the pious profile of the storyteller(s) telling the tales included in anthologies that were produced in ecclesiastical and monastic contexts between the fifth and seventh centuries. These anthologies include the *Apophthegmata Patrum*, collective biographies, miracle tale collections, and beneficial tale collections. In our corpus, the storyteller, usually a man (i.e. monk, priest, or bishop), might identify with the anthology's composer or he might be another character who undertakes to share with the author-storyteller his own story or that of a previous storyteller

---

as Resumption: From Litany to Thinking in Byzantium", *Revista Portuguesa de Filosofia* 69.2 (2013) 205–213.

4 See, e.g., Sophronios of Jerusalem, *Miracles of Kyros and John* (BHG 477–479), ed. N.F. Marcos, *Los 'Thaumata' di Sofronio: Contribución al estudio de la 'incubatio' cristiana* (Madrid: 1975), where miraculous cures significantly outnumber other types of tales.

5 See, e.g., Artemios appearing as a butcher and terrifying a patient by pulling out his intestines while, in fact, performing a healing; *Miracles of Artemios* (BHG 173–173c), ed. A. Papadopoulos-Kerameus, *Varia Graeca sacra* (St. Petersburg: 1909) 1–75, at ch. 25. For useful comments on the text see the trans. of V.S. Crisafulli and J.W. Nesbitt in *The Miracles of St. Artemios: A Collection of Miracle Stories by an Anonymous Author of Seventh-Century Byzantium* (Leiden – New York – Cologne: 1997).

6 Ascetic fathers are, for instance, recurrent protagonists in Palladios of Hellenopolis, *Lausiac History*, ed. D.C. Butler, *The Lausiac History of Palladius*, vol. 2: *Introduction and Text* (Cambridge: 1898–1904) 1–169.

7 Kosmas and Damian, for example, repeatedly perform their healings in the patients' dreams; *Miracles of Kosmas and Damian* (BHG 385–391), ed. L. Deubner, *Kosmas und Damian: Texte und Einleitung* (Leipzig – Berlin: 1907) 193–206; E. Rupprecht, *Cosmae et Damiani sanctorum medicorum vita(m) et miracula e codice Londinensi* (Berlin: 1935). On healing dreams see also Constantinou S., "Healing Dreams in Early Byzantine Miracle Collections", in Oberhelman S. (ed.), *Dreams, Healing, and Medicine in Greece: From Antiquity to the Present* (Aldershot: 2013) 189–198 and eadem, "The Morphology of Healing Dreams: Dream and Therapy in Byzantine Collections of Miracle Stories", in Angelidi C. – Calofonos G. (eds.), *Dreaming in Byzantium and Beyond* (Aldershot: 2014) 21–34.

8 For instance, the tales included in the *Miracles of Artemios* repeatedly present a standard structure whereby the patient's profile is followed by the description of the patient's illness and the saint's healing intervention. The tales usually conclude with praise of the miraculous saint.

9 See Introduction.

REPETITION AND THE STORYTELLER'S PROFILE

who might, in turn, share someone else's story, thus creating a storytelling chain.[10]

As we will show, repetition in the examined texts functions as a powerful tool in the authors' hands in their attempt to present themselves and their sources as trustworthy, wise, pious, and exemplary storytellers. In short, the storyteller's profile is strongly associated with repetition and its various forms, including the repetition of the very act of storytelling. For reasons of space, the following analysis will focus on three texts belonging to three different types of early Byzantine tale collections: collective biography (*History of the Monks in Egypt*), miracle collection (*Miracle Collection of Thekla*), and beneficial tale collection (Daniel of Sketis' *Narrations*). The three texts under investigation illustrate three different types of storytellers as these are created through the employment of repetition: the holy, the chosen, and the repentant storyteller.

2   The Holy Storyteller: *History of the Monks in Egypt*

The *History of the Monks in Egypt* (hereafter HME), the oldest text examined here, was composed at the end of the fourth century.[11] Its anonymous author belonged to a group of seven monks who departed from their monastery on the Mount of Olives in Jerusalem to visit the famous monks of the Egyptian desert. The backbone of HME, which includes twenty-six stories featuring mostly the ascetics that our group of monks meet, is created by the latter's itinerary, which starts from Asyût and ends at Diolcos. In between, the seven monks appear to have visited many places, including Bahr Yûsuf, Eshmûnen, Behnesa, Shêkh 'Abâda, Bawit, Tehna, Akhnasia el-Medina, Der el-Memun, Kôm Fâris, Babylon, Memphis, El Barnugi, and Alexandria. In most stories, the storyteller's role is undertaken by the author of HME. Some of the Egyptian monks populating the above-mentioned places also act as storytellers, telling

---

10   For a more thorough analysis of the storyteller in the early Byzantine tale see Constantinou S. – Andreou A., "The Voices of the Tale: The Storyteller in Early Byzantine Collective Biographies, Miracle Collections, and Collections of Edifying Tales", *Byzantine and Modern Greek Studies* 46.1 (2021) 24–40, DOI: 10.1017/byz.2021.31.

11   For dating, authorship, and the collection see Cain A., *The Greek Historia Monachorum in Aegypto* (Oxford: 2016) 33–53; Ward B., "Introduction", in Ward B. – Russell N. (eds.), *The Lives of the Desert Fathers*, Cistercian Studies 34 (Kalamazoo, MI: 1980) 1–46. For a discussion of the Greek and Latin versions see Festugière A.-J., "Le problème littéraire de l'*Historia monachorum*", *Hermes* 83.3 (1955) 257–284; Frank G., "The *Historia Monachorum in Aegypto* and Ancient Travel Writing", *Studia Patristica* 30 (1997) 191–195. For the text (BHG 1333–1334), see Festugière A.-J. (ed.), *Historia monachorum in Aegypto*, Subsidia hagiographica 34 (Brussels: 1961).

their own stories and/or those of other previous and contemporary ascetics whom the travelers do not meet in person.

But let us discuss one such storyteller and how he interacts with the author-storyteller. The storyteller in question is John of Lykopolis, the central hero of the collection's first and longest tale, consisting of 439 printed lines. As for repetition, this frame tale is structured around triple repetitions both in terms of style (language and rhetoric) and narrative (types of characters and structure). Even though triple repetitions are common in our corpus (the number three is a holy number symbolizing the Holy Trinity), as well as in *HME* in particular,[12] the tale on John of Lykopolis stands out for its persistent and recurrent employment of the triple repetition. This repetition plays an instrumental role in the creation of John's profile as a holy and humble storyteller and monk that trusts the author-storyteller and the fellow travelers with whom he shares his storytelling art and wisdom. To provide a better understanding of how triple repetition works in this frame tale, it is important first to present its individual single-episode tales and its structure as a frame tale.[13]

The first frame of the tale consists of eight single-episode tales which are told by the author-storyteller who introduces himself and the central hero at the outset: 'In the territory of Lyko in the Thebaid I saw the great and blessed John, a truly holy and virtuous man' ('Ἐθεασάμην οὖν ἐν τοῖς ὁρίοις Λυκῶ τῆς Θηβαΐδος τὸν μέγαν καὶ μακάριον Ἰωάννην, ἄνδρα ἅγιον ἀληθῶς καὶ ἐνάρετον).[14] The tale's second frame is marked by the introduction of a new storytelling voice, that of John, who tells tales concerning other monks in his attempt to exemplify the teachings he addresses to the author-storyteller and his fellow travelers in the previous tale. When John's frame narratives end there is a return to the first frame, that of the author-storyteller, who now confirms the realization of John's prophecies that were mentioned in the first tale of the first frame and reports on John's death. The frame tale's structure is summarized as follows:

> **FRAME 1:** Introduction of the author-storyteller's voice (ch. 1, 1).
> **Tale 1:** The author-storyteller gives an account of John's prophecies (ch. 1, 1–20).

---

12   See, e.g., *HME* ch. 2, 48–51, where an angel appears every three days to feed an ascetic who hasn't tasted human food for three years.

13   For the episodic structure of early Byzantine tales and their categorization into single-episode tales, multiple-episode tales, and frame tales, see Chapter 8.

14   *HME* ch. 1, 1–2; trans. N. Russell, "The Lives of the Desert Fathers", in Ward B. – Russell N. (eds.), *The Lives of the Desert Fathers: The Historia Monachorum in Aegypto*, Cistercian Publications 34 (Kalamazoo, MI: 1980) 47–119, at 52, with minor amendments.

REPETITION AND THE STORYTELLER'S PROFILE

Tale 2: The author-storyteller tells a tale about an official who convinces John to meet his wife, whom the ascetic visits in a dream (ch. 1, 21–53).

Tale 3: The author-storyteller tells how John informs an officer about the difficult birth of his son and the boy's future (ch. 1, 54–69).

Tale 4: The author-storyteller tells how John heals the blind wife of a senator remotely (ch. 1, 70–78).

Tale 5: The author-storyteller describes their arrival at John's dwelling and how John reveals the secret priestly identity of one of his visitors (ch. 1, 79–99).

Tale 6: The author-storyteller tells how John heals one of the seven monks, who has fever (ch. 1, 100–107).

Tale 7: The author-storyteller describes John's harsh ascetic life and reports the teachings he addresses to the seven monks upon the latter's request (ch. 1, 108–196).

FRAME 2: John assumes the storyteller's role (ch. 1, 197).

Tale 1: John tells a tale about a monk who fails in his spiritual battle as result of the evil of pride (ch. 1, 197–235).

Tale 2: John tells a tale about a sinful layman who changes his life, becomes a monk, and gains salvation because of his humility (ch. 1, 236–289).

Tale 3: John tells a tale about a monk who falls into the sin of pride and repents (ch. 1, 290–425).

FRAME 1: The author resumes his storytelling function (ch. 1, 426).

Tale 7: Return to and continuation of the seventh tale presented above; the author-storyteller describes how he and his fellow monks say goodbye to John. He then goes on to confirm the realization of John's prophecies that were presented in Tale 1 of Frame 1 (ch. 1, 426–433).

Tale 8: The author-storyteller tells how during meetings with other ascetics they were informed about John's death and his last wishes (ch. 1, 434–439).

As becomes evident from this breakdown of frames and their internal tales, each frame has one or more groups consisting of three tales that present a similar theme and purpose. Frame 1 includes two tale groups, and Frame 2 has one such group. Tales 2–4 of the first frame concern John's contactless interaction with three different women, who are espoused to three officials. These tales manifest John's gifts of clairvoyance and miracle-working. They involve a miraculous dream bringing John to the first official's wife (Tale 2), revelations about the pregnant wife's difficult labor and the fate of the second official's newborn son (Tale 3), and the miraculous healing of the third official's wife

(Tale 4). John's divine gifts are also stressed through the repeated use of the word γάρ ('for example').[15]

Following John's meeting with our company of monks, three additional tales (5–7) of the first frame that constitute narrativizations of events taking place in front of the author-storyteller highlight once again John's gift of clairvoyance (Tale 5) and his healing powers (Tale 6), while his exemplary asceticism is also stressed (Tale 7). In short, in Frame 1 and within the framework of two groups of tales that have repetitive elements, John is conveniently established as a holy and exemplary character. It is as such that he assumes first the teacher's and then the storyteller's role, thus introducing the second frame, which has parallels with the first frame.

But before undertaking these two roles for the benefit of the seven monks, John washes their feet. Even though he undermines his teaching and storytelling abilities – 'what remarkable thing did you expect to find, my dearest children, that you have undertaken such a long journey with so much labor in your desire to visit some poor simple men who possess nothing worth seeing or admiring?' (Καὶ τί θαυμαστὸν ὀψόμενοι, ὦ προσφιλέστατοι παῖδες, τοσαύτην ὁδὸν καὶ κάματον ὑπήλθατε ἀνθρώπους ταπεινοὺς καὶ εὐτελεῖς ὁρᾶν ἐπιθυμήσαντες οὐδὲν ἄξιον θεωρίας οὐδὲ θαύματος ἔχοντας;)[16] – he does embark on a lengthy teaching exposition about how a monk could achieve eternal salvation, thus proving himself a competent monastic teacher. A recurrent theme of John's teachings is the virtue of humility, a virtue he himself embodies when he washes the feet of his seven visitors and proclaims that he has nothing worthy to teach them. Yet, John teaches humility not only through his example and teachings, but also through his role as a storyteller telling three tales that repeatedly thematize the importance of a monk's humility.

John's first tale concerns a monk who, misperceiving himself as being spiritually perfect ('he came eventually to trust in himself, placing his reliance on his good way of life'; ἐφ' ἑαυτῷ λοιπὸν ἐπεποίθει θαρρῶν ἐπὶ τῇ καλῇ πολιτείᾳ),[17] is fooled by a demon transformed into a beautiful woman. The woman asks to spend the night with the ascetic as she does not desire to dwell alone in the desert at night. The ascetic agrees and unavoidable chatting with the woman leads to her bodily touching, and this touching, in turn, arouses the ascetic's sexual desire. As the ascetic rushes to satisfy his lust, the woman vanishes like a shadow. The demons make fun of him and triumph over his spiritual fall. The

---

15   *HME*, ch. 1, 21 and ch. 1, 72; trans. Russell, "The Lives of the Desert Fathers" 63, 64.

16   *HME*, ch. 1, 127–128; trans. Russell, "The Lives of the Desert Fathers" 55.

17   *HME*, ch. 1, 200–201; trans. Russell, "The Lives of the Desert Fathers" 56–57. See also *HME*, ch. 1, 223–224.

REPETITION AND THE STORYTELLER'S PROFILE 113

monk wakes up in the morning and laments for his lost piety. Despairing of his salvation and spending the day in lamentation, he abandons his ascetic life and returns to the world. As one may readily infer, the tale's events take place in three acts and on three consecutive days: the woman spending a night with the monk; the monk realizing his fault the next day; and the monk returning to the world the following day.

The next tale, too, involves a man who decides to change his way of life, but in the opposite direction. This is a sinful layman who leaves the world behind to adopt an ascetic life. After he has spent a week in the desert, a group of demons starts tempting him with the worldly pleasures he used to enjoy. At the same time, the demons shout at him and attack him physically. They reappear in the same fashion for another two consecutive nights. The new monk's thrice-repetitive struggle with the demons leads to his eventual release from temptation, with the demons admitting their defeat in a repetitive, and consequently emphatic, way: 'You have won, you have won, you have won' (ἐνίκησας, ἐνίκησας, ἐνίκησας).[18]

In the third and final tale, a pious monk falls prey to the sin of pride: 'he began without realizing it to think that he was superior to most men, and that he had attained something greater than others, and having arrived at this opinion he began to trust in himself' (ἔλαθεν ἑαυτὸν οἰόμενος πλεῖον εἶναί τι τῶν πολλῶν καὶ ὡς ἤδη τι παρὰ τοὺς ἄλλους ἀνθρώπους μεῖζόν [τι] κεκτημένος, καὶ τοιοῦτος ὢν λοιπὸν ἑαυτῷ ἐπεποίθει).[19] This monk used to miraculously find bread in his cell that was provided by God. Nevertheless, at a certain point he begins to exhibit signs of laziness, thinking he has already reached spiritual perfection. The first day he shows such signs we are told that he finds his bread as it was on the previous days. On the second day, however, his bread starts getting dirty. On the following day, lustful thoughts are added to his laziness, and he becomes distracted from his prayer. As a result, the bread becomes extremely dirty, while by night its state deteriorates to such a degree that it appears to have been eaten by dogs or mice. In the course of three consecutive days, the bread is marked by different stages of freshness reflecting the man's deteriorating spiritual state. Eventually, the monk recognizes his sin and undertakes a long-lasting repentance.

Interestingly, as soon as John assumes the storyteller's role, he is no longer one of the characters of the tales he tells. However, his exemplary ascetic life is implicitly recalled within the framework of each of his three tales. The three protagonists of John's tales represent three different types of monks whom the

---

18   *HME*, ch. 1, 279; trans. Russell, "The Lives of the Desert Fathers" 59.
19   *HME*, ch. 1, 319–321; trans. Russell, "The Lives of the Desert Fathers" 60.

reader or listener cannot help but compare with John. Tempted by the devil in a woman's disguise, the first monk falls prey to lust. The monk's bodily contact with the woman is reminiscent of John's three contactless interactions with the officials' wives represented in the three tales told by the author-storyteller. Although all these women are noble and presumably pious, with two of them in a state of health emergency, John resists having any physical contact with them – unlike the monk of his first tale who allows a female stranger to enter his cell. This unavoidable comparison stresses once again John's bodily integrity and humility over the first monk's lust and carelessness. Despite the innumerable years of his asceticism and his great monastic experience, John is careful enough not to think that he has reached a state of perfection.

Introduced in between two failing monks, the resisting monk of John's second tale is still inferior to the holy man. Even though he has performed no sin and has, therefore, nothing to repent for, John remains humble throughout his monastic life. Not even in the last three days of his life does his divine zeal diminish. Moreover, John's high spiritual state allows him to perform miracles, to help, and to edify others through teaching and storytelling. The second monk, in contrast, retreats to the desert to fight against his temptations and to make up for his previously sinful life. This story builds upon John's lesson on humility, since it is due to his humility that the second monk manages to defeat the demons. As for the third and final monk, besides his falling prey to pride and thus proving once again John's warning about the disastrous effect of such a sin, he seems to be inferior to John even in his 'good days'. This monk consumes bread. John, by contrast, 'ate nothing apart from fruit, and after sunset at that, in spite of his advanced age, having formerly lived a life of great ascetic discipline. And he never ate bread or anything that needed to be cooked' (ἤσθιεν γὰρ οὐδὲν ἕτερον πλὴν ὀπώρας, καὶ τοῦτο μετὰ τὴν ἡλίου δύσιν ἐν τῷ γήρει, πολλὰ προασκήσας πρότερον καὶ μήτε ἄρτου μετειληφὼς μήτε ὅσα διὰ πυρὸς ἔχει τὴν χρῆσιν).[20]

In between his three tales, John continues his teachings about the importance of humility. By the end of the third tale, the author-storyteller resumes his storytelling role to point out that John has been telling stories for three consecutive days. Even though it is not clear how many tales he tells each day, it is inferred that John is a tireless storyteller and an inexhaustible source of tales. After completing his storytelling task, as the author-storyteller reports, John prays for another three days. In so doing, he pays equal attention to the practice of prayer and that of storytelling. Both practices appear equally important for achieving holiness. After three days of continuous storytelling followed by

---

20   *HME*, ch. 1, 110–113; trans. Russell, "The Lives of the Desert Fathers" 54.

REPETITION AND THE STORYTELLER'S PROFILE   115

another three days of uninterrupted prayer, John is united with God: 'he died and departed for God, to whom be glory for all eternity. Amen' (ἐτελειώθη πρὸς θεὸν ἀπερχόμενος· ᾧ ἡ δόξα εἰς τοὺς αἰῶνας, ἀμήν).[21]

'Amen' does not just refer to the end of John's life, but also marks the end of *HME*'s first frame tale, which is to a large degree a tale about storytelling and story-listening. Our company of monks has the privilege to live with John during three of the last six days of his earthly life and to repeatedly listen to his last tales. Possessing the gift of clairvoyance, John is aware of this very reality, namely that the seven monks will be his last visitors. He therefore provides them with the experience of his best storytelling-self, the one that the author-storyteller commemorates in the very first tale of his monumental work. Evidently, the author-storyteller becomes John's primary storyteller both for turning into tales the last episodes of his life and for transmitting his saintly storytelling voice through the composition of *HME*.

3   The Chosen Storyteller: *Miracles of Thekla*

The *Miracles of Thekla* (hereafter *MT*),[22] a work including forty-six miracle tales, was composed in the mid-fifth century by an anonymous author who also wrote Thekla's *Life*.[23] The tales of *MT*, as is the case with most tales of the miracle collections included in our corpus, are told by a single voice – that of the author-storyteller – and not by the chain of storytellers found in collective biographies such as *HME*. In *MT*, however, there are three tales in which the author-storyteller also acts as the protagonist and beneficiary of the saint's miracles. The autobiographical tales in question are found close to the beginning, the middle, and the end of the collection (chs. 12, 31, and 41). In what follows, we will show how Thekla's repeated manifestations within the framework of a triple repetition of autobiographical tales, which are strategically placed

---

21   *HME*, ch. 1, 438–439; trans. Russell, "The Lives of the Desert Fathers" 62.
22   *Miracles of Thekla* (BHG 1718), ed. G. Dagron, *Vie et miracles de sainte Thècle: Texte grec, traduction et commentaire*, Subsidia hagiographica 6 (Paris: 1978) 285–412.
23   For the collection, its date and authorship see Dagron, *Vie et miracles* 13–30; Efthymiadis S., "Collections of Miracles: Fifth to Fifteenth Centuries", in idem (ed.), *The Ashgate Research Companion to Byzantine Hagiography*, vol. 2: *Genres and Contexts* (Farnham: 2014) 103–131, at 106. For stylistic matters see Johnson S.F., *The Life and Miracles of Thekla: A Literary Study*, Hellenic Studies 13 (Cambridge, MA – London: 2006) 172–220; Narro Á., "Lo scontro tra formazione classica e pensiero cristiano: La vita e miracoli di santa Tecla", *Greco-Latina Brunensia* 15 (2010) 127–138.

in *MT*, aim at confirming the author as the saint's chosen hagiographer, story-teller, encomiast, and priest.

Triple repetition is a characteristic of the first autobiographical tale (ch. 12), too. The opening lines of the tale read as follows: 'I blush to tell the miracle concerning myself – which happened once and even a second and a third time' (Τὸ δὲ περὶ ἐμὲ αὐτὸν θαῦμα, γεγονὸς ἅπαξ που καὶ δεύτερον καὶ τρίτον ἐπερυθριῶ μὲν εἰπεῖν).[24] This autobiographical multiple-episode tale includes three divine manifestations that are experienced by the author-storyteller through the same narrative device. This is the device of the dream around which the tale's episodes are structured. The first dream leads to the cure of the author-storyteller's dangerous disease. The second is a prophetic dream warning him about the excommunication that the local bishop, Basil, prepares against him. The last dream, which is also premonitory and complements the second one, informs the author-storyteller about the excommunication's revocation.

The author-storyteller tells his first dream thus:

> I saw the virgin entering the place where I was sleeping. [...] After enter-ing and witnessing the wasps' attack against me, taking the top part of her *himation*, which covered her head as well as the rest of her body, and swinging it around with her hand, she scared away the whole swarm of the wasps, destroyed them, trampled them with her feet and set me free from all those terrible enemies.

> Ἐδόκουν [...] καθεύδειν [...] ἐπεισελθοῦσαν [τὴν παρθένον] δὲ καὶ θεασαμένην τὸν κατ' ἐμοῦ τῶν σφηκῶν πόλεμον, καὶ λαβομένην ἄκρου τοῦ ἱματίου τοῦ τὴν κεφαλὴν μετὰ καὶ τοῦ λοιποῦ σκέποντος σώματος καὶ περιστρέψασαν τῇ χειρί, τὸν πολὺν ἐκεῖνον ὅμαδον τῶν σφηκῶν ἀποσοβῆσαί τε καὶ καθελεῖν καὶ συμπα-τῆσαι τοῖς ποσί, καὶ ἐμὲ πάντων ἐκείνων ἐλευθερῶσαι τῶν δεινῶν πολεμίων.[25]

By appearing in person to save her hagiographer from a life-threatening dis-ease symbolized by the fierce wasps, Thekla not only solves a serious health problem that is associated with the hero's strong emotional crisis, but also initiates an intimate relationship with him which is strengthened each time she performs a miracle on his behalf. Waking from his first divine dream, the author-storyteller realises that the martyr has become his protectress and

---

24   *MT*, ch. 12, 1–2; trans. S.F. Johnson, "The Miracles of Thekla", in Talbot A.M. – Johnson S.F. (trans.), *Miracle Tales from Byzantium*, Dumbarton Oaks Medieval Library 12 (Cambridge, MA – London: 2012) 1–201, at 47.

25   *MT*, ch. 12, 24–32; trans. Johnson, "The Miracles of Thekla" 49.

REPETITION AND THE STORYTELLER'S PROFILE

savior: 'I found I had been delivered from that fierce pain and suffering, so that I was even smiling and gladdened at the blessed vision [...]. [T]hey [the doctors] lost their payment on account of her visitation and healing' (ἐγὼ μὲν ἀπηλλάγμην τῶν ἀγρίων ἐκείνων πόνων καὶ ἀλγηδόνων, ὡς καὶ μειδιᾶν καὶ γάννυσθαι ἐπὶ τῇ μακαρίᾳ ὄψει, οἱ δὲ ἰατροὶ [...] διὰ τὴν αὐτῆς ἐπίσκεψιν καὶ ἰατρείαν καὶ ἀπόμισθοι γεγονότες).[26]

Even though it is quite different, the premonitory dream that follows repeats some of the elements of the first dream:

Zamaras [...] seemed to approach me while I was sleeping, and held out what we commonly call a *tremisis* [...]. This coin, too, was dark and very black, or at least it seemed to be dark. I took it against my will and without pleasure, I must confess. For the dream seemed to me to be the sort of prophecy auguring nothing good.

Ζαμαρᾶς [...] καθεύδοντί μοι προσιέναι τε ἔδοξε καὶ ὀρέγειν ὃ καλεῖν ἔθος ἡμῖν τριμίσιον [...]. ζοφῶδες δὲ καὶ τοῦτο ἦν καὶ μελάντατον, ἢ ἐδόκει ζοφῶδες εἶναι. Τοῦτο ἄκων ἐδεξάμην καὶ οὐχ ἡδέως, ὁμολογῶ· καὶ γὰρ ὄναρ ἔδοξέ μοι οὐκ ἀγαθοῦ τινος εἶναι μάντευμα τὸ τοιοῦτο.[27]

The hagiographer has the two dreams at approximately the same time: 'when daylight appeared and began to shine' (τῆς δὲ ἡμέρας ἤδη φανείσης καὶ ὑπολάμπειν ἀρχομένης); 'just as day was coming on' (ἄρτι δὲ ἡμέρας γεγονυίας).[28] This time correlation underlines the divine origin and purpose of the dreams, which occur at the right time, revealing the strategy that lies behind them. The healing dream comes to cancel an operation through which the hero's finger is about to be amputated. The premonitory dream aims at warning the hagiographer about his excommunication, which is announced soon after he wakes up from the dream. In both cases, the author-storyteller sees himself being approached by a figure while sleeping (Thekla and the evil Zamaras). When he awakes from each dream, the hagiographer comes to an important realization concerning himself. Yet, while the realization from the first dream (the restoration of his health) is positive, that of the second (his upcoming excommunication) is negative. The first dream frees the author-storyteller from his bodily and emotional suffering, while the second dream foretells his upcoming, yet short-lived, emotional suffering through the excommunication.

---

26   *MT*, ch. 12, 34–35, 39–40; trans. Johnson, "The Miracles of Thekla" 49.
27   *MT*, ch. 12, 58–63; trans. Johnson, "The Miracles of Thekla" 51.
28   *MT*, ch. 12, 33, 64; trans. Johnson, "The Miracles of Thekla" 49, 51.

The third dream comes to solve the problem that is foretold by the second dream. In the last dream, Thekla visits the author-storyteller once again, to express her opposition to his unjustified excommunication and to offer her emotional support and help. Thekla's treatment of her protégé is once again remarkable:

> The martyr stood at my side in a girl's appearance, with a white *tribonion* wrapped around her, from her back to her chest, then fastened there [at the shoulder] with a pin. And taking my right hand, she gave me that very thing of which Basil had wickedly deprived me. 'Take this and be courageous, my child', she said to me. [...] Having uttered [these words], she flew away [...]. But I stood up and found my hand filled with an extraordinary fragrance. I [...] said to my friends who were present: 'Today [...] Basil will revoke the excommunication'.

> ἐφίσταταί μοι ἡ μάρτυς ἐν κορικῷ σχήματι καὶ τριβωνίῳ λευκῷ ἐκ τῶν μεταφρένων μὲν ἐπὶ τὰ στέρνα περιηγμένῳ, αὐτόθι δὲ λοιπὸν ἐμπεπορημένῳ, καὶ λαβομένη μου τῆς δεξιᾶς χειρὸς ἐντίθησί μοι ὅπερ Βασίλειος οὐκ οἶδα εἰ καλῶς ἀφείλετο· Ἔχε καὶ θάρρει, τέκνον' – ἐπιφθεγξαμένη μοι [...]. Καὶ ἡ μὲν ταῦτα εἰποῦσα ἀπέπτη [...], ἐγὼ δὲ διαναστὰς τὴν μὲν χεῖρα ἐξαισίου τινὸς εὐωδίας εὗρον πεπληρωμένην [...] τοῖς παραγεγονόσι τῶν φίλων εἶπον εὐθὺς ὡς· 'Σήμερον, [...] Βασίλειος λύσει τὴν ἀκοινωνησίαν'.[29]

While in her previous dream epiphany Thekla behaves fiercely and violently, hitting, repelling, and crushing the wasps that threaten the hagiographer, here she appears in a gentle manner. Having the appearance of a maiden wearing elegant attire, she gently takes the hero's hand and gives him a token symbolizing the excommunication's revocation. Even though they are in one sense antithetical, the martyr's repeated appearances, along with the recurrent divine dreams, serve the same purposes: to provide divine solutions to urgent personal problems and to highlight through the sequence of dreams the martyr's role as the hagiographer's constant guardian and protectress.

In the second autobiographical tale of MT, Thekla appears to support the hagiographer in his very role as her approved author-storyteller. Specifically, while finishing up the writing of the preceding tale (ch. 30) the hagiographer remarks: 'I had been neglectful in collecting and committing these events to writing, I confess, and I was lazily holding my writing tablet and stylus, as if I had already given up researching and collecting these miracles' ('Ὀλιγώρως

---

29   MT, ch. 12, 95–106; trans. Johnson, "The Miracles of Thekla" 47, 49, 51, 53, 55, modified.

REPETITION AND THE STORYTELLER'S PROFILE   119

μὲν γὰρ εἶχον ἤδη περὶ τοῦ συλλέγειν καὶ γράφειν αὐτὰ ταῦτα, ὁμολογῶ, καὶ ῥαθύ-
μως ἡπτόμην λοιπὸν καὶ δέλτου καὶ γραφίδος, ὡς ἂν καὶ ἀπειρηκὼς λοιπὸν περὶ τὴν
τῶν θαυμάτων τούτων ἔρευνάν τε καὶ συλλογήν).[30] At this point when the hagiographer is about to give up his work on Thekla's miracle collection, she visits him in his workplace to encourage him not to abandon such an important
undertaking.

This time the martyr appears seated 'in the place where he consults his
books' (οὗπερ καὶ ἔθος ἦν μοι τὴν πρὸς βιβλία ποιεῖσθαι συνουσίαν).[31] She takes the
manuscript from his hands and reads the previous miracle tale approvingly. In
so doing, she becomes the tale's first reader. Through her reactions – she seems
to smile, to enjoy, and to be pleased with what she reads – she determines
the reactions of the work's future audiences, who are invited to enjoy and find
pleasant what the saint herself enjoys and approves. As the author-storyteller
points out, 'I was consumed with fear, but even greater was my desire to take
up my writing tablet and stylus once again and to continue this work as long
as she might command' (με [...] δέους τε πληρωθῆναι καὶ προθυμίας ὑποπλη-
σθῆναι καὶ ἅψασθαι πάλιν δέλτου καὶ γραφίδος, καὶ τοῦτο ποιεῖν μέχρι περ ἂν αὐτὴ
κελεύη).[32] He thus embraces the tasks of writing and storytelling as a saintly
plan designed only for himself. Being a sequel of the author-storyteller's legiti-
mization as a person (physical integrity) and a personality (social integrity) in
the first autobiographical tale, this second tale illustrates his emergence as the
saint's chosen hagiographer and storyteller.

In the third autobiographical tale (ch. 41), the author-storyteller shines as
an orator, public encomiast, and priest of Thekla. This is the last tale of a group
of miracles having orators as their beneficiaries. The author-storyteller introduces into the collection this group of oratory miracle tales as follows:

> Now oratory is accusing me and complaining on behalf of eloquent
> scholars: should it alone remain neglected in my stories, given that it has
> not been neglected by the martyr but, on the contrary, wise and eloquent
> men have often obtained miracles? Come on, let me tell what I have
> learned up to the present moment, so that oratory may grace my pages,
> because it has been included in such a blessed chorus of miracles.
>
> Εἶτα οὐ καρτεροῦσιν ἡμῶν οἱ λόγοι, καὶ καταβοήσουσι πρὸς τοὺς ἐλλογίμους
> τῶν ἀνδρῶν, εἰ μόνοι παροφθεῖεν ὑφ' ἡμῶν, καὶ ταῦτα οὐ παροφθέντες ὑπὸ τῆς

---

30   *MT*, ch. 31, 3–7; trans. Johnson, "The Miracles of Thekla" 127.
31   *MT*, ch. 31, 8–9; trans. Johnson, "The Miracles of Thekla" 127.
32   *MT*, ch. 31, 16–18; trans. Johnson, "The Miracles of Thekla" 129.

μάρτυρος, ἀλλὰ γὰρ καὶ πολλάκις τετυχηκότες θαυμάτων ἐν ἀνδράσι σοφοῖς τε καὶ ἐλλογίμοις; Φέρε οὖν, ἃ τέως μεμαθήκαμεν εἴπωμεν, ἵνα ἔχοιεν ἡμῖν καὶ οἱ λόγοι χάριν, ὡς τῆς οὕτω καὶ αὐτοὶ μακαρίας τῶν θαυμάτων χοροστασίας ἀξιωθέντες.[33]

As suggested by the above-quoted passage, our author envisions his work as excelling in oratory and thus becoming 'blessed' by the martyr herself. As he points out later, addressing his audience, 'You see then how fond of oratory the martyr is, and how she enjoys the praise that comes to her through speeches' (Οὕτω δὴ φιλόλογός τε ἐστιν ἡ μάρτυς καὶ χαίρει ταῖς διὰ τῶν λόγων ταύταις εὐφημίαις).[34] The third autobiographical tale, where he features as an orator receiving the martyr's miraculous powers, places him amongst the 'wise and eloquent men who obtain miracles'. This tale revolves around a problem that puts into danger the delivery of the author-storyteller's encomium for the saint that is scheduled for her feast day, just as in the previous autobiographical tale the completion of Thekla's miracle collection was put into jeopardy due to the hagiographer's tiredness and loss of motivation. Now, the problem is physical rather than psychological. A day before the delivery of the oration, the author-storyteller gets an ear infection preventing him from acting as the orator of Thekla's holiness. He thus finds himself once again in a desperate position: 'I despaired of speaking at all' (με καὶ τοῦ ἐρεῖν ἀπογνῶναι παντελῶς).[35]

Thekla reappears at the author-storyteller's side, taking immediate action. She repeats her violent approach toward the treatment of his disease by abruptly taking and aggressively shaking the author-storyteller's infected ear. Yet, this time, she does not flee as soon as the cure is achieved through the evacuation of the pus that had accumulated in the ear. She stays next to the man while he delivers the oration:

> I spoke a few words but then the martyr offered her helping hand and her grace to such an extent that, first, I seemed to be a man of some reputation; second I spoke passably well and third, I received substantial admiration for my words which had no admirable feature.

> καὶ εἶπον μὲν ἄττα, οὕτω δε μοι τὴν χεῖρα καὶ χάριν συνεπέδωκεν ἡ μάρτυς, ὡς εἶναί τι καὶ δόξαι, καὶ εἰρηκέναι μετρίως, καὶ θαῦμα πλεῖστον ἐπὶ μηδενὶ θαυμαστῷ τῶν ἐμῶν ἀπενέγκασθαι λόγων.[36]

---

33   *MT*, ch. 37, 5–11; trans. Johnson, "The Miracles of Thekla" 153.
34   *MT*, ch. 41, 1–2; trans. Johnson, "The Miracles of Thekla" 163.
35   *MT*, ch. 41, 14; trans. Johnson, "The Miracles of Thekla" 165.
36   *MT*, ch. 41, 24–27; trans. Johnson, "The Miracles of Thekla" 165.

REPETITION AND THE STORYTELLER'S PROFILE   121

Through the saint's constant presence and support, the author-storyteller does not just succeed in what he sets out to do (to effectively deliver his first oration on Thekla). His divinely inspired eloquence, which wins the listeners' admiration and respect, renders him a much finer orator than the ones receiving Thekla's miraculous powers in the previous oratory tales. The saint's repeated manifestations during his public performances as orator and priest are the most striking indications of her approval and support. As he points out toward the end of the tale,

> Thekla assisted me constantly. Appearing to me at night she always held out a book or a sheet of parchment, which was and always appeared to be a symbol of her substantial favor toward me. ⟨Since this is her pattern of behavior,⟩ if ever she fails to appear to me when I am about to speak, the inverse conclusion [i.e., that she is not favorable] is equally clear to me.

> συμπαρῆν τε ὡς τὰ πολλά, καὶ νύκτωρ ἐπιφαινομένη βιβλίον τί μοι πάντως ἢ χάρτην ὤρεγεν, ὃ πάντως μοι πλείστης εὐδοκιμήσεως σύμβολον ἦν τε καὶ ἐδόκει. Εἰ δὲ μέλλοντί μοι λέγειν τι μὴ ὀφθῇ τοῦτο ποιοῦσα, τό γε ἀποβησόμενον πάλιν εὔδηλον ἦν.[37]

By repeatedly narrativizing Thekla's recurring manifestations in both dream and vision, the author-storyteller seems to have created autobiographical tales that repeat and thus establish the same belief, namely that the saint never abandons her chosen and favorite hagiographer, storyteller, orator, encomiast, and priest. Not only does she support him in his writings and public performances that are divinely inspired, but she also rushes to save him whenever his health and reputation are at serious risk. In so doing, the saint highlights his special value and legitimizes his authority as the text's writer.

4   The Repentant Storyteller: Daniel of Sketis' *Narrations*

Our final collection of tales, Daniel of Sketis' *Narrations* (hereafter simply *Narrations*), is associated with Daniel, the sixth-century renowned ascetic and abbot of the monastic community of Skete in Egypt. The collection, which is ascribed to Daniel, was presumably produced by one of his disciples at some point toward the end of the sixth century.[38] It contains tales which have monks

---

37   *MT*, ch. 41, 28–32; trans. Johnson, "The Miracles of Thekla" 167.
38   Daniel of Sketis, *Narrations* (BHG 2099z–2102f, 79–80, 121–122, 618, 2255, 2453), ed. B. Dahlman, *Saint Daniel of Sketis: A Group of Hagiographic Texts*, Studia Byzantina Upsaliensia 10 (Uppsala: 2007) 108–187.

but also laymen as their protagonists, and whose main activities are set in and around the monastic centers of Alexandria, Skete, and the Thebaid.[39] Being the lengthiest story of *Narrations*, the sixth tale examined here presents through repetition a new type of storyteller: the repentant storyteller.[40]

The tale features two protagonists: a layman, Eulogios the Stone-Cutter, and Daniel. Eulogios gathers strangers in from the street of Thebais, offering them hospice. Observing the man's philanthropy, Daniel prays for Eulogios to become rich so that he can offer more and be able to support a greater number of people in need. However, as soon as he gains wealth, Eulogios completely changes his disposition, thus endangering Daniel's salvation. Unavoidably, Daniel's spiritual destiny becomes intertwined with that of Eulogios. Daniel undertakes the storyteller's role to tell an autobiographical tale revolving around his personal journey of repentance and forgiveness which evidently also secures that of Eulogios. Once again, triple repetition is an essential characteristic of the storyteller's autobiographical tale. Decisive moments concerning Daniel's spiritual status are linked to three dreams of divine origin which repeat one another. But let us first briefly present the tale's structure.

The tale in question is a frame tale consisting of two frames. The first frame is initiated by the author-storyteller, who undertakes to tell the story of the trip of Daniel and his disciple to Thebais, the dispute between the two men about where to spend the night, and their meeting with Eulogios, whose identity the disciple ignores. On their way back to Skete, the disciple forces Daniel to tell him Eulogios' story. It is at this point that the tale's second frame is introduced. Daniel becomes the storyteller of the story involving himself and Eulogios. The frame tale's structure can be presented as follows:

> **FRAME 1:** The author-storyteller introduces the heroes of his tale: Daniel and his disciple (ch. 1, 1).
> **Tale 1:** The author-storyteller tells the story of the two men's trip (ch. 1, 1–56).
> **FRAME 2:** Daniel assumes the role of the storyteller.
> **Tale 1:** Daniel narrates Eulogios' current vocation of offering care and hospice to foreigners (ch. 1, 57–66).

---

39   Binggeli A., "Collections of Edifying Stories", in Efthymiadis, *The Ashgate Research Companion* 2:143–159, at 149–150; Dahlman, *Saint Daniel* 41–89. For beneficial tales see also Ivanov S., (ed.) *Spiritually Beneficial Tales in Byzantine and Slavic Literature*, Special Issue, *Scripta* 8/9.

40   The tale numbers 235 printed lines in Dalman's edition.

REPETITION AND THE STORYTELLER'S PROFILE

Tale 2: Daniel narrates his mistake and repentance in four episodes (ch. 1, 67–229).

Episode 1: Daniel observes Eulogios' philanthropy and guarantees for his soul in a dream where Christ is present (ch. 1, 67–95).

Episode 2: A second divine dream informs Daniel about Eulogios' shift to an impious lifestyle and Daniel's pending spiritual destruction. He attempts to meet Eulogios, but he fails (ch. 1, 95–144).

Episode 3: In a third divine dream, Christ releases Daniel from his sin through the Virgin's intercession and informs Daniel that He will restore Eulogios to his former pious life (ch. 1, 145–206).

Episode 4: Daniel meets Eulogios, who has now returned to his pious lifestyle (ch. 1, 207–229).

FRAME 1: The author-storyteller resumes his function and brings the tale to a closure (ch. 1, 230–235).

Triple repetition is firstly detected in the tale of the first frame. Daniel insists three times that he and his disciple stay in the middle of the street, without explaining the reason for this unexpected demand. Daniel's repetitive insistence provokes the disciple's repetitive resistance:

> The elder said: 'We are going to stay here today.' His disciple began to grumble, saying: 'How much longer are we going to wander around? Let us go to Sketis.' But the elder said: 'No, we are staying here today.' And they sat down in the centre of the village like strangers. The brother said to the elder: 'Will it please God that we sit here like brothers of these men? Let us at least go to a martyrion.' The elder said: 'No, we will sit here.' And there they remained sitting until late evening. And the brother began to quarrel with the elder, saying: 'Because of you I am going to die a miserable death'.

> καὶ λέγει ὁ γέρων· ὧδε ἔχομεν μεῖναι τὴν σήμερον. καὶ ἤρξατο ὁ μαθητὴς αὐτοῦ γογγύζειν λέγων· ἕως πότε γυρεύομεν; ἄγωμεν λοιπὸν εἰς τὴν Σκῆτιν. ὁ δὲ γέρων φησίν· οὐχί, ἀλλ' ὧδε μένομεν σήμερον. καὶ ἐκάθισαν εἰς τὸ μέσον τοῦ χωρίου ὡς ξένοι. καὶ λέγει ὁ ἀδελφὸς τῷ γέροντι· ἆρα ἀρέσκει τῷ Θεῷ ὅτι ὡς συνάδελφοι καθήμεθα ὧδε; ἄγωμεν κἂν εἰς μαρτύριον. καὶ λέγει ὁ γέρων· οὐχί, ἀλλ' ὧδε καθεζόμεθα. καὶ ἔμειναν ἐκεῖ καθεζόμενοι μέχρις ἑσπέρας βαθείας. καὶ ἤρξατο ὁ ἀδελφὸς μάχην ποιεῖν μετὰ τοῦ γέροντος λέγων· διὰ σὲ ἔχω ἀποθανεῖν κακῶς.[41]

---

41   *Narrations*, ch. 6, 5–14; trans. Dahlman, *Saint Daniel* 149.

This first cycle of repetitions underlines the importance of the public space the two men inhabit, which eventually becomes the stage of action that leads Daniel to assume the role of the storyteller. Indeed, while Daniel and his disciple are sitting on the street as if homeless, suddenly an old man arrives, Eulogios, who takes the two men to his home, along with some other people he finds on the street, and offers them hospice, food, and words of salvation. This development becomes the cause of a second, heated, exchange between Daniel and his disciple, since, upon their return to Skete, the former does not agree to reveal the old man's identity. In fact, Daniel's almost frantic insistence on staying in the middle of the street without explaining why and his original refusal to share Eulogios' story with his disciple are at odds with his corresponding behavior in the other tales of the collection. In those tales, Daniel features as the wise storyteller and teacher who readily discloses the true identities of secretly pious protagonists, offering his disciples and other monks or laymen beneficial lessons. This is possibly the reason why the disciple accompanying Daniel to Thebais gets irritated by his unusual insistence on not sharing Eulogios' story.

As we will show, Daniel's uncommon behavior becomes fathomable only in retrospect – after he fulfills his storytelling role that is part of the tale's second frame.[42] Having first described Eulogios' present situation, Daniel goes on to explain how he became a guarantor of the man's soul. When Daniel saw Eulogios' great philanthropy he was so impressed that he fervently prayed for the man's acquisition of riches, which would support him in his God-pleasing work. Daniel's prayers were answered by Christ, who visited the ascetic in a dream:

> And I saw that we were standing in the Church of the Holy Resurrection, and a young man was sitting on the holy stone with Eulogios standing on his right. He sent one of those who stood by him to me and said to me: 'Is this the person who stands guarantor for Eulogios?' And everybody said: 'Yes, master.' Again, he said: 'Tell him that I shall require the guarantee.' I said to him: 'Yes, master – it is my responsibility. Only give it to him.' And I saw how they were pouring a large amount of money into Eulogios' lap, which received as much as they poured. When I awoke, I knew that my prayer had been heard and I glorified God.

> καὶ βλέπω ὡς ὅτι εἰς τὴν Ἁγίαν Ἀνάστασιν ἐστήκαμεν, καὶ μειράκιον ἐκάθητο ἐπάνω τοῦ ἁγίου λίθου, καὶ τὸν Εὐλόγιον ἐκ δεξιῶν αὐτοῦ ἱστάμενον.

---

42   *Narrations*, ch. 6, 57–229.

REPETITION AND THE STORYTELLER'S PROFILE

καὶ πέμπει πρός μέ τινα τῶν παρισταμένων αὐτῷ καὶ λέγει μοι· οὗτός ἐστιν
ὁ ἐγγυησάμενος Εὐλόγιον; καὶ λέγουσι πάντες· ναί, Δέσποτα. καὶ πάλιν λέγει·
εἴπατε αὐτῷ ὅτι τὴν ἐγγύην ἀπαιτῆσαι ἔχω. καὶ λέγω αὐτῷ· ναί, Δέσποτα, πρός
ἐμέ· μόνον δὸς αὐτῷ. καὶ βλέπω ὅτι ἐκένουν εἰς τὸν κόλπον Εὐλογίου χρήματα
πολλὰ πάνυ· καὶ ὅσον ἐκεῖνοι ἐκένουν τοσοῦτον ἐπεδέχετο ὁ κόλπος Εὐλογίου.
καὶ διυπνισθεὶς ἔγνων ὅτι εἰσηκούσθην, καὶ ἐδόξασα τὸν Θεόν.[43]

The Church of the Resurrection where the dream is set directly recalls the
Day of Judgment, while the young man sitting in a prominent place stands
for Christ in His role as the Judge in the Second Coming. Acting unwisely and
arrogantly within the realm of the divine dream, Daniel ties his spiritual fate
with that of Eulogios, whom he does not really know. Despite Christ's warning,
Daniel does not realize that he is putting his own salvation into jeopardy, a sign
of his initial immaturity and lack of judgment.

It is only after receiving the second divine dream that Daniel comes to realize how mistaken he was to tie his own salvation to that of another man:

> Two years later, in a dream, I saw that young man in the Church of the
> Holy Resurrection again, as before, and, shortly after, I saw Eulogios being
> dragged away from the young man by an Ethiopian. I woke up and said to
> myself: 'Woe to me, sinful man! I have lost my soul'.

> καὶ μετὰ δύο ἔτη βλέπω κατ' ὄναρ πάλιν τὸ μειράκιον ἐκεῖνο εἰς τὴν Ἁγίαν
> Ἀνάστασιν, ὥσπερ πρότερον, καὶ μετὰ μικρὸν βλέπω τὸν Εὐλόγιον συρόμε-
> νον ἀπὸ προσώπου τοῦ μειρακίου ὑπὸ ἑνὸς Αἰθίοπος. καὶ διυπνισθεὶς λέγω ἐν
> ἐαυτῷ· ἀβάλα μοι τῷ ἁμαρτωλῷ. ἀπώλεσα τὴν ψυχήν μου.[44]

Essential elements of the first dream are repeated in the second dream, which
is also set in the Church of the Resurrection, featuring once again Christ as a
young man sitting on the holy stone. This time, however, Eulogios does not
stand by Christ's right side, but is dragged away by an Ethiopian, a symbol of
the devil. Despite being almost identical with the first dream in terms of space
and characters, the second dream overturns the first one, where Daniel sees
himself and Eulogios as men of high spiritual status approaching salvation.
The key to unraveling the meaning of the second dream is found in its new element: the addition of an Ethiopian who violently takes Eulogios away. Having
tied himself to Eulogios, Daniel apprehends that he is also condemned to the

---

43   *Narrations*, ch. 6, 86–95; trans. Dahlman, *Saint Daniel* 153–155.
44   *Narrations*, ch. 6, 111–115; trans. Dahlman, *Saint Daniel* 155.

same fate, a realization that allows him to comprehend Christ's behavior in the first dream, and thus to reach for the first time a better understanding of himself: he is not as perfect as he thought he was when he was taking full responsibility for Eulogios. His immediate reaction is to abandon Skete to look for Eulogios, because if he manages to save the man from the devil's hands, he will also save his own soul.

Daniel's repeatedly failing attempts to meet Eulogios augment his distress. He begs the Virgin Mary to intercede on his behalf, but she informs him that he needs to pay his spiritual debt no matter what. He then makes a third failing attempt to meet Eulogios, which results in further desperation, which is released in the following dream:

> Once again I saw myself in the Church of the Holy Resurrection and that young man sitting upon the holy stone. He turned towards me and said to me threatening: 'Will you not fulfil your guarantee?' I stood trembling and could not speak because of fear. He ordered two of those standing beside him to hang me up with my arms tied up behind my back and they said to me: 'Do not offer guarantees beyond your power, and do not contradict God.' I could not open my mouth hanging there. And there was a voice saying: 'The Augusta is coming!' When I saw her, I took a little comfort and said to her in a low voice: 'Have mercy on me, lady of the World.' She said to me: 'What do you want again?' I said to her: 'It is because of the guarantee I gave for Eulogios that I am hanging here.' She said to me: 'I am going to intercede for you.' And I saw how she went and kissed the feet of the young man. And that holy young man said to me: 'Do not ever act like that again.' I said: 'I have sinned, master, please forgive me. I prayed that he would be useful and not useless.' He gave the order and they released me. He said to me: 'Go to your cell, and do not ask how I will bring Eulogios to his former position.' I awoke and rejoiced with great joy, having been released from such a guarantee.

> καὶ βλέπω ἐμαυτὸν πάλιν εἰς τὴν Ἁγίαν Ἀνάστασιν, καὶ τὸ μειράκιον ἐκεῖνο καθήμενον ἐπὶ τοῦ ἁγίου λίθου, καὶ προσέχων μοι μετὰ ἀπειλῆς λέγει μοι· οὐχ ὑπάγεις πληροῖς τὴν ἐγγύην; ἐγὼ δὲ ἱστάμην τρέμων καὶ μὴ δυνάμενος λαλῆσαι ἀπὸ τοῦ φόβου. καὶ κελεύει δύο τῶν παρισταμένων αὐτῷ καὶ κρεμῶσί με ὀπισθάγκωνα, καὶ λέγουσί μοι· μὴ ὑπὲρ τὴν δύναμίν σου ἐγγυῶ, καὶ μὴ ἀντίλεγε Θεῷ. καὶ οὐκ ἠδυνάμην ἀνοῖξαι τὸ στόμα μου κρεμάμενος. καὶ ἰδοὺ φωνὴ λέγουσα· ἡ Αὐγοῦστα προέρχεται. καὶ ἰδὼν αὐτὴν ἔλαβον μικρὰν παραμυθίαν καὶ λέγω αὐτῇ λεπτῇ τῇ φωνῇ· ἐλέησόν με, Δέσποινα τοῦ κόσμου. καὶ λέγει μοι· τί πάλιν θέλεις; λέγω αὐτῇ· περὶ τῆς ἐγγύης Εὐλογίου κρέμαμαι. καὶ λέγει

REPETITION AND THE STORYTELLER'S PROFILE 127

μοι· ἐγὼ παρακαλῶ ὑπὲρ σοῦ. καὶ βλέπω ὅτι ἀπῆλθε καὶ κατεφίλει τοὺς πόδας τοῦ μειρακίου. καὶ λέγει μοι τὸ ἅγιον μειράκιον ἐκεῖνο· ὕπαγε μηκέτι ποιήσῃς τὸ πρᾶγμα τοῦτο. καὶ λέγω· ἥμαρτον, Δέσποτα· συγχώρησόν μοι. ἐγὼ γὰρ παρεκάλεσα ἵνα χρήσιμος γένηται, οὐχὶ δὲ ἀχρήσιμος. καὶ κελεύει, καὶ λύουσί με. καὶ λέγει μοι· ὕπαγε εἰς τὸ κελλίον σου, καὶ πῶς φέρω τὸν Εὐλόγιον εἰς τὴν προτέραν αὐτοῦ τάξιν μὴ ζήτει. καὶ διυπνισθεὶς ἐχάρην χαρὰν μεγάλην, ἀπαλ-λαγεὶς τῆς τοιαύτης ἐγγύης.[45]

As is the case with the two dreams discussed above, the setting and important dream characters remain the same. The dreamer finds himself for a third time in the Church of the Resurrection standing before Christ as a young man who sits on the holy stone. Yet this time it is Daniel's and not Eulogios' condemnation that materializes. In contrast to the talkative and confident Daniel of the first dream, here we encounter a petrified, silenced, and immobile man. His situation changes when the Virgin arrives as a *deus ex machina* to intercede on his behalf. Of course, the promised salvation, like the previous condemnation, is a double one. Daniel's release becomes at the same time Eulogios' release.

What then does repetition in this tale reveal about its storyteller? This storyteller exposes himself to his disciple and the tale's audiences in ways that set him apart from the two previous storytellers acting as protagonists of their tales (John of Lykopolis in *HME* and the author-storyteller of *MT*). At the beginning, Daniel hesitates to tell his story because he is embarrassed about his mistake. Both John and Thekla's protégé might appear equally hesitant to talk about themselves, yet in their case it is their humility that determines their behavior. Furthermore, Daniel, in contrast to Thekla's protégé, develops as a character through the three dreams. He moves from self-ignorance to self-knowledge while at the same time he contributes to the salvation of Eulogios, who also reaches a state of self-knowledge. Daniel has neither the perfection of John nor the divine favoritism of Thekla's hagiographer. Being a sinful man, an ignorant ascetic committing mistakes at the early stages of his religious life, Daniel emerges as a more humanized storyteller. As such he is brought closer to his disciples and the audiences of his tale who, as humans, have their own imperfections and falls. This storyteller shares his experience of how, as human beings, we jump into deep pitfalls of mistakes and how we can be forgiven through incessant prayer and fervent faith. In short, he shows that it is acceptable to make mistakes – because everyone, even the most renowned ascetic, may go wrong – as long as people do not fail to come to terms with their errors and sins, through which they become better persons.

---

45   *Narrations*, ch. 6, 162–181; trans. Dahlman, *Saint Daniel* 159–161.

5 Conclusions

The aim of the preceding analysis was to unravel the mechanisms at work when (triple) repetition is employed to create the storyteller's profile in three texts (*HME*, *MT*, and *Narrations*) belonging to different types of early Byzantine collections of tales (collective biography, miracle collection, and collection of beneficial tales). As the investigation of the three texts has hopefully shown, repetition may construct at least three different types of storytellers: the saintly, the chosen, and the repentant storyteller. In *HME*, repetitions reveal a storyteller who is a saintly monk that manages to perfect his asceticism in every aspect, thus conquering a monk's most feared and most committed sin – pride. Being also an eloquent and untiring storyteller, John earns his audiences' great trust and admiration for both his monastic and storytelling virtues. Through his three autobiographical tales, the anonymous storyteller of *MT* emerges as someone who is always under the wing of the saint – whether as a hagiographer, storyteller, encomiast, or priest. As such, he appears as a storytelling authority and as the right storyteller for the martyr's miraculous deeds. Finally, Daniel constructs himself as a repentant storyteller coming closer to his audiences, to whom he offers a feasible recipe for salvation. Evidently, the various ways in which the examined authors use repetition to create a profile of their storytellers that suits the religious purposes and aesthetic values of their works provides a good answer to Toolan's aforementioned question concerning how something repetitive can create a fresh, exciting, and original tale – and let us add here that repetition can also create three fresh, exciting, and original storytellers.

Bibliography

Primary Sources

Daniel of Sketis, *Narrations* (BHG 2099z–2102f, 79–80, 121–122, 618, 2255, 2453). In ed. B. Dahlman, *Saint Daniel of Sketis: A Group of Hagiographic Texts*, Studia Byzantina Upsaliensia 10 (Uppsala: 2007) 108–187.

History of the Monks in Egypt (BHG 1333–1334). In ed. A.-J. Festugière, *Historia monachorum in Aegypto*, Subsidia hagiographica 34 (Brussels: 1961).

John Moschos, *Spiritual Meadow* (BHG 1440f–1442z). In *Patrologia Graeca* 87.3:2852–3112.

Miracles of Thekla (BHG 1718). In ed. G. Dagron, *Vie et miracles de sainte Thècle: Texte grec, traduction et commentaire*, Subsidia hagiographica 6 (Paris: 1978) 285–412.

Miracles of Artemios (BHG 173–173c). In ed. A. Papadopoulos-Kerameus, *Varia Graeca sacra* (St. Petersburg: 1909) 1–75.

Miracles of Kosmas and Damian (BHG 385–391). In ed. L. Deubner, *Kosmas und Damian: Texte und Einleitung* (Leipzig – Berlin: 1907) 193–206; E. Rupprecht, *Cosmae et Damiani sanctorum medicorum vita(m) et miracula e codice Londinensi* (Berlin: 1935).

Palladios of Hellenopolis, *Lausiac History*. In ed. D.C. Butler, *The Lausiac History of Palladius*, vol. 2: *Introduction and Text* (Cambridge: 1904) 1–169.

Sophronios of Jerusalem, *Miracles of Kyros and John* (BHG 477–479). In ed. N.F. Marcos, *Los 'Thaumata' di Sofronio: Contribución al estudio de la 'incubatio' cristiana* (Madrid: 1975).

Secondary Works

Binggeli A., "Collections of Edifying Stories", in Efthymiadis S. (ed.), *The Ashgate Research Companion to Byzantine Hagiography*, vol. 2: *Genres and Contexts* (Farnham: 2014) 143–159.

Cain A., *The Greek Historia Monachorum in Aegypto* (Oxford: 2016).

Chitoiu D., "Repetition as Resumption: From Litany to Thinking in Byzantium", *Revista Portuguesa de Filosofia* 69.2 (2013) 205–213.

Constantinou S., "Healing Dreams in Early Byzantine Miracle Collections", in Oberhelman S. (ed.), *Dreams, Healing, and Medicine in Greece: From Antiquity to the Present* (Aldershot: 2013) 189–198.

Constantinou S., "The Morphology of Healing Dreams: Dream and Therapy in Byzantine Collections of Miracle Stories", in Angelidi C. – Calofonos G. (eds.), *Dreaming in Byzantium and Beyond* (Aldershot: 2014) 21–34.

Constantinou S. – Andreou A., "The Voices of the Tale: The Storyteller in Early Byzantine Collective Biographies, Miracle Collections, and Collections of Edifying Tales", *Byzantine and Modern Greek Studies* 46.1 (2021) 24–40, DOI: 10.1017/byz.2021.31.

Crisafulli V.S. – Nesbitt J.W. (trans.), *The Miracles of St. Artemios: A Collection of Miracle Stories by an Anonymous Author of Seventh-Century Byzantium* (Leiden – New York – Cologne: 1997).

Dagron G. (ed.), *Vie et miracles de sainte Thècle: Texte grec, traduction et commentaire*, Subsidia hagiographica 62 (Paris: 1978).

Dahlman B. (trans.), *Saint Daniel of Sketis: A Group of Hagiographic Texts*, Studia Byzantina Upsaliensia 10 (Uppsala: 2007).

Efthymiadis S., "Collections of Miracles: Fifth to Fifteenth Centuries", in *The Ashgate Research Companion to Byzantine Hagiography*, vol. 2: *Genres and Contexts* (Farnham: 2014) 103–131.

Festugière A.-J. (ed.), *Historia monachorum in Aegypto*, Subsidia hagiographica 34 (Brussels: 1961).

Festugière A.-J., "Le problème littéraire de l'*Historia monachorum*", *Hermes* 83.3 (1955) 257–284.

Frank G., "The *Historia Monachorum in Aegypto* and Ancient Travel Writing", *Studia Patristica* 30 (1997) 191–195.

Ivanov S., (ed.) *Spiritually Beneficial Tales in Byzantine and Slavic Literature*, Special Issue, *Scripta* 8/9.

Johnson S.F., *The Life and Miracles of Thekla: A Literary Study*, Hellenic Studies 13 (Cambridge, MA – London: 2006).

Johnson S.F. (trans.), "The Miracles of Thekla", in Talbot A.M. – Johnson S.F. (trans.), *Miracle Tales from Byzantium*, Dumbarton Oaks Medieval Library 12 (Cambridge, MA – London: 2012) 1–201.

Narro Á., "Lo scontro tra formazione classica e pensiero cristiano: La vita e miracoli di santa Tecla", *Greco-Latina Brunensia* 15 (2010) 127–138.

Russell N. (trans.), "The Lives of the Desert Fathers", in Ward B. – Russell N. (eds.), *The Lives of the Desert Fathers*, Cistercian Studies 34 (Kalamazoo, MI: 1981) 47–119.

Toolan M., *Making Sense of Narrative Text: Situation, Repetition, and Picturing in the Reading of Short Stories*, Routledge Studies in Rhetoric and Stylistics (New York – London: 2016).

Ward B., "Introduction", in Ward B. – Russell N. (eds.), *The Lives of the Desert Fathers*, Cistercian Studies 34 (Kalamazoo, MI: 1980) 1–46.

CHAPTER 6

Circulation of Hagiographical Tales along the Incense Route: Storytelling as Technology of Enchantment

Nicolò Sassi

1 Introduction

The University Library of Heidelberg, Germany, preserves a tenth-century manuscript containing the Greek Περίπλους τῆς Ἐρυθρᾶς Θαλάσσης (lit. *Periplus of the Erythraean Sea*).[1] The *Periplus* is an ancient traveling guide for merchants, offering a first-hand description of navigation routes and trading opportunities in the area that stretches from the harbors of Roman Egypt to the coastal towns of southwestern India.[2] Opening a window on a world of marketplaces, bazaars, and caravanserais, the *Periplus* sheds light on a complex network of land and sea ways that connected Alexandria to Yemen and India through the coastal plains of Tihamah and the cities, marts, and trading posts of inner Egypt and the Arabic Peninsula such as Berenice and Najran. Somewhat similarly to the much better-known Silk Road, this trading network represented a generative system of interaction and exchange bridging major empires of the ancient and medieval world, crossing the Mediterranean, Eastern Africa, the Persian Gulf, and India.

By virtue of the main trading good that traveled along it, the network of land and sea ways described in the *Periplus* came to be known over time as the Incense Route.[3] Beside the *Periplus*, multiple ancient and medieval texts

---

1   I want to deeply thank here Douglas Boin, Jacob Boss, Laura Carlson Hasler, Mary Dunn, Constance Furey, Lily Jiang, Atria Larson, Filippo Marsili, Peter Martens, John Purcell, James Redfield, and Jeremy Schott for asking important questions and providing precious advice in key moments of the conceptualization and writing of this chapter; Andria Andreou and Stavroula Constantinou for shepherding the project throughout its various phases; the peer-reviewers for their insightful and encouraging comments.

2   Codex Palatinus Graecus 398 (tenth century), fols. 40v–54v, Universitätsbibliothek, Heidelberg. The text is edited and translated in Casson L., *The Periplus Maris Erythraei: Text with Introduction, Translation, and Commentary* (Princeton: 1989; repr. 2012).

3   The earliest mention of this name I was able to locate is in Ingrams H., "Burton Memorial Lecture: From Cana (Husn Ghorab) to Sabbatha (Shabwa): The South Arabian Incense Road", *Journal of the Royal Asiatic Society* 77.3–4 (1945) 169–185. In time this name became common:

© NICOLÒ SASSI, 2025 | DOI:10.1163/9789004707351_008

This is an open access chapter distributed under the terms of the CC BY-NC-ND 4.0 license.

offer descriptions and accounts of this route: Agatharchides of Cnidus' *On the Erythraean Sea* (second century BC),[4] Strabo's *Geography* (first century BC–first century AD),[5] Pliny the Elder's *Natural History* (first century AD),[6] Kosmas Indicopleustes' *Christian Geography* (sixth century AD).[7] In describing this system of land and sea ways traversed by Egyptian, Roman, East African, and Arabian merchants, these texts offer insight into otherwise unknown aspects of premodern travel, cross-cultural relations, geographical imagination, trade, but also local folklore, fashion trends in clothing and jewels, and olfactory tastes. For instance, we learn that in Barbarikon (today Karachi, Pakistan) a great deal of thin clothing and figured linens were imported, but also gems and precious stones like peridot and coral, or the balsamic resins used to produce the incense burnt during religious rites, like styrax and frankincense. From this little town, in turn, there were exported nard (an aromatic essential oil), turquoise, lapis lazuli, Seric skins, cotton cloths, silk yarn, and above all indigo, the natural dye that became the most important dye plant for blue color in the western portion of the world and whose popularity and economic value reached a peak during the Middle Ages.[8]

The Incense Route was not just a system of exchange of precious trading goods but also of what Fernand Braudel called *biens culturels*: philosophical ideas, languages of worlds far and near, technologies, theological and scientific worldviews, songs, religions, art forms, and stories.[9] The circulation of the

---

see for instance Brozyna J.M., *The Incense Route: A Study of Its Origin and Development* (M.A. dissertation, San Jose State University: 1999); Sidebotham S. – Willemina W.Z., "Berenike: A Ptolemaic-Roman Port on the Ancient Maritime Spice and Incense Route", *Minerva* 13.3 (2002) 28–31; David C.B. – Isaac B., "Six Milestone Stations and New Inscriptions Discovered in the Negev along the Petra–Gaza Incense Route", *Palestine Exploration Quarterly* 152.3 (2020) 234–247. For an overview on the incense trade in the ancient and medieval world see Van Beek W., "Frankincense and Myrrh in Ancient South Arabia", *Journal of the American Oriental Society* 78 (1958) 141–151; idem, "Frankincense and Myrrh", *Biblical Archeologist* 23 (1960) 69–95; Groom N., *Frankincense and Myrrh: A Study of Arabian Incense Trade* (London: 1981); Crone P., *Meccan Trade and the Rise of Islam* (Princeton: 1987).

4 Agatharchides of Cnidus, *On the Eyrthraean Sea*, ed. and trans. S.M. Burstein, *Agatharchides of Cnidus: On the Erythraean Sea* (London: 1989) *passim*.

5 Strabo, *Geography*, 15.1.4.C686, ed. and trans. E.L. Jones, *The Geography of Strabo* (Cambridge, MA: 1983) 5.

6 Pliny the Elder, *Natural History*, 6.26.22–36, trans. J. Bostock, *The Natural History of Pliny* (London: 1855) 60–65.

7 Kosmas Indicopleustes, *Christian Geography*, 11, ed. J.M.W. Crindle, *The Christian Topography of Cosmas, an Egyptian Monk* (Edinburgh: 1897) 358–373.

8 Casson, *The Periplus* 75. On the trade of indigo during antiquity and the Middle Ages, see Balfour-Paul J., "Indigo in South and South-East Asia", *Textile History* 30.1 (1999) 98–112.

9 Braudel F., *La Méditerranée et le monde méditérranéen à l'époque de Philippe II* (Paris: 1949) 555: 'Voyages des hommes; voyages des biens aussi, des biens culturels les plus usuels comme

STORYTELLING AS TECHNOLOGY OF ENCHANTMENT   133

last is particularly well attested, especially in the realm of hagiography. For instance, the legend of Longinos, originally written in Greek, started moving southwards along the Incense Route sometime between the twilight of antiquity and the dawn of the Middle Ages, resurfacing in a later Arabic version and, subsequently, in Ethiopic. Another example of dissemination of tales across time, space, and languages along the Incense Route can be seen in the hagiographical tradition related to Menas. The cult of the saint originated in Egypt, where we find an early Coptic version of the legend of his life dating between the seventh and the eighth centuries. This legend transformed and reappeared in later Arabic and Ethiopic versions, and another text belonging to the hagiographical dossier of the saint, the collection of miracles, is found in Old Nubian, another language spoken along the Incense Route.[10]

The present study asks what the textual transmission of hagiographical tales along the Incense Route reveals about their cultural and religious function. How did these tales transform across their various translations and reworkings, and what does this process of textual dissemination and manipulation reveal about the role that these texts played within the Eastern Christian communities of the Incense Route? As the breadth of this analysis would greatly exceed the limits of a single essay, the present study focuses exclusively on the two hagiographical traditions mentioned above, centered around Longinos and Menas. My aim in this study is threefold: (1) to track the genesis of these narrative traditions, delineating their seminal literary structure; (2) to identify their transformations during the process of textual transmission, isolating the elements that stuck, those that were dropped, and those that changed across versions; (3) to delineate what human efforts are at work within these textual manipulations, using these findings to reflect on the function of these tales as cultural and religious technology.[11] My contention is that a major dimension

---

les plus inattendus. Ils ne cessent de se déplacer avec les hommes eux-mêmes. Apportés ici par les uns cette année, repris par d'autres l'année suivante ou un siècle plus tard, on les voit sans cesse transportés, abandonnés, ressaisis, et par des mains parfois ignorantes' ('Travel of men, travel of goods as well, of cultural goods, both the everyday and the unexpected, unceasingly traveling with traveling men. Arriving with a group of men one year, they might be carried on by others a year or a century after, ferried from place to place, left behind or taken up again, often by ignorant hands'; my translation).

10   See below for a more thorough analysis of these traditions.

11   I borrow the term 'technology' from the recent work of Eva-Maria Simms (Simms E.-M., "A Phenomenology of Reading: Textual Technology and Virtual Worlds", in Howard P. – Saevi T. – Foran A. – Biesta G. (eds.), *Phenomenology and Educational Theory in Conversation* (London: 2020) 88–99). Leveraging the theoretical legacy of Maurice Merleau-Ponty, *Phenomenology of Perception*, trans. C. Smith (London: 1962), as well as Ivan Illich and Barry Sanders, *ABC: The Alphabetization of the Popular Mind* (San Francisco: 1988),

of the cultural work performed by these tales lies in leveraging storytelling to transform the readers' vision and experience of the world, redefining the geography of their everyday life as enchanted. It is in this effort to bring enchantment into everyday reality that I detect one of the major functions of these narrative traditions.[12]

2 Tales of Saints between Byzantium and Aksum: At the Origin of the Hagiographical Traditions on Longinos and Menas

Both narrative traditions we are concerned with here survive in multiple versions. Legends of the centurion who witnessed the death of Christ and the miracles that followed it, later identified as Longinos, date back to the fourth century, when we find mentions of them in John Chrysostom[13] and Gregory of Nyssa.[14] Throughout late antiquity and the Middle Ages these legends were disseminated in the Mediterranean and Eastern Christian world, multiplying in a variety of versions in Greek, Latin, Armenian, Georgian, Arabic, and Ethiopic.[15] However, not all of these different legends traveled along the Incense Route. In fact, only one tale appears to have moved southwards among the Christian communities of Northern and Eastern Africa. The oldest known form of this tale is found in the 19th homily attributed to Hesychios of Jerusalem.[16] Michel Aubineau, the most recent editor of the text, contests the traditional attribution of this homily to Hesychios and the resulting dating to the fifth century, proposing instead the sixth or seventh century as more likely dates of

---

     Simms develops a productive understanding of text and textuality as 'a consciousness technology', namely as a conceptual tool that 'alters the very way we perceive, think, and believe in what is real' by shaping 'the perceptual and epistemological structure' of one's consciousness (Simms, "A Phenomenology" 90–91). As we shall see below, this understanding of text and narrative as formative forces in the structuring of one's experience and interpretation of the world also informs the work of Hanna Meretoja, whom I will rely on later to illuminate the form and function of the hagiographical tales under scrutiny.

12   On the meaning of the term 'enchantment' in the present study see definition and analysis below.

13   John Chrysostom, *In Matthaeum homilia* 88.2, ed. in *Patrologia Graeca* (PG) 58:777, lines 40–41.

14   Gregory of Nyssa, *Letter* 17.15, ed. in PG 46:1061d–1064a.

15   On the Greek, Latin, Armenian, and Georgian versions see Aubineau M. (ed.), *Les homelies festales d'Hesychius de Jérusalem*, 2 vols. (Brussels: 1980) 2:778–816 *passim*. On the Arabic and Ethiopic see below.

16   Hesychios of Jerusalem, *Martyrdom of St. Longinus the Holy and Glorious Martyr* (BHG 988), ed. in PG 93:1545–1560. The most updated edition of the text is in Aubineau, *Les homelies festales* 778–844.

STORYTELLING AS TECHNOLOGY OF ENCHANTMENT 135

composition.[17] Among the languages of the Incense Route, this tale is found in several Greek reworkings: one by Symeon the Metaphrast, one anonymous, and one in the *Synaxarion of Constantinople*.[18] In addition, two other versions survive in Eastern Christian languages: an Arabic version, found in the Alexandrian synaxarion dating to the thirteenth century, and an Ethiopian version, based on the Arabic one, dating between the end of the fourteenth and the beginning of the fifteenth century.[19]

In the version of the story of Longinos that traveled along the Incense Route, the protagonist is immediately identified with one of the centurions that in Matthew 27:54 say 'Truly he is the son of God' (Ἀληθῶς θεοῦ υἱὸς ἦν οὗτος). In its oldest version (= Pseudo-Hesychios), the tale begins with the Jewish leaders and priests planning to conceal the facts surrounding the death of Christ and the miracles that followed it. They try to bribe Longinos into not revealing what he saw, but the experience of witnessing the death of Christ profoundly transformed him: having chosen to 'belong completely to Christ' (ὅλως Χριστοῦ γενέσθαι, Aubineau 4.4–5), Longinos refuses the bribe, leaves Jerusalem, and moves to his homeland of Cappadocia to pursue an ascetic life and proclaim the gospel of Jesus. At this point the Jewish leaders and priests, having decided to silence him, collude with Roman authorities to send Roman soldiers to Cappadocia to kill Longinos. The soldiers arrive in Cappadocia but, after spending time with and talking to Longinos, they are so moved by his words

---

17   Ibidem, 796–800. Because of this, I will occasionally refer to this text as 'Pseudo-Hesychios'.

18   The *Passion* by Symeon the Metaphrast (BHG 989) is found in PG 115:31–44. The anonymous version (BHG 990) can be found in *Acta Sanctorum* Mar. II:739–740. The version in the synaxarion of Constantinople can be found in H. Delehaye, *Synaxarium ecclesiae constantinopolitanae* (Brussels: 1902) 141–144. The story of Longinos exists in three other known Greek versions that, however, are not edited and were therefore left out of the present analysis. They are: BHG Novum Auctarium 988abc, briefly discussed by Aubineau, *Les homelies festales* 779 and 809–811; BHG Novum Auctarium 988z; BHG Novum Auctarium 990c, again briefly discussed in Aubineau, *Les homelies festales* 800–801.

19   The Arabic synaxarion was composed by Michael, Bishop of Atrib and Malig, around 1250. On the authorship and dating of the Arabic synaxarion, see Graf G., *Geschichte der christlichen arabischen Literatur*, vol. 2: *Die Schriftsteller bis zur Mitte des 15. Jahrhunderts*, Studi e testi 118 (Vatican City: 1944–1953) 414–427 (see esp. 416–420), and Colin G., "Le synaxaire éthiopien: État actuel de la question", *Analecta Bollandiana* 106.3/4 (1988) 273–317 (see esp. 274). On the dating of the Ethiopian synaxarion, see Colin, "Le synaxaire éthiopien" *passim*. The critical edition of the life of Longinos in the Alexandrian synaxarion is found in ed. I. Forget, *Synaxarium alexandrinum*, Corpus Scriptorum Christianorum Orientalium (CSCO), vols. 47, 48, 49, 67, 78, and 90: *Scriptores arabici*, series 3 (Louvain: 1953); the Latin translation can be found in Forget, *Synaxarium alexandrinum* 78:99–100. The critical edition and translation of the Life of Longinos in the Ethiopian synaxarion can be found in ed. G. Colin, *Le synaxaire éthiopien: Mois de Ḥedar* (Turnhout 1988) 309–313.

and hospitality that they decide not to kill him. But Longinos wants to witness his faith with martyrdom, so at his behest the recalcitrant soldiers eventually execute him by decapitation. Longinos' head is brought back to Jerusalem. At this point the tale moves on to a new main character, a blind, unnamed widow from Cappadocia who, after hearing of the miracles performed by Jesus, takes her only son and travels to Jerusalem to seek healing for her blindness. Here a tragedy strikes her: her son suddenly dies. But, soon after, she receives a vision: Longinos speaks to her, telling her where to recover his head and that, upon finding it, she will regain her sight. The widow finds Longinos' head and is healed from her blindness. The following night, the widow experiences a new dream vision and sees her son conscripted in the celestial army and enjoying the bliss of heaven. After having recovered both her son's body and Longinos' head, the widow heads back to Cappadocia, where she buries the two together and spends the rest of her life proclaiming the glory of heaven.[20]

Unlike Longinos, whose popularity stretches from the late ancient Christian East to the Arthurian legends of medieval Europe, the tales about Menas had a more markedly Eastern Christian area of dissemination. Multiple stories related to the cult of this saint survive. The oldest known text is the Coptic *Encomium of Apa Mena*, dating to the seventh or eighth century and edited by James Drescher in 1946.[21] At least five tales associated with the saint are known in Greek: the *Acta Sancti Menae*, two *Passiones*, the Ἐγκώμιον εἰς τὸν μεγαλομάρτυρα Μῆνα, and a collection of *Miracula*.[22] Later tales about Menas are found in other languages of the Christian East, such as Arabic and Ethiopic, in the respective synaxaria, as well as in a short collection of miracles preserved in

---

20   The tale is particularly rich in themes relevant for the study of late ancient Christian *mentalités* (from the anti-Jewish topos of the initial narrative to the theme of pilgrimage to the holy places, passing through supernatural and martyrological ideologies and the late ancient culture of hospitality), but even a cursory analysis of them is beyond the scope of this paper. For a good seminal breakdown of the major themes of this tale see Aubineau, *Les homelies festales* 784–786.

21   *Encomium of Apa Mena* (Coptic), ed. J. Drescher, *Apa Mena: A Selection of Coptic Texts Relating to Saint Menas. Edited, with Translation and Commentary* (Cairo: 1946) 126–149.

22   The *Acts of Menas* (*Acta Sancti Menae*, BHG 1250) is edited (with Latin translation) by G. van Hoof, "Acta Sancti Menae: Martyris Aegyptis", *Analecta Bollandiana* 3 (1884) 258–270. The two *Passiones* (BHG 1251 and 1254) are edited, respectively, in T. Ioannou's Μνημεῖα ἁγιολογικά, Subsidia Byzantina 8 (Venice: 1884) 284–324, and in K. Krumbacher, *Miscellen zu Romanos* (Munich: 1907) 31–43. The *Encomium to the Great Martyr Menas* (Ἐγκώμιον, BHG 1255) is found in Ioannou, Μνημεῖα 324–327. The collection of *Miracles* (*Miracula*, BHG 1226–1269 *passim*) is edited in N. Pomjalovskij, *Žitije prepodovnago Paisija velikago i Timotheja part. Aleks. povestvovanie o čudesah sv. velikomučenika Miny* (St. Petersburg: 1900) 62–89.

STORYTELLING AS TECHNOLOGY OF ENCHANTMENT

Old Nubian and Old Slavic.[23] Just as in the case of Longinos, however, only one of these multiple narrative traditions traveled along the Incense Route, namely the legend of the oldest Coptic *Encomium*, which resurfaces in the medieval tales in Arabic and Ge'ez of the Alexandrian and Ethiopian synaxaria. It is this tale, in the Coptic–Arabic–Ethiopic line of transmission, that we are concerned with here, and for this reason we will leave aside the fascinating yet unrelated history of the textual transmission of the *Passiones* and the *Miracula*.[24]

In the narrative fiction of the oldest, Coptic version of the tale, the events surrounding the life and death of Menas take place between the end of the third and the beginning of the fourth century. The end of the Severan dynasty had led to military anarchy and political chaos, and in order not to tear the already unstable social fabric of the empire any further through the spread of a relatively new religion, several major persecutions of Christianity were being carried out. The story of Menas takes place during the last and most violent of these persecutions, namely that of Diocletian. The tale begins with Menas' conception. Menas' family is Christian: his father Eudoxos is an Egyptian governor from Nikiu as well as a devout Christian; his mother, Eudoxia, is a pious Christian too. Eudoxos and his wife struggle for a long time to have children. One day, during a celebration for the mother of God, Menas' mother enters a church and prays in front of an image of the Virgin Mary for the grace of getting pregnant. A voice comes out of the image and utters 'amen', 'so be it'. After this miraculous event, Eudoxos and his wife finally conceive a baby and call him Menas in honor of the miracle. Growing up, Menas learns the scriptures and spiritual science. When Menas is eleven Eudoxos dies, and the mother dies three years later. At that point, Menas himself becomes a soldier, but because of the persecution of Diocletian flees into the African desert. There Menas receives a vision: the sky opens, and the martyrs crown him with beautiful crowns. Menas understands then that martyrdom is his destiny and goes back into the city. Here he is tortured, imprisoned, and decapitated in front of the masses. His body is thrown into fire but is later retrieved by a group of

---

23   Alexandrian synaxarion: Forget, *Synaxarium* 78:124–126. Ethiopian synaxarion: Colin, *Le synaxaire* 309–313. Old Nubian: ed. G.M. Brown, *The Old Nubian Miracles of Saint Menas* (Vienna: 1994). Old Slavic: ed. V. Jagić, "Ein mittelbulgarisches Bruchstück des ersten Wunders des Großmärtyrers Menas (aus dem XIV. Jahrh.)", *Archiv für slavischen Philologie* 30 (1909) 392–399 and 392–393; D. Atanassova, "The Miracles of the Great Martyr Menas in the Medieval Slavic Pre-Metaphrastic Menaia-Čet'i (Critical Edition of the Text, Based on Manuscript No. 1039 from the SS. Cyril and Methodius National Library in Sofia)", *Scripta & e-Scripta* 6 (2008) 305–324.

24   For a concise and updated analysis of the *status quaestionis* on the hagiographical dossier on Menas, with a special focus on the *Miracles*, see Silvano L. – Varalda P., "Per l'edizione dei *Miracula Sancti Menae* (BHG 1256–1269)", *Philologia antiqua* 12 (2019) 51–86.

Christians, who leave the city and embark on a ship to Alexandria. During the navigation horrible monsters come out of the sea and start licking the body of the saint, which gives off flames and burns their faces, thus allowing the Christians to continue their journey and reach Alexandria. Upon arrival, the Christians decide to carry the body of the saint to a village of inner Egypt, but the camel on which they put it refuses to move. They try a second camel, and it refuses too, and then a third, and a fourth, until the Christians decide to bury the body of the saint in that place as they 'understand that this was the ordinance of God that the martyr's remains should stay there'.[25] In time, God decides to reveal the supernatural powers of the body of Menas to the autochthonous population through a miracle. A boy, crippled since his birth, arrives at the sepulcher of Menas and after falling into a mystical slumber wakes up healed. Through this miracle many people come to believe and the site becomes a place of worship.

Although virtually no work has explored the concrete venues and opportunities of fruition of these (and other) hagiographical tales among the communities of the Incense Route, certain features of these texts offer us an insight into their potential spaces and modalities of use. One of the major collections of stories about the life, deeds, miracles, and death of saints and martyrs found among the communities of the Incense Route is the above-mentioned synaxarion, a term that in the context of the present investigation describes a big liturgical book containing one (or sometimes more than one) life of a saint or martyr for each day of the year, to be read during the daily liturgy.[26] The major synaxaria produced and used along the Incense Route were the Alexandrian and the Ethiopic, written respectively in Arabic and Ge'ez. These collections contain stories short enough (in the most recent critical editions each story covers an average of one or two pages) that, unlike the long hagiographies of a Byzantine menologion like that of Symeon the Metaphrast, we can assume

---

25   Drescher, *Apa Mena* 142.

26   The reading of hagiographical texts from the synaxarion or the menologion takes place at different moments of the liturgy across the different Eastern Christian churches. In the Greek Orthodox Byzantine rite, the reading from the menologion takes place during the *orthros*, after the sixth ode of canons (Buchberger M., *Lexikon für Theologie und Kirche*, 11 vols. (Freibourg: 1964) 9:1224, and McDonald W.J., *New Catholic Encyclopedia*, 17 vols. (Palatine, IL: 1981) 13:881). In the Coptic Church the reading from the synaxarion takes place either during Mass, between the reading from the Acts of the Apostles and the Gospel, or during the office of incense if there is no Eucharistic service (Burmester O.H.E. KHS, *The Egyptian or Coptic Church* (Cairo: 1967) 44 and 108 n. 3). In the Ethiopian Church the reading from the synaxarion takes place right before the end of the liturgy (see Cohen M., "Review of W. Budge's *Book of Saints*", *Revue de l'histoire des religions* 99 (1929) 310).

they were indeed read in their entirety during liturgy. In addition, as we saw in the case of Pseudo-Hesychios' homily on Longinos, stories on the lives of saints were woven into homilies, again revealing that liturgy was a major channel of access to hagiographical tales for the Christians of the Incense Route. Some hagiographical texts in languages of the area survive in longer versions whose precise forms of fruition are harder to guess, but that were unlikely to be read during liturgy because of their length (e.g. the Coptic *Encomium* of Menas). For these texts, we can conjecture that a potential venue of use could be a monastic setting, where they could be read individually for devotional purposes, during the monastic mealtime reading, or possibly as a reservoir of exempla for catechetical education and edification.

As mentioned in the beginning, the tales on Longinos and Menas transformed as they traveled along the Incense Route, being translated and reworked in a variety of ancient and medieval languages of the area. How precisely did these stories transform as they moved across cultural and linguistic boundaries?

3   Comparative Analysis of the Textual Variance of the Hagiographical Traditions of the Incense Route on Longinos and Menas

The following table contains a synopsis of the textual variance of the tale of Longinos across the various versions in languages of the Incense Route. The first column contains the oldest form of the tale (i.e. the Greek version attributed to Hesychios of Jerusalem) broken down into its main sections in their order of appearance:

1. Introduction containing a *recusatio*, a typical rhetorical feature of premodern Eastern Christian texts in which the author declares his lowliness and inability to carry out the task of writing.
2. The anti-Jewish narrative on the Jewish leaders and priests planning Longinos' death.
3. Longinos' move to Cappadocia followed by his speech in praise of martyrdom.
4. The narrative of Longinos' decapitation.
5. The episode of the blind widow from Cappadocia, etc.

The text is rich and diverse in its composition. Beside the purely narrative sections detailed in the summary above, this earliest version of the life of Longinos also contains rhetorical sections (like the initial *recusatio* and the final conclusion), miracle narratives (like the dream visions of the widow and the healing from blindness), speeches in praise of martyrdom, and prayers. In Table 6.1, I have broken down the later rewritings in languages of the Incense Route mentioned above (the three Greek rewritings, the Arabic version, and the Ethiopic one), highlighting in RED the missing elements (namely the sections of the text that appear in the original but are not found in the later rewritings), in BLACK the elements that are maintained across different versions, and in GREEN the later interpolations (namely sections of texts that are found in a given later version but do not appear in the original Greek text). For instance, the narrative of the widow appears in all versions, with the only difference being that the first Greek rewriting adds an extra supernatural element by transforming the affliction of the widow from blindness to demonic haunting. Conversely, the narrative on the Jewish leaders planning Longinos' death is missing in three different later rewritings: the first Greek rewriting, the Arabic, and the Ethiopic.

A comparative reading of the various versions of this tale reveals that certain elements were occasionally dropped throughout the transmission across the Incense Route, whereas others consistently stuck. Specifically, the miracle narratives appear to be less disposable than any other literary element. In most cases, the number of miracle narratives across versions either remained the same or increased, whereas other kinds of sections – speeches, prayers, narrative sections not containing miracles, rhetorical sections – were occasionally dropped. Why did certain elements stick instead of/more than others? A potential answer to this question could be textual corruption. Later versions of the tale might have been copied from a manuscript, say, eaten by mice, and for this reason such versions are missing certain sections already missing in their antigraph. But this does not seem to be the case, as becomes evident through examining comparatively the textual traditions of multiple tales. Looking at multiple hagiographical traditions that traveled along the Incense Route, it becomes clear that *there is a trend in the modalities of textual transmission of these tales*. Table 6.2 contains a breakdown of the tale of Menas analogous to the table discussed above on the tale of Longinos and its reworkings in languages of the Incense Route.

STORYTELLING AS TECHNOLOGY OF ENCHANTMENT

141

TABLE 6.1 Synopsis of the textual variance of the hagiographical tradition on Longinos in the languages of the Incense Route

	Greek I Hesychios of Jerusalem (BHG 988; 6th/7th c.)a	Greek II "Inventio Capitis" (BHG 990; Unknown Dating)	Greek III Constantin. Synaxarion (BHG Novum Auctarium 990e; Pre-Metaphrastic)b	Greek IV Symeon the Metaphrast (BHG 989; 10th c.)	Arabic Synaxarion (13th c.)	Ethiopic Synaxarion (14th c.)
1.	Intro + *Recusatio*	MISSING	Intro — List of miracles following death of Jesus witnessed by Longinos	MISSING	MISSING	MISSING
2.	Narrative: Jewish leaders planning Longinos' death / Longinos' conversion / Move to Cappadocia / Roman soldiers after Longinos	MISSING	Narrative: Jewish leaders planning Longinos' death / Longinos' conversion / Move to Cappadocia / Roman soldiers after Longinos	Narrative: Jewish leaders planning Longinos' death / Longinos' conversion / Move to Cappadocia / Roman soldiers after Longinos	Narrative: Roman soldiers after Longinos in Cappadocia	Narrative: Roman soldiers after Longinos in Cappadocia

a Aubineau, *Les homelies festales* 796–800
b Ibidem, 801

TABLE 6.1   Synopsis of the textual variance of the hagiographical tradition (*cont.*)

	Greek I Hesychios of Jerusalem (BHG 988; 6th/7th c.)	Greek II "*Inventio Capitis*" (BHG 990; Unknown Dating)	Greek III Constantin. Synaxarion (BHG Novum Auctarium 990e; Pre-Metaphrastic)	Greek IV Symeon the Metaphrast (BHG 989; 10th c.)	Arabic Synaxarion (13th c.)	Ethiopic Synaxarion (14th c.)
3.	**Martyrological Speech**	MISSING	MISSING	**Martyrological Speech**	MISSING	MISSING
4.	**Narrative:** Longinos invites the soldiers to his house/ They convert/ He still chooses martyrdom	MISSING	MISSING	**Narrative:** Longinos invites the soldiers to his house/ They convert/ He still chooses martyrdom	MISSING	MISSING
5.	**Martyrological Speech**	MISSING	MISSING	**Martyrological Speech**	MISSING	MISSING
6.	**Narrative:** Decapitation/ Head brought to Jerusalem	MISSING	**Narrative:** Decapitation/ Head brought to Jerusalem	**Narrative:** Decapitation/ Head brought to Jerusalem	**Narrative:** Decapitation/ Head brought to Jerusalem/ The Jews rejoice	**Narrative:** Decapitation/ Head brought to Jerusalem/ The Jews rejoice

TABLE 6.1 Synopsis of the textual variance of the hagiographical tradition (*cont.*)

	Greek I Hesychios of Jerusalem (BHG 988; 6th/7th c.)	Greek II "*Inventio Capitis*" (BHG 990; Unknown Dating)	Greek III Constantin. Synaxarion (BHG Novum Auctarium 990e; Pre-Metaphrastic)	Greek IV Symeon the Metaphrast (BHG 989; 10th c.)	Arabic Synaxarion (13th c.)	Ethiopic Synaxarion (14th c.)
7.	Narrative: Blind widow from Cappadocia heads to Jerusalem/ Son dies	Narrative: Widow haunted by a demon/ Vision of Longinos/ heads to Jerusalem	Narrative: Blind widow from Cappadocia heads to Jerusalem/ MISSING NARRATIVE OF THE DYING SON	Narrative: Blind widow from Cappadocia heads to Jerusalem/ Son dies	Narrative: Blind widow from Cappadocia heads to Jerusalem/ Son dies	Narrative: Blind widow from Cappadocia heads to Jerusalem/ Son dies
8.	Prayer of the Widow	MISSING	MISSING	Prayer of the Widow	MISSING	MISSING
9.	Narrative: Dream of Longinos I/ Retrieval of the Head	Narrative: Retrieval of the Head/ Vision of 3 angels	Narrative: Dream of Longinos I/ Retrieval of the Head	Narrative: Dream of Longinos I/ Retrieval of the Head	Narrative: Dream of Longinos I/ Retrieval of the Head through perfume	Narrative: Dream of Longinos I/ Retrieval of the Head through perfume

TABLE 6.1   Synopsis of the textual variance of the hagiographical tradition (*cont.*)

	Greek I Hesychios of Jerusalem (BHG 988; 6th/7th c.)	Greek II "*Inventio Capitis*" (BHG 990; Unknown Dating)	Greek III Constantin. Synaxarion (BHG Novum Auctarium 990e; Pre-Metaphrastic)	Greek IV Symeon the Metaphrast (BHG 989; 10th c.)	Arabic Synaxarion (13th c.)	Ethiopic Synaxarion (14th c.)
10.	**Narrative:** Dream of Longinos II / The son is happy	**Narrative:** Vision of Longinos to the widow/ Vision of Longinos to Son/ Son dies	MISSING	**Narrative:** Dream of Longinos II / The son is happy	MISSING	MISSING
11.	**Speech:** (By Longinos) On the son in heaven	**Narrative:** Widow is sad/ Angel appears/Widow still sad	MISSING	**Speech:** (By Longinos) On the son in heaven	MISSING	MISSING
12.	**Narrative:** Widow brings Longinos' head to Sandralis	**Narrative:** Vision of Longinos to the widow	MISSING	**Narrative:** Widow brings Longinos' head to Sandralis	MISSING	MISSING
13.	**Speech:** The widow preaches on the glory of heaven	MISSING	MISSING	**Speech:** The widow preaches the glory of heaven	MISSING	MISSING
14.	**Conclusion by Hesychios**	MISSING	MISSING	MISSING	MISSING	MISSING

STORYTELLING AS TECHNOLOGY OF ENCHANTMENT 145

TABLE 6.2   Synopsis of the textual variance of the hagiographical tradition on Menas in the languages of the Incense Route

	Coptic Encomium (7th–8th c.)	Arabic Synaxarion (13th c.)	Ethiopic Synaxarion (14th c.)
1.	**Intro**	MISSING	MISSING
2.	**Narrative:** Conception of Menas through miracle	**Narrative:** Conception of Menas through miracle	**Narrative:** Conception of Menas through miracle
3.	**Narrative:** Childhood / Death of parents / Conscription / Withdrawal in the desert	**Narrative:** Childhood / Death of parents / Conscription / Withdrawal in the desert	**Narrative:** Childhood / Death of parents / Conscription / Withdrawal in the desert
4.	**Vision:** Crown of martyrdom	**Vision:** Crown of martyrdom	**Vision:** Crown of martyrdom
5.	**Narrative:** Back in the city / Dialogue with governor	**Narrative:** Back in the city / Dialogue with governor	**Narrative:** Back in the city / Dialogue with governor
6.	**Praise of Martyrdom**	MISSING	MISSING
7.	**Narrative:** Tortures / Interrogation / Tortures	MISSING	MISSING
8.	**Narrative:** Menas brought to the *comes* / Voice from heaven to Menas in prison and vision of Jesus	MISSING	MISSING
9.	**Miracle:** Saw melts	MISSING	MISSING
10.	**Martyrdom**	**Martyrdom** Body of the martyr doesn't burn	**Martyrdom** Body of the martyr doesn't burn
11.	**Narrative:** Body brought to Egypt / Travel by sea / Sea monsters	**Narrative:** Body brought to Egypt / Travel by sea / Sea monsters	**Narrative:** Body brought to Egypt / Travel by sea / Sea monsters

146 SASSI

TABLE 6.2 Synopsis of the textual variance of the hagiographical tradition (*cont.*)

	Coptic Encomium (7th–8th c.)	Arabic Synaxarion (13th c.)	Ethiopic Synaxarion (14th c.)
12.	**Miracle of the Camels**	**Miracle of the Camels**	**Miracle of the Camels**
13.	**Miracle:** Healing by the tomb of sick boy	**Miracle:** Sheep healed / Constantine's daughter healed	**Miracle:** Sheep healed / Constantine's daughter healed
14.	**Narrative:** Building of the shrine and city	**Narrative:** Building of the shrine and city	**Narrative:** Building of the shrine and city
15.	**Conclusion and Prayer:** May the saint intercede for us	MISSING	MISSING

Similarly to the tale of Longinos, the tale of Menas mostly retained the number of miracle narratives while dropping other sections that did not contain miracle or supernatural elements. The introductory section, for instance, found in the oldest version of the tale, is not found in the later rewritings. The long torture narratives and interrogations/dialogues, too, were similarly dropped. Conversely, most miracles stuck across versions and new ones were interpolated. The Arabic and Ethiopic rewritings contain one extra miracle at the end: after the first healing occurring on the burial site of the saint (which in the original version has a crippled boy as its protagonist, whereas in the later versions the recipient of the healing is a sheep),[27] a second healing takes place, involving the daughter of the emperor Constantine, who is miraculously healed from leprosy. In the case of textual manipulations that entail a significant shortening, for instance in the textual reworking of the tale of Means from the long version of the Coptic *Encomium* to the short one of the Arabic synaxarion, we notice that, although a brief mention of a supernatural element might occasionally be dropped (such as the tortures that fail because of supernatural interventions, found in the Coptic but lost in the Arabic and Ethiopic

---

27 The shift in the receiver of the healing doesn't change the narratological function of the episode, which lies in revealing the supernatural power of the saint through a posthumous miracle.

versions),[28] miracle narratives still appear to have a heavier narrative *weight*. Such weight appears to protect them from erosion throughout the process of textual transmission, preventing substantial losses of miracle material. To summarize: generally, the number of miracle narratives across the process of textual transmission either stays the same or increases. When stories shorten significantly, they still appear to concentrate miracle narratives in contrast to all other kinds of literary elements, thus displaying a peculiarly high level of retention of miracle and supernatural narratives.

Looking at the textual transmission of multiple hagiographical tales brings to light a trend in the modes of transformation of these tales. Thus, unless we are willing to envision mice, bugs, and other corrupting agents with a special predilection for non-miracle narrative sections of manuscripts across time and space, we shall acknowledge that this process of textual transmission illuminates a human effort, and thus a promising window into a human way of maneuvering storytelling. Yet what is this effort? What is it that these miracle narratives are made (and manipulated) to do?

4 What Do Miracle Narratives Achieve? Storytelling as Technology of Enchantment

In asking what miracle narratives do, I seek answers on how texts are simultaneously reflective and constitutive of human ways of feeling, thinking, and acting. I follow in this the productive methodological lead of, among others, Laura Carlson Hasler[29] and Tim Whitmarsh, who effectively summarized this approach in this way:

> Cultural history focuses upon the role of texts and other media not simply as 'reflections' of history, but as *active participants* in the struggle to define and popularize certain perceptions of the current state of society; upon, that is to say, the role of *representation* in the dissemination of ideas. 'Reality' is to be understood not as a concrete, static 'structure' that lies behind representation in literature and other media, but as a collection of ways of perceiving the world. Texts, then, are not second-order 'evidence' for a society; they are primarily building-blocks of that society, as it is experienced and understood by its members.[30]

---

28 Drescher, *Apa Mina* 137–139 *passim*.
29 Carlson Hasler L., *Archival Historiography in Jewish Antiquity* (Oxford: 2020) 110–125.
30 Whitmarsh T., *Ancient Greek Literature* (Cambridge: 2004) 6, emphasis added.

Thus, an inquiry into the domain of literary form and representation can bring to light an endeavor to invite (or discourage) a certain posture toward the world, a certain way of feeling, imagining, being in, acting on, and perceiving reality. Therefore, in order to understand what efforts are embedded in the miracle narratives under scrutiny here, and consequently shed light on one or more of the functions that these narratives played/were made to play within the communities in which they were produced and disseminated, we need to focus on what these miracle narratives look like.

Miracle narratives in the hagiographical tales of the Incense Route are consistently associated with concrete and specific geographical locations. For instance, the textual tradition of the tale of Longinos displays a multiplicity of miracles (e.g. dream visions, a miraculous perfume wafting from a corpse, the healing of the widow's blindness) taking place in Jerusalem, a city that would have been familiar to a Christian of the Incense Route because of its ties with sacred history. In the tale of Menas, on the other hand, multiple miracles take place in Phrygia, a well-known region of the late ancient world, and Alexandria, one of the gateways into the Incense Route. In other hagiographical traditions that traveled along the Incense Route we find a similar recurrence of miracle narratives associated with specific geographical locations in or around the area, such as Egypt, Palestine, and Ethiopia. Both the Life of Menas and the Life of Longinos are found in the Ethiopian synaxarion as readings for the month of Ḥedar (roughly the equivalent of November in the Gregorian calendar): if we survey even just the hagiographies found in the month of Ḥedar as a case study, we find this phenomenon reflected in most miracle narratives. On the 7th of Ḥedar, namely November 16 on the Gregorian calendar, the story of George the Great is told, who performed miracles through his icon in the shrine dedicated to him in the city of Lydda, 15 km from today's Tel Aviv.[31] On the 16th of Ḥedar, the equivalent of November 25, the story of Daniel tells us about the miracle of an angel who came down to earth in Sketis, in the Egyptian desert.[32] On the 20th of Ḥedar, November 29, the story of Anianos is told, who was miraculously cured by Saint Mark in the city of Alexandria.[33] On the 3rd of Ḥedar, November 12, the tale of 'Āmda Mikā'ēl instructs readers on this saint, buried in the church of 'Atronsa Māryām in the Amhara region of Ethiopia, who was fed the Eucharist by the Archangel Michael himself, and whose corpse after death was surrounded by heavenly light.

---

31   Colin, *Le synaxaire* 257–259.
32   Ibidem, 319–321.
33   Ibidem, 337–339.

STORYTELLING AS TECHNOLOGY OF ENCHANTMENT 149

By associating miracle narratives with concrete places, most often on or around the Incense Route, these tales encouraged readers to see their everyday reality in a new light: specifically, as a site where the divine presence manifests itself. This is the effort, this is one of the fundamental functions of these tales: to transform the reader's vision and experience of the world, revealing that physical reality is filled with traces of the divine. These tales endeavor to reshape the readers' attention, as if they were speaking to them, saying, 'Look around, in that one place you know an angel appeared; in that other place, the dead body of a glorious martyr performed a miraculous healing; transcendent powers, the divine presence are all around you'. These textual traditions were born and disseminated in the heart of the Christian East, one of the birthplaces of apophaticism and negative theology, all forms of theological discourse that invite a way of imagining the divine as remote, ineffable, and transcendent. What these hagiographical tales do is, in a way, the opposite of that: they invite readers to perceive the divine as near and present.[34]

This rewiring of the readers' perception and meaning-making capacities emerges from the power of stories to enable alternative possibilities of thought, experience, and action by offering hermeneutical resources that bear on the limits and qualities of the readers' mindscape. Hanna Meretoja has lucidly described the functioning of this capacity of stories to transform reality:

> We are always already entangled in webs of narratives. They are integral to the world that precedes us, and they make it possible for us to develop into subjects who are capable of narrating their experiences, sharing them with others, and telling their own versions of the stories they have inherited. Each cultural and historical world functions as a *space of possibilities* that encourages certain modes of experience, thought, and action, and discourages or disallows others, and stories play a constitutive role in establishing the limits of these worlds – both enabling experience and delimiting it.[35]

Stories effected this rewiring of the reader's mindscape during liturgy, individual devotional reading, catechetical instruction, and edification. Such religious practices do not just reflect but produce, articulate, and maintain norms

---

34 I am invoking negative theology in order to underscore, by contrast, the specificity of the cultural work performed by the hagiographies under scrutiny here. We have no reason to believe that these texts show an intentionally polemic effort directed against apophatic and negative theologies.

35 Meretoja H., *The Ethics of Storytelling: Narrative Hermeneutics, History, and the Possible* (Oxford: 2015) 96.

for understanding the self, the world, the divine, and the relationship between them. Through hours of liturgical and devotional experience, stories inculcate specific narrative patterns that shape one's encounter and commerce with reality. Derek Krueger has convincingly demonstrated how liturgy acted as a mechanism for the formation of the Byzantine self by offering 'templates telling Christians who they were in relation to God, each other, the Church, and the state'.[36] The process I am describing here is analogous inasmuch as it leverages texts as technology to shape one's resources for meaning-making. However, instead of working specifically on self-understanding and subjectivity like the liturgical poems studied by Krueger, the hagiographical tales of the Incense Route reveal an effort to affect the readers' experience of their external reality and its relationship with the divine.

The specific form of encounter with reality encouraged by these hagiographical tales I call enchantment. Since Weber's seminal work on the notion of *Entzauberung*, 'disenchantment', the term enchantment has blossomed in a variety of contexts and with a multiplicity of meanings in religious and literary studies.[37] The way I use the term in the present chapter is most attuned to the definition offered by Jason Crawford in his *Allegory and Enchantment*:

> When we talk about enchantment, we often talk about the medieval church, with its vast sacramental economies and its theology of bodily presence; about medieval political life, with its magical conceptions of authority and social bond; or about the medieval natural order, with its occult affinities and its daemonic agents. If disenchantment entails 'the impoverishment of the reign of the invisible', enchantment, as many of our narratives imagine it, indicates the immanent operations of the invisible, whether the invisible agent takes the form of God whom Akeel Bilgrami has described as 'present in nature itself and therefore providing an inner source of dynamism' or of the 'host of demons, threatening from all sides' that Charles Taylor takes as the defining mark of an enchanted

---

36 Krueger D., *Liturgical Subjects: Christian Ritual, Biblical Narrative, and the Formation of the Self in Byzantium* (Philadelphia: 2014) 7.

37 Weber's mention of *Entzauberung* is found in his lecture "Science as Vocation" in Weber M., *Essays in Sociology*, trans. H.H. Gerth – C. Wright Mills (Oxford: 1946) 155. For broader explorations of the term 'enchantment' (although with a chronological focus limited to the transition between the late Middle Ages and early modernity) see Bilgrami A., "What Is Enchantment?", in Warner M. – VanAntwerpen J. – Calhoun C. (eds.), *Varieties of Secularism in a Secular Age* (Cambridge, MA: 2010) 145–165, and Morgan D., "Enchantment, Disenchantment, Re-enchantment", in Morgan D. – Elkins J. (eds.), *Re-enchantment* (New York – London: 2009) 9–18.

cosmos. *The language of enchantment therefore tends to indicate forms of commerce or approach, channels by which the material world and the immaterial divine come into contact with one another.*[38]

Although we could texture the notion of enchantment in a variety of ways and through the work of a variety of thinkers, from Tolkien's notion of the *Faërie* to Brown's identification of enchantment with the sacramental,[39] it is Crawford's definition in the last sentence of the passage quoted above that I choose as best representation of the kind of human experience that the hagiographical tales of the Incense Route invite. What these texts endeavor to do is to re-signify the geography of being of their readers, joining heaven to earth through the invitation to discover reality as permeated by the holy. Be it the city of Jerusalem, shimmering with the memory of the miraculous apparitions of Longinos, or the deserts of Sketis, where, the tale of Daniel reminds us, angels walked, the Greek, Coptic, Arabic, Ethiopic, and Old Nubian hagiographical tales of the Incense Route reveal reality anew, gesturing toward the infinite mystery that burns under the ashes of the physical world.

I began this exploration by asking what the transmission of these tales can reveal about their cultural and religious role within the Christian communities of the Incense Route. We saw that hagiographical tales traveled far and wide across this ancient network of sea and land routes, surviving and morphing for centuries after their initial composition. The way these tales morphed and changed points decidedly toward the conclusion that at least one, specific effort undergirds their literary form across translations and reworkings, namely offering a new way to imagine and be in the world where corners of everyday life radiate with enchantment. Within and through these tales the shrine of Menas or the city of Lydda could become places where the otherwise ineffable and remote Godhead could be perceived powerfully, although mysteriously, as close and present. It is in the unique way that these tales re-signify and reshape the cosmology of the reader and their experience of the world that one of the major cultural and religious functions of these tales is to be found.

---

38   Crawford J., *Allegory and Enchantment: An Early Modern Poetics* (Oxford: 2017) 2–3, emphasis added.

39   Tolkien J.R.R., "On Fairy-Stories", in idem, *Tree and Leaf* (London: 1988) 9–73; Brown D., *God and Enchantment of Place* (Oxford: 2004) *passim*.

5 Conclusions: Narrative Technologies Joining Heaven to Earth

Throughout the present analysis I have underscored repeatedly how stories shape the human encounter with the world. But this is not new. The history of literature is full of figures whose reality is profoundly transformed, for better or for worse, by interacting with stories: from Don Quixote and his maddening thirst for adventure to Emma Bovary and her luring love fantasies, from King Shahryar in the *Arabian Nights* to Paolo and Francesca in the fifth canto of Dante's *Divine Comedy*. In addition, plenty of work – in philosophy, literary theory, religious studies, theology, some of which I have quoted throughout this analysis – has long demonstrated the power of literature and stories to extend, diminish, and transform reality. The present chapter augments these studies by revealing that the study of textual transmission of the late ancient and medieval Eastern Christian hagiographies of the Incense Route brings to light *a specific aspect* of that broader phenomenon, a specifically *religious* aspect, namely the capacity of stories to transform the reader's imagination and perception of the world, making a tear in the fabric of reality so as to let the transcendent shine through. A merchant, traveler, pilgrim, or soldier passing by the shrine of Menas near Alexandria would have experienced this place differently after reading the related tale, because they would have known that that place was the site where the body of a martyr performed miracles of healing; a place where the divine powers were manifested; a place permeated by the holy.

If, on the one hand, the study of the textual transmission of these tales offers meaningful insight into the relationship between storytelling and religious experience (and, more specifically, on the transformative power of the former on the latter), such a study also has potential to gesture toward the fact that cross-cultural exchange is empowering for religious imagination. For as we track the complex, unpredictable migrations of these tales across the eastern Mediterranean and northeastern Africa, we witness how originally Greek and Coptic tales brought outward, into the regions that are now Sudan, Ethiopia, Eritrea, Djibouti, and Somalia, new cultural resources to conceptualize the relationship between the physical and the spiritual, the visible and the invisible, the immanent and the transcendent. By acquiring the new cultural codes embedded in these tales' vision of the world and the miraculous, the communities of the Incense Route extended the limits of what they could imagine, experience, and do. It is in this multiplication and diversification of one's resources to imagine oneself, the universe, and the divine that the story of the transmission of hagiographical tales along the Incense Route becomes not just a fascinating episode of intellectual history but a story of religious

STORYTELLING AS TECHNOLOGY OF ENCHANTMENT

empowerment through the encounter and the intrareligious compenetration of cultures (I use the term 'intrareligious' to indicate a form of exchange between different cultural complexes within the same religious tradition, e.g. Greek Christianity and Ethiopian Christianity).

As this analysis nears its conclusion, one wonders what else would emerge from a more sustained study of a broader corpus of sources. If, on the one hand, this study has pointed to the conclusion that the analysis of multiple hagiographical traditions reveals a trend in the textual manipulation of these narratives (i.e. miracles stick, other sections are occasionally dropped), on the other hand one may wonder if, when, and why this trend is ever disrupted. Additionally, one might ask what other textual elements stick in a similar fashion to miracle narratives in other textual traditions, and what is accomplished by maintaining (or losing) those. And what about other genres among the literatures of the Incense Route? Is it possible that a similar analysis, focused on the close study of textual transmission as a window into the late ancient and medieval religious imagination, could bring to light other, unexpected ways texts function as religious technologies, similarly to how the hagiographical tales of the Incense Route function as technologies of enchantment? What other 'technologies of' can be retrieved by an analogous study of the circulation and transformation of texts in the late ancient Eastern Christian world? It goes without saying that these questions go well beyond the limits of a single chapter and cannot be addressed here, yet it is useful, I believe, to point out their promising lead. May those qualified come to complete this fragment.

Bibliography

Primary Sources

Acts of Menas (BHG 1250). In ed. G. van Hoof, "Acta Sancti Menae: Martyris Aegyptis", *Analecta Bollandiana* 3 (1884) 258–270.

Agatharchides of Cnidus, *On the Eyrthraean Sea*. In ed. S.M. Burstein, *Agatharchides of Cnidus: On the Erythraean Sea* (London: 1989).

Encomium of Apa Mena (Coptic). In ed. J. Drescher, *Apa Mena: A Selection of Coptic Texts Relating to Saint Menas. Edited, with Translation and Commentary* (Cairo: 1946) 126–149.

Encomium to the Great Martyr Menas (BHG 1255). In ed. T. Ioannou, *Μνημεῖα ἁγιολογικά*, Subsidia Byzantina 8 (Venice: 1884) 324–327.

Gregory of Nyssa, *Letter* 17. In *Patrologia Graeca* 46:1057–1068.

154 SASSI

Hesychios of Jerusalem, *Martyrdom of St. Longinus the Holy and Glorious Martyr* (BHG 988). In *Patrologia Graeca* 93:1545–1560; ed. in Aubineau M., *Les homelies festales d'Hesychius de Jérusalem*, 2 vols. (Brussels: 1980) 2:778–844.

John Chrysostom, *In Matthaeum homilia* 88. In *Patrologia Graeca* 58:775–782.

Kosmas Indicopleustes, *Christian Geography*. In ed. J.M.W. Crindle, *The Christian Topography of Cosmas, an Egyptian Monk* (Edinburgh: 1897) 358–373.

Miracles of Menas (BHG 1226–1269). In ed. N. Pomjalovskij, *Žitije prepodovnago Paisija velikago i Timotheja part. Aleks. povestvovanie o čudesah sv. velikomučenika Miny* (St. Petersburg: 1900) 62–89.

Miracles of Menas (Old Nubian). In ed. G.M. Brown, *The Old Nubian Miracles of Saint Menas* (Vienna: 1994).

Miracles of Menas (Old Slavic). In ed. V. Jagić, "Ein mittelbulgarisches Bruchstück des ersten Wunders des Großmärtyrers Menas (aus dem XIV. Jahrh.)", *Archiv für slavischen Philologie* 30 (1909) 392–399 and 392–393; D. Atanassova, "The Miracles of the Great Martyr Menas in the Medieval Slavic Pre-Metaphrastic Menaia-Čet'i (Critical Edition of the Text, Based on Manuscript No. 1039 from the SS. Cyril and Methodius National Library in Sofia)", *Scripta & e-Scripta* 6 (2008) 305–324.

Passion of Longinos (Alexandrian Synaxarion). In ed. I. Forget, *Synaxarium alexandrinum*, Corpus Scriptorum Christianorum Orientalium (CSCO), vols. 47, 48, 49, 67, 78 and 90: *Scriptores arabici*, series 3 (Louvain: 1953).

Passion of Longinos (Alexandrian Synaxarion, Latin). In ed. I. Forget, *Synaxarium alexandrinum*, Corpus Scriptorum Christianorum Orientalium (CSCO), vol. 78: *Scriptores arabici*, series 3 (Louvain: 1953) 99–100.

Passion of Longinos (anonymous). In *Acta Sanctorum* Mar. II:739–740.

Passion of Longinos (Ethiopian Synaxarion). In ed. G. Colin, *Le synaxaire éthiopien: Mois de Ḥedar* (Turnhout: 1988) 309–313.

Passion of Longinos (Synaxarion). In ed. H. Delehaye, *Synaxarium ecclesiae constantinopolitanae* (Brussels: 1902) 141–144.

Passion of Menas (BHG 1251). In ed. T. Ioannou, *Μνημεῖα ἁγιολογικά*, Subsidia Byzantina 8 (Venice: 1884) 284–324.

Passion of Menas (BHG 1254). In ed. K. Krumbacher, *Miscellen zu Romanos* (Munich: 1907) 31–43.

Passion of Menas (Alexandrian Synaxarion). In ed. I. Forget, *Synaxarium alexandrinum*, Corpus Scriptorum Christianorum Orientalium (CSCO), vol. 78: *Scriptores arabici*, series 3 (Louvain: 1953) 124–126.

Passion of Menas (Ethiopian Synaxarion). In ed. G. Colin, *Le synaxaire éthiopien: Mois de Ḥedar* (Turnhout: 1988) 309–313.

Periplus of the Erythraean Sea (Περίπλους τῆς Ἐρυθρᾶς Θαλάσσης). In ed. L. Casson, *The Periplus Maris Erythraei: Text with Introduction, Translation, and Commentary* (Princeton: 1989; repr. 2012).

Strabo, *Geography*. In ed. E.L. Jones, *The Geography of Strabo* (Cambridge, MA: 1983).

Symeon the Metaphrast, *Metaphrasis of the Passion of Longinos* (BHG 989). In *Patrologia Graeca* 115:31–44.

Secondary Works

Aubineau M. (ed.), *Les homelies festales d'Hesychius de Jérusalem*, 2 vols. (Brussels: 1980).

Balfour-Paul J., "Indigo in South and South-East Asia", *Textile History* 30.1 (1999) 98–112.

Bilgrami A., "What Is Enchantment?", in Warner M. – VanAntwerpen J. – Calhoun C. (eds.), *Varieties of Secularism in a Secular Age* (Cambridge, MA: 2010) 145–165.

Bostock J. (trans.), *The Natural History of Pliny* (London: 1855).

Braudel F., *La Méditerranée et le monde méditérranéen à l'époque de Philippe II* (Paris: 1949).

Brown D., *God and Enchantment of Place* (Oxford: 2004).

Brozyna J.M., *The Incense Route: A Study of Its Origin and Development* (M.A. dissertation, San Jose State University: 1999).

Buchberger M., *Lexikon für Theologie und Kirche*, 11 vols. (Freibourg: 1964) 9.

Burmester O.H.E. KHS, *The Egyptian or Coptic Church* (Cairo: 1967).

Burstein S.M. (ed. and trans.), *Agatharchides of Cnidus: On the Erythraean Sea* (London: 1989).

Carlson Hasler L., *Archival Historiography in Jewish Antiquity* (Oxford: 2020).

Casson L. (ed. and trans.), *The Periplus Maris Erythraei: Text with Introduction, Translation, and Commentary* (Princeton: 1989; repr. 2012).

Cohen M., "Review of W. Budge's *Book of Saints*", *Revue de l'histoire des religions* 99 (1929) 310.

Colin G., "Le synaxaire éthiopien: État actuel de la question", *Analecta Bollandiana* 106.3/4 (1988) 273–317.

Crawford J., *Allegory and Enchantment: An Early Modern Poetics* (Oxford: 2017).

Crone P., *Meccan Trade and the Rise of Islam* (Princeton: 1987).

David C.B. – Isaac B., "Six Milestone Stations and New Inscriptions Discovered in the Negev along the Petra–Gaza Incense Route", *Palestine Exploration Quarterly* 152.3 (2020) 234–247.

Drescher J., *Apa Mena: A Selection of Coptic Texts Relating to Saint Menas. Edited, with Translation and Commentary* (Cairo: 1946).

Graf G., *Geschichte der christlichen arabischen Literatur*, vol. 2: *Die Schriftsteller bis zur Mitte des 15. Jahrhunderts*, Studi e testi 118 (Vatican City: 1944–1953).

Groom N., *Frankincense and Myrrh: A Study of Arabian Incense Trade* (London: 1981).

Illich I. – Sanders B., *ABC: The Alphabetization of the Popular Mind* (San Francisco: 1988).

Ingrams H., "Burton Memorial Lecture: From Cana (Husn Ghorab) to Sabbatha (Shabwa): The South Arabian Incense Road", *Journal of the Royal Asiatic Society* 77.3–4 (1945) 169–185.

Jones E.L. (ed. and trans.), *The Geography of Strabo* (Cambridge, MA: 1983).

Krueger D., *Liturgical Subjects: Christian Ritual, Biblical Narrative, and the Formation of the Self in Byzantium* (Philadelphia: 2014).

McDonald W.J., *New Catholic Encyclopedia*, 17 vols. (Palatine, IL: 1981) 13.

Meretoja H., *The Ethics of Storytelling: Narrative Hermeneutics, History, and the Possible* (Oxford: 2015).

Merleau-Ponty M., *Phenomenology of Perception*, trans. C. Smith (London: 1962).

Morgan D., "Enchantment, Disenchantment, Re-enchantment", in Morgan D. – Elkins J. (eds.), *Re-enchantment* (New York – London: 2009) 9–18.

Sidebotham S. – Willemina W.Z., "Berenike: A Ptolemaic-Roman Port on the Ancient Maritime Spice and Incense Route", *Minerva* 13.3 (2002) 28–31.

Silvano L. – Varalda P., "Per l'edizione dei *Miracula Sancti Menae* (BHG 1256–1269)", *Philologia antiqua* 12 (2019) 51–86.

Simms E.-M., "A Phenomenology of Reading: Textual Technology and Virtual Worlds", in Howard P. – Saevi T. – Foran A. – Biesta G. (eds.), *Phenomenology and Educational Theory in Conversation* (London: 2020) 88–99.

Tolkien J.R.R., "On Fairy-Stories", in Tolkien J.R.R., *Tree and Leaf* (London: 1988) 9–73.

Van Beek W., "Frankincense and Myrrh", *Biblical Archeologist* 23 (1960) 69–95.

Van Beek W., "Frankincense and Myrrh in Ancient South Arabia", *Journal of the American Oriental Society* 78 (1958) 141–151.

Weber M., *Essays in Sociology*, trans. H.H. Gerth – C. Wright Mills (Oxford: 1946).

Whitmarsh T., *Ancient Greek Literature* (Cambridge: 2004).

PART 3

Tales in Collections

CHAPTER 7

Stunning with a List, Dazzling with a Catalogue: The Form of Paradoxographical and Christian Miracle Collections Revisited

Julia Doroszewska

1 Introduction

In his seminal book *La vertigine della lista*, published in 2009, Umberto Eco reflects on the form of the list or the catalogue (used interchangeably) as a particular mode of artistic representation that continually recurs in Western thought from Homer onward.[1] Epic and prosaic catalogues, collections of *mirabilia*, bestiaries, treasuries, genealogical lists, visual collections of things pictured on paintings, cabinets of curiosities: these and other instances are embraced by the capacious definition of the list applied by him. All of them, Eco argues, manifest a specific way of seeing and describing the world that appears in certain circumstances: when a comprehensive definition of a phenomenon that would grasp its essence cannot be provided because its boundaries are unknown or unimaginably large. To this he adds a situation where the existing definition is unsatisfactory or where defining is not a concern at all. Then there comes the other option: a list. A list that enumerates all the known properties of the phenomenon in lieu of a synthetic summary. Such intellectual inadequacy may explain the curious prolixity of the famous catalogue of ships in Book 2 of the *Iliad*, that cornerstone of all literary catalogues. In his account of the Trojan War, the poet, faced with the astronomically large number of people involved in the hostilities on the Greek side, limits himself to listing 'merely' the commanders and ships. This measure allows the catalogue to take up only 274 lines of the total 892 in Book 2.[2]

---

1 Eco U., *La vertigine della lista* (Milan: 2009). I used the English translation: Eco U., *The Infinity of Lists*, trans. A. MacEwen (London: 2009). Cf. also Kirk A., *Ancient Greek Lists: Catalogue and Inventory across Genres* (Cambridge: 2021).
    This chapter is funded by the National Science Centre in Poland under the project 'Epiphanies of the Saints in Late Antique Greek Literature', no. UMO-2018/31/D/HS3/00870.
2 Homer, *Iliad*, 2.488–759. On a detailed examination of Homer's strategies of counting the uncountable in the catalogue of ships and other passages, see the chapter "A Number of

---

© JULIA DOROSZEWSKA, 2025 | DOI:10.1163/9789004707351_009

This is an open access chapter distributed under the terms of the CC BY-NC-ND 4.0 license.

Eco proposes to contrast the Homeric enumeration of the ships with another form of representation: the description of the shield of Achilles in Book 18 of the *Iliad*.[3] While the list suggests infinity through its open-ended form itself, the shield's round shape signifies the opposite: a completeness expressed and enhanced by the detailed and minute description of the world represented on it. While the number of Greek warriors at Troy was uncountable, here the poet is capable of offering an exhaustive depiction of an entire universe, since its essence and limits are known and comprehensible to him. In this light, the list would thus be an admission of defeat and a desperate ploy to merely approach the inexpressible by providing a sample of its iterations or properties. The philosopher observes, however, that the reasons for choosing to list and enumerate rather than to delimit and delineate may vary. In other words, the eponymous vertigo embedded in the notion of the list may hint at different underpinnings and different goals depending on the context.[4]

Inspired by the Italian philosopher's insights, I would like to test them with relation to two literary genres that he discusses either very briefly or not at all, that is paradoxographical and early Byzantine miracle collections, respectively. Both focus on recording extraordinary phenomena and both use the form of the list or the catalogue to present and organize their content. Therefore, it seems very plausible that the paradoxographical collections of *mirabilia* inspired the late antique Christian authors of *miracula*. The parallels they display call for a comparison, the dissimilarities demand an examination. In this chapter, I will analyze how the list is handled in *mirabilia* and *miracula* and discuss their authors' possible motivations and purposes in adopting this particular form of expression. My main focus, however, will be on the latter genre and its potential dependence on the former, since much has already been said on paradoxographical structure and strategies, while *miracula* have so far been understudied in this respect. Furthermore, I will argue that there is also another literary model that might have influenced the authors of miracle collections, namely the epic catalogue.

Things: Homeric Catalogue, Numerical Authority, and the Uncountable" in Kirk, *Ancient Greek Lists* 17–47.

3 Homer, *Iliad*, 18.478–608; Eco, *The Infinity of Lists* 9–18.
4 Eco, *The Infinity of Lists* 18.

STUNNING WITH A LIST, DAZZLING WITH A CATALOGUE

2 Paradoxographical Lists

Admittedly, paradoxographical collections had their origin in quite different historical and cultural circumstances than Christian miracle collections. Nonetheless, both genres adopted cataloguing as their form. Let us look into their possible motivations and aims and consider their potential interconnectedness.

Although many studies have been dedicated to paradoxography, the genre still remains quite enigmatic.[5] This is because in these collections we are treated to nothing but series of pieces of information about diverse extraordinary phenomena. As a rule, there are no introductions, no prefaces, no commentaries that would shed light on the rationale behind the selection of these particular facts and not others. Even more importantly, we are not provided with any explanation as to why such collections were compiled at all. This authorial omission is probably even more astonishing than the unusual occurrences themselves, assembled in their mass in paradoxographical compilations. Some scholars have thus suspected that these collections were created as notes rather than works written with publication in mind.[6] This does not seem to have been the case, however, given the general cataloguing frenzy manifesting itself particularly since the Hellenistic period, of which paradoxography was just a narrow subset.[7]

Obviously, the lack of introductions may result from the poor state of preservation of the bulk of the collections, with key opening parts often missing, which makes many of them inconclusive cases. I agree, however, with Chris Delcroix, who argues that these works were originally conceived purely as collections of barely processed material with no literary pretensions.[8] I would add to this another telling fact: paradoxographers entirely refrained from explaining the very unusual phenomena recorded. On the contrary, they actually tweaked the content to render it more wondrous and extraordinary than

---

5   The most important and comprehensive studies are those by Ziegler K., "Paradoxographoi", *Paulys Realencyclopädie der classischen Altertumswissenschaft* 18 (1949) 1137–1166; Giannini A., "Studi sulla paradossografia greca I. Da Omero a Callimaco: Motive e forme del meraviglioso", *Istituto Lombardo (Rendiconti di Lettere)* 97 (1963) 247–266; idem, "Studi sulla paradossografia greca II. Da Callimaco all'età imperiale: La lettura paradossografica", *Acme* 17 (1964) 99–140; Schepens G. – Delcroix K., "Ancient Paradoxography: Origin, Evolution, Production and Reception", in Pecere O. – Stramaglia A. (eds.), *La letteratura di consumo nel mondo greco-latino: Atti del Convegno Internazionale, Cassino, 14–17 settembre 1994* (Cassino: 1996) 410–460.

6   Schepens – Delcroix, "Ancient Paradoxography" 403.

7   Ibidem, 380.

8   Ibidem, 427.

originally presented in their sources. However, they achieved their goals not through stylistic means, but by truncating the context surrounding a given 'curiosity' or even omitting the rational exegesis if it happened to be provided in the source.[9]

Thus, this new category of collection emerged to focus solely on assembling the marvelous, as may be inferred from Antigonos, who passingly mentions that the scope of his interest is 'the strange and the paradox' (τὸ ξένον καὶ παράδοξον).[10] The most frequent term denoting its main concern is, however, *thauma* and its cognates, which appear already in the titles of such collections.[11] In addition to their extraordinary content, which is still very appealing to us, their great strength lies precisely in the form in which they present this content. These collections simply dazzle us with a series of unconnected pieces of information, which are linked in a paratactic style with the word καί that can be explicit or implicit. It may occur simply as a conjunction and mean 'and', or adverbially as 'also' (δὲ καί). Two entries in Antigonos of Karystos' *Collection of Paradoxical Stories*, both concerning cicadas, may be quoted as an exemplar:

> 2: And (καί) another such fabulous story is being told among the inhabitants of Rhegium [...].
> 3: And (καί) in Kefallenia a river divides the land [...].

> 2: Καὶ ἄλλο δὲ παρὰ τοῖς Ῥηγίνοις τοιοῦτον ὡς μυθικὸν ἱστορεῖται [...].
> 3: Καὶ ἐν Κεφαλληνίᾳ δὲ ποταμὸς διείργει [...].[12]

Likewise, in Phlegon of Tralles' *Mirabilia*, three consecutive entries, of which two concern a ghost story and one mentions a case of sex change:

> 2: Also (δὲ καί) Hieron of Alexandria or of Ephesos recounts that a ghost also (καί) appeared in Aetolia.
> 3: Also (δὲ καί) Antisthenes, the Peripatetic philosopher, relates that the consul Acilius Glabrio along with the legates Porcius Cato and

---

9   For an examination of the procedures used by paradoxographers see ibidem, 391–394.

10 Antigonos of Karystos, *Collection of Paradoxical Stories*, 60b, ed. A. Giannini, *Paradoxographorum Graecorum reliquiae* (Milan: 1965) 32–106.

11 The word that most frequently appears in various configurations in roughly half of the extant titles of paradoxographical collections is the adjective *thaumasios* (περὶ θαυμασίων, θαυμασίων συναγωγή, etc.), while the other half are based on the adjective *paradoxos* (παράδοξος ἱστορία, ἱστοριῶν παραδόξων συναγωγή, etc.); see Schepens – Delcroix, "Ancient Paradoxography" 381.

12 Antigonos, *Collection of Paradoxical Stories*, 2–3; translation mine.

STUNNING WITH A LIST, DAZZLING WITH A CATALOGUE   163

Lucius Valerius Flaccus drew up in battle-order against Antiochos in
Thermopylai and fought nobly.

4: Also (δὲ καί) Hesiod, Dikaiarchos, Klearchos, Kallimachos and certain
other authors relate the following incident about Teiresias.

2: Ἱστορεῖ δὲ καὶ Ἱέρων ὁ Ἀλεξανδρεὺς ἢ Ἐφέσιος καὶ ἐν Αἰτωλίᾳ φάσμα
γενέσθαι.
3: Ἱστορεῖ δὲ καὶ Ἀντισθένης, ὁ Περιπατητικὸς φιλόσοφος, Ἀκείλιον Γλαβρίωνα
τὸν ὕπατον, μετὰ πρεσβευτῶν Πορκίου Κάτωνος καὶ Λουκίου Οὐαλερίου
Φλάκκου, παραταξάμενον Ἀντιόχῳ ἐν Θερμοπύλαις γενναίως τε ἀγωνισάμενον.
4: Ἱστορεῖ δὲ καὶ Ἡσίοδος καὶ Δικαίαρχος καὶ Κλέ{ιτ}αρχος καὶ Καλλίμαχος
καὶ ἄλλοι τινὲς περὶ Τειρεσίου τάδε.[13]

Since there is neither a clear beginning nor an end, they seem to suggest that
there is still something more that could be added.[14] This poetics of etcetera,[15]
which hints at an implied infinity of instances that display only a superfi-
cial affinity, makes us feel what Eco called 'the vertigo of the list'. In his view,
this dizziness is a psychological symptom of mental anxiety in the face of an
uncountable number of facts that cannot be clearly reduced to a common
denominator. Although Eco is not very precise in his general diagnosis, which
aims to explain the practice of list-making, if it embraces also the conditions
underlying collections of *mirabilia*, it may be true on a deeper level. The first
paradoxographical compilations appeared at that specific historical moment
when the Greeks had to reformulate their definition of the world due to a sudden expansion of its boundaries.[16] More superficially, however, it is likely that
these collections display an admiration for the diversity of the world driven by
scientific interests, as well as a true passion for collecting information about
that which is 'against expectation' (*para-doxon*). The compilers' purpose was
to extract the very essence of the marvelous and serve it plain. They do not

---

13   Phlegon of Tralles, *The Book of Marvels*, ed. A. Stramaglia, *Phlegon Trallianus: Opuscula
      de rebus mirabilibus et de longaevis*, Bibliotheca Scriptorum Graecorum et Romanorum
      Teubneriana 2008 (Berlin – New York: 2011) 1–60; trans. W. Hansen, *Phlegon of Tralles'
      Book of Marvels* (Exeter: 1996) 37, slightly modified.
14   On *mirabilia* as open structures see Jacob C. – de Polignac F., *Alexandria, Third Century
      BC: The Knowledge of the World in a Single City*, trans. C. Clement (Alexandria: 2000) 93.
15   Eco, *The Infinity of Lists* 7.
16   The conquest of the East by the Hellenistic kings and the cultural rift it triggered is sug-
      gested to be a direct factor stimulating the emergence of the paradoxographical genre
      (Gabba E., "True History and False History in Classical Antiquity", *Journal of Roman
      Studies* 71 (1981) 50–62, at 52–53), as well as the establishment and organization of
      research institutes and libraries (Schepens – Delcroix, "Ancient Paradoxography" 402).

164   DOROSZEWSKA

seem to have been interested in seeking explanations or definitions of the facts they gathered, since this would have been simply counterproductive. The charm and force of paradoxography stems mainly from its specific form, which makes the sensational and marvelous content shine.

3 Christian Miracle Collections

There can be no doubt that within the broad tradition of literary collections, paradoxography paved the way for the *miracula* that appeared in the early Byzantine period,[17] and was their immediate predecessor. Scott Johnson showed this very nicely in his study of the *Miracles of Thekla* and pointed out a set of structural similarities between the two genres.[18] To sum them up briefly: both collection types share a simple paratactic order that repeats itself in each story. As a rule, there is a brief introduction that names the source of the story or gives some reason for mentioning it, followed by a narrative of varying length which always ends abruptly after its climax and closes with a very brief

---

17   My corpus includes eight extant texts: from the fifth century, the anonymous *Miracles of Thekla*, hereafter MT (BHG 1718, ed. G. Dagron, *Vie et miracles de sainte Thècle: Texte grec, traduction et commentaire*, Subsidia hagiographica 62 (Brussels: 1978) 285–412) and the *Miracles of Theodore Teron*, hereafter *MThT* (twelve miracles appended to the short *Encomium*, BHG 1765c) by Chrysippos of Jerusalem (ed. A. Sigalas, *Des Chrysippos von Jerusalem Enkomion auf den hl. Theodoros Teron*, Byzantinisches Archiv 7 (Leipzig: 1921) 50–79); from the sixth century, the *Miracles of Menas*, hereafter MM (BHG 1256–1269), possibly by Timothy of Alexandria (ed. N. Pomjalovskij, *Žitije prepodovnago Paisija velikago i Timotheja part. Aleks. povestvovanie o čudesah sv. velikomučenika Miny* (St. Petersburg: 1900) 62–89), and the anonymous *Miracles of Kosmas and Damian*, hereafter MKD (BHG 385–391, ed. L. Deubner, *Kosmas und Damian: Texte und Einleitung* (Leipzig – Berlin: 1907) 193–206); and from the seventh century, the *Miracles of Kyros and John*, hereafter MKJ (BHG 477–479) by Sophronios of Jerusalem (ed. N. Fernández Marcos, *Los 'Thaumata' de Sofronio: Contribucion al estudio de la 'incubatio' cristiana* (Madrid: 1975)), the *Miracles of Demetrios*, hereafter MD (BHG 516z–522) by John of Thessalonike (the first fifteen miracles; the other six are anonymous), ed. P. Lemerle, *Les plus anciens recueils des Miracles de Saint Démétrius*, vol. 1: *Le texte* (Paris: 1979) 4–165 (John of Thessalonike), 168–241 (anonymous)), the anonymous *Miracles of Anastasios the Persian*, hereafter MAP (BHG 89g–90), ed. B. Flusin, *Saint Anastase le Perse et l'histoire de la Palestine au début du VIIe siècle*, vol. 1: *Les textes* (Paris: 1992) 117–153, and the anonymous *Miracles of Artemios*, hereafter MA (BHG 173–173c, ed. A. Papadopoulos-Kerameus, *Varia Graeca sacra* (St. Petersburg: 1909) 1–75).

18   Johnson S.F., *The Life and Miracles of Thekla: A Literary Study* (Cambridge, MA – London: 2006) 172–194.

STUNNING WITH A LIST, DAZZLING WITH A CATALOGUE   165

conclusion. In both cases the source and inspiration are the style, form, and content adopted and presented by Herodotus in his *Histories*.[19]

Johnson also rightly observes that they are linked by their focus on the *thaumata* and *paradoxa*, whose semantic range expanded over time from natural wonders to human oddities, as seen for example in Phlegon of Tralles, and to healing miracles in Byzantine hagiography.[20] Furthermore, he aptly argues that in the Thekla collection one will find neither terms such as *semeia* or *terata* that are typical for the New Testament, nor *iamata*, which are characteristic of Asclepian healing miracles. His argumentation, based on the technical vocabulary related to the miracles, aims for the most part to disconnect the form employed in the *Miracles of Thekla* from the one seen in the Asclepian *iamata* inscribed on *stelai* that are best known from Epidauros.[21] It is not so true for other miracle collections, however. Despite the unquestionable prevalence of terms cognate to *thauma*,[22] other terms denoting a miracle also recur throughout the later collections.[23]

I nonetheless agree with Johnson that the form of the *miracula* was consciously drawn from paradoxography. However, it was used for different purposes, which I will discuss below. Before doing so, I would like to argue that there is also another literary model that could have influenced the miracle collections: the epic catalogue.

4   Epic Catalogues and the Inexpressibility Topos

Umberto Eco observes that when preparing to enumerate the ships, Homer stipulates that what he is going to offer us will only be a sample. Even if he had ten mouths and ten tongues and a heart of bronze, a narrative encompassing the whole would be beyond his power of speech.[24] Through these means, the

---

19   The structure of this work, which is thought of as a paratactic sequence of narrative units, combines the historiographical strand of literature with the ethnographic one. The former diachronically recounts unique events from the past presented as a chronological and causal continuity, while the latter relies on synchronic description of permanent conditions and customary actions in the present in discontinuous catalogue form; see Munson R., *Telling Wonders: Ethnographic and Political Discourse in the Work of Herodotus* (Ann Arbor: 2001) 2.

20   Johnson, *The Life and Miracles of Thekla* 196.

21   Ibidem, 172–174.

22   θαῦμα: *MT*: 90 times; *MKJ*: 110; *MKD*: 80; *MA*: 40. θαυματουργός: *MKJ*: 1; *MKD*: 3; *MA*: 10. θαυματουργία: *MT*: 3; *MA*: 11; *MKJ*: 10. παράδοξον: *MT*: 5; *MKD*: 17.

23   σημεῖον: *MKJ*: 2; τέρας: *MKJ*: 13; *MA*: 1. ἴαμα: *MKJ*: 9; *MA*: 8.

24   Homer, *Iliad*, 2.488–493.

poet introduced the so-called inexpressibility topos to literature, which would make a great career in the epic and other genres of subsequent ages. As a matter of fact, this commonplace, termed *Unsagbarkeitstopos*, was discerned by Ernst Robert Curtius, who defined it as 'an emphasis upon inability to cope with the subject'.[25] The paradox embedded in this poetic form of conventional reticence and hesitation, as Morgane Cariou aptly points out, is that it usually goes hand in hand with a wordy catalogue which nevertheless evokes a significant portion of the presumed plethoric or even infinite remainder.[26] It thus somewhat combines the figure of preterition, which draws attention to something by the act of pretending to pass over it, with the adynaton, which expresses a paradoxical or impossible fact.[27]

Next to Homer, Hesiod's *Theogony* is another foundational text that is a genealogical catalogue par excellence. Even though the poet bravely begins it by enumerating fifty Nereids, he loses confidence when he proceeds to the other offspring of Ocean and Thetis, who are too numerous to be told by a mortal man.[28] With this conclusion he abandons the attempt, thereby having creatively modified the inexpressibility topos by shifting it from the preamble of the catalogue to its closing formula.[29] From the Hellenistic period onward this commonplace would come to be exploited by both Greek and Latin authors of epic poetry, and of didactic poetry in particular. Since it would be impossible to discuss them all here, I will limit myself to just a few examples.[30] For instance, Aratos uses it to talk about the stars, while Virgil employs it in the *Aeneid* after providing a catalogue of torture victims and the great number of crime types. In the *Georgics*, he talks about the countless variety of grapes and wines. Oppian mentions the limitless number of species in the sea. Nonnos, referring directly to Homer, gives up before enumerating all the companions of Dionysos, and so forth.[31]

---

25   Curtius E., *European Literature and the Latin Middle Ages*, trans. W. Trask (Princeton – Oxford: 2013) 159.

26   Cariou M., "Le topos de l'ineffable dans les catalogues poétiques", *Revue de philologie, de littérature et d'histoire anciennes* 88.2 (2014) 27–58, at 27.

27   Ibidem, 28.

28   Hesiod, *Theogony*, 362–370, ed. M.L. West, *Hesiod: Theogony* (Oxford: 1966) 111–149.

29   Cariou, "Le topos de l'ineffable" 31.

30   For a detailed study see Cariou, "Le topos de l'ineffable".

31   Aratos, *Phaenomena*, 373–377, ed. A.W. Mair – G.R. Mair, *Callimachus, Lycophron, Aratus. Hymns and Epigrams. Lycophron: Alexandra. Aratus: Phaenomena* (Cambridge, MA: 1921) 206–297, at 236; Virgil, *Aeneid*, 6.625–627, and *Georgics*, 2.102–108, ed. H. Rushton Fairclough, rev. G. Goold, *Virgil. Eclogues. Georgics. Aeneid: Books 1-6* (Cambridge, MA: 1916) 262–597, at 576 and 98–259, at 144–146; Oppian, *Halieutica*, 1.80–82, ed. A.W. Mair, *Oppian, Colluthus, Tryphiodorus* (Cambridge, MA: 1928; repr. 1963) 200–514, at

STUNNING WITH A LIST, DAZZLING WITH A CATALOGUE 167

More importantly, perhaps, the inexpressibility topos is echoed in the epilogue to the Gospel of John, where we learn that Jesus did many more things, but the world is unable to accommodate enough books to describe every one of them.[32] This is an interesting conclusion in that it essentially envisions a catalogue of Jesus' remaining deeds. Its existence, however, is deemed impossible not so much because their number exceeds the capacity of the author, but that of the world itself. This particular passage may have influenced the collections of miracles, as their holy protagonists and their miracle activity certainly took the figure of Jesus as a model. His prophesized legacy that his believers would cast out demons and cure the sick, quoted at the end of Mark's Gospel, laid the foundation for thaumaturgical discourse in late antiquity.[33]

In what follows, I would like to show that the miracle collections deliberately adopted the form of extended catalogues. Unlike works of paradoxography, they not infrequently offer quite elaborate prefaces and prologues in which they give an insight into or at least declare the motivations and purposes underlying their composition.[34] Their authors often comment on the reason for compiling the miracles performed by a given saint. The most interesting case is perhaps our earliest extant collection of the *MT*, dating to the mid-fifth century. Its anonymous author claims that he had been moved to make the truth about his holy patron shine. For this reason he collected Thekla's 'miracles scattered here and there'.[35] Testimony to the truth seems to be a particular consideration in this case, because the author states that there exist what may be considered rival collections of 'oracles about many subjects and cures of diseases' that are said to have been recorded by 'the priests and attendants of pagan soothsaying demons'.[36] While the author believes them to be quite false and misleading, he sees the need to show those that are connected to the source of truth.

     206; Nonnos, *Dionysiaca*, 13.47–52, ed. W. Rouse, *Nonnos. Dionysiaca*, vol. 1: *Books 1-15* (Cambridge, MA: 1940) 2–533, at 430–432.

32   John, 21:25.

33   Mark, 16:17–18; cf. Efthymiadis S., "Collections of Miracles (Fifth–Fifteenth Centuries)", in idem (ed.), *The Ashgate Research Companion to Byzantine Hagiography*, vol. 2: *Genres and Contexts* (Farnham: 2014) 103–142, at 103.

34   Sometimes the miracle collections are appended to the saint's Life or *Encomium* with which they share an introduction.

35   *MT*, Preface, 1: τὰ σποράδην [...] τυγχάνοντα θαύματα. All translations from the *MT* are by S.F. Johnson, "The Miracles of Thekla", in Talbot A.M. – Johnson S.F. (trans.), *Miracle Tales from Byzantium*, Dumbarton Oaks Medieval Library 12 (Cambridge, MA – London: 2012) 1–201.

36   *MT*, Preface, 2; trans. Johnson, "The Miracles of Thekla" 5.

The need to collect miracles that are dispersed in different works also drives the author of the Prologue to the *MAP*. Likewise, the author of the prologue to the fifth series of the *MKD* mentions that he was motivated by a desire to add some more testimonies of acts of miraculous healing to those that were already circulating orally. Both the *MA* and those of Demetrios are said in their prologues to have been composed to thank God and glorify him. In the prologue to the third series of the *MKD*, the author addresses a certain Florentios, who is said to have asked him to write them down. According to Curtius, such alleged inspirations by a third party also belong to the repertory of topoi and should not be taken literally.[37]

All the authors describe in various ways how they will cope with the material they are to recount. The *Leitmotiv* is the enormous number of miracles performed by a given saint, which is evoked as a rule via the inexpressibility topos. In the *MT*, the author repeats in a somewhat obsessive manner that he can offer us but a sample of the miracles. He juggles phrases such as a 'very small portion', 'small collection', and 'not even a greater part of the whole'.[38] The author of the *MA* asserts that there are so 'many miracles of the martyr' that he is 'naturally at a loss to recall all of them since they are boundless in their multitude'.[39] In the prologue to the first series of the *MKD* we read that 'although the deeds of the saints are great and innumerable', the author 'will dare to recount a small portion of them and truly the smallest one, even if in an unbefitting way', which he 'put in this poor piece'.[40] From the Prologue to the third series we learn that 'a man faced with this multitude and excess of miracles refrains from writing'. In the substantial preface to the *Encomium of Kyros and John* (hereafter *EKJ*) which precedes the proper collection of their miracles,[41] Sophronios of Jerusalem says that he wrote of 'seven tens of miracles', although he 'should have had thousands of tens to write'.[42] In the prologue to the *MThT* the author rhetorically asks 'who could recount the cures of all sorts of diseases that took place there' and 'enumerate the people who

---

37   Such statements often accompany the modesty topos: Curtius, *European Literature* 85.

38   *MT*, Preface, 1; trans. Johnson, "The Miracles of Thekla" 3.

39   All translations from the *MA* are from V.S. Crisafulli and J.W. Nesbitt, *The Miracles of St. Artemios: A Collection of Miracle Stories by an Anonymous Author of Seventh-Century Byzantium* (Leiden – New York – Cologne: 1997).

40   All translations from the *MKD* are mine.

41   Sophronios of Jerusalem, *Encomium of Kyros and John*, ed. P. Bringel, *Sophrone de Jérusalem*, "Panégyrique des saints Cyr et Jean", *Patrologia Orientalis* 226 (Turnhout: 2008) 16–72.

42   All translations from the *EKJ* and *MKJ* are mine.

STUNNING WITH A LIST, DAZZLING WITH A CATALOGUE

enter there continually'.[43] Sophronios poses the same question in a passage that betrays a direct inspiration from Homer:

> Who is able to count the wonders accomplished by the saints, who would have a tongue bold enough or a mouth eloquent enough to relate them? No man, even if he had ten tongues and ten mouths and even if such a man had a breath of brass and a voice that cannot be broken.

> Τὰ δὲ τοῖς ἁγίοις ἐντεῦθεν τερατουργούμενα τίς ἱκανὸς ἀριθμήσασθαι, ἢ γλώττῃ τολμηρᾷ διηγήσασθαι, ἢ πολυρρήμονι φθέγξασθαι στόματι; Ἀνθρώπων μὲν οὐδείς, οὐδὲ εἰ δέκα μὲν εἶεν γλῶτταί τινι, δέκα δὲ στόματα, ψυχήν τε χαλκείαν καὶ φωνὴν ὁ τοιοῦτος ἄρρηκτον κτήσαιτο.[44]

In the prologue to the *Miracles of Demetrios* the author wonders where he should start his account of the martyr's incessant protection.[45] When explaining the order he has necessarily adopted, he expresses the fear that he will be accused of not doing justice to the saint; his only excuse is that he has but one tongue.[46] The miracle collections thus draw on the above-mentioned epic catalogues and transform the inexpressibility topos featured therein in its secular, rhetorical-literary use into its religious variant, which implies that its divine subject matter transcends all human discourse.[47]

Also frequently encountered is a rhetorical device intimately linked with the inexpressibility topos that Curtius calls 'affected modesty'. Through humble self-depreciation, the authors enhance the effect exerted by the uncountability of the miracles. We have already seen some evidence of this in the examples quoted above, such as when an author calls his work a 'poor piece' that is written in an 'unbefitting way', or when another only 'dares' to recount the miracles. Phrases of this kind are sometimes very frequent and still more elaborate. Sophronios expresses doubts both as to his rhetorical capability to render the tens of thousands of tens of miracles, and as to his audience's strength to listen to them.

---

43 *MThT*, Prologue, 58. All translations from the *MThT* are from J. Haldon, *A Tale of Two Saints: The Martyrdoms and Miracles of Saints Theodore 'the Recruit' and 'the General'. Critical Introduction, Translation and Commentary by John Haldon* (Liverpool: 2016).

44 *EKJ*, 30.

45 *MD*, Prologue, 6.

46 Ibidem, Prologue, 6.

47 Brook C., *The Expression of the Inexpressible in Eugenio Montale's Poetry: Metaphor, Negation and Silence* (Oxford: 2002) 2.

In Anastasios the Persian's collection, the author confesses that he is not able to adequately depict the glory of the martyr because of his own life, wasted in laziness and ignorance, and his lack of rhetorical skills. In the prologue of the third series of the *MKD*, the author says that the valor of the martyrs' miracles is beyond anyone's talent of speech, giving the eye which is too weak to look at the sun as a comparison. Likewise, in the *MThT*, the inexpressibility of the subject matter is suggested through the lack of sufficient time to retell it and the inadequacy of speech to encompass it.[48] The author of the prologue of the *MAP* uses a variant of this commonplace distinguished by Curtius,[49] when he humbly says that he will skip most of the miracles so as not to bore his listeners.

5   Metaphors for Infinity

Yet another device exploited in the *miracula* to express the plethora of miracles is the stock metaphor that draws on the natural world and is once again rooted in epic poetry. Most prominently, images of the sea and the sky are evoked as having no clear limits or dimensions. While Sophronios rather passingly mentions 'waves of healings' of the saints Kyros and John, nautical metaphors recur several times in the prologue of the first series of the *MKD*, which are used to describe a cultic shrine that is compared to an 'ocean of miracles' (πέλαγος θαυμάτων) and 'an inexhaustible and immeasurable and eternal spring or rather a sea' that 'pours forth miracles at any time' (ἀνεξάντλητος καὶ ἀκατάληπτος καὶ ἀέννανος πηγὴ μᾶλλον δὲ θάλασσα).[50] In the third series, depicting all the miracles is likened to measuring the sea and counting the stars.

Like the image of counting the waves or grains of sand, this simile is exploited in poetry, but in fact it also features as early as in Herodotus. He puts it into the mouth of the Delphic oracle, who told the Lydians that it 'knows the number of the grains of sand and the extent of the sea'.[51] In Artemios and Theodore Teron, another somewhat clichéd image is employed: one referring to a garden or meadow in bloom, which stands for the beauty and multitude of a saint's deeds. In the former, the author compares his eagerness to recount the miracles to the desire to share memories of beautiful views seen in a delightful park with trees and fragrant flowers. In the latter, Chrysippos of Jerusalem,

---

48   *MThT*, 58.

49   Curtius, *European Literature* 85.

50   *MKD*, 1st series, Prologue.

51   Herodotos, *Histories*, 1.47, trans. A. Godley, *Herodotus: The Histories* (Cambridge, MA – London: 1920) 55. Cf. Cariou, "Le topos de l'ineffable" 37 n. 34.

STUNNING WITH A LIST, DAZZLING WITH A CATALOGUE

alluding to the practice of crowning victors, wonders how to weave a crown for the martyr: whether the first blossoms should be provided by the meadow of his martyrdom or by that of his miracles.[52]

Both authors invoke the motifs traditionally used in titles of compilations and miscellaneous compositions, from the *Garland* (Στέφανος) by Meleager of Gadara, which formed the kernel of the later *Greek Anthology*, to variations on a similar floral or vegetal theme that were mocked already by Aulus Gellius.[53] Also an author of miscellanies, he dissociates himself from his predecessors, who in his opinion gave pretentious titles to their works. In the spirit of conscientious cataloguing, he ironically enumerates typical examples of such collections, among them those related to the idea of a group of trees, flowers, or plants in general, such as 'Woods' (*Silvarum*), 'Meads' (Λειμῶνας), or 'Field' (*Pratum*).[54]

Although these works vaguely allude to the topos of ideal landscape (*locus amoenus*), their late antique equivalents are much more explicit as to why they employ the image of the meadow as an umbrella concept for their collections. The most prominent example is John Moschos' *Spiritual Meadow*, where the author explains the symbolism of his work's title to his dedicatee Sophronios. He states that springtime meadows are most delightful prospects by virtue of the rich diversity of innumerable flowers, their colors and fragrances. His intention is thus to offer an equivalent delight composed of spiritually beneficial deeds of the fathers. The parallel drawn between flowers and miracles of holy men and saints gains a more concrete sense in a passage in the Thekla collection which describes the beauty of the martyr's shrine at Dalisandos.[55] An interesting modification of this canonical example of the *locus amoenus* topos is that the ideal landscape at Dalisandos is itself said to have miraculous healing powers that restore some sick people to health simply by virtue of their visiting that place.[56]

6   Holy Calculation

All the above-mentioned devices serve to express the multitude and diversity of the issues to be listed in the miracle collections, subsequently allowing the

---

52   *MThT*, 51.
53   Aulus Gellius, *Attic Nights*, ed. J.C. Rolfe, *The Attic Nights of Aulus Gellius: With an English Translation* (Cambridge, MA – London: 1927) XXVIII–XXX.
54   Ibidem.
55   *MT*, ch. 26.
56   Ibidem, ch. 26, 3.

authors to offer only a sample that gives a sense of the rest. To quote the author of the prologue of the third series of the MKD, we are given 'the chance to calculate, so to say, the total number of miracles, basing on these few' (ἀφορμὴν ἐκ τῶν ὀλίγων τὰ πάντα ὡς εἰπεῖν ἀναλογίζεσθαι θαύματα).[57] We may thus ask whether what we are offered is a representative sample or, in other words, what the selection criteria used by the compilers were. Authors generally have the credibility of their stories at heart. Thekla's collection is once again a most curious case in this respect, since its author keeps rather circularly repeating which miracle stories he decided to include, and why he chose them while excluding others. These passages are worth quoting at length here, as they convey well the sense of somewhat obsessive repetition that is characteristic of the style of the entire collection, which I will discuss below.

> This is not all of them [sc. miracles], and not even the greater part of the whole, but a very small portion, and only those that happened in my time or among those who lived a short time before us. And of these, again only a small portion of the whole, and only as many as I have been able to collect from reputable men and women, in order that the audience should not distrust the events we have previously described but, from the miracles she is performing even now and from those already performed, may reap the fruits of belief in her former struggles and contests. For this reason I have made mention of people, places, and names, so that the audience has no doubts about these events, but rather can consider them from close up and examine the truth of what I have said.

> οὐ πάντα μέν, ἀλλ᾽ οὐδὲ τὸ πολλοστὸν τῶν πάντων μέρος, ὀλίγιστα δὲ παντελῶς, καὶ τὰ καθ᾽ ἡμᾶς καὶ τοῖς ὀλίγῳ πρὸ ἡμῶν συμβεβηκότα μόνον· καὶ τούτων δὲ ὀλίγιστα πάλιν καὶ ὅσα παρ᾽ ἀληθευόντων ἀνδρῶν ἢ γυναικῶν ἀναλέξασθαι ἰσχύσαμεν, ὅπως ἐξῇ τοῖς ἐντυγχάνουσι μηδὲ περὶ ὧν προειρήκαμεν ἀπιστεῖν, ἀλλ᾽ ἐκ τῶν νῦν ἐπιτελουμένων τε καὶ ἐπιτελεσθέντων ἤδη θαυμάτων καὶ τὰς περὶ τῶν προλαβόντων αὐτῆς ἀγώνων καὶ ἀθλήσεων πίστεις καρποῦσθαι. Διὰ τοῦτο δὲ προσώπων καὶ τόπων καὶ ὀνομάτων ἐμνημονεύσαμεν, ὥστε μηδὲ περὶ αὐτῶν τοὺς ἐντυγχάνοντας ἀμφιβάλλειν, ἀλλ᾽ ἐγγύθεν ἔχειν καὶ ποιεῖσθαι τὴν περὶ ὧν εἰρήκαμεν ἐξέτασιν τῆς ἀληθείας.[58]

This somewhat muddled piece of prose is intended to dazzle us with the alleged astronomically large number of miracles, and eventually concludes

---

57   MKD, 3rd series, Prologue.
58   MT, Preface, 1; trans. Johnson, "The Miracles of Thekla" 3.

STUNNING WITH A LIST, DAZZLING WITH A CATALOGUE 173

that the sample offered was selected with credibility as the criterion, guaranteed by the reputation of the author's sources. The logical conclusion to be drawn from this is that most of this bulk of miracles is unreliable, particularly as the author sums up in the last paragraph of his preface:

> In order that we may relate a very few of all these many miracles, let me recount those which we have known hitherto, which are commonly acknowledged by many, and which we all know and have experienced, some of us to our own personal benefit, while others have heard tell from those who themselves benefited.

> Καὶ ἵνα ἐκ πάνυ πολλῶν ἄγαν ὀλίγα εἴπωμεν, φέρε εἴπωμεν ἅ τε ἡμεῖς ἴσμεν τέως, ἅ τε συνομολογεῖται τοῖς πολλοῖς, καὶ ὧν πάντες ἴστορές τε καὶ ἐν πείρᾳ καθεστήκαμεν, οἱ μὲν καὶ αὐτῷ τῷ εὖ παθεῖν, οἱ δὲ καὶ παρ' αὐτῶν τῶν εὖ πεπονθότων ἀκηκοότες.[59]

In the prologue of the third series of the MKD the author also relies on his own experience and hearsay obtained during his sojourn in the healing shrine where the relics of the martyrs were deposited. Likewise, in the MA, the author applies the criterion of time and selects those miracles performed in his generation that are known to him personally and from hearsay in order to ensure credibility. In the MThT it is the vague concept of the 'appropriateness of the tale' (πρὸς τὸ τοῦ λόγου μέτρον) that determines which miracles, elsewhere described as 'fitting',[60] are included and which are not. Since almost all of them concern a theft, this theme may have been a tacit selection criterion. In the MAP, the author does not want us to disbelieve what he recounts, and therefore he too chooses the miracles of his times.[61] In a similar manner, in the MD the author rejects ancient miracles and includes those known to him either from his own experience or credible witnesses.[62]

Having analyzed the selection criteria applied by the authors of the miracle collections, let us now calculate, from the alleged vastness, the actual number of miracles we are offered. The most impressive is the collection assembled by Sophronios in his MKJ, numbering seventy, while one of the smallest is that for Theodore Teron, which consists of just twelve tales. Only the authors of these two texts explain the arithmetic behind these particular numbers, citing

---

59   MT, Preface, 9; trans. Johnson, "The Miracles of Thekla" 11.
60   MThT, 58.
61   MAP, Prologue, 3.
62   MD, Prologue, 8.

174   DOROSZEWSKA

their mystical meaning. The latter states that twelve is the most holy number and thus best suits the martyr's crown. The former provides more complicated mathematical operations, multiplying the mystic number seven by the perfect number ten. Thekla's and Artemios' collections are also quite large, with their forty-six and forty-five miracles respectively.

There is, however, yet another means of enhancing the impression of numerousness of miracles performed by the saints. In paradoxographical collections, we encounter the passionless and monotonous καί that begins each successive entry according to the poetics of etcetera, and which creates an overall feeling of an infinite number of wondrous 'facts'. In the *miracula*, in turn, the authors play with the concept of sequence and order, frequently evoking images of haste and the pressure that they exerted on themselves, or even that the miracles themselves exerted, each one urging that it be told. This strategy is employed in the last paragraph (or just words) of various miracle tales, as in the following examples:

> *MT*, ch. 21, 1: Let us pass again to the accomplishment of another miracle.[63]

> Ἰτέον δὲ καὶ πρὸς ἑτέρου πάλιν θαύματος ἔργον.

> *MT*, ch. 23, 1: Who would wish to overlook the miracle accomplished on Pausikakos' behalf?[64]

> Τὴν δὲ κατὰ Παυσίκακον θαυματουργίαν, τίς ἂν ἑκὼν παραδράμοι;

> *MT*, ch. 12, 8 (the last sentence of the tale): These events concluded at this point [...] and now I will discuss that which I was hastening to tell long ago.[65]

> Καὶ ταῦτα μὲν εἰς τοῦτο ἔληξε [...] ἐφ' ὃ δὲ καὶ πάλαι ἠπειγόμην ῥητέον.

> *MT*, ch. 13, 4 (the last paragraph of the tale): While I am still dazzled by the radiance of this miracle, another miracle shines forth which happened in the past [...]. Therefore let us not delay, but since the miracle is

---

63   Trans. Johnson, "The Miracles of Thekla" 89.
64   Ibidem, 93.
65   Ibidem, 55.

STUNNING WITH A LIST, DAZZLING WITH A CATALOGUE

impatient to bound swiftly into view, let us grant it speed. What, then, is this miracle?[66]

Ἔτι δέ με ὑπὸ τῆς αἴγλης τοῦδε τοῦ θαύματος καταλαμπόμενον, θαῦμα ἕτερον ὑπολάμψαν ποτὲ γεγονὸς [...]. Μήτε οὖν ἡμεῖς μελλήσωμεν, καὶ τῷ θᾶττον βουλομένῳ προπηδῆσαι θαύματι χαρισώμεθα τάχος. Ποῖον δὲ δὴ τοῦτό ἐστιν;

MKJ, ch. 8, 1: Why and for how long will we leave Christodoros waiting?

Τί δὲ καὶ τίνος ἄχρι καταλείψομεν τὸν Χριστόδωρον;

MKJ, ch. 22, 1: Why do we put off the illustrious Sarapammon, even though we do not want to omit him?

Τί δὲ τὸν λαμπρὸν Σαραπάμμωνα μέλλομεν, εἴπερ αὐτὸν παρελθεῖν οὐ βουλόμεθα;

MKD, ch. 2, 11: Therefore the extraordinary grace of their healings [...] pushes [me] to recount another of their miracles.

ὅθεν ἡ τῶν ἰαμάτων αὐτῶν ὑπερβάλλουσα χάρις [...] ἄγει εἰς ἑτέρου θαύματος αὐτῶν διήγησιν.

The closing part of a tale is sometimes coupled with the first words of the next tale, as illustrated by the following examples:

MKJ, ch. 1, 14 (the last words of the story of Ammonios): Let us praise the saints [...] and then pass to their other astonishing healings.

Καὶ ἡμεῖς δὲ τοὺς ἁγίους ὑμνήσαντες [...], ἐπ' ἄλλας ἀξιαγάστους αὐτῶν ἰατρείας χωρήσωμεν.

MKJ, ch. 2, 1 (the beginning of the next tale): After Ammonios, Theodoros enters our account.

Θεόδωρος δὲ μετὰ Ἀμμώνιον εἰς διήγησιν πρόεισι.

---

66   Ibidem, 59.

Alternatively, the preceding tale can be briefly concluded in the opening of the next:

> MKD, ch. 6, 1: When the aforementioned man praised the gift from the servants of Christ Kosmas and Damian and left their dwelling, another man arrived at the far-famed saints' home.

> τοῦ προειρημένου τοίνυν ἀπολαύσαντος καθὰ ἔφαμεν τῆς τῶν θεραπόντων τοῦ Χριστοῦ Κοσμᾶ καὶ Δαμιανοῦ παροχῆς καὶ τὸν ἴδιον οἶκον καταλαβόντος ἕτερος ἀνὴρ ἐφίσταται τῷ περιβοήτῳ τῶν ἁγίων τούτῳ οἴκῳ.

Nevertheless, sometimes the links between neighboring miracles are articulated in a more moderate manner. This is the case when an author proposes to add another miracle to those he has already gathered, as in Theodore Teron's collection:

> 1. Come, therefore, let us add to these things something no less wondrous or joyful.

> Φέρε οὖν τούτοις ἐπισυνάψωμέν τι καὶ ἕτερον οὐκ ἐλάττονος οὔτε θαύματος, οὔτε χάριτος.[67]

> 2. Hear now in addition another wonderful deed.

> Ἀκούσατε ἔτι τούτοις ἕτερον θαυμαστὸν λίαν.[68]

> 4. Would you like to know another tale of sympathy surpassing all bounds?

> Βούλεσθε δὲ καὶ ἑτέραν ἰδεῖν συμπάθειαν πᾶσαν παραδραμοῦσαν ὑπερβολήν;[69]

While in Artemios' collection we find no trace of this strategy at all, in Anastasios the Persian miracles are linked both by the figure of the monk who accompanied the martyr's relics in their journey (e.g. at the beginning of ch. 6: 'The above-mentioned [*sc.* in the previous account] monk took the relics [...]'; Λαβὼν οὖν ὁ προρρηθεὶς μοναχὸς τὸ ἅγιον λείψανον [...]) and by references to events that were recounted in the preceding miracle, like the construction of

---

67   *Encomium of Saint Theodore Teron*, 63; trans. Haldon, *Tale* 69.
68   *Encomium of Saint Theodore Teron*, 64; trans. Haldon, *Tale* 70.
69   *Encomium of Saint Theodore Teron*, 68; trans. Haldon, *Tale* 73.

the Tetrapylon dedicated to the saint, which is mentioned in the beginning of ch. 8, but described in ch. 7.[70]

This strategy, whose primary function is to link the tales to each other, is also successfully employed to enhance the impression of a vast number of miracles that seem to press on and approach one after the other as if on a production line before jumping straight under the author's pen. As we have seen, the authors of the miracle collections draw on a rich repertoire of literary devices and strategies to dazzle us with the idea of limitless divine powers that work through the saints. They exploit commonplaces and stock metaphors to promote the image of the saints as potent and holy intercessors who grant incalculable graces to their followers.

7   Lists of Lists, Lists in Lists

Miracle collections certainly catalogue not only the miracles themselves but also other data. Many scholars, predominantly historians, comb them in search of the evidence on religious, social, and cultural life recorded there. In this way they make their own lists. For example, the introductory essays to the MA provide a table that comprises lists of the names of the miracle recipients, as well as their occupations, ages, and places of origin and residence. There follows another list, of Artemios' disguised epiphanies, which enumerates the forms and garb the martyr adopted in contacts with his patients. It is possible to imagine many more such lists. The miracles themselves are lists of lists of various facts or phenomena, such as diseases, healing treatments and medications, or vices and sins. What scholars often do with the collections is reduce them to a dry list of facts, a move that resembles the work of paradoxographers, but with the opposite vector. Paradoxographers squeezed the essence out of the marvelous, while scholars often truncate the marvelous to get to the bare data, such as biographical details.

Listing can be not only a form, but also a rhetorical device, called enumeration. Thekla's miracle collection exploits this technique particularly often, which can be viewed as a hallmark of its style, but we also sporadically find it in Demetrios.[71] In the prologue to the MT, the author begins his refutation of the rival pagan collections of oracles by listing cultic shrines linked to them:

---

70   *MAP*, ch. 6.

71   Cf. Dagron G., *Vie et miracles de sainte Thècle: Texte grec, traduction et commentaire*, Subsidia hagiographica 62 (Brussels: 1978) 158.

The priests and attendants of the soothsaying demons and the interpreters of the Pythian portents – I mean the celebrated Zeus in Dodona, of the Pythian Apollo in Delphi, especially his prophet by the waters of the Kastalian spring, of Asclepius in Pergamum, Epidaurus, and our neighbor Aigai – have recorded many oracles about many subjects and cures of diseases. Among these, some are myths, some fictions, and some, inventions of their authors, aiming to attribute potency, strength, and foreknowledge to the demons.

Ὑποφῆται μὲν καὶ ὑπηρέται δαιμόνων χρησμολόγων καὶ πυθικῶν τερατευμάτων ἐξηγηταί, τοῦ ἐν Δωδώνῃ θρυλουμένου λέγω Διός, τοῦ πυθικοῦ καὶ ἐν Δελφοῖς Ἀπόλλωνος, ἢ καὶ τοῦ παρὰ τὰ Κασταλίας νάματα ποιουμένου τὰς μαντείας, τοῦ ἐν Περγάμῳ καὶ ἐν Ἐπιδαύρῳ ἢ καὶ ἐν Αἰγαῖς ταύταις Ἀσκληπιοῦ, πολλὰ περὶ πολλῶν ἀναγεγράφασι χρηστήριά τε καὶ παθῶν λυτήρια. Ὧν τὰ μέν εἰσι μῦθοι καὶ πλάσματα καὶ αὐτῶν τῶν συγγεγραφότων κομψεύματα, ἐνέργειαν καὶ ἰσχύν τινα καὶ πρόγνωσιν βουλομένων περιθεῖναι τοῖς δαίμοσι.[72]

Here, the author takes a broad view of the phenomenon of the oracle, listing the most important ones to eventually discredit them all as pure fraud. Further on, he concludes his polemic by juxtaposing in neat symmetry a concise list of invectives against the prophecies of pagan demons with an analogous catalogue of the merits of Christian saints:

But the predictions of demons, to list (εἰπεῖν) only a few out of many, are such as the following: deceitful, evil, dishonest, hollow, treacherous, possessing much that is obscure and fraudulent. But of what nature, then, are the healings and oracular sayings of the saints? Clear, true, simple, holy, complete, and truly worthy of the God who has granted them.

Ἀλλὰ τὰ μὲν τῶν δαιμόνων, ὡς ἐκ πάνυ πολλῶν ὀλίγα εἰπεῖν, τοιαῦτα· ἀπατηλά, πονηρά, κίβδηλα, ὕπουλα, δολερά, πολὺ τὸ ἀχλυῶδες καὶ διεψευσμένον ἔχοντα. Τὰ δὲ τῶν ἁγίων ἄρα λοιπὸν ἰάματα καὶ θεσπίσματα ποῖα; Σαφῆ, ἀληθῆ, ἁπλᾶ, ἅγια, ὁλόκληρα καὶ τοῦ δεδωκότος θεοῦ ἀληθῶς ἐπάξια.[73]

We are thus offered two parallel catalogues of features pertaining to the supernatural activities of the good and the evil side, preceded by an allusion to the inexpressibility topos.

---

72 *MT*, Preface, 2; trans. Johnson, "The Miracles of Thekla" 5.
73 *MT*, Preface, 6; trans. Johnson, "The Miracles of Thekla" 9.

The peak of rhetorical enumeration, however, is reached in the description of Thekla's thaumaturgical activities. We could very easily imagine this passage written graphically in the form of a list, like this:

Of these saints the greatest witness is Thekla,
always present,
always making visitation,
continually hearkening to those who make entreaty,
watching over all people bountifully –
those who are physically sound,
those who are unwell,
those who are of good cheer,
those who are despondent,
sailors,
wayfarers,
those in danger,
those safe from danger,
individually,
in groups,
house by house,
people by people,
city by city,
district by district,
foreigners and citizens alike,
locals and aliens,
men and women,
masters and servants,
the elderly and the young,
the wealthy and the poor,
those in power,
those in the military,
those in the courts,
those at war,
those at peace.

Τούτων τῶν ἁγίων καὶ ἡ μεγίστη μάρτυς ἐστὶ Θέκλα,
ἀεὶ παροῦσα,
ἀεὶ φοιτῶσα,
τῶν δεομένων ἐπαΐουσα πάντοτε,
καὶ πάντας ἀφθόνως ἐφορῶσα,

180 DOROSZEWSKA

ὑγιαίνοντας,
ἀρρωστοῦντας,
εὐθυμοῦντας,
ἀθυμοῦντας,
πλέοντας,
ὁδοιποροῦντας,
κινδυνεύοντας,
μὴ κινδυνεύοντας,
κατὰ ἕνα,
κατὰ πολλούς,
κατὰ οἴκους,
κατὰ γένη,
κατὰ πόλεις,
κατὰ δήμους,
ξένους ὁμοίως καὶ πολίτας,
ἐγχωρίους καὶ ὑπερορίους,
ἄνδρας καὶ γυναῖκας,
δεσπότας καὶ οἰκέτας,
ἀφηλικεστέρους καὶ νέους,
πλουσίους καὶ πένητας,
τοὺς ἐν ἀρχαῖς,
τοὺς ἐν στρατείαις,
τοὺς ἐν δίκαις,
τοὺς ἐν πολέμοις,
τοὺς ἐν εἰρήνῃ.[74]

It draws on panegyric enumeration, focused here on promoting the martyr's all-encompassing protection and patronage, but it clearly evokes a prayer in this context – like a litany or a chaplet. The accumulation of Thekla's properties and attributes, intriguingly described through the naming of the groups of her followers, lends itself to rhythmic recitation, which hints at another possible aspect of this rhetorical device, namely a meditative one.

The above passage resonates with another, which once again opens with the inexpressibility topos, strengthened by the metaphor of snowflakes falling on the ground, which the miracles performed by Thekla are likened to by virtue of their uncountability. It concludes with a brief categorization of the addressees of Thekla's mercy and beneficial activity, who include 'all nations, all races, all cities, all towns, all fields and houses, all who make supplication to the martyr':

---

74   *MT*, Preface, 6; trans. Johnson, "The Miracles of Thekla" 9.

STUNNING WITH A LIST, DAZZLING WITH A CATALOGUE

It would be an impossible feat to discover all the miracles and, once they have been recovered, to recount them. In the same way, when snowflakes fall thickly upon the earth, since God sent the storm, it is impossible to say how many of them God lets fall. So also the number of Thekla's miracles is incalculable. For she did not cease working miracles in the past, nor will she ever cease doing so, since she is good and is always inclined to mercy toward each person who supplicates her. This means everyone: all nations, all races, all cities, all towns, all fields and houses, all who make supplication to the martyr.

Καὶ γὰρ τῶν ἀμηχάνων εὑρεῖν τε πάντα καὶ εὑρόντα εἰπεῖν· ὥσπερ γὰρ ὅτε νιφάδες ἐπὶ γῆς φέρονται πολλάκις ὕοντος τοῦ Θεοῦ τῶν ἀμηχάνων ἐστὶ φράσαι πόσας ταύτας ἀφίησιν ὁ Θεός, οὕτω καὶ τῶν Θέκλας θαυμάτων ἀνεξερεύνητος ὁ ἀριθμός· οὔτε γὰρ ἔληξεν, οὔτε μὴν λήξει ποτὲ τοῦ θαυματουργεῖν, ἀγαθή τε οὖσα καὶ πρὸς ἕκαστον ἀεὶ τῶν αἰτούντων ἐπικαμπτομένη. Οὗτοι δέ εἰσι πάντες ἄνθρωποι· ὅσα γὰρ ἔθνη, ὅσα γένη, ὅσαι πόλεις, ὅσαι κῶμαι, ὅσοι ἀγροὶ καὶ οἶκοι, πάντες τῆς μάρτυρος δέονται.[75]

A few lines on, the same rhetoric recurs when all the places embraced by the martyr's miraculous powers are listed, namely mountains, plains, a sea, stops along a route, rivers, lakes, the Maeotis, the Pillars of Herakles, and the Ocean itself:

For there is nothing which restricts her grace and power from reaching every place and hearing every request: neither mountains, nor plains, nor sea, nor stops around a route (however numerous they may be), nor overflowing rivers, nor lakes which cover a great part of the earth, neither the Maeotis, nor the Pillars of Herakles, and not even the immense Ocean itself.

Οὔτε γὰρ εἴργει τὴν χάριν αὐτῆς καὶ δύναμιν οὐδὲν μὴ οὐκ ἐπὶ πάντα φοιτᾶν καὶ πάντων ἀκούειν, οὐκ ὄρη, οὐ πεδία, οὐ θάλαττα, οὐχ ὁδοῦ σταθμοὶ τόσοι καὶ τόσοι, οὐ ποταμοὶ πελαγίζοντες, οὐ λίμναι ἐπὶ πολὺ τῆς γῆς ἡπλωμέναι, οὐχ ἡ Μαιῶτις, οὐχ Ἡράκλειοι στῆλαι, οὐδ' αὐτὸς ὁ μέγιστος Ὠκεανός.[76]

A similar concept is employed in yet another passage, which specifies the groups of people who assembled in Seleukeia to celebrate the martyr's festival:

---

75   *MT*, ch. 10, 3; trans. Johnson, "The Miracles of Thekla" 41.
76   Ibidem.

On this day, everyone, both citizen and foreigner, man, woman, and child, both ruler and ruled, general and soldier, magistrate and private citizen, young and old, seaman and farmer, simply everyone who was zealous would eagerly hasten to assemble.

Ἐν ταύτῃ πᾶς τις ἐπείγεται καὶ ἀστὸς καὶ ξένος, καὶ ἀνὴρ καὶ γυνὴ καὶ παιδίον, καὶ ἄρχων καὶ ἀρχόμενος, καὶ στρατηγὸς καὶ στρατιώτης, καὶ δημαγωγὸς καὶ ἰδιώτης, καὶ νέος καὶ πρεσβύτης, καὶ ναυτίλος καὶ γεωργός, καὶ πᾶς τις ἁπλῶς πρόθυμος συλλεγῆναι σπουδαιότερον.[77]

Further on, the assembled talk about the festivities, and this is again framed as an enumeration, which then flows smoothly into another list presenting people's actions that made up the overall holiday confusion:

One spoke about its brilliance and splendor, another about the immense multitude of people that gathered together, another about the assembly of so many bishops, another about the artistic talent of the preachers, another about the melodiousness of the psalmody, another about the length of the night vigil, another about the well-paced arrangement of the rest of the liturgy, another about the intensity of those who prayed, another about the press of the crowd, another about the excessive stifling heat, another about the jostling back and forth during the awesome mysteries, as some were just coming forward, others already leaving, others coming back in again, and others withdrawing again, all the while shouting, competing with each other, entangled one with another and not ceding ground to others in the slightest because each wanted to be the first to partake of the holy elements.

ὁ μὲν τὸ λαμπρὸν αὐτῆς καὶ φαιδρόν, ὁ δὲ τῶν συνεληλυθότων τὸ μυρίον πλῆθος, ὁ δὲ τῶν ἀρχιερέων τὸν πολὺν σύλλογον, ὁ δὲ τῶν διδασκάλων τὸ εὔμουσον, ὁ δὲ τῆς ψαλμῳδίας τὸ εὔηχον, ὁ δὲ τῆς νυκτεγερσίας τὸ διαρκές, ὁ δὲ τῆς λοιπῆς λειτουργίας τὸ τεταγμένον καὶ εὔρυθμον, ὁ δὲ τῶν εὐχομένων τὸ ἔντονον, ὁ δὲ καὶ τοῦ ὄχλου τὸν ὠθισμόν, ὁ δὲ καὶ τοῦ πνίγους τὴν ὑπερβολήν, ὁ δὲ καὶ τῶν ἐπὶ τῆς φρικτῆς μυσταγωγίας τὴν ἔνστασιν ἅμα καὶ σύστασιν τῶν ἄρτι προσιόντων, τῶν ἤδη ἀπιόντων, τῶν ἐπεισιόντων πάλιν, τῶν ὑποχωρούντων αὖθις, τῶν

---

77   *MT*, ch. 33, 1; trans. Johnson, "The Miracles of Thekla" 133.

STUNNING WITH A LIST, DAZZLING WITH A CATALOGUE   183

βοώντων, τῶν φιλονεικούντων, τῶν ἀλλήλοις ἐμπλεκομένων καὶ μὴ εἰκόντων ἀλλήλοις διὰ τὸ πρῶτός τις μάλιστα βούλεσθαι μετασχεῖν τῶν ἁγιασμάτων.[78]

We are also provided with a list of general saintly powers, which is immediately mirrored in a catalogue that shows how Thekla used them:

> They could accomplish through God's grace and power such great miracles as may require his special assistance, through intercession, consolation, and entreaty on behalf of nations, cities, races and peoples, against plagues, famines, wars, droughts, earthquakes, and as many disasters as the hand of God alone can mightily subdue and alleviate. Appropriately also, the great martyr – since she can accomplish great things and was appointed for this purpose by our common king Christ – often halted famine, put an end to plague, quenched drought, terminated war, handed over enemies, saved cities, protected houses, and gave out bountifully, to the collective and to each individual, the very things which each asked for.

> τὰ δὲ καὶ διὰ τῆς αὐτοῦ χάριτος καὶ δυνάμεως μεγαλουργεῖν ὅσα καὶ τῆς αὐτοῦ μάλιστα δεῖται βοηθείας, πρεσβεύοντας, παρακαλοῦντας, δυσωποῦντας ὑπὲρ ἐθνῶν, ὑπὲρ πόλεων, ὑπὲρ γενῶν καὶ δήμων, κατὰ λοιμῶν καὶ λιμῶν καὶ πολέμων καὶ αὐχμῶν καὶ σεισμῶν καὶ ὅσων οἷόν τε μάλιστα τὴν τοῦ Θεοῦ χεῖρα μόνην ὑπερέχειν τε καὶ ἀντιλαβέσθαι κραταιῶς. Εἰκότως οὖν καὶ ἡ μεγάλη μάρτυς, ὡς μεγάλα τε δυναμένη καὶ ἐπὶ τοῦτο ταχθεῖσα παρὰ τοῦ κοινοῦ βασιλέως Χριστοῦ, πολλάκις καὶ λιμὸν ἔπαυσε, καὶ λοιμὸν ἔλυσε, καὶ αὐχμὸν ἔσβεσε, καὶ πόλεμον ἔθραυσε, καὶ πολεμίους παρέδωκε, καὶ πόλεις ἔσωσε, καὶ οἴκους ἐφύλαξε, καὶ κοινῇ τε πᾶσι καὶ τοῖς καθ᾽ ἕκαστον ἅπερ ἕκαστος ᾔτησεν ἀφθόνως ἔδωκε.[79]

Another small catalogue encompasses all the animal species affected by a plague that were eventually healed by Thekla ('mules, horses, cows, donkeys, sheep, and simply every species of livestock'; ὀρέας, ἵππους, βόας, ὄνους, πρόβατα, καὶ πάντα ἁπλῶς ὅσα τῆς τῶν βοσκημάτων ἐστὶ φύσεως) and which the author does not fail to list again even more accurately in an image depicting them filling all the roads and hastening to the martyr's shrine: 'One could see that every path, as well as every highway, leading to this one spot from the flatlands and

---

78   *MT*, ch. 33, 2; trans. Johnson, "The Miracles of Thekla" 133. Cf. another image of crowds gathering for the martyr's festival in ch. 29, 10.

79   *MT*, ch. 4, 3–4; trans. Johnson, "Miracles of Thekla" 19 and 21.

the high places alike, was filled with horses, mules, cows, sheep, goats, donkeys, and even dogs and pigs' (Ἦν γοῦν ἰδεῖν πᾶσαν μὲν ἀτραπόν, πᾶσαν δὲ λεωφόρον, ἐκ τῶν ὑπτίων καὶ ὑπερτέρων τόπων ὧδέ τε βλέπουσαν καὶ ὧδε ἄγουσαν, καὶ πλή-θουσαν ἵππων, ὀρέων, βοῶν, προβάτων, αἰγῶν, ὄνων, ἤδη δὲ καὶ κυνῶν καὶ συῶν).[80]

Eventually, we are offered a catalogue of holy men and women who followed Thekla in ascetism. It is introduced by yet another instance of the inexpressibility topos:

> Her [Thekla's] miracles are not few, not even many, but quite simply of an infinite number. It is not possible for me to sprout wings or become strong as steel and cover every land and sea so as to make my collection from each city, or region, or village, or house. For neither would the collection be possible for me, nor would the composition be feasible, nor my life long enough to do justice to such an infinite multitude of miracles.

> Ἀλλ' οὔτε ὀλίγα, οὔτε πολλῶν πλείονα, οὔτε ὅλως ἀριθμητά ἐστιν. Οὔτε δ' ἐμοὶ δυνατὸν πτηνῷ τὴν φύσιν ἢ ἀδαμαντίνῳ γενέσθαι, καὶ διὰ πάσης χωρῆσαι γῆς καὶ θαλάσσης, ὡς ἐξ ἑκάστης πόλεως ἢ χώρας ἢ κώμης ἢ οἰκίας ἀναλέξασθαι· μήτε γὰρ ἂν τὴν συλλογὴν γενέσθαι μοι δυνατήν, μήτε τὴν συγγραφὴν ἐφικτήν, μήτε τὴν ζωὴν οὕτω μακρὰν ὡς ἐξαρκέσαι τοσούτῳ καὶ οὕτως ἀπείρῳ πλήθει θαυμάτων.[81]

The author then begins to list and discuss individuals who have displayed extraordinary virtue, only to conclude his enumeration of female characters with an overt reference to Hesiod's *Catalogue of Women*:[82]

> Among the women are, in turn, Marthana, Xenarchis, our own Dionysia, Sosanna, Theodoule, and all the others whom time does not permit me to name, even if I wished, like Hesiod, to write a catalogue of the most distinguished women of our time.

> Καὶ τῶν γυναικῶν δ' αὖ πάλιν τὴν Μαρθάναν, τὴν Ξεναρχίδα, τὴν Διονυσίαν ταύτην, τὴν Σωσάνναν, τὴν Θεοδούλην, τὰς ἄλλας πάσας, ἃς οὔτε καταλέγειν μοι καιρός, εἰ μήπου καθ' Ἡσίοδον ἄρα καὶ αὐτὸς βουλοίμην γυναικῶν ἀρίστων ἄρτι κατάλογον γράφειν.[83]

---

80   *MT*, ch. 36, 1 and 3: trans. Johnson, "Miracles of Thekla" 147 and 151.
81   *MT*, ch. 44, 3; trans. Johnson, "Miracles of Thekla" 173.
82   On this work of Hesiod, now fragmentary, see West M., *Hesiodic Catalogue of Women: Its Nature, Structure, and Origins* (Oxford: 1985).
83   *MT*, ch. 44, 3; trans. Johnson, "Miracles of Thekla" 175.

STUNNING WITH A LIST, DAZZLING WITH A CATALOGUE 185

This paragraph betrays direct inspiration from the practice of cataloguing and the form of the catalogue, pointing to the most classical example of this genre as its model. This emphasizes all the more the conscious use of this form of expression underlying the entire collection.

This rhetoric of enumeration thus permeates all parts of the work.[84] Its ubiquity is a hallmark of the authorial style, which may partially have a psychological explanation. There is one significant passage depicting the author's dream that, if taken to be authentic, may give us a small insight into his mind. It is actually more of a nightmare featuring Thekla, in which he is attacked by a swarm of wasps:[85] 'Having fallen asleep only a little [...] I saw many terrible wasps brandishing their stingers, pointing them at me like spears'; (Μικρὸν δὲ ὅσον ἀποκαθευδήσας [...] ὁρῶ σφῆκας πολλούς τε καὶ δεινοὺς καὶ τὰ κέντρα ἠρκότας καὶ ὥσπερ αἰχμὰς προτείνοντας κατ' ἐμοῦ).[86] This image of an uncountable number of dangerous objects encircling the subject is very telling. However, his fear gives way to relief when the martyr springs into action to save him. Inevitably, this scene is also given in the form of a catalogue:

> After entering and witnessing the wasps' attack against me, taking the top part of her *himation*, which covered her head as well as the rest of the body, and swinging it around with her hand, she scared away the great swarm of wasps, destroyed them, trampled them with her feet, and set me free from all those terrible enemies.

> ἐπεισελθοῦσαν δὲ καὶ θεασαμένην τὸν κατ' ἐμοῦ τῶν σφηκῶν πόλεμον, καὶ λαβομένην ἄκρου τοῦ ἱματίου τοῦ τὴν κεφαλὴν μετὰ καὶ τοῦ λοιποῦ σκέποντος σώματος καὶ περιστρέψασαν τῇ χειρί, τὸν πολὺν ἐκεῖνον ὅμαδον τῶν σφηκῶν ἀποσοβῆσαί τε καὶ καθελεῖν καὶ συμπατῆσαι τοῖς ποσί, καὶ ἐμὲ πάντων ἐκείνων ἐλευθερῶσαι τῶν δεινῶν πολεμίων.[87]

The fear of plethoras of things, perhaps bordering on *horror vacui*, may shed some light on the somewhat obsessive and circular manner of writing abundantly manifested in Thekla's collection. Such frequent passages based on enumeration nonetheless seem to be simply a favorite device of an author with a penchant for rhetorical display. However, it cannot be ruled out that he composed his work with recitation in mind, and that the miracle tales were meant

---

84   And, as Dagron, *Vie et miracles de sainte Thècle* 158, observes, also in the *Life of Thekla*, see the following passages: ch. 6, 42–48, ch. 27, 40–45.

85   A discussion of this dream is provided in Chapter 5.

86   *MT*, ch. 12, 2; trans. Johnson, "Miracles of Thekla" 49, slightly modified.

87   *MT*, ch. 12, 2; trans. Johnson, "Miracles of Thekla" 49.

186 DOROSZEWSKA

to be read aloud in the shrine. In any case, they are all intended to emphasize Thekla's role as a patron of an infinite number of both individuals and entire social groups, and even animals, and as a protector against innumerable misfortunes and evils, with geographically limitless thaumaturgical powers; all this is in tune with her boundless miracles.

A similar enumerative technique is also occasionally employed in the MD. In particular, it features in several passages of the first miracle narrative. In one of them, Satan launches an attack on Marianos, an eparch of Illyria, trying to drive him to commit the seven deadly sins one by one, each time without success. Having failed in this, he bitterly states:

> In your case, gluttony has been subdued; the unbridled passion for carnal pleasures has been tamed; avarice has been trampled down; anger has been overwhelmed by gentleness; worldly sorrow has been banished by hope of immortality; the acedia of the virtues, through faith and its sister, that is, perseverance, has died; vanity, or in other words the love of fame and praise, has been destroyed by concealment of the virtues.

> παρὰ σοῦ ἡ γαστριμαργία δεδούλωται, τὸ τῆς σαρκὸς ἀκρατὲς τῆς φιληδονίας πάθος πεπέδηται, ἡ φιλαργυρία πεπάτηται, ὁ θυμὸς ὑπὸ τῆς πραότητος κατεπόθη, ἡ λύπη τῶν κοσμικῶν τῇ τῆς ἀφθαρσίας ἐλπίδι διερράγη, ἡ ἀκηδία τῶν ἀρετῶν διὰ τῆς πίστεως καὶ τῆς θυγατρὸς αὐτῆς, λέγω δὴ τῆς ὑπομονῆς, ἐνεκρώθη, ἡ κενοδοξία, ταυτὸ δὲ εἰπεῖν φιλοδοξία, καὶ ἀνθρωπαρέσκεια τῷ κρυφίῳ τῶν ἀρετῶν ἐξαπόλωλε.[88]

The effect of this panegyric, which is based on enumeration of the seven deadly sins avoided by the addressee, is reinforced by the very figure of the speaker, i.e. the devil himself. Further on, Marianos glorifies God, offering Him the following prayer:

> You are the teacher of knowledge to man, maker of the soul and shaper of the body and connector of their harmony and governor of their permanence and manager of their profitable separation, and provider and *thaumatourgos* of their re-formation in resurrection and unconfused union and eternal life in immortality.

> σὺ εἶ ὁ θεὸς ὁ διδάσκων ἄνθρωπον γνῶσιν, ὁ τῆς ψυχῆς ποιητὴς καὶ τοῦ σώματος πλάστης, καὶ τῆς ἁρμονίας αὐτῶν συμπήκτωρ, καὶ τῆς διαμονῆς αὐτῶν κυβερνήτης, καὶ τῆς διαζεύξεως αὐτῶν πρὸς τὸ συμφέρον οἰκονόμος, καὶ πάλιν

---

88   MD, ch. 1, 1.13. All translations from the MD are mine.

STUNNING WITH A LIST, DAZZLING WITH A CATALOGUE 187

τῆς ἀναπλάσεως τῆς ἐν τῇ ἀναστάσει καὶ τῆς ἀσυγχύτου συγκράσεως αὐτῶν καὶ τῆς ἐν ἀφθαρσίᾳ ζωῆς αἰωνίου προνοητὴς καὶ θαυματουργός.[89]

In a similar vein, elsewhere in a passage praising Demetrios he asks: 'What am I thenceforth to admire? What am I to glorify about the martyr? Hospitality? Or simply his mercy? Or his quick reaction toward those who invoke him with faith? Or rather [his reaction despite] not being summoned to have pity on those in need?' (*Τί τοίνυν ἀπεντεῦθεν θαυμάσω, τί δὲ δοξάσω τοῦ μάρτυρος· τὸ φιλόξενον; ἀλλὰ τὸ ἁπλῶς φιλάνθρωπον; ἀλλὰ τὸ ταχυήκοον πρὸς τοὺς ἐπικαλουμένους ἐν πίστει; ἢ μᾶλλον τὸ μηδὲ καλούμενον ἐλεεῖν τοὺς ἐν ἀνάγκαις;*).[90]

In the first miracle narrative we are also offered a catalogue of symptoms experienced by the diseased Marianos, who describes them to Saint Demetrios, disguised as his friend who bears the same name:

> What do I share with the living, what do I not share with those who lie in the grave? My whole head has been terribly affected, all my senses have been held in vain, for I have no eyes to see clearly, nor ears to hear except for the loudest noises, nor a nose to distinguish well the quality of odors, nor the sweet taste to distinguish from the bitter on my tongue, my whole body has changed so much, that I seem to be cooled when I touch hot things, and when I cling to cold things I believe I am being warmed. My shoulders, arms, and hands just dangle idly along my body, carried wherever motion would lead them and not my own will.

> *Τί γὰρ ἔχω τῶν ἐν ζῶσι, τί δὲ τῶν ἐν τάφῳ κειμένων οὐκ ἔχω; κεφαλὴ μὲν γὰρ πᾶσα κεκακωμένη δεινῶς, πάντα τὰ αἰσθητήρια μάτην κέκτηται, οὔτε γὰρ ὀφθαλμοὺς ἔχω βλέποντας ἐναργῶς, οὔτε ἀκοὴν ἐπαΐουσαν πλὴν τῶν μεγίστων ψόφων, ἀλλ' οὔτε ἡ ῥὶς διακρίνει σαφῶς τῶν ὀσφραινομένων τὴν ποιότητα, οὔτε παρὰ τῇ γλώττῃ μου διαφορὰν ἔχει τὰ γλυκέα πρὸς τὰ πικρά· οὕτω δὲ ἠλλοίωταί μου τὸ πᾶν σῶμα ὅτι καὶ τῶν θερμῶν ἁπτόμενος ψύχεσθαι δοκῶ, καὶ τοῖς ψυχροῖς κολλώμενος ὑπολαμβάνω θερμαίνεσθαι· ὦμοι δὲ καὶ ἀγκῶνες καὶ χεῖρες ἀποκρέμανται μόνον τοῦ σώματος ἀεργεῖς, ὅπῃ δ' ἂν ἡ κίνησις ἄγοι φερόμεναι, οὐχ ὅπῃ βούλησις ἡ ἐμή.*[91]

The passages discussed above serve to emphasize certain aspects of the narrative, such as the virtues and glory of their subjects (Marianos, God himself), or specific conditions important for the plot to develop (the woeful state of the

---

89 Ibidem, ch. 1, 1.14.
90 Ibidem, ch. 1, 4.48.
91 Ibidem, ch. 1, 1.16.

protagonist). They also slow the narrative down and provide some embellishment of the otherwise schematic story of a miraculous healing.

Unlike in the *MT*, however, where enumeration was employed profusely, and often piled with elaborate cascades or multiplied with echoes of parallel lists, in the *MD* the strategy seems to be used more casually. It may certainly be a matter of individual aesthetic taste. Whereas the author of Thekla's collection did not hesitate to employ what seems to be his favorite strategy to an almost excessive degree, the author of the *Miracles of Demetrios* could hardly be accused of overusing it. Aside from the purely aesthetic issue, however, what in Demetrios' miracles can be considered a conventional rhetorical device, in Thekla's miracles may be seen as part of a broader authorial program that seeks to exploit the potential of the list and the catalogue and their analogous means of expression.

8 Conclusions

The paradoxographical authors did not leave us any clues as to why they adopted the list form to present the material they gathered for their collections of *mirabilia*. If it was their conscious decision not to provide introductions, they must have been aware of the potency of the list itself. They sought to dazzle us with a multitude of paradoxical curiosities and mysteries of the world that could render this very world hard to define. *Mirabilia* offer the thrill of interacting with a *thauma* that is divided into hundreds of small pieces. In turn, the authors of Christian miracle collections shared with their pagan predecessors a belief in the enchanting power of listing. Therefore, in composing their works they drew on the repertory of available literary models that had been developed to evoke the inexpressible. However, they had a clear definition of the world, ruled by an omnipotent divinity for whom there are no limits. That is why they focused on constantly highlighting the boundless powers of the holy martyrs that are proven by their incalculable miracles. The power of God which works through His saints thus lurks behind all the stories gathered in the miracle collections and provides them with an overarching narrative. These texts were thus created for two purposes: one of them is more pragmatic, while the other is more important. The former is targeted at promoting the cult of a given saint and their cultic shrine. The latter, however, conveys the profound moral message that divine arithmetic is beyond human comprehension.

STUNNING WITH A LIST, DAZZLING WITH A CATALOGUE

Bibliography

Primary Sources

Antigonos of Karystos, *Collection of Paradoxical Stories*. In ed. A. Giannini, *Paradoxographorum Graecorum reliquiae* (Milan: 1965) 32–106.

Aratos, *Phaenomena*. In ed. A.W. Mair – G.R. Mair, *Callimachus, Lycophron, Aratus. Hymns and Epigrams. Lycophron: Alexandra. Aratus: Phaenomena* (Cambridge, MA: 1921) 206–297.

Aulus Gellius, *Attic Nights*. In ed. J.C. Rolfe, *The Attic Nights of Aulus Gellius: With an English Translation* (Cambridge, MA – London: 1927).

Chrysippos Presbyter of Jerusalem, *Encomium and Miracles of Theodore Teron* (BHG *1765c*). In ed. A. Sigalas, *Des Chrysippos von Jerusalem Enkomion auf den hl. Theodoros Teron*, Byzantinisches Archiv 7 (Leipzig: 1921) 50–79.

Hesiod, *Theogony*. In ed. M.L. West, *Hesiod: Theogony* (Oxford: 1966) 111–149.

John, Archbishop of Thessalonike, *Miracles of Demetrios* (BHG 499–523). In ed. P. Lemerle, *Les plus anciens recueils des Miracles de Saint Démétrius*, vol. 1: *Le texte* (Paris: 1979) 4–165.

Miracles of Thekla (BHG 1718). In ed. G. Dagron, *Vie et miracles de sainte Thècle: Texte grec, traduction et commentaire*, Subsidia hagiographica 62 (Brussels: 1978) 285–412.

Miracles of Anastasios the Persian (BHG 89g–90). In ed. B. Flusin, *Saint Anastase le Perse et l'histoire de la Palestine au début du VIIᵉ siècle*, vol. 1: *Les textes* (Paris: 1992) 117–153.

Miracles of Artemios (BHG 173–173c). In ed. A. Papadopoulos-Kerameus, *Varia Graeca sacra* (St. Petersburg: 1909) 1–75.

Miracles of Demetrios (anonymous) (BHG 516z–522). In ed. P. Lemerle, *Les plus anciens recueils des Miracles de Saint Démétrius*, vol. 1: *Le texte* (Paris: 1979) 168–241.

Miracles of Kosmas and Damian (BHG 385–391). In (partial) ed. L. Deubner, *Kosmas und Damian: Texte und Einleitung* (Leipzig – Berlin: 1907) 193–206.

Nonnos of Panopolis, *Dionysiaca*. In ed. W. Rouse, *Nonnos. Dionysiaca*, vol. 1: *Books 1–15* (Cambridge, MA: 1940) 2–533.

Oppian, *Halieutica*. In ed. A.W. Mair, *Oppian, Colluthus, Tryphiodorus* (Cambridge, MA: 1928; repr. 1963) 200–514.

Phlegon of Tralles, *The Book of Marvels*. In ed. A. Stramaglia, *Phlegon Trallianus: Opuscula de rebus mirabilibus et de longaevis*, Bibliotheca Scriptorum Graecorum et Romanorum Teubneriana 2008 (Berlin – New York: 2011) 1–60.

Sophronios of Jerusalem, *Encomium of Kyros and John* (BHG 475). In ed. P. Bringel, *Sophrone de Jérusalem*, "Panégyrique des saints Cyr et Jean", *Patrologia Orientalis* 226 (Turnhout: 2008) 16–72.

Sophronios of Jerusalem, *Miracles of Kyros and John* (BHG 477–479). In ed. N. Fernández Marcos, *Los 'Thaumata' de Sofronio: Contribución al estudio de la 'incubatio' cristiana* (Madrid: 1975).

Timothy of Alexandria, *Miracles of Menas* (BHG 1256–1269). In ed. N. Pomjalovskij, *Žitije prepodovnago Paisija velikago i Timotheja part. Aleks. povestvovanie o čudesah sv. velikomučenika Miny* (St. Petersburg: 1900) 62–89.

Virgil, *Aeneid.* In ed. H. Rushton Fairclough, rev. G. Goold, *Virgil. Eclogues. Georgics. Aeneid: Books 1–6* (Cambridge, MA: 1916) 262–597.

Virgil, *Georgics.* In ed. H. Rushton Fairclough, rev. G. Goold, *Virgil. Eclogues. Georgics. Aeneid: Books 1–6* (Cambridge, MA: 1916) 98–259.

Secondary Works

Brook C., *The Expression of the Inexpressible in Eugenio Montale's Poetry: Metaphor, Negation and Silence* (Oxford: 2002).

Cariou M., "Le topos de l'ineffable dans les catalogues poétiques", *Revue de philologie, de littérature et d'histoire anciennes* 88.2 (2014) 27–58.

Crisafulli V.S. – Nesbitt J.W. (trans.), *The Miracles of St. Artemios: A Collection of Miracle Stories by an Anonymous Author of Seventh-Century Byzantium* (Leiden – New York – Cologne: 1997).

Curtius E., *European Literature and the Latin Middle Ages*, trans. W. Trask (Princeton – Oxford: 2013).

Dagron G., *Vie et miracles de sainte Thècle: Texte grec, traduction et commentaire*, Subsidia hagiographica 62 (Brussels: 1978).

Eco U., *La vertigine della lista* (Milan: 2009).

Eco U., *The Infinity of Lists*, trans. A. MacEwen (London: 2009).

Efthymiadis S., "Collections of Miracles (Fifth–Fifteenth Centuries)", in Efthymiadis S. (ed.), *The Ashgate Research Companion to Byzantine Hagiography*, vol. 2: *Genres and Contexts* (Farnham: 2014) 103–142.

Gabba E., "True History and False History in Classical Antiquity", *Journal of Roman Studies* 71 (1981) 50–62.

Giannini A., "Studi sulla paradossografia greca I. Da Omero a Callimaco: Motive e forme del meraviglioso", *Istituto Lombardo* (*Rendiconti di Lettere*) 97 (1963) 247–266.

Giannini A., "Studi sulla paradossografia greca II. Da Callimaco all'età imperiale: La lettura paradossografica", *Acme* 17 (1964) 99–140.

Godley A. (trans.), *Herodotus: The Histories* (Cambridge, MA – London: 1920).

Haldon J. (trans.), *A Tale of Two Saints: The Martyrdoms and Miracles of Saints Theodore 'the Recruit' and 'the General'. Critical Introduction, Translation and Commentary by John Haldon* (Liverpool: 2016).

Hansen W. (trans.), *Phlegon of Tralles' Book of Marvels* (Exeter: 1996).

Jacob C. – de Polignac F., *Alexandria, Third Century BC: The Knowledge of the World in a Single City*, trans. C. Clement (Alexandria: 2000).

Johnson S.F., *The Life and Miracles of Thekla: A Literary Study* (Cambridge, MA – London: 2006).

Johnson S.F. (trans.), "The Miracles of Thekla" in Talbot A.-M. – Johnson S.F. (trans.), *Miracle Tales from Byzantium*, Dumbarton Oaks Medieval Library 12 (Cambridge, MA – London: 2012) 1–201.

Kirk A., *Ancient Greek Lists: Catalogue and Inventory across Genres* (Cambridge: 2021).

Munson R., *Telling Wonders: Ethnographic and Political Discourse in the Work of Herodotus* (Ann Arbor: 2001).

Schepens G. – Delcroix K., "Ancient Paradoxography: Origin, Evolution, Production and Reception", in Pecere O. – Stramaglia A. (eds.), *La letteratura di consumo nel mondo greco-latino: Atti del Convegno Internazionale, Cassino, 14–17 settembre 1994* (Cassino: 1996) 410–460.

West M., *Hesiodic Catalogue of Women: Its Nature, Structure, and Origins* (Oxford: 1985).

Ziegler K., "Paradoxographoi", *Paulys Realencyclopädie der classischen Altertumswissenschaft* 18 (1949) 1137–1166.

CHAPTER 8

(Auto)biographical, Marvelous, and Supernatural Stories in Early Byzantine Hagiographical Anthologies

Stavroula Constantinou and Andria Andreou

Based on hagiographical tale collections (i.e. collective biographies, miracle collections, and collections of edifying tales) and miscellanies (i.e. *Apophthegmata Patrum*) from the early Byzantine period (fourth–seventh century), this chapter will attempt to provide a criterion for the examined tales' classification, which could prove useful also for approaching other and later tales. This criterion is what we call 'the agent' of the story, that is the force or the element which initiates a tale's episode(s) and drives it forward, defining its form and general structure. Tale episodes in early Byzantine hagiographical collections are like those explained by Tzvetan Todorov in his *Introduction to Poetics*, namely 'episodes [...] that describe a state (an equilibrium or of disequilibrium) and those that describe the transition from one state to the other'.[1]

In our corpus, three main types of agents have been detected: the human agent, the marvelous agent, and the supernatural agent. These agents form, in turn, three corresponding tale categories, which are as follows: (1) the (auto)biographical tale, (2) the marvelous tale, and (3) the supernatural tale. Each of these categories, which will be analyzed below, assumes three different structural forms: (1) the single-episode tale, (2) the multiple-episode tale, and (3) the frame tale. As suggested by these structural forms, just one episode might sustain a whole (auto)biographical, marvelous, or supernatural tale, that is, what we have termed 'the single-episode tale', while the sequence of episodes is characteristic of multiple-episode tales and frame tales.

A multiple-episode tale might have episodes from the same category ((auto)biographical, marvelous, or supernatural) or a combination of episodes from two or three categories (biographical and marvelous; (auto)biographical and supernatural; marvelous and supernatural; (auto)biographical, marvelous, and supernatural). Finally, a frame tale has a tale-within-a-tale arrangement. The principal storyteller of a given tale tells the story of another storyteller who,

---

1 Todorov T., *Introduction to Poetics*, trans. R. Howard, Theory and History of Literature 1 (Minneapolis: 1981) 51.

© STAVROULA CONSTANTINOU AND ANDRIA ANDREOU, 2025 | DOI:10.1163/9789004707351_010

This is an open access chapter distributed under the terms of the CC BY-NC-ND 4.0 license.

(AUTO)BIOGRAPHICAL, MARVELOUS, AND SUPERNATURAL STORIES   193

in turn, tells his or her own story and/or those of other storytellers or characters.[2] Thus, in contrast to the single- or multiple-episode tale, the frame tale has
one or more characters who are simultaneously the storytellers of the interpolated tales. The frame tale, therefore, involves more than one narrative level –
the so-called frames that include embedded tales each of which might have a
single- or a multiple-episode structure. Each embedded multiple-episode tale,
as is the case with the non-embedded ones, might contain tales from the same
category ((auto)biographical, marvelous, or supernatural) or combinations of
different categories.[3]

1   The Single-Episode Tale

In terms of length and density, the episode of a tale might be described as
simple or complex. In general, tales with simple episodes have up to two or
three characters, while tales having complex episodes involve more than two
or three characters and are therefore longer. In general, single-episode tales
are, as expected, shorter than those belonging to the other two structural types,
which include more than one episode. The shortest tale with a simple episode
comprises three printed lines, and the longest tale with a complex episode has
around fifty-five printed lines. A single-episode tale is shaped and structured
according to the characteristics of its distinct category: (auto)biographical,
marvelous, or supernatural. In our attempt to provide a better understanding of the (structural) character of the single-episode tale, as well as that of

---

2   For the storyteller's role in early Byzantine tale collections see Constantinou S. – Andreou A.,
     "The Voices of the Tale: The Storyteller in Early Byzantine Collective Biographies, Miracle
     Collections, and Collections of Edifying Tales", *Byzantine and Modern Greek Studies* 46.1
     (2021) 24–40, DOI: 10.1017/byz.2021.31.
3   Of course, the three tale categories ((auto)biographical, marvelous, or supernatural) with
     their corresponding structures (single-episode, multiple-episode, and frame tale) are not
     only found in the examined texts, but are also included in later anthologies, while at the
     same time they are inserted into other types of texts. Yet, for reasons of time and space,
     this study discusses the three tale categories and their structures as they appear in early
     Byzantine hagiographical collections and miscellanies. It should be noted that no discus-
     sion of the conception, production, and consumption of the tales' particular arrangements
     in hagiographical anthologies or miscellanies is undertaken here. These issues concerning
     anthologies in general are certainly important and deserve a thorough examination; nev-
     ertheless, this is beyond the scope of the present chapter, which focuses on hagiographical
     tales' structural forms (single-episode tale, multiple-episode tale, and frame tale) and dis-
     cusses their 'how' and main characteristics.

multiple-episode tales and frame tales, in this larger section we discuss each tale category separately.

1.1 *The (Auto)biographical Tale*

The agent driving the single-episode (auto)biographical tale is a human figure performing remarkable conduct which is manifested in a series of actions and/or physical and spiritual trials. Biographical tales are, as described by Patricia Cox Miller, 'biographical sketches'. They do 'not analyse character so much as present it in striking images, using a [...] "peculiarly expressionistic manner"'. The character is portrayed in a 'vividly visual and emotional' way, while 'conventional biographical data like ancestry, place of birth and death' are absent.[4] Most single-episode (auto)biographical tales follow a similar pattern that, through its frequent repetitions, provides a work with a ritual structure. These repetitions render (auto)biographical tales easily recognizable, memorable, and adaptable – particularly for later authors who intend to create biographical sketches of new heroes and heroines.

As for the (auto)biographical tales' most common arrangement, they first introduce the protagonist into the narrative by sketching his or her profile, which is constructed through a selection of brief pieces of information including the character's name, origin, age, monastic career (e.g. hermit, cenobitic monk, or nun) or profession (e.g. merchant, actor, herdsman), sexual/marital status, and geographical location. Then follows an account of the character's bodily and/or spiritual deeds, which are often witnessed by the tale's storyteller, who also appears as the protagonist's biographer and adds his or her own perspective to the biographical sketch. (Auto)biographical tales are mostly open-ended narratives inviting the tales' readers or listeners to think of more similar episodes featuring in the protagonist's daily life, which seems an endless repetition of admirable deeds. The lack of a clear end, along with the protagonist's striking image(s), provides (auto)biographical tales with their distinctiveness and power. Sometimes, (auto)biographical tales, like their marvelous and supernatural counterparts, might at the end include the storyteller's final comments, which mostly take the form of a short moral lesson.

An indicative example of a single-episode biographical tale is the story of John from the *History of the Monks in Egypt*, a very brief narrative with a simple episode involving two types of characters: the biographer who sees and reports, and his protagonist. The tale reads as follows:

---

4 Cox Miller P., "Strategies of Representation in Collective Biography: Constructing the Subject as Holy", in Hägg T. – Rousseau P. (eds.), *Greek Biography and Panegyric in Late Antiquity* (Berkeley: 2000) 209–254, at 209–210 and 230.

(AUTO)BIOGRAPHICAL, MARVELOUS, AND SUPERNATURAL STORIES 195

26. We also visited another John in Diolcos, who was the father of hermitages. He, too, was endowed with much grace. He looked like Abraham and had a beard like Aaron's. He had performed many miracles and cures, and he was especially successful at healing people afflicted with paralysis and gout.

κϛ΄. Περὶ Ἰωάννου
Εἴδομεν δὲ καὶ ἄλλον Ἰωάννην ἐν Διόλκῳ, πατέρα μοναστηρίων καὶ αὐτὸν πολλὴν χάριν ἔχοντα τό τε Ἀβραμιαῖον σχῆμα καὶ τὸν πώγωνα τὸν Ἀαρών, δυνάμεις τε καὶ ἰάσεις ἐπιτελέσαντα καὶ πολλοὺς παραλυτικοὺς καὶ ποδαλγοὺς θεραπεύσαντα.[5]

In Todorov's words, the biographical episode involving John 'describes an equilibrium'. Despite its extreme brevity, this biographical tale is constructed on two elements: the biographer's image of John, and the information he has managed to collect about the ascetic. In John's face, the biographer-storyteller sees two biblical figures, Abraham and Aaron. Being the father of many monasteries, John appears to the biographer's eyes as another Abraham, whose name meant 'father of height' and whom God chose to make the spiritual father and leader of a new people.

As for Aaron, in Ps. 133.2 he is described as someone whose beard was so long that it covered his garments. By presenting John as both another Abraham and Aaron,[6] the biographer brings to the memory of his audience the stories of these important biblical figures, who become part of John's own biographical tale too. Through this identification, John's biographical information becomes longer than the written text quoted above, which simply mentions that John established and led monasteries and that he also performed many miracles and particularly healings of paralysis and gout. The biographical tale's audiences are invited to think that while establishing and leading monasteries, John shared Abraham's monumental patience, his active and living faith, and his righteousness. At the same time, he had the eloquence of Aaron, his high and holy calling, and his monumental penitence during which he suffered for his own sins and those of others.

Single-episode biographical tales, such as that of John, are less frequently found in miracle collections, whereas they are common in the *History of the*

---

5 *History of the Monks in Egypt* (BHG 1333–1334), ed. A.-J. Festugière, *Historia monachorum in Aegypto*, Subsidia hagiographica 34 (Brussels: 1961); trans. N. Russell, "The Lives of the Desert Fathers", in Ward B. – Russell N. (eds.), *The Lives of the Desert Fathers*, Cistercian Publications 34 (Kalamazoo, MI: 1980) 47–119, at 117.
6 The descriptions of Abraham and Aaron in the Old Testament are presented in Lockyer H., *All the Men of the Bible* (Grand Rapids, MI: 1958) 28–29 and 19–21.

Monks in Egypt, Palladios' *Lausiac History*, Daniel of Sketis' *Narrations*, John Moschos' *Spiritual Meadow*, Anastasios of Sinai's *Edifying Tales*, and the *Apophthegmata Patrum*. Miracle collections are less concerned with (auto)biographical tales, since they are attached to a saint's specific shrine (e.g. that of Thekla in Seleukeia, Artemios in Oxia in Constantinople, etc.) and their primary aims are to encourage pilgrimage to the shrine and to promote the saint's cult through the circulation of stories that manifest his or her posthumous miraculous powers. The miraculous saint's biography, which is equally important for the establishment and promotion of his or her cult, is provided in a separate text, the saint's Passion, Life, or Encomium.

1.2 *The Marvelous Tale*

In a pioneering study on medieval wonder, Caroline Walker Bynum presents Western medieval ways of relating and reacting to strange, bizarre, and marvelous phenomena that, as such, were at the limits of knowledge and rational insight.[7] As the famous historian shows, there was a fascination with the marvelous in the Middle Ages, which fostered a cultivation of the extraordinary and the bizarre in various types of writing: the devotional genres of sermon and hagiography, and the literature of entertainment (i.e. writings on travel, chronicles, and collections of odd stories). The Western medieval approach to the marvelous referred to manifestations which challenged and exceeded the limits of the reasonable and the known. These manifestations took many forms, including, for example, spatial manipulation and metamorphosis. In fact, the latter probably represents the most common manifestation of the marvelous in the examined corpus. According to Walker Bynum, the marvelous incites strong emotional reactions that 'range from terror and disgust to solemn astonishment and playful delight'.[8] Walker Bynum's descriptions of the marvelous in Western medieval genres are to a great extent valid also for the marvelous tales of the examined texts.

Being normally shorter than most single-episode (auto)biographical tales, the length of marvelous tales ranges from approximately five to forty printed lines. In contrast to (auto)biographical tales, marvelous tales do not focus on the extraordinary deeds of a particular human character, but concentrate on happenings or phenomena that exceed human understanding and perception. The marvelous event, which is witnessed by the author-storyteller and/or

---

7   Walker Bynum C., *Metamorphosis and Identity* (New York: 2005) 37–75. For medieval marvels see also Le Goff J., *The Medieval Imagination*, trans. A. Goldhammer (Chicago – London: 1988) 27–44.

8   Walker Bynum, *Metamorphosis and Identity* 57.

(AUTO)BIOGRAPHICAL, MARVELOUS, AND SUPERNATURAL STORIES   197

other, mostly secondary, characters of the tale, constitutes a sudden, unexpected, and, at times, violent intrusion of mystery into the order of normal life. Marvelous tales do not just cause the feeling of admiration that is evoked by (auto)biographical tales, but also a series of often antithetical feelings, including dread, wonder, pleasure, and joy, which, like the admiration of the (auto)biographical tales, are experienced by both the tales' characters and the texts' actual audiences.

Whether the extraordinary in our corpus is manifested in the form of an animal exhibiting human behavior,[9] a walking headless body,[10] the soil spitting out corpses,[11] a small source filling up of its own accord and retaining water until Pentecost,[12] or the transformation of eucharistic bread into human flesh,[13] for the Byzantine listener, reader, or observer the marvelous is received in its individuality and veracity. As John Moschos concludes his marvelous tale on the said tiny source that once a year – on the day of the paschal feast of the Resurrection – fills up with water, 'these [...] wonders are in the Province of Lycia and if one does not believe in them, it is no burdensome journey to Lycia where they can be informed of the truth' (Ταῦτα [...] θαύματα, ἐν τῇ ἐπαρχίᾳ τῆς Λυκίας. Εἰ δὲ τούτοις τις ἀπιστήσει, οὐ πολὺς μέχρι τῆς Λυκίας ὁ σκυλμός, πρὸς πληροφορίαν τῆς ἀληθείας).[14]

The marvelous episodes in our monastic and ecclesiastical tales appear to have a divine origin. Even though they are Christianized and thus normalized, marvelous episodes are not always specifically religious. A case in point is a tale in the Anonymous Collection of the *Apophthegmata Patrum* about a lion that behaves like a human being. The lion lives in a cave in which a hermit finds shelter from the heat. Upon seeing the elder, the lion shows its dismay

---

9   John Moschos, *Spiritual Meadow* (BHG 1440f–1442z), ed. in *Patrologia Graeca* (PG) 87.3:2852–3112, at ch. 108, 2965–1971.

10   Anastasios of Sinai, *Edifying Tales* (BHG 1448q–1448qo), ed. F. Nau, "Le texte grec des récits utiles à l'âme d'Anastase (le Sinaïte)", *Oriens Christianus* 3 (1903) 56–75; S. Heid, "Die C-Reihe erbaulicher Erzählungen des Anastasios vom Sinai im Codex Vaticanus Graecus 2592", *Orientalia Christiana periodica* 74 (2008) 71–114 [second collection], at ch. 6, 89–90 (Heid).

11   John Moschos, *Spiritual Meadow*, ch. 88, 2945.

12   Ibidem, ch. 215, 3108.

13   *Sayings of the Desert Fathers* (*Apophthegmata Patrum*), Anonymous Collection, ed. F. Nau, "Histoires des solitaires égyptiens", *Revue de l'Orient chrétien* 12 (1907) 43–69, (1908) 171–189 and 393–413; 13 (1909) 47–66, 266–297; 14 (1912) 357–379; 17 (1913) 204–211, 294–301; and 18 (1913) 137–146; trans. J. Wortley, *The Anonymous Sayings of the Desert Fathers: A Select Edition and Complete English Translation* (Cambridge: 2013), at 3, ch. 18.4 (Nau).

14   John Moschos, *Spiritual Meadow*, ch. 215; trans. J. Wortley, *John Moschus, The Spiritual Meadow: Introduction, Translation and Notes*, Cistercian Studies Series 139 (Kalamazoo, MI: 1992) 192, with minor adjustments.

by grinding its teeth. Yet it does not attack the elder, as one would expect, but peacefully abandons the cave, thus following the man's advice, as he tells the animal: 'This is a place with room for you and me. Get up and leave if you do not like it' (ἔνι τόπος χωρῶν ἐμὲ καὶ σέ. Εἰ δὲ οὐ θέλεις, ἀνάστα ἔξελθε).[15] By creating a Christian frame of reference, the authors under discussion make a distinction between their own marvelous tales and the non-Christian paradoxography that nevertheless appears to inform their works.[16] In so doing, our authors aim at liberating their tales from the fictional character they see in ancient paradoxography. Their marvelous tales, by contrast, depict real phenomena that constitute parts of the Christian God's economy.[17]

The marvelous tales under discussion seem to be more effective and powerful when their readers or listeners are invited not only to gaze at what the characters see, but also to perceive *how* these characters see. Sometimes it is only select characters (mostly pious Christians) who can see the bizarre, whereas other characters (mostly heathens and heretics) are denied the reality of the extraordinary. In these cases, the tales are structured around two forms of reality: one allowing the marvelous manifestation and one that denies its existence. Yet the first reality is deemed higher, and that is the reason why it is eventually disclosed to the narratives' good characters, who, in turn, share their experience of the marvelous with their fellows and/or the tales' storytellers that afterwards transmit it to the texts' audiences. One such marvelous tale is the following:

> In this same Clysma, there was a certain other sailor, who was also called Theodore. Even though he was a Christian, when the ships entered the land of Saracens, he was lured by the one who hates the good, and he became an apostate of the Christian faith, and he rejected the cross and the baptism.
>
> After some days passed, when in the evening one of his colleagues named Menas was going to the church he met the renouncer Theodore. And behold, he saw a headless human being walking. Feeling wonder before this strange sight he asked the creature a question, saying: 'Headless being, who are you?' He replied, saying: 'I am Theodore the

---

15 *Apophthegmata Patrum*, Anonymous Collection N.333/19.19, ed. Wortley, *Anonymous Sayings of the Desert Fathers* 216; trans. ibidem, 217.

16 *Miracles of Thekla* (BHG 1718), ed. G. Dagron, *Vie et miracles de sainte Thècle: Texte grec, traduction et commentaire*, Subsidia hagiographica 62 (Paris: 1978) 285–412; see Johnson S.F., *The Life and Miracles of Thekla: A Literary Study*, Hellenic Studies 13 (Cambridge, MA – London: 2006) 172–220.

17 For *thauma* in paradoxography and hagiography, see Chapter 2.

(AUTO)BIOGRAPHICAL, MARVELOUS, AND SUPERNATURAL STORIES 199

sailor who died three months ago.' Menas then said: 'Where is your head?' Theodore replied, saying: 'Ninety days ago now I lost my head, because I joined the faith of the headless.' Then he immediately disappeared.

When Menas entered the church, he was trembling with fear because of what he had seen and heard. When he was asked by his colleagues, who are still alive and live in Clysma, for the reason of his fear, he narrated this story so that we might know that there is no godly faith other than that of Christians.

Ἐν τῷ αὐτῷ Κλύσματι γέγονε καὶ ἔτερός τις ναύτης, Θεόδωρος καὶ αὐτὸς λεγόμενος. Οὗτος Χριστιανὸς ὑπάρχων, εἰσελθόντων πλοίων ἐν τῇ χώρᾳ τῶν Σαρακηνῶν, ἀπατηθεὶς ὑπὸ τοῦ μισοκάλου ἐκεῖσε ἀποστάτης τῆς Χριστοῦ πίστεως γέγονεν ἀρνησάμενος καὶ τὸν σταυρὸν καὶ τὸ βάπτισμα.

Μετ' ὀλίγας οὖν ἡμέρας ἀπήντησεν ἐν νυκτὶ τῷ ἀρνησαμένῳ Θεοδώρῳ τις ἐκ τῶν σὺν αὐτῷ[ν] Μηνᾶς λεγόμενος εἰς τὴν ἐκκλησίαν ἀπερχόμενος. Καὶ ἰδοὺ θεωρεῖ ἄνθρωπον περιπατοῦντα, κεφαλὴν δὲ μὴ ἔχοντα. Καὶ θαμβηθεὶς ἐπὶ τῷ ξένῳ θεάματι ἠρώτα τὸν ὀφθέντα αὐτῷ· Ἀκέφαλον, λέγων, τίς εἶ σύ; Ὁ δὲ ἀπεκρίθη αὐτῷ λέγων· Ἐγώ εἰμι Θεόδωρος ὁ ναύτης ὁ γενόμενος μακαρίτης πρὸ τριῶν μηνῶν. Λέγει πρὸς αὐτὸν ὁ Μηνᾶς· Καὶ ποῦ ἐστιν ἡ κεφαλή σου; Ἀπεκρίθη αὐτῷ ὁ Θεόδωρος λέγων· Ἔχω ἐνενήκοντα ἡμέρας, ὅτι ἀπώλεσα τὴν κεφαλήν μου καὶ ἐπίστευσα μετὰ ἀκεφάλων, καὶ εὐθέως ἐγένετο ἄφαντος.

Ἐλθὼν οὖν ὁ Μηνᾶς ἐν τῇ ἐκκλησίᾳ ἦν σύντρομος ἐκ τοῦ φόβου τῶν ὀφθέντων καὶ λαληθέντων αὐτῷ. ἐπερωτηθεὶς τὴν αἰτίαν τοῦ κατέχοντος αὐτὸν τρόμου ταῦτα διηγήσατο τοῖς ἑταίροις αὐτοῦ τοῖς ἔτι ζῶσι καὶ ἐν τῷ Κλύσματι διάγουσιν, ὅπως καὶ διὰ τούτου μάθωμεν, ὅτι οὐκ ἔστιν ἄλλη θεοῦ πίστις εἰ μὴ μόνη τῶν Χριστιανῶν.[18]

This tale has the typical beginning of a biographical tale. Its first sentence introduces into the narrative the hero whose body will soon become the space of the marvelous. This is Theodore, a Christian sailor from Clysma (an Egyptian city located at the head of the Gulf of Suez) whose conversion to Islam causes a bodily transformation that one evening is witnessed by his colleague Menas on the latter's way to the church. Being a practicing Christian, Menas is deemed worthy of the marvelous manifestation, which takes place in a setting that is specifically designed both to prepare and to sustain the threat caused by Theodore's headless apparition.

A theatrical scene is created featuring Menas walking alone in the darkness. Suddenly, he sees an absurd and grotesque sight: a headless human body

---

18   Anastasios of Sinai, *Edifying Tales*, ch. 6 (89–90 Heid); our own translation.

walking. Through the storyteller's use of the phrase 'and behold' (καὶ ἰδού), the gaze of the tale's audience turns to *what* Menas sees and *how* he sees it. He is startled by and feels curious about the apparition moving before his eyes. He speaks to it, and his words, which are given in direct speech, are heard by the tale's listeners, who, along with Menas, hear the apparition's voice. After satisfying Menas' curiosity, the apparition disappears, and thus the hero's initial feelings of astonishment and curiosity are replaced by a strong fear that becomes known to his fellows through his bodily trembling. His fear diminishes as he narrates his experience of the marvelous.

The tale concludes with a moral lesson taught by Theodore's religious conversion and subsequent monstrosity: Christianity is the only true religion, and those who deny their Christianity lose their identity and humanity. This serious loss is allegorically represented through a headless body moving around, violating physical order and thus provoking both wonder and fear. At the same time, Theodore's headless body reproduces his new, yet 'godless', religion that is represented by a headless god (Akephalos) who in ancient magical texts (dating from the second century BC to the fifth century AD) is diversely identified with Osiris, Seth/Typhon, Bes, Helios, and Apollo, and is, among others, associated with apparitions.[19] By espousing an Akephalos god and joining his followers, Theodore becomes headless, too.

In general, marvelous tales are characterized by a mysteriousness that is accepted as part and parcel of everyday reality. While the marvelous defies empirically defined reality by exaggerating the real, it also serves to assert the impossible. Insofar as the tales tend to make repeated, yet restricted, use of comparatively few marvelous features, these become predictable and therefore, at least to some extent, acceptable. Thus, the marvelous elements are just as capable of reproducing, and thus valorizing, social situations as the 'realistic' features are. For example, marvelous representations of the body, as Theodore's tale shows, are imbued with desires as well as fears: the desire to learn about the grotesque apparition and the fear that this knowledge brings. The marvelous phenomenon, in whatever manifestation, is best seen and known in person, thus functioning as the greatest proof of the claim to truth of the witness, who, like Menas, will then share the marvelous experience with others. The transformation of the experience into a tale constitutes not only a challenge to available paradigms for making sense of an otherwise unfamiliar world, but also a challenge to the subjectivity of the witness-narrator who,

---

19   Goodison L., "Sunlight, Divination, and the Dead in Aegean Ritual Tradition", in Papadopoulos C. – Moyes H. (eds.), *The Oxford Handbook of Light in Archaeology* (Oxford: 2022) 185–206, at 197.

(AUTO)BIOGRAPHICAL, MARVELOUS, AND SUPERNATURAL STORIES   201

through the narration, tries to make sense of a strange phenomenon that functions as a means of edification.

1.3 *The Supernatural Tale*

Supernatural tales are the most frequent single-episode tales and the richest in terms of their agents' variations. As already suggested, the agents of supernatural tales are either divine or demonic figures that enter the human world and interact with a human protagonist (e.g. in an ascetic's battle against demons and demonic temptations; in a person's dreamlike or visionary encounter with a saintly figure) or bring about the performance of a miracle (e.g. a dead person's resurrection; the healing of a deadly disease). In this category, we also include tales whose episode centres on a protagonist's descent into hell or ascent to heaven through dreamlike or visionary experiences.

In addition to their variety of forms, the supernatural figures depicted in the tales under investigation also serve different functions. There are angels, appearing mostly as handsome men or eunuchs, who are dressed in expensive attire and who frequently undertake roles such as that of the messenger, escort, savior, and punisher. There are biblical and saintly figures (e.g. prophets, the Virgin, apostles, martyrs, confessors, and bishops) in various appearances who perform miracles, foretell the future, instruct, and punish. There are demons in various guises who use various tricks attempting to make pious characters abandon their Christian way of life, and who possess other individuals with the intention of destroying them. Finally, there are undefined divine or demonic figures manifesting themselves through bodiless voices and grotesque forms that help or hinder the protagonists in their endeavors, either pious or sinful. Concerning the supernatural figures who appear in person, they are often depicted as quite fleshy. As such, they possess what Cox Miller has described as 'ephemeral corporeality': 'the supernatural agent's body is invisible yet seen as quite physical, touching both the man in the story and the reader'.[20] This is particularly relevant in the cases in which a supernatural figure touches a character violently to serve various purposes (e.g. to achieve a cure; to punish; to shake an ascetic's steadfastness).

The great majority of supernatural episodes belong to the second type of episodes identified by Todorov, since they 'describe the transition from one state' to another.[21] Through supernatural agency, for example, a seriously ill character is healed completely, or the other way round: a healthy character

---

20   Cox Miller P., *The Corporeal Imagination: Signifying the Holy in Late Ancient Christianity* (Philadelphia: 2009) 107.

21   Todorov, *Introduction to Poetics* 51.

develops a disease; a sinful character repents, or vice versa: a pious character commits a sin; a character's ignorance turns into knowledge; and calamity changes into blessing or blessing turns into calamity. The supernatural tales included in miracle collections chiefly concern the transition from a state of illness to that of health, while most supernatural tales incorporated into our other collections deal with a character's transition from ignorance to self-knowledge and divine wisdom.

The following supernatural tale from Artemios' miracle collection involves a double transition: from illness to health and from ignorance to self- and divine knowledge.

> Another man, a Phrygian by birth named George, had swollen testicles and, suffering in the extreme, was waiting for a cure by the martyred saint. But this man chattered incessantly; for neither by night nor by day was his mouth at rest, nor would he allow anyone to rest, and although everyone censured him, he would not be quiet. So the saint appeared to him in the small hours saying: 'When day comes, withdraw from here. Since if you remain another moment, I will double your hernia. For I hate babblers.' Rising early, he knew that he was cured and in accordance with what was said to him by the holy martyr, so he acted and did not remain but rejoicing went off blessing God.

> Ἄλλος ἀνὴρ τοὔνομα Γεώργιος, Φρύγιος τῷ γένει, ἐξωγκωμένους τοὺς διδύμους αὐτοῦ ἔχων καὶ τὰ ἔσχατα ὀδυνώμενος προσεκαρτέρει πρὸς τὸ ἰαθῆναι αὐτὸν τῷ ἁγίῳ ἀθλοφόρῳ. ἦν δὲ οὗτος λαλῶν πολλά· οὐκ ἠρέμει γὰρ αὐτοῦ τὸ στόμα οὔτε νυκτὸς οὔτε ἡμέρας, λοιπὸν οὐδὲ συνεχώρει ἀναπαύεσθαί τινα, καὶ πάντων αὐτῷ ἐπιτιμώντων οὐκ ἐσιώπα. Φαίνεται οὖν αὐτῷ ταῖς πολλαῖς ὁ ἅγιος λέγων· "Ἡνίκα ἡμέρα γένηται, ἀναχώρει τῶν ἔνθεν, ἐπεὶ ἐὰν μείνῃς ἄλλην ῥοπήν, διπλῆν ποιῶ τὴν κήλην σου· ἐγὼ γὰρ μισῶ τοὺς φλυάρους.' ἀναστὰς δὲ τῷ πρωῒ ἔγνω ἑαυτὸν ὑγιῆ, καὶ κατὰ τὸ ῥηθὲν αὐτῷ ἐκ τοῦ ἁγίου μάρτυρος, οὕτως ἐποίησεν καὶ οὐκ ἔστη, ἀλλὰ χαίρων ἀπῆλθεν εὐλογῶν τὸν θεόν.[22]

George, the human character of this supernatural tale, grows impatient as Saint Artemios, who specializes in the healing of testicular diseases, postpones his miraculous cure. Despite his extreme suffering, George 'chatters

---

22   *Miracles of Artemios*, ch. 8, ed. A. Papadopoulos-Kerameus, *Varia Graeca sacra* (St. Petersburg: 1909) 1–75; trans. V.S. Crisafulli – J.W. Nesbitt, *The Miracles of St. Artemios: A Collection of Miracle Stories by an Anonymous Author of Seventh-Century Byzantium* (Leiden – New York – Cologne: 1997) 93.

incessantly' without realizing that this is not proper behavior in the sacred space housing Artemios' relics (i.e. the church of John the Forerunner in Oxia in Constantinople), and without paying any attention to the fact that he becomes a real nuisance for his fellow patients also waiting, but patiently, for the saint's healing. It is primarily his (self-)ignorance and indifference to the others' situation that initiate the dreamlike epiphany of Artemios, whose words have a humoristic effect which is created by the saint's ambivalent behavior: it appears both human and supernatural. By stating his disgust for babblers, Artemios behaves like George's fellow patients who, as pointed out, also reveal their discomfort with the continuous chattering. By threatening to worsen George's suffering, on the other hand, Artemios exhibits his power to miraculously cause – but also heal – testicular diseases.

As George and, along with him, the tale's audiences realize when he wakes up, Artemios was performing his cure while reproaching him within the dream. Following the saint's instructions, George leaves the church, yet he does not cease talking, though in a completely different manner: his initial words of misery are now replaced by words of eulogy which in contrast to the previous ones are most desirable and welcome. In sum, supernatural agency in this episode effects both bodily and spiritual transformation. George's great suffering is transformed into grand happiness, and his ignorance concerning unpleasant aspects of his character and saintly intentions turns into self-knowledge and divine wisdom. He becomes both a healthy and a better man.

As the preceding analysis has hopefully made clear, despite their extreme brevity and simplicity, single-episode tales from early Byzantium constitute powerful narratives whose human, superhuman, and marvelous agents manage to engage their audiences' senses and emotions. The episode, as defined through its agent type, constitutes the building block of the early Byzantine tale. It is a complete and free-standing narrative unit. As such, the episode becomes essential not only for the tale's creation, but also for its further development, which is materialized in longer and more complex structures, such as those of the multiple-episode tale and the frame tale. Multiple-episode tales unroll through a series of episodes, whereas the even more complicated frame tales develop through series of embedded episodes. But let us first examine how a multiple-episode tale is structured.

2   The Multiple-Episode Tale

The multiple-episode tale does not have a unified or consistent length and structure: the more the episodes, the longer the tale, and the longer the tale, the more complicated the structure. In terms of the types of episodes they involve, multiple-episode tales might be divided into two groups: monothematic and polythematic tales. Monothematic tales are those having episodes with the same agent, (auto)biographical, marvelous, or supernatural. Polythematic tales, on the other hand, include combinations of episodes with two different agents (i.e. (auto)biographical and marvelous; (auto)biographical and supernatural; marvelous and supernatural) or episodes with all three agents (i.e. (auto)biographical, marvelous, and supernatural). The arrangement of episodes in polythematic tales, which varies from tale to tale, is determined by the author's individual purposes, aesthetic, didactic, or other.

An indicative example of a short monothematic multiple-episode tale comprising just two episodes is the biographical story of Makarios the Younger from Palladios' *Lausiac History*. The tale reads as follows:

> A young man named Makarios about eighteen years of age was playing with his comrades along Lake Marea. He was pasturing animals and accidentally killed someone. Telling no one about it, he went off to the desert; he was so afraid of God and of man that he had no regard for himself, and he stayed in the desert for three years without a shelter. [...] Afterwards he built himself a cell and lived another twenty-five years there. He was deemed worthy of the gift of spitting upon demons, and he rejoiced in his solitude.
>
> I spent quite some time with him, and I asked him how he felt about his sin and homicide. He said that it was far from his thoughts, and that he even rejoiced in it, since it was actually the starting point of his salvation. He said, bringing testimony from Holy Writ, that Moses would not have been deemed worthy of the divine vision and the great gift of writing inspired words if he had not fled to Mount Sinai in fear of Pharaoh, because of the homicide he had committed in Egypt.
>
> I do not say this to make light of homicide, but rather to show that there are virtues which are due to circumstances, when a man does not advance to good of himself. For some virtues are deliberately chosen and others are dependent upon circumstances.

> Νεώτερός τις ὀνόματι Μακάριος, ὡς ἐτῶν δεκαοκτώ, ἐν τῷ παίζειν μετὰ τῶν συνηλικιωτῶν παρὰ τὴν λίμνην τὴν λεγομένην Μαρίαν, τετράποδα νέμων, ἀκούσιον εἰργάσατο φόνον. Καὶ μηδενὶ μηδὲν εἰρηκὼς καταλαμβάνει τὴν ἔρημον, καὶ εἰς τοσοῦτον ἤλασε φόβον θεῖόν τε καὶ ἀνθρώπινον, ὡς ἀναισθητῆσαι αὐτὸν καὶ ἐπὶ τριετίαν ἄστεγον μεῖναι ἐν τῇ ἐρήμῳ. [...] Οὗτος ὕστερον

(AUTO)BIOGRAPHICAL, MARVELOUS, AND SUPERNATURAL STORIES

ᾠκοδόμησε κέλλαν ἑαυτῷ· καὶ ζήσας ἄλλα εἰκοσιπέντε ἔτη ἐν τῷ κελλίῳ ἐκείνῳ χαρίσματος ἠξιώθη καταπτύειν δαιμόνων, ἐντρυφῶν τῇ μονότητι.

Τούτῳ πολλὰ συγχρονίσας ἠρώτων πῶς αὐτοῦ διάκειται ὁ λογισμὸς ἐπὶ τῇ τοῦ φόνου ἁμαρτίᾳ· ὃς τοσοῦτον ἔλεγεν ἀπέχειν λύπης ὡς καὶ προσευχαριστεῖν ἐπὶ τῷ φόνῳ· γεγένηται γὰρ αὐτῷ ὑπόθεσις σωτηρίας ὁ ἀκούσιος φόνος. Ἔλεγε δὲ ἀπὸ γραφῶν φέρων τὴν μαρτυρίαν ὅτι οὐκ ἂν Μωσῆς ἠξιοῦτο τῆς θεϊκῆς ὀπτασίας ⌜καὶ τῆς τοσαύτης δωρεᾶς καὶ τῆς συγγραφῆς τῶν ἁγίων λόγων⌝, εἰ μὴ φόβῳ τοῦ Φαραὼ διὰ τὸν φόνον ὃν ἔδρασεν ἐν τῇ Αἰγύπτῳ κατειλήφει τὸ ὄρος τὸ Σινᾶ.

Ταῦτα δὲ λέγω οὐχ ὁδοποιῶν εἰς φόνον, δεικνύων δὲ ὅτι εἰσὶ καὶ περιστατικαὶ ἀρεταί, ὅταν μὴ ἑκουσίως τις τῷ ἀγαθῷ προσέλθῃ· τῶν γὰρ ἀρετῶν αἱ μέν εἰσι προαιρετικαί, αἱ δὲ περιστατικαί.[23]

The first two lines of the tale introduce the protagonist by giving just his name (Makarios), age (18 years old), and occupation (herdsman). Makarios' accidental killing of an anonymous young man initiates plot movement. Wishing to repent for his crime, Makarios withdraws secretly to the desert. The severity of his bodily renunciation is quite striking: he lives alone in the open air, enduring the desert's difficult weather conditions. No further explanation is provided concerning the homeless phase of Makarios' asceticism, but its specified time frame (three years) highlights the hero's continuous suffering, which renders it even more praiseworthy. The second phase of Makarios' ascetic life, which is equally elliptically described, is marked by his sheltered feats and his ability to perform exorcisms, which constitute the strongest proof of his deliverance from his serious sin. The duration of this second phase is also given. It lasts twenty-five years, that is, about eight times longer than the first phase, which functions as a preparation for the second phase.

A third phase in the hero's ascetic life – marked by a new paragraph in the above quotation – is initiated through the appearance of another hero, the storyteller and Makarios' biographer, who is Palladios himself. In this third phase, Makarios' total isolation, characterizing the first two phases, is broken. Now Makarios acquires disciples and becomes a teacher of repentance. Palladios, who, as he explains, had the chance to spend considerable time with the protagonist, is very interested in hearing about Makarios' experience of

---

23   Palladios of Hellenopolis, *Lausiac History* (BHG 1435–1438), ed. D.C. Butler, *The Lausiac History of Palladius*, vol. 2: *Introduction and Text* (Cambridge: 1904) 1–169, ch. 15; trans. R. Meyer, *Palladius: The Lausiac History*, Ancient Christian Writers: The Works of the Fathers in Translation 34 (New York – Mahwah, NJ: 1964) 51–52.

homicide and sin. However, he allows the tale's audience to get only a very sketchy impression of this experience, which appears as a duplication of the biblical Moses' corresponding experience. At this point Makarios' biographical tale ends.

In the last paragraph of the above quotation, Palladios briefly explains his choice as a storyteller. In so doing, Palladios recalls Menas, the previously discussed sailor from Anastasios of Sinai's *Edifying Tales*, who, as Anastasios remarks, narrates his experience of the marvelous – which is related to another religion that is condemned by the author – to prove the truth of Christianity. Here, Palladios highlights the reason why he is sharing Makarios' previous experience of such a serious sin as homicide. His intention, as he points out, is to use this very experience as a moral lesson for the tale's readers or listeners. For Palladios, Makarios' example constitutes a strong manifestation of the fact that goodness might be a result of circumstances and not of innate ability. He thus implies that had Makarios not committed homicide he would never have become such a holy man. It is, in fact, due to the life he acquired in penitence that his *bios* could be turned into the biographical tale which Palladios includes in his *Lausiac History*, a work aiming at 'increasing the [moral] strength' of its audiences, particularly when they are 'afflicted with spiritual dryness' (ἐνδυνα-μώσει σε, κἂν ἐν ἀκηδίᾳ τυγχάνῃς).[24] As already remarked, the function of a tale as a moral lesson is common in the examined texts. This moral lesson often appears as the very reason for a given tale's inclusion in a particular anthology.

As for an example of a polythematic multiple-episode tale, a case in point is the following narrative from the miracle collection of Thekla:

> The miracle concerning myself [...] I will tell. 'Anthrax' is the name given [...] to a certain malady [...]. I was greatly afraid [...] that the infection [...] might put my entire life in jeopardy. [...]
>
> I saw the virgin entering the place where I was sleeping. [...] After entering and witnessing the wasps' attack against me, [...] she scared away that great swarm of wasps [...] and set me free from all those terrible enemies. This is the vision which happened to me. But when daylight appeared and began to shine, I found I had been delivered from that fierce pain and suffering [...]. The miracle happened in this way and such was its resolution. I will now recount the one which followed [...].
>
> This youngster Basil – let me pass by now how he came to be bishop and gained control of the church, ⟨a tale⟩ which does not deserve to be

---

24   *Lausiac History*, Prologue, 16.4; trans. Meyer, *Palladius* 29.

(AUTO)BIOGRAPHICAL, MARVELOUS, AND SUPERNATURAL STORIES 207

narrated – began to rage against me [...] – for I [...] opposed this destructive election, as being an impure, unjust and profane act – and he continued to plot against me in every way possible.

Once he even fabricated a charge [...] and he excluded me from the divine mysteries, as it is customary to exclude those who truly sin. [...] A black pygmy filled with darkness and doom [...] – Zamaras was the name of this black man – this fellow seemed to approach me while I was sleeping, and held out what we commonly call a *tremisis* [...]. This coin, too, was dark and very black [...]. I took it against my will and without pleasure, I must confess. For the dream seemed to me to be the sort of prophecy auguring nothing good. The dream ceased at that point, just as day was coming on, and, while I was still ruminating and disturbed by this vision, our own white Zamaras [i.e. Basil] [...] imposed upon me the sentence of my excommunication [...].

Once this had occurred, a great disorderly tumult of shouting arose in the church and in the city, since everyone was amazed at the shamelessness and irregularity of the deed. My friends were downcast, as were all those in authority, as many of them as knew what had befallen me. Thomas, a holy man and beloved of God, [...] railed against Basil and Euboulos, reproaching their ridiculous machination against me [...]. Relatives and friends were already preparing for battle against Basil and Euboulos and were ready to do something rash against them. But I restrained them from their impulse. [...] Then [...] I recalled my vision of Zamaras, recognizing that those images had been symbols of these current events, even a forewarning, and that now the evil would cease.

I was already in the second day of my excommunication and night was falling. [...] The martyr stood at my side in a girl's appearance [...]. And taking my right hand, she gave me that very thing of which Basil had wickedly deprived me. 'Take this and be courageous, my child [...].' Having uttered [these words], she flew away [...]. But I stood up and found my hand filled with an extraordinary fragrance. I [...] said to my friends who were present: 'Today [...] Basil will revoke the excommunication [...].' When the third day arrived, Basil summoned me and revoked the sentence against me.

Τὸ δὲ περὶ ἐμὲ αὐτὸν θαῦμα, [...] λέξω. Ἄνθραξ καλεῖταί τι πάθος [...] καὶ ἦν πολὺς ὁ φόβος ἐμοί [...] μὴ [...] τῇ πάσῃ μου λυμήνηται ζωῇ. [...]

Ἐδόκουν [...] καθεύδειν [...] ἐπεισελθοῦσαν [τὴν παρθένον] δὲ καὶ θεασαμένην τὸν κατ᾽ ἐμοῦ τῶν σφηκῶν πόλεμον [...] τὸν πολὺν ἐκεῖνον ὅμαδον τῶν σφηκῶν ἀποσοβῆσαί [...] καὶ ἐμὲ πάντων ἐκείνων ἐλευθερῶσαι τῶν δεινῶν πολεμίων. Καὶ ἡ μὲν ὄψις ἡ γεγονυῖά μοι αὕτη· τῆς δὲ ἡμέρας ἤδη φανείσης καὶ ὑπολάμπειν ἀρχομένης, ἐγὼ μὲν ἀπηλλάγμην τῶν ἀγρίων ἐκείνων πόνων καὶ ἀλγηδόνων [...]. Καὶ τόδε μὲν τὸ θαῦμα ὧδέ τε ἔσχε καὶ ὧδε ἐτελεύτησεν· ὃ δὲ ἐφεξῆς εἰμι ἐρῶν.

[...] Τὸ μειράκιον τοῦτο Βασίλειος, τὸ μὲν ὅπως ἐπίσκοπός τε ἐγένετο καὶ τῆς ἐκκλησίας ἐκράτησε, τὸ μηδὲ σκηνῆς ἄξιον, ἀφείσθω τὰ νῦν· [...] ἀρξάμενον ὑπομηνιᾶν μοι – καὶ γὰρ [...] ταῖς περὶ αὐτοῦ κακαῖς καὶ ὀλεθρίοις ψήφοις ἀντέκρουσα, ὡς οὔτε εὐαγέσιν, οὔτε τὸ δίκαιον, οὔτε τὸ ὅσιον ἐχούσαις –, πάντα τρόπον ἐπιβουλεῦόν μοι διετέλει.

Καὶ δή ποτε καὶ πλασάμενος αἰτίαν [...] τῶν θείων εἴργει με μυστηρίων, ᾗ νόμος τοὺς ἀληθῶς πταίοντας εἴργειν. [...] Ἀνθρωπίσκος γάρ τις αἰθίοψ, ζόφου καὶ ἀχλύος πεπληρωμένος [...] – Ζαμαρᾶς δὲ ἦν ὄνομα τούτῳ τῷ Αἰθίοπι –, οὗτος καθεύδοντί μοι προσιέναι τε ἔδοξε καὶ ὀρέγειν ὃ καλεῖν ἔθος ἡμῖν τριμίσιον [...] ζοφῶδες δὲ καὶ τοῦτο ἦν καὶ μελάντατον [...]. Τοῦτο ἄκων ἐδεξάμην καὶ οὐχ ἡδέως, ὁμολογῶ· καὶ γὰρ ὄναρ ἔδοξέ μοι οὐκ ἀγαθοῦ τινος εἶναι μάντευμα τὸ τοιοῦτο. Καὶ τὸ μὲν ὄναρ εἰς τοῦτο ἔληξεν, ἄρτι δὲ ἡμέρας γεγονυίας, καὶ ἔτι μοι τὰ κατὰ τὴν ὄψιν ταύτην διανοουμένῳ καὶ ἀσχάλλοντι ὁ λευκὸς οὗτος Ζαμαρᾶς [...] ἐπάγει μοι τὴν τῆς ἀκοινωνησίας ψῆφον [...].

Τούτου δὲ γεγονότος, θόρυβός τε πολὺς καὶ θροῦς ἄτακτος κατὰ τὴν ἐκκλησίαν, κατὰ τὴν πόλιν, πάντων τὸ τοῦ πράγματος ἀναιδὲς καὶ ἄτοπον θαυμαζόντων, κατηφεῖς δὲ οἱ φίλοι καὶ οἱ ἐν τέλει πάντες, ὅσοι δὴ καὶ τὰ καθ' ἡμᾶς ᾔδεσαν. Ὁ δὲ Θωμᾶς, ἀνὴρ ἅγιος καὶ Θεῷ φίλος [...] κατεβόα μὲν τοῦ Βασιλείου καὶ Εὐβούλου, τὴν καταγέλαστον αὐτῶν ἐπ' ἐμοὶ σκαιωρίαν ὀνειδίζων [...]. ἤδη δὲ καὶ συγγενῶν καὶ φίλων ὁπλιζομένων κατὰ τοῦ Βασιλείου καὶ Εὐβούλου καὶ δρᾶσαι κατ' αὐτῶν νεανικόν τι βουλευομένων, ἐκείνους μὲν τῆς ὁρμῆς ἐπέσχον [...]. Ἐπὶ τούτοις [...] ἦλθον καὶ εἰς μνήμην τῆς κατὰ Ζαμαρᾶν ὄψεως, καὶ ὡς τῶν γεγονότων τούτων ἐκεῖνα σύμβολα ἦν καὶ προάγγελσις, καὶ ὡς ἤδη λωφήσει τὸ κακόν.

Δευτέρας γοῦν ἡμέρας ἤδη μοι οὔσης ἐπὶ τῇ ἀκοινωνησίᾳ καὶ τῆς νυκτὸς ἐπιλαβούσης, [...] ἐφίσταταί μοι ἡ μάρτυς ἐν κορικῷ σχήματι [...] καὶ λαβομένη μου τῆς δεξιᾶς χειρὸς ἐντίθησί μοι ὅπερ Βασίλειος οὐκ οἶδα εἰ καλῶς ἀφείλετο· Ἔχε καὶ θάρρει, τέκνον [...]. Καὶ ἡ μὲν ταῦτα εἰποῦσα ἀπέπτη [...], ἐγὼ δὲ διαναστὰς τὴν μὲν χεῖρα ἐξαισίου τινὸς εὐωδίας εὗρον πεπληρωμένην [...] τοῖς παραγεγονόσι τῶν φίλων εἶπον εὐθὺς ὡς· Σήμερον [...] Βασίλειος λύσει τὴν ἀκοινωνησίαν [...]. τῆς γὰρ τρίτης ἡμέρας ἐπιγενομένης, μεταπεμψάμενός με ὁ Βασίλειος λύει τὴν ἐπ' ἐμοὶ ψῆφον.[25]

---

25 *Miracles of Thekla*, ch. 12; trans. S.F. Johnson, "The Miracles of Thekla", in Talbot A.M. – Johnson S.F. (trans.), *Miracle Tales from Byzantium*, Dumbarton Oaks Medieval Library 12

(AUTO)BIOGRAPHICAL, MARVELOUS, AND SUPERNATURAL STORIES 209

This tale consists of six episodes which, as above, we have made discernible by presenting each episode in a new paragraph. There are four autobiographical and two supernatural episodes, which are organized in the following manner: autobiographical – supernatural – autobiographical – autobiographical – autobiographical – supernatural. In other words, the tale starts with an autobiographical episode and ends with a supernatural one. The two supernatural episodes provide solutions to the hagiographer's health and personal problems as exemplified in the autobiographical episodes. Thematically, the six episodes might be divided into two units, which the hagiographer presents as two distinct miracles that are combined in one tale: the hagiographer's miraculous cure (the first autobiographical episode and the following supernatural episode), and the enmity of Basil against the hagiographer followed by the miraculous end of the latter's excommunication (the subsequent three autobiographical episodes and the last supernatural episode).

The first and shorter unit, which consists of two episodes, concerns the hagiographer's life-threatening disease (described in some detail) and its miraculous healing. The night before his scheduled surgery in which one of his fingers was to be amputated to prevent the infection's spreading throughout his body, Saint Thekla appears in a dream (also described in some detail) to rescue the author's finger and life through a healing that takes place in an allegorical way.[26] The martyr's destruction of the murderous wasps that attack the author in his dream functions as a symbol for the cure of a disease that 'feels like a hotly burning inflammation' (διακαὲς ἄγαν καὶ φλογῶδες),[27] and, as we shall understand by reading the tale's second unit, it also symbolizes the subsequent vanishing of Basil's burning enmity against the hagiographer. Thekla's dreamlike epiphany does not just provide a supernatural solution to the hero's dangerous health problem. It also constitutes a powerful manifestation of the fact that he is the martyr's favorite protégé, who will once again be protected when facing Basil's enmity – the central thread of the tale's second unit.

The episode introducing the second unit explains the source and initiation of Basil's hatred against the hagiographer. The latter refrains from embedding another tale into this tale – 'which does not deserve to be narrated'. This other account concerns Basil's ascendance to the bishopric throne, which, as

---

(Cambridge, MA – London: 2012) 1–201, at 47, 49, 51, 53, 55. For ch. 12 from Thekla's collection, see also Chapter 5 in this volume.

26   For allegorical healing dreams, and mainly for this particular one, see Constantinou S., "The Morphology of Healing Dreams: Dream and Therapy in Byzantine Collections of Miracle Stories", in Angelidi C. – Calofonos G. (eds.), *Dreaming in Byzantium and Beyond* (Aldershot: 2014) 21–34, at 33–34.

27   Trans. Johnson, "The Miracles of Thekla" 47, with minor changes.

the hagiographer believes, being achieved by 'impure' and 'unjust' means and machinations, deserves to remain untold.[28] According to the hagiographer, Basil developed a strong hatred against him because he openly opposed his treacherous election as a bishop.

The following episode develops around the most striking display of Basil's hatred: the hagiographer's excommunication, a charge normally imposed against true sinners. The hagiographer is warned of this development by an unpleasant premonitory dream that is an allegory of Basil's villainous charge. The last autobiographical episode revolves around the stark reactions of both churchmen and laymen against the hagiographer's excommunication. Our hero undertakes immediate action in an attempt to prevent his friends from preparing a battle against Basil and his supporter Euboulos.

The last episode has many parallels with the first episode. Here, too, the author is greatly distressed. His previously imminent biological death is now replaced by a social death provoked by the excommunication. The martyr arrives once again in a dream to act as a *deus ex machina*. This time, however, she looks different: she has the guise of a young girl. Yet her behavior does not cease to be allegorical. She places something in the hero's hand that symbolizes his right to be member of the church. This mystical substance is transformed into an extraordinary fragrance when the hagiographer wakes up from the dream. This very fragrance has a function key to the dream's interpretation. The hagiographer concludes that the excommunication will soon end. The next day – the excommunication's third day – Basil is forced by the martyr to summon the hagiographer and cancel the punishment. The excommunication's end also brings an end to Basil's enmity, and the two men are on good terms thereafter.

As the previous discussion of a monothematic multiple-episode tale and its polythematic counterpart has shown, each episode of such a tale can be approached and apprehended on its own, but its actual narrative power lies in the fact that it constitutes part of a series of episodes that shape the tale. These episodes are frequently connected with each other through transition words or phrases. For example, these might indicate time (e.g. 'it was still night', νὺξ δὲ ἦν ἔτι; 'once this had occurred', τούτου δὲ γεγονότος; 'I was already in the second day of my excommunication and night was falling', δευτέρας γοῦν ἡμέρας ἤδη μοι οὔσης ἐπὶ τῇ ἀκοινωνησίᾳ καὶ τῆς νυκτὸς ἐπιλαβούσης).[29] They might also be short interventions made by the storyteller pointing to the end of the previous episode and the beginning of the next one (e.g. 'The miracle happened in this

---

28   Ibidem, 51.

29   *Miracles of Thekla*, ch. 12, 18, 72, 91; trans. Johnson, "The Miracles of Thekla" 49, 53, 55.

(AUTO)BIOGRAPHICAL, MARVELOUS, AND SUPERNATURAL STORIES   211

way and such was its resolution. I will now recount the one which followed',
Καὶ τόδε μὲν τὸ θαῦμα ὧδέ τε ἔσχε καὶ ὧδε ἐτελεύτησεν. ὃ δὲ ἐφεξῆς εἰμι ἐρῶν).[30]
In multiple-episode tales, episodes are stitched together both thematically
and chronologically. For example, a series of (auto)biographical episodes is
strung together following the course of the protagonist's life after the performance of certain actions (e.g. homicide leading to repentance leading to
spiritual teaching) or in situations such as disease and enmity (e.g. the beginning and development of the disease or enmity). The interchange of (auto)bio-
graphical and supernatural episodes, for instance, might serve purposes related
to the protagonist's situation, with the latter episodes being the result of the
first ones. As the case of chapter 12 from the *Miracles of Thekla* indicates, supernatural episodes follow autobiographical episodes to provide divine solutions
to central issues in the protagonist's life.

3   The Frame Tale

Being anthologies, the examined texts are unavoidably framed by a prologue
and/or an epilogue in which the redactor-storyteller directly addresses his
audience, presenting among other things the general character of his work and
its sources, authenticity, purpose, and importance. The function of such frames
is as what the famous narratologist Gérard Genette has termed 'paratexts'.[31]
According to Genette, a paratext 'surrounds and extends' a text 'in order to *present* it [...] to ensure the text's presence [...], its "reception" and consumption'.[32]
In short, Genette proposes that paratexts attempt to 'frame' both positive
reception and 'correct' text understanding and interpretation. Likewise, the
paratexts of our texts – namely their prologues and epilogues – legitimize and
contextualize their collective and polyphonic character. Without this frame,
the texts would appear to be a haphazard accumulation of tales. Through the
frame, by contrast, the tales become part of a whole – a work that constitutes
a conscious gathering of oral tales which were written down by a pilgrim visiting desert fathers or an ecclesiastic related to a miraculous saint's shrine.
Surrounded by such a frame, the tales are *presented* as worthy of consumption and consideration. All in all, the frame makes visible the necessity and

---

30   *Miracles of Thekla*, ch. 12, 41; trans. Johnson, "The Miracles of Thekla" 51.
31   Genette G., *Paratexts: Thresholds of Interpretation*, trans. J.E. Lewin, Literature, Culture,
     Theory 20 (Cambridge: 1997).
32   Ibidem, 1, emphasis in original.

importance of the work of the redactor, who seeks to provide the tales with validity as fundamental cultural documents of early Byzantine Christianity.

In addition to their external frame, the works under discussion have several internal frames which can be detected within their individual tales. One of these internal frames might be another prologue and/or epilogue that reproduces on a smaller scale the external frame of an anthology. The rest of the internal frames, which form what we call here a 'frame tale', establish a tale-within-a-tale arrangement created through the presence of a primary storyteller who introduces further storytellers telling new tales that are embedded in the frame tale. It is these storytelling frames that we are examining in this final part of the present analysis.

In the *History of Monks in Egypt*, we read the following frame tale:

ON KOPRES
There was a priest called Kopres [...]. He was a holy man, nearly ninety years old and the superior of fifty brothers. [...] When he saw us, he embraced us and prayed for us. [...] But we asked him rather to explain to us the virtues of his own rule of life. [...] He gave us an account of his own life and that of his great predecessors [...].

ON PATERMUTHIOS
'For example, there was a father who lived before us called Patermuthios. He was the first of the monks in this place and was also the first to devise the monastic habit. In his former life as a pagan, he had been a brigand chief and a tomb robber, and he had become notorious for his crimes. But he found the following occasion of salvation. [...]

He once [...] was taken up in a vision into the heavens. [...] He related how he had eaten of the fruits of paradise, and he showed evidence of the fact. For he had brought the disciples a large choice fig, deliciously scented, to prove to them that what he said was true.'

The priest Kopres who was telling us this story, being at a time a young man, saw this fig in the hands of Patermuthios' disciples, and kissed it, and admired its scent. 'For many years', he said, 'it remained with his disciples, being kept as evidence of the father's visit to paradise. It was of enormous size. Indeed, a sick man had only to smell it and he was at once cured of his illness [...].'

'These and even greater things', said Kopres, 'were achieved by our Father Patermuthios while performing signs and wonders. And other such men have lived before us of whom the world was not worthy [...].'

(AUTO)BIOGRAPHICAL, MARVELOUS, AND SUPERNATURAL STORIES

While Father Kopres was telling us these stories, one of our party, overcome with incredulity at what was being said, dozed off. [...]

He immediately woke up and told the rest of us who were listening to Kopres, in Latin, what he had seen.

While he was still speaking to us about these things, a peasant carrying a shovelful of sand came up and stood by him, waiting for him to finish his discourse. We asked the father what the peasant wanted the sand for. He replied '[...] for the sake of your zeal and edification, because you have come so far to see us, I will not deprive you of what may be edifying, but will explain in the presence of the brethren what God in his providence has effected through us.

The land bordering us was infertile. [...] For a worm developed in the ear and destroyed the whole crop. Those farmers who had been catechized by us and had become Christians asked us to pray for the harvest. [...] at once their land became extremely fertile, more than anywhere else in Egypt [...].'

ON ABBA SOUROUS

'Once Abba Sourous', said Kopres, 'and Isaiah and Paul, all of them devout men and ascetics, met one another unexpectedly at the river bank as they were on their way to visit the great confessor Anough [...].

Abba Anough said to them, "[...] Everything I have asked from God I have received at once. I have often seen tens of thousands of angels standing before God [...]."

Having spoken to us about these things and much else for three days, he delivered us his soul. At once angels received it, and choirs of martyrs led it up to heaven, while the fathers looked on and heard the hymns.'

ON ABBA HELLE

'Another father, called Abba Helle, had preserved since childhood the ascetic life. He often carried fire to his neighbouring brethren in the fold of his tunic [...].'

When father Kopres had finished telling us these amazing stories and other things even more wonderful, and had treated us with all customary kindness, he took us into his own garden and showed us date-palms and other fruit trees which he had planted himself in the desert. This had been suggested to him by the faith of those peasants to whom he had said that even the desert can bear fruit for those who have faith in God: 'For when I saw that they sowed sand and their land bore fruit', he said, 'I tried to do the same and I succeeded'.

Περὶ Κόπρη

Ἦν δέ τις πρεσβύτερος [...] Κόπρης λεγόμενος, ἀνὴρ ἅγιος ἐτῶν σχεδὸν ἐνενήκοντα, ἡγούμενος ἀδελφῶν πεντήκοντα [...]. ὡς οὖν ἡμᾶς ἐθεάσατο, ἠσπάσατο
καὶ ὑπερηύξατο [...]. ἡμεῖς δὲ ἠξιοῦμεν αὐτὸν μᾶλλον ἡμῖν τῆς οἰκείας πολι-
τείας τὰς ἀρετὰς ὑφηγήσασθαι [...]. ὑφηγεῖτο ἡμῖν τόν τε ἑαυτοῦ βίον καὶ τῶν
αὐτοῦ προγενεστέρων [...].

⟨Περὶ Πατερμουθίου⟩

Ἦν γὰρ πατήρ τις πρὸ ἡμῶν, ὀνόματι Πατερμούθιος, πρῶτος τῶν ἐν τῷ τόπῳ
τούτῳ μοναχῶν αὐτὸς γενόμενος καὶ τὸ μοναδικὸν ἔνδυμα τοῦτο πρῶτος ἐφευ-
ρών. οὗτος ἀρχιληστὴς πρῶτον καὶ νεκροτάφος Ἑλλήνων ὑπάρχων καὶ διαβόη-
τος ἐπὶ κακίᾳ γενόμενος πρόφασιν εὕρατο σωτηρίας τοιαύτην [...].

καὶ ἀπῆχθαι δὲ αὐτὸν ἐν σαρκὶ ἔφη εἰς τὸν παράδεισον [...]. μετειληφέναι
δὲ αὐτὸν ἔλεγεν ἐκ τῶν καρπῶν τοῦ παραδείσου καὶ μάρτυρα τοῦ πράγματος
ἐδείκνυεν· σῦκον γὰρ ἓν μέγα καὶ ἐξαίρετον καὶ εὐωδίας πολλῆς μεστὸν πρὸς
τοὺς ἑαυτοῦ μαθητὰς ἀπεκόμισεν ἐπιδεικνύων αὐτοῖς ὅτι ἀληθές ἐστι τὰ παρ'
αὐτοῦ λεγόμενα.'

ὅπερ σῦκον ὁ διηγούμενος ἡμῖν ταῦτα Κόπρης ὁ πρεσβύτερος νεανίας τότε
ὑπάρχων ἐν ταῖς χερσὶ τῶν μαθητῶν αὐτοῦ ἐθεάσατο καὶ κατεφίλησεν καὶ τὴν
πνοὴν ἐθαύμασεν. 'Πολλοῖς γὰρ ἔτεσι', φησί, 'διέμεινεν παρὰ τοῖς αὐτοῦ μαθη-
ταῖς εἰς ἐπίδειξιν φυλαττόμενον. ἦν γὰρ παμμέγεθες. μόνον γάρ τις ὀσφρήσατο
αὐτοῦ τῶν κακουμένων, εὐθέως τῆς νόσου ἀπηλλάττετο [...].'

'Ταῦτά τε καὶ ἄλλα πλείονα καὶ μεγάλα', φησίν, 'κατώρθωσεν ὁ πατὴρ ἡμῶν
Πατερμούθιος ποιῶν σημεῖα καὶ τέρατα. καὶ ἄλλοι τοιοῦτοί τινες πρὸ ἡμῶν
γεγόνασιν, ὧν οὐκ ἦν ἄξιος ὁ κόσμος. [...].'

Καὶ ὡς ἦν ἔτι ταῦτα διηγούμενος ἡμῖν Κόπρης ὁ πατήρ, ἀπονυστάξας εἷς ἐξ
ἡμῶν ἀδελφὸς ἀπιστίᾳ περὶ τῶν λεγομένων φερόμενος [...].

ὁ δὲ ταραχθεὶς εὐθὺς ἡμῖν ἀκρωμένοις αὐτοῦ τὸ ὁραθὲν ῥωμαϊστὶ ἐξέφηνεν.

ἔτι δὲ τούτου λαλοῦντος πρὸς ἡμᾶς ταῦτα ἐπῆλθέν τις ἄγροικος κύαθον
ἔχων μεστὸν ψάμμου καὶ παρειστήκει πληρῶσαι αὐτὸν ἐκδεχόμενος τὴν
διήγησιν. ἐπυνθανόμεθα δὲ ἡμεῖς αὐτοῦ τοῦ πατρός τί ἄρα θέλει ὁ ἄγροικος
μετὰ τῆς ψάμμου. ἀπεκρίνατο δὲ πρὸς ἡμᾶς ὁ πατὴρ λέγων· '[...] διὰ δὲ τὴν
ὑμῶν σπουδὴν καὶ ὠφέλειαν, ὅτι ἐκ τοσούτου μήκους πρὸς ἡμᾶς ἐληλύθατε, οὐ
ζημιῶ ὑμᾶς τῆς ὠφελείας, ἀλλ' ἅπερ δι' ἡμῶν ὁ θεὸς ᾠκονόμησεν παρόντων τῶν
ἀδελφῶν διηγήσομαι.

Ἄκαρπος ἦν ἡ πλησίον ἡμῶν χώρα. [...] σκώληξ γὰρ γεννώμενος ἐν τῷ
στάχυϊ ὅλον τὸν ἄμητον διέφθειρεν. οἱ δὲ κατηχηθέντες παρ' ἡμῶν γεωργοὶ καὶ
Χριστιανοὶ γεγονότες ἠξίουν ἡμᾶς εὔχεσθαι ὑπὲρ τοῦ θερισμοῦ. [...] καὶ ἐξαίφνης πολύκαρπος ἡ χώρα γεγένηται παρὰ πᾶσαν τὴν Αἴγυπτον [...].'

Περὶ ἀββᾶ Σούρους.

(AUTO)BIOGRAPHICAL, MARVELOUS, AND SUPERNATURAL STORIES 215

Ἀββᾶ Σούρους δέ ποτε᾽, φησίν, ‘καὶ Ἡσαΐας καὶ Παῦλος συνέτυχον ἀλλήλοις ἐξαπίνης ἅμα ἐπὶ τῷ ποταμῷ εὑρεθέντες, ἄνδρες εὐλαβεῖς καὶ ἀσκηταί, ὡς
τὸν μέγαν ὁμολογητὴν ἀββᾶν Ἀνοὺφ ἐπισκεψόμενοι [...].

Εἶπεν δὲ ἀββᾶ Ἀνοὺφ πρὸς αὐτούς· “[...] πᾶν αἴτημα παρὰ τοῦ θεοῦ μου
εὐθὺς ἐλάμβανον. εἶδον πολλάκις μυριάδας ἀγγέλων τῷ θεῷ παρεστώσας [...].”

Ταῦτά τε καὶ ἄλλα πολλὰ διηγούμενος ἐπὶ τρεῖς ἡμέρας παραδίδωσι τὴν
ψυχήν. τὴν δὲ εὐθὺς ἄγγελοι ὑποδεξάμενοι καὶ χοροὶ μαρτύρων εἰς οὐρανὸν
ἀνῆγον αὐτῶν ὁρώντων καὶ ἀκουόντων τοὺς ὕμνους.᾽
Περὶ ἀββᾶ Ἑλλῆ.

Ἄλλος δέ τις πατήρ, ἀββᾶ Ἑλλῆ καλούμενος, ἐκ παιδόθεν τῇ ἀσκήσει προσ-
καρτερήσας τοῖς πλησίον ἀδελφοῖς αὐτοῦ πολλάκις πῦρ ἐν κόλπῳ ἐβάσταζεν
[...].᾽

Ταῦτά τε καὶ ἄλλα πλείονα θαυμαστὰ ὁ πατὴρ Κόπρης ὑφηγησάμενος καὶ
φιλοφρονησάμενος ἡμᾶς κατὰ τρόπον εἰς τὸν ἑαυτοῦ κῆπον εἰσῆγεν δεικνύων
ἡμῖν φοίνικας καὶ ἄλλα ὀπωρικὰ ἅπερ αὐτὸς ἐν τῇ ἐρήμῳ ἐφύτευσεν ὑπὸ τῆς
τῶν ἀγροίκων πίστεως ὑπομνησθείς, πρὸς οὓς εἶπεν ὅτι δύναται καὶ ἡ ἔρημος
καρποφορῆσαι τοῖς ἔχουσι πίστιν πρὸς τὸν θεόν· “Ὡς γὰρ εἶδον᾽, φησίν, ‘αὐτοὺς
τὴν ψάμμον σπείραντας καὶ τὴν χώραν αὐτῶν καρποφορήσασαν, κἀγὼ τὸ αὐτὸ
ἐπιχειρήσας ἐπέτυχον᾽.[33]

Being one of the longest frame tales included in the *History of Monks of Egypt*,
comprising 360 printed lines, this frame tale consists of four different frames,
which together include eight embedded tales. The first frame is created by the
primary storyteller and author of the text, who starts telling the biographical
tale of Kopres, which involves two episodes until the point at which a second
frame or storyteller is introduced. The first episode concerns Kopres' ascetic
and miraculous deeds. The second episode refers to the author's and his companions' meeting with Kopres. So far, the tale appears to follow the pattern
and structure of two-episode biographical tales, such as that of Makarios the
Younger from Palladios' *Lausiac History*, which was examined earlier. When
the primary storyteller and his companions ask Kopres to tell his own story, the
ascetic promises to 'give an account of his own life and that of his predecessors'. In so doing, Kopres initiates a second frame that is in turn interrupted by
other storytellers.

Kopres' first story is a multiple-episode tale involving one of his predecessors and teachers, Patermuthios. This rather long tale has fifteen episodes and
is polythematic, as it includes episodes from all three categories: biographical,

---

33 *History of the Monks in Egypt*, ch. 10–12; trans. Russell, "The Lives of the Desert Fathers"
82–92, with slight modifications.

marvelous, and supernatural. It is possibly due to the tale's many marvelous and supernatural episodes that one of the listeners, a member of the author's group, is 'overcome with incredulity' and falls asleep. The episode with the sleeping man breaks down Kopres' second frame and brings us back to the first frame. The primary storyteller takes over to tell the episode of the sleeping man. In the meantime, the sleeping man, who receives a divine dream, wakes up and starts telling his own supernatural experience, thus disrupting the first frame once again and opening a third frame. Yet, while the man shares his experience, we are informed by the primary narrator that a peasant arrives, and we thus return to the first frame. The first frame is interrupted again by Kopres, who is asked about the reason for the peasant's presence.

At this point Kopres starts the narration of his second tale. This shorter monothematic tale consists of four autobiographical episodes. Kopres explains how he transformed the surrounding infertile land into a fertile one; how he exposed the wrongness of a Manichaean who was leading people astray; how he showed the incorrectness of pagan religion, convincing some pagans to convert to Christianity; and what happened to the vegetables that a pagan stole from his garden. Kopres' second tale, like his first one, is open-ended. Without any intervention from another storyteller, Kopres moves to this third tale, which involves three other ascetics: Sourous, Isaiah, and Paul. After having been miraculously informed about the imminent death of another ascetic called Anough, the three men decide to visit him, wishing to hear from him for one last time.

This single-episode tale on the three men's mission is interrupted by Anough's own tale, as he introduces the fourth frame. This tale – the seventh in sequence – has an autobiographical and a supernatural episode. He talks about his acquisition of ascetic virtues and his supernatural experiences with angels, saints (i.e. martyrs and confessors), and Satan. His storytelling is abruptly interrupted by Kopres, who talks about Anough's death, thus marking the return to the second frame. Kopres, however, does not return to the story of Anough's three visitors. He goes on to relate another tale instead – his fourth tale, that is, the eighth story of the frame tale. Kopres' last tale is another polythematic multiple-episode tale involving another desert father called Helle. Like all his previous tales, Kopres' final tale has no proper end. It is once again interrupted by the primary storyteller, who brings us back to the first frame, which closes with a third and last episode that belongs to the storyteller's first tale. The primary storyteller resumes the first frame through the phrase 'When Father Kopres had finished telling us these amazing stories [...]'. He then goes on to describe Kopres' hospitality, which included a guided visit to his garden. The primary storyteller's tale on Kopres is another open-ended tale, which

(AUTO)BIOGRAPHICAL, MARVELOUS, AND SUPERNATURAL STORIES 217

closes with Kopres' words: 'For when I saw that they sowed sand and their land bore fruit, I tried to do the same and I succeeded'.

As the analysis of this frame tale reveals, storytelling in this third and most complex structure of early Byzantine tales operates on multiple levels with diverse combinations of storytellers, tale structures (single-episode tale; multiple-episode tale, either monothematic or polythematic), and audiences. The first frame or level consists of the primary storyteller – the redactor of the collection as a whole – and his audience of all readers and listeners at different places and times throughout the centuries. The primary storyteller starts his art of storytelling (level 1) by constructing a frame that will come to support a highly elaborate tale structure.

While introducing the first frame, or the main framing story, the primary storyteller introduces a new protagonist, Kopres, who becomes a storyteller too, and initiates a second narrative level (level 2) containing its own audience, who are Kopres' visitors, including the primary storyteller and his fellow travellers. At some point, the primary storyteller breaks the second level to initiate the third one (level 3) through the episode of the sleeping monk who undertakes to tell his own dreamlike experience. The now awakened monk's listeners are those of Kopres plus Kopres himself. When Kopres resumes his storytelling, he creates a fourth narrative level (level 4) by introducing a fourth storyteller, the hermit Anough.

Through the four storytellers and the narrative levels they create, a number of tales are enclosed within others. The primary storyteller's tale boxes eight tales, while Kopres' tale on Sourous, Isaiah, and Paul embeds Anough's tale. Even though different storytelling levels are at work simultaneously, each boxed tale is completed before the tale within which it is enclosed closes. The variety of storytelling voices also creates an uncertainty concerning who is telling the tale each time. The open-endedness of most tales, including those of the first frame, gives the impression that the frame tale and the *History of the Monks in Egypt* as a whole, and by implication all tales involving Egyptian ascetics, are ongoing. They could go on forever.

In general, the arrangement of tales within the frame tales of the examined corpus shows certain patterns of balance and repetition, stressing either similarity between individual tales or contrast. For example, Kopres' autobiographical tales and those he tells about his predecessors stress the similarities that bring together their exemplary protagonists. The episode of the disbelieving man, by contrast, highlights the differences among tale protagonists and also audiences: those who believe the stories and use them as exemplars and those who do not. The associations of resemblance and difference are established by various devices, such as imagery, characters, situations, and words or phrases.

These devices function independently to strengthen the internal cohesion of a frame tale, but they also tighten a collection's internal structure.

4 Conclusions

Through the preceding analysis, we have sought to establish a new theoretical framework for the study of hagiographical tales in early Byzantine hagiographical collections. These tales may be divided into categories according to their agents: biographical, marvelous, and supernatural. Their structural forms are also three in number: the single-episode tale, the multiple-episode tale, and the frame tale. An episode creates and sustains a single tale, while a series of episodes form the more complicated structures of the multiple-episode tale and the frame tale. In the two latter cases, episodes that, in one sense, are complete, independent narrative units with a certain intrinsic value in themselves are connected with other episodes and with a given frame. These connective threads weave a broader context from which the tales or episodes derive a certain meaning that might be quite distinct from that of the tales told in isolation.

Early Byzantine hagiographical authors used the agents and structural forms of tales in diverse ways according to the types of their collections and their personal needs and tastes, as well as those of their audiences. Although the biographical, supernatural, and marvelous agents are present in the tales of all the examined works, certain collections showcase a preference for one or another. For example, collective biographies favor (auto)biographical tales, miracle collections are more interested in the supernatural, while collections of edifying tales have the tendency to include marvelous tales.

Bibliography

Primary Sources

Anastasios of Sinai, *Edifying Tales* (BHG 1448q–1448qo). In ed. F. Nau, "Le texte grec du moine Anastase sur les saints pères du Sinaï", *Oriens Christianus* 2 (1902) 58–89 [first collection]; F. Nau, "Le texte grec des récits utiles à l'âme d'Anastase (le Sinaïte)", *Oriens Christianus* 3 (1903) 56–75 and S. Heid, "Die C-Reihe erbaulicher Erzählungen des Anastasios vom Sinai im Codex Vaticanus Graecus 2592", *Orientalia Christiana periodica* 74 (2008) 71–114 [second collection].

History of the Monks in Egypt (BHG 1333–1334). In ed. A.-J. Festugière, *Historia monachorum in Aegypto*, Subsidia hagiographica 34 (Brussels: 1961).

John Moschos, *Spiritual Meadow* (BHG 1440f–1442z). In *Patrologia Graeca* 87.3:2852–3112.

Miracles of Thekla (BHG 1718). In ed. G. Dagron, *Vie et miracles de sainte Thècle: Texte grec, traduction et commentaire*, Subsidia hagiographica 62 (Paris: 1978) 285–412.

Miracles of Artemios (BHG 173–173c). In ed. A. Papadopoulos-Kerameus, *Varia Graeca sacra* (St. Petersburg: 1909) 1–75.

Palladios of Hellenopolis, *Lausiac History* (BHG 1435–1438). In ed. D.C. Butler, *The Lausiac History of Palladius*, vol. 2: *Introduction and Text* (Cambridge: 1904) 1–169.

Sayings of the Desert Fathers (*Apophthegmata Patrum*), Anonymous Collection. In ed. F. Nau, "Histoires des solitaires égyptiens", *Revue de l'Orient chrétien* 12 (1907) 43–69, (1908) 171–189 and 393–413; 13 (1909) 47–66, 266–297; 14 (1912) 357–379; 17 (1913) 204–211, 294–301; and 18 (1913) 137–146; J. Wortley, *The Anonymous Sayings of the Desert Fathers: A Select Edition and Complete English Translation* (Cambridge: 2013).

Secondary Works

Constantinou S., "The Morphology of Healing Dreams: Dream and Therapy in Byzantine Collections of Miracle Stories", in Angelidi C. – Calofonos G. (eds.), *Dreaming in Byzantium and Beyond* (Aldershot: 2014) 21–34.

Constantinou S. – Andreou A., "The Voices of the Tale: The Storyteller in Early Byzantine Collective Biographies, Miracle Collections, and Collections of Edifying Tales", *Byzantine and Modern Greek Studies* 46.1 (2021) 24–40, DOI: 10.1017/byz.2021.31.

Cox Miller P., *The Corporeal Imagination: Signifying the Holy in Late Ancient Christianity* (Philadelphia: 2009).

Cox Miller P., "Strategies of Representation in Collective Biography: Constructing the Subject as Holy", in Hägg T. – Rousseau P. (eds.), *Greek Biography and Panegyric in Late Antiquity* (Berkeley: 2000) 209–254.

Crisafulli V.S. – Nesbitt J.W. (trans.), *The Miracles of St. Artemios: A Collection of Miracle Stories by an Anonymous Author of Seventh-Century Byzantium* (Leiden – New York – Cologne: 1997).

Genette G., *Paratexts: Thresholds of Interpretation*, trans. J.E. Lewin, Literature, Culture, Theory 20 (Cambridge: 1997).

Goodison L., "Sunlight, Divination, and the Dead in Aegean Ritual Tradition", in Papadopoulos C. – Moyes H. (eds.), *The Oxford Handbook of Light in Archaeology* (Oxford: 2022) 185–206.

Johnson S.F., *The Life and Miracles of Thekla: A Literary Study*, Hellenic Studies 13 (Cambridge, MA – London: 2006).

Johnson S.F. (trans.), "The Miracles of Thekla", in Talbot A.M. – Johnson S.F. (trans.), *Miracle Tales from Byzantium*, Dumbarton Oaks Medieval Library 12 (Cambridge, MA – London: 2012) 1–201.

Le Goff J., *The Medieval Imagination*, trans. A. Goldhammer (Chicago – London: 1988).

Lockyer H., *All the Men of the Bible* (Grand Rapids, MI: 1958).

Meyer R. (trans.), *Palladius: The Lausiac History*, Ancient Christian Writers: The Works of the Fathers in Translation 34 (New York – Mahwah, NJ: 1964).

Russell N. (trans.), "The Lives of the Desert Fathers", in Ward B. – Russell N. (eds.), *The Lives of the Desert Fathers*, Cistercian Studies 34 (Kalamazoo, MI: 1981) 47–119.

Todorov T., *Introduction to Poetics*, trans. R. Howard, Theory and History of Literature 1 (Minneapolis: 1981).

Walker Bynum C., *Metamorphosis and Identity* (New York: 2005).

Wortley J. (ed. and trans.), *The Anonymous Sayings of the Desert Fathers: A Select Edition and Complete English Translation* (Cambridge: 2013).

Wortley J. (trans.), *John Moschus, The Spiritual Meadow: Introduction, Translation and Notes*, Cistercian Studies Series 139 (Kalamazoo, MI: 1992).

Wortley J., "Judgment, Heaven and Hell in Byzantine 'Beneficial Tales'", *Dumbarton Oaks Papers* 55 (2001) 53–69.

CHAPTER 9

Space in Edifying Stories: The Case of Anastasios Sinaites

Markéta Kulhánková

1 Introduction

The edifying story (or spiritually beneficial tale) is one of the most prolific genres of early Byzantine hagiography.[1] At the same time, it is one of the most concise Byzantine narrative genres, comprising one simple plot and its message and reducing other elements of narration to a minimum, including descriptions of space. That, however, does not mean that space is not important in this genre. On the contrary: narrative space performs a series of functions and often plays a decisive role in the overall effect of the story. As Charis Messis noted, edifying stories usually focus on a relatively limited time span, but often extend the narration in space – a feature that brings the genre closer to the novel.[2] The aim of this chapter is to look closer at the construction and function of space in this genre and to illustrate some principles with examples from a rather neglected representative: the first collection of stories by Anastasios Sinaites (*c.*630–701). I will suggest that, alongside substantial analogies and genre-specific common features with other collections, the uniqueness of this collection lies in the prominent function of space as narrative device.

---

1 The most complete and useful overviews of the genre are Binggeli A., "Collections of Edifying Stories", in Efthymiadis S. (ed.), *The Ashgate Research Companion to Byzantine Hagiography*, vol. 2: *Genres and Contexts* (Farnham: 2014) 143–159 and Wortley J., "The Genre of the Spiritually Beneficial Tale", *Scripta & e-Scripta* 8/9 (2010) 71–91. See also the (incomplete) list of the stories with abstracts in idem, "The Repertoire of Byzantine 'Spiritually Beneficial Tales'", *Scripta & e-Scripta* 8/9 (2010) 93–306. For the treatment of the edifying story as an independent genre, see also Kulhánková M., *Das gottgefällige Abenteuer: Eine narratologische Analyse der byzantinischen erbaulichen Erzählungen* (Červeny Kostelec: 2015) 13–21.

2 See Messis C., "Fiction and/or Novelisation in Byzantine Hagiography", in Efthymiadis, *The Ashgate Research Companion* 2:313–341. Some prominent examples of an extended story space that includes many relocations in a broad area from various locations of the Egyptian desert, villages, and cities to Jerusalem and Constantinople are offered by the *Daniel-Sketiotes-Dossier*, see Kulhánková M. "'I Went Aboard a Ship and Reached Byzantium': The Motif of Travel in Edifying Stories", in Mitrea M. (ed.), *Holiness on the Move: Mobility and Space in Byzantine Hagiography* (London – New York: 2023) 90–101, at 95–97.

© MARKÉTA KULHÁNKOVÁ, 2025 | DOI:10.1163/9789004707351_011

This is an open access chapter distributed under the terms of the CC BY-NC-ND 4.0 license.

2 Anastasios' *Edifying Tales*

While such collections of tales as the anonymous *History of the Monks in Egypt*, Palladios' *Lausiac History*, or Moschos' *Spiritual Meadow* are widely known and studied,[3] it is not the same case with Anastasios' *Edifying Tales*. One of the reasons for this is that it falls outside the period of early monasticism, in which the genre emerged, and the collections from this period are studied as a novelty illustrating the changed social and spiritual environment.[4] Second, Anastasios' oeuvre is rich, and some of his other works attract more scholarly attention, again as important representatives of the period. This is the case with the apologetic *Viae dux*, the didactic *Questiones et responsiones*, or the exegetical *Hexaemeron*.[5] On the other hand, the *Edifying Tales* could seem, at first sight, to be one more item in the series varying the already established themes and motifs. A third and perhaps the most important reason for the relative neglect of the collection is the lack of an accessible modern critical edition.[6] The two collections (thirty-nine and twenty-eight tales) were first

---

3 For a discussion of the *History of the Monks in Egypt* and the *Spiritual Meadow*, see also Chapters 1, 5, and 8 of this volume.

4 See, e.g., Frank G., *The Memory of the Eyes: Pilgrims to Living Saints in Christian Late Antiquity* (Berkeley – Los Angeles – London: 2000); Harmless W., *Desert Christians: An Introduction to the Literature of Early Monasticism* (Oxford – New York: 2004); Minets J., "Palladius of Helenopolis: One Author, Two Ways to Write", *Journal of Early Christian Studies* 25 (2017) 411–440.

5 For a short and useful outline of Anastasios' position in the Byzantine literature of the seventh century see Haldon J., "The Works of Anastasius of Sinai: A Key Source for the History of Seventh-Century East Mediterranean Society and Belief", in Cameron A. – Conrad L.I. (eds.), *The Byzantine and Early Islamic Near East*, vol. 1: *Problems in the Literary Source Material* (Princeton: 1992) 107–147. For detailed analyses of various aspects of Anastasios' work, with a focus on biographical, theological, and editorial issues, see Uthemann K.-H., *Anastasios Sinaites* (Berlin – Boston: 2015) and idem, *Studien zu Anastasios Sinaites* (Berlin – Boston: 2017).

6 A similar case is the nearly contemporary *Spiritual Meadow* by John Moschos, which, although much more popular than Anastasios' *Edifying Tales*, lacks a modern critical edition as well. In Moschos' case the reason is the plethora of manuscripts and the complicated textual tradition, but the result is the same: very poor scholarly literature compared to the importance of the collection. See the short accounts of this collection in Flusin B., "Palestinian Hagiography (Fourth–Eighth Centuries)", in Efthymiadis S., *The Ashgate Research Companion to Byzantine Hagiography*, vol. 1: *Periods and Places* (Farnham: 2011) 199–226, at 213; and Binggeli, "Collections of Edifying Stories" 146–147; for a more recent and detailed account see Detoraki M., "Récits édifiants et hagiographie: À propos du Pré spiritual", in Rigo A. (ed.), *Byzantine Hagiography: Texts, Themes and Projects* (Turnhout: 2017) 167–178.

SPACE IN EDIFYING STORIES   223

edited by François Nau in 1902 and 1903.[7] The modern edition by André Binggeli remains unpublished,[8] but one well accessible English translation of the first collection is that by Daniel F. Caner, which is based on Binggeli's new edition.[9] Literary analysis supports the division of the material in two collections, suggested first by Bernard Flusin and followed in Binggeli's edition:[10] the two groups display differences in themes, focus, and narrative strategies; the different character of the two collections is indicated already by their titles: *Various Tales about the Fathers of the Desert of the Holy Mount Sinai* (Διηγήσεις διάφοροι περὶ τῶν ἐν τῇ ἐρήμῳ τοῦ Σινᾶ ὅρους ὁσίων πατέρων) and *Spiritually Beneficial and Supportive Tales That Happened in Various Locations in Our Years* (Διηγήματα ψυχωφελῆ καὶ στηρικτικὰ γενόμενα ἐν διαφόροις τόποις ἐπὶ τῶν ἡμετέρων χρόνων). As is obvious, the connecting message of the latter collection is the evidence of the superiority of the Christian faith over the Muslim one, while the first one concentrates geographically on a particular monastic region and thematically on experiences and events of the anchorites and monks living there, and thus resembles the spirit of earlier monastic collections.[11] Most scholars agree that the collection was written around 660, i.e. shortly after the Arab conquest of the Sinai Peninsula.[12] Karl-Heinz Uthemann, on the other hand, argued for an earlier date, the third decade of the seventh century.[13] Similarly, whereas most scholars agree on Anastasios' authorship of both collections, Uthemann considers the first collection inauthentic.[14] The present chapter does not aim to contribute to the debate on these questions of dating or authenticity. Instead, it will argue that, regardless of when and by whom precisely the first collection, as edited by Binggeli, was written down, it consists not of randomly collected

---

7   Anastasios of Sinai, *Edifying Tales*, ed. F. Nau, "Le texte grec du moine Anastase sur les saints pères du Sinaï", *Oriens Christianus* 2 (1902) 58–89; and F. Nau, "Le texte grec des récits utiles à l'âme d'Anastase (le Sinaïte)", *Oriens Christianus* 3 (1903) 56–75.

8   Binggeli A., *Anastase le Sinaite: Récits sur le Sinaï et Récits utiles à l'âme* (Ph.D. dissertation, University of Paris IV: 2001).

9   Caner D.F. (trans.), *History and Hagiography from the Late Antique Sinai* (Liverpool: 2010) 174–196. There is also a modern edition of the Vatican manuscript containing the so-called third collection, which is in fact a version of the second collection; ed. S. Heid, "Die C-Reihe erbaulicher Erzählungen des Anastasios vom Sinai im Codex Vaticanus Graecus 2592", *Orientalia Christiana periodica* 74 (2008) 71–114.

10   Flusin B., "Démons et Sarrasins: L'auteur et le propos des *Diègèmata stèriktika* d'Anastase le Sinaïte", *Travaux et mémoires* 11 (1991) 380–409.

11   Binggeli, "Collections of Edifying Stories" 149.

12   Chitty D., *The Desert a City* (Oxford: 1966) 171; Caner, *History and Hagiography* 173.

13   Uthemann, *Anastasios Sinaites* 422–460.

14   Ibidem, 462–463.

tales, but of carefully organized material, while space plays an important role both as an organizing and as a characterizing element that contributes to the construction of character.[15]

3 Narrative Space and Spatial Reality

In comparison to other narratological categories, such as the narrator, focalization, and especially time, space was considerably late in attracting the attention not only of literary theorists,[16] but also of scholars of humanities and social sciences in general, and this is even more true for Byzantine Studies.[17] With regard to Byzantine literature, until recently there was only one topic related to space that received much scholarly attention: the *ekphrasis*.[18] Only in the last few years have various aspects of space as narratological category and device started being explored and appreciated by students of Byzantine literature, often with the help of methods and tools of narratology,[19] a branch of research which this chapter aims to join.

It is well known that, regardless of how much attention is devoted to the presentation of space in a narrative, it can never be presented in totality: only a – richer or poorer – selection of details is ever offered to the recipient.[20] To outline the facets of space offered in Anastasios' stories to the recipients, as a base on which they construct the narrative world in their imagination, I will

---

15 For various functions of space in narrative see, e.g., de Jong I.J.F., *Narratology and Classics: A Practical Guide* (Oxford: 2014) 122–129.

16 Cf., e.g., ibidem, 105–106. It is symptomatic that in the founding work of classical narratology, there are three chapters devoted to different aspects of narrative time (order, duration, frequency), but no single section focused on space; cf. Genette G., *Narrative Discourse: An Essay in Method*, trans. J.E. Levin (Ithaca, NY: 1980 [1972]).

17 Cf. Veikou M., "Space in Texts and Space as Text: A New Approach to Byzantine Spatial Notions", *Scandinavian Journal of Byzantine and Modern Greek Studies* 2 (2016) 143–175, at 143–147.

18 For bibliography see, e.g., Veikou M. "'Telling Spaces' in Byzantium: Ekphraseis, Place-Making and 'Thick Description'", in Messis C. – Mullett M. – Nilsson I. (eds.), *Storytelling in Byzantium: Narratological Approaches to Byzantine Texts and Images* (Uppsala: 2018) 15–32.

19 Cf., e.g., Roilos P. (ed.), *Medieval Greek Storytelling* (Wiesbaden: 2014), see esp. chapters by Dirkse S. and Cupane C.; the section "Space and Storyworlds" in Messis – Mullett – Nilsson, *Storytelling in Byzantium*, see esp. chapters by Söderblom Saarela E., Vukašinović M., and Weller A.; Mantova Y., "Space Representation in the Life of St. Gregentios and the Life of St. Nikon *the Metanoite*", in Rigo, *Byzantine Hagiography* 157–165.

20 de Jong, *Narratology and Classics* 105.

SPACE IN EDIFYING STORIES 225

use the categorization proposed by Marie-Laure Ryan.[21] In each narrative, she distinguishes five levels of space: spatial frames, setting, story space, narrative world, and narrative universe.

Spatial frames are 'the immediate surroundings of the actual events'. In Anastasios' first collection these are typically open-air locations such as places somewhere in the desert or gardens near monks' abodes. When the action takes place inside, it is mostly in chapels, monks' cells, or caves. Setting is, according to Ryan, 'the general socio-historico-geographical environment in which the action takes place'.[22] In the case of the text in question, it is the Sinai desert during the first half of the seventh century.[23] Story space is 'the space relevant to the plot, as mapped by the actions and thoughts of the characters'.[24] It is formed also by locations that are just mentioned in the text, without becoming the setting of the narrated events. Thus, although the setting of the tales in the discussed collection does not move from the Sinai region, the story space also includes, e.g., Constantinople or Cyprus, which are mentioned from time to time.

A further layer is the narrative (or story) world: 'the story space supplemented by the reader's imagination on the basis of cultural knowledge and real-world experience'.[25] Since the recipient's imagination is involved, different audiences may construct very different narrative worlds: Anastasios' fellow monks would create one narrative world, Anastasios' contemporaries living in the capital who never visited Sinai a different one. Yet other narrative worlds are created by modern readers, again depending on their own experience or lack of experience with the location. The fifth and last layer, according to Ryan, is the narrative universe. It is the world 'presented as actual by the text plus all the counterfactual worlds constructed by characters as beliefs, wishes, fears, speculations, hypothetical thinking, dreams, and fantasies',[26] and we can add, for the type of literature we deal with, also visions and miracles. In Anastasios' stories, the narrative universe is completed by various spaces, typically gardens,

---

21 Ryan M.-L., "Space", in Hühn P. – Pier J. – Schmid W. – Schönert J. (eds.), *The Living Handbook of Narratology* (Hamburg: 2014) 420–433, at 421–423.

22 Ibidem, 421–422.

23 Note that the terminology is not unified. As with many other narratological terms, individual scholars coin their own terminologies, which are often not compatible. So, de Jong uses these two terms in quite opposite meanings: *setting* means for her roughly the same as *spatial frames* for Ryan, while she understands *frames* as 'locations that occur in thoughts, dreams, memories, or reports', cf. de Jong, *Narratology and Classics* 107.

24 Ryan, "Space" 422.

25 Ibidem.

26 Ibidem.

appearing and disappearing in the desert, with which I will deal in more detail below.

As a hagiographical genre, the beneficial tale aims to communicate religious truths and to achieve edifying purposes rather than to mirror the full objective reality in the sense in which it is claimed by historiography. But still the narrated stories are set in existing locations that the recipients, at least theoretically, could reach and experience by themselves – and especially the tales whose actions take place in the 'exotic' monastic and eremitic regions as a part of their beneficial purpose claimed to mediate the spatial reality of this special environment.

Nevertheless, the spaces of the examined tales are fundamentally affected by cultural and personal circumstances. The cultural part, as Catia Galatariotou has pointed out, is 'built with the symbolic bricks and mortar of assumptions, attitudes, and mentalities collectively held by members of the culture in which the text was produced'.[27] The personal circumstances consist of the author's actual physical and psychical condition, intentions, and experiences, all that being mirrored in the narrative. Margaret Mullett pointed out that there is one more layer that has to be taken into consideration, namely the literary one: 'the literary context, generic discourse and the horizon of expectations of the textual community'.[28] Thus, regarding the construction of space, we have to look at whether a certain motif or way of expression is part of the literary tradition and conventions, before we ascribe it to the personal subjective experience of the author. This is doubly important for Byzantine literature, whose main artistic principles were imitation and variation of literary predecessors.[29]

In sum, when interpreting a (Byzantine) text which makes some claim to reflect reality – and let us limit ourselves to the spatial reality which is the focus of this chapter – we have always to keep in mind that there are four degrees of mirroring reality which together produce the final image. First, there is the level of factual reality, which provides generally indisputable and independently verifiable information. To take an example from the first collection of Anastasios Sinaites: there is a chapel on the Holy Peak of Sinai. Second, there is the level of cultural reality, which renders a collectively held interpretation of factual reality influenced by the system of convictions and ideologies of a particular culture. For example, for Anastasios Sinaites and his

---

27 Galatariotou C., "Travel and Perception in Byzantium", *Dumbarton Oaks Papers* 47 (1993) 221–241, at 222–223.

28 Mullett M., "In Peril on the Sea: Travel Genres and the Unexpected", in Macrides R. (ed.), *Travel in the Byzantine World* (Aldershot: 2002) 259–284, at 283–284.

29 Cf. Papaioannou S., "Theory of Literature", in idem (ed.), *The Oxford Handbook of Byzantine Literature* (Oxford: 2021) 76–109.

SPACE IN EDIFYING STORIES 227

contemporaries and religious companions, Mount Sinai is the Christian holy peak par excellence.

Further, there is the level of personal reality, which mirrors the subjective perception of the author: the desert of Sinai is inhospitable, inaccessible, and terrible,[30] but, simultaneously, it is 'our desert' (ἡ καθ' ἡμᾶς ἔρημος),[31] a miraculous space, now, in the times of the storyteller, stained and defiled by the arrival of barbarians.[32] We have to be especially cautious about confusing the personal reality with the fourth and last level, that of textual reality, which includes the use of certain motifs, strategies, or intertextual allusions determined by the rules of the genre rather than by extra-literary experience.

To take again an example from Anastasios' first collection, the frequent biblical allusions and parallels, both in motifs and in wording, can be mentioned. So, for example, in I.11 Abba John the Sabaïte washes the feet of a young disciple who is going to be the future abbot of the Sinai monastery, specifically the most known until modern times, John Klimax.[33] This prophetic gesture follows the passage taken from the Gospel of John where Jesus washes the feet of his disciples. The spatial constellation remains the same: 'When the old man – the Sabaïte – saw them, he got up, poured water into a small basin and washed the feet of the disciple and kissed his hand'[34] ('Ως οὖν εἶδεν αὐτοὺς ὁ γέρων, ὁ Σαβαΐτης, ἀναστὰς ἔβαλεν ὕδωρ εἰς μακρὰν λεκάνην καὶ ἔνιψε τοὺς πόδας τοῦ μαθητοῦ καὶ ἠσπάσατο αὐτοῦ τὴν χεῖρα).[35] In another tale, the same Abba John the Sabaïte heals a blind coney pup with mud made from clay and his own spit just as Jesus does for a blind man in the New Testament.[36] Similarly, the repeated challenge to those who have experienced a miracle not to reveal it to anyone is to be read in connection with similar appeals in the Bible.[37]

---

30   Cf. e.g. Anastasios, *Edifying Tales*, I.3.1; I.8.1–2; I.17.2. I adopt the numbering of the tales according to Binggeli's edition (Binggeli, *Anastase le Sinaite*), which is also used by Caner, *History and Hagiography from the Late Antique Sinai* where also references to Nau's numbering are included.

31   Ibidem, I.8.1–2, I.17.2.

32   Ibidem, I.5.1–2. According to Uthemann, *Anastasios Sinaites* 423–430, these barbarians were not Arabs, but Persians.

33   John Klimax, whom Anastasios knew personally, acts or is mentioned in several tales of the collection: Anastasios, *Edifying Tales*, I.3, 9–12, and 16. For Klimax's agency at the Sinai monastery see Chitty, *The Desert a City* 172–175.

34   Trans. Caner, *History and Hagiography* 181. Cf. John, 13:5: 'After that, he poured water into a basin and began to wash his disciples' feet, drying them with the towel that was wrapped around him'; εἶτα βάλλει ὕδωρ εἰς τὸν νιπτῆρα καὶ ἤρξατο νίπτειν τοὺς πόδας τῶν μαθητῶν καὶ ἐκμάσσειν τῷ λεντίῳ ᾧ ἦν διεζωσμένος.

35   Anastasios, *Edifying Tales*, I.11.5–7.

36   Ibidem, I.23.5–7, cf. John, 9:6.

37   Ibidem, I.1.20–21; I.19, cf. John, 5:14.

Another example of the genre's textual reality concerns the almost formulaic incipits of the tales, responding to three basic wh- questions: 'who, when, and where', imposed by the already established tradition of the genre: 'Five years ago another brother became an attendant on the same Holy summit. He was an Armenian called Elisha'[38] (Καὶ ἕτερος δὲ τῶν ἀδελφῶν πρὸ τούτων τῶν πέντε χρόνων γενόμενος διακονητὴς ἐν τῇ ἁγίᾳ Κορυφῇ. Ἐλισσαῖος λεγόμενος).[39] In the next section, we will have a look at how the cultural reality of a model text or group of texts gradually becomes part of the textual reality of the genre in connection to space.

4   Spatial Principles: Dichotomy, Liminality, Heterotopia

I suggest that there are three principles chiefly constituting the cultural reality of space in the genre of beneficial tale: the dichotomy between the profane and the sacred space, the liminal character of the space, and the specific character of space which deviates from its normal, everyday functioning – the Foucaultian 'heterotopia'.

The story space of the early monastic tradition was constructed upon the contrast between the 'secular world' and the 'desert', *oikoumenē* and *erēmos*, the profane and the sacred space.[40] With edifying stories, a gradual convergence and mingling of the two (at first wholly separated) spaces of the monastic and secular worlds can be traced. In the earliest collection, the *History of the Monks in Egypt*,[41] the opposition between the desert and the world outside is determining; in the *Daniel-Sketiotes-Dossier*,[42] the desert serves as a peaceful harbor but the holy is mostly hidden (and uncovered in the course of the narration) in the secular world; and in the *Spiritual Meadow* of John Moschos,[43] the sacred and the secular space are consistently mingled and brought together.

---

38   Trans. Caner, *History and Hagiography* 178.

39   Anastasios, *Edifying Tales*, 1.6.1–2.

40   See especially Chitty, *The Desert a City* passim; cf. also Saradi H.G., "The City in Byzantine Hagiography", in Efthymiadis, *The Ashgate Research Companion* 2:412–452.

41   *History of the Monks in Egypt* (BHG 1333–1334), ed. A.-J. Festugière, *Historia monachorum in Aegypto*, Subsidia hagiographica 34 (Brussels: 1961).

42   Daniel of Sketis, *Narrations* (BHG 2099z–2102f, 79–80, 121–122, 618, 2255, 2453), ed. B. Dahlman, *Saint Daniel of Sketis: A Group of Hagiographic Texts*, Studia Byzantina Upsaliensia 10 (Uppsala: 2007).

43   John Moschos, *Spiritual Meadow* (BHG 1440f–1442z), ed. in *Patrologia Graeca* 87.3:2852–3112.

SPACE IN EDIFYING STORIES

The case is the same for Anastasios' second collection,[44] whereas in the first collection this dichotomy is almost entirely cancelled. Not only does the secular world not form part of the setting, but almost not even of the story space and the narrative universe. Only a handful of scattered mentions of the world beyond the Holy Mountain can be found in the whole collection.[45] The dichotomy of the story space is replaced by a continuum, both in the vertical and in the horizontal direction. There are places that are, so to speak, more sacred than others: the closer one approaches to the Holy Peak,[46] or the further one goes into the desert,[47] the more dangerous the space is and, simultaneously, the closer is the sanctity and the bigger the miraculous power of the place.[48] Other dichotomies are also present, such as the contrast between the human and the animal worlds and between life and death,[49] but these do not determine the story space.

If we proceed to the level of the narrative world, another kind of dichotomy emerges: it is the one between the human and the divine. To put it differently, the narrative space of the first collection is a liminal space where the human world meets the divine. The concept of cultural liminality, first described by Arnold van Gennep as the state and process of transition from one phase of a transitional ritual to another,[50] can be linked to many situations, connected not only to religions but to any transformative or transitional phase of human life.[51]

For the needs of the analysis of edifying story as a genre, it seems useful to combine liminality with Michel Foucault's concept of 'heterotopias': a term designating places whose function and order are different from those of normal,

---

44   Cf. Kulhánková M., "Zwischen Wüste und Welt: Die Konstruktion des Raumes in den byzantinischen erbaulichen Erzählungen", *Byzantinische Zeitschrift* 108 (2015) 715–733; Della Dora V., *Landscape, Nature and the Sacred in Byzantium* (Cambridge: 2016) 132–134.
45   Anastasios, *Edifying Tales*, I.9.3–4, 15, 20, 26, 29.
46   Ibidem, I.1–7.
47   Ibidem, I.25.3.
48   Ibidem, I.9, 14, 17, 21, 25.
49   Ibidem, I.21, 23, 24.
50   Van Gennep A., *The Rites of Passage* (Chicago: 1960 [1909]).
51   With a special focus on Christianity and pilgrimage, the concept was further developed by Victor and Edith Turner, who also focused on the specifics of the sharing of a liminoid experience by a group of people (*communitas*). In contrast to *liminal* experience, the *liminoid* experience is optional and does not result in a change of status; cf. Turner V.W. – Turner E., *Image and Pilgrimage in Christian Culture: Anthropological Perspectives* (New York: 1978) 1–39 and 253–254. This type of liminality is most characteristic for the *History of the Monks in Egypt*, where the frame story depicts the pilgrimage of a group of monks.

everyday life.[52] This concept is no longer unknown in the study of Byzantine literature and culture. Recently, Myrto Veikou and Ingela Nilsson have used it to show how the heterotopic character of ports and harbors is represented in Byzantine literature.[53] In a previous publication, I have also pointed out the heterotopic function of ships and graves particularly in the edifying story.[54]

In her recent dissertation, Myrto Veikou took an important step forward in the theoretical approach of space in Byzantine hagiography while complementing the two aforementioned concepts with more recent approaches of cultural geography. She suggested the conception of in-between spaces which 'lay in a continuum that has two very different extremes – such as "human" and "divine" [...] – as distinct hybrid categories'.[55] These in-between spaces are liminal worlds, often 'pending between the earthly and the heavenly, where space is simply fluidified on a vertical axis', as Veikou put it.[56] In the edifying stories, typical in-between spaces include a grave, a temple, an ascetic's cell,[57] and other spaces where a kind of communication between the earthly and the divine is enabled.[58] Turning back to Anastasios' first collection, it can be argued that the whole story space of the Sinai desert is an in-between space filled in with smaller in-between spaces that form the spatial frames of the particular tales, as will be illustrated in the following section.

---

52 Foucault M., "Of Other Spaces: Utopias and Heterotopias", in Leach N. (ed.), *Rethinking Architecture: A Reader in Cultural Theory* (New York: 1997 [1967]) 330–336.

53 Veikou M. – Nilsson I., "Ports and Harbours as Heterotopic Entities in Byzantine Literary Texts", in Carnap-von Bornheim C. – Daim F. – Ettel P. – Warnke U. (eds.), *Harbours as Objects of Interdisciplinary Research: Archaeology, History, Geosciences* (Mainz: 2018) 265–277.

54 Kulhánková M., *Das gottgefällige Abenteuer* 86–89.

55 Veikou M., *Spatial Paths to Holiness: Literary 'Lived Spaces' in Eleventh-Century Byzantine Saints' Lives*, Studia Byzantina Upsaliensia 22 (Uppsala: 2023) 84–85.

56 Ibidem, 111.

57 Cf. Brooks Hedstrom D.L., "The Geography of the Monastic Cell in Early Egyptian Monastic Literature", *Church History* 78 (2009) 756–791.

58 Cf. also Brown P., *The World of Late Antiquity: AD 150–750* (London 1971) 96–102, and idem, *The Body and Society* (New York 1988) 216–219. For some of the heterotopias in edifying stories, e.g. monastic cells, cf. also the concept of 'hierotopy' defined by Alexei Lidov for the creation of sacred spaces: Lidov A., "Hierotopy: The Creation of Sacred Spaces as a Form of Creativity and Subject of Cultural History", in idem (ed.), *Hierotopy: Creation of Sacred Spaces in Byzantium and Medieval Russia* (Moscow: 2006) 32–58.

SPACE IN EDIFYING STORIES   231

5   Organizing and Characterizing the Function of Space

Anastasios exploits in numerous ways the potential of three chief topoi of
Christian monastic topography that Veronica della Dora pointed out: the
mountain, the desert, and the garden.[59] Sometimes he uses them separately
and at other times he combines them with each other. In the first collection,
topography decisively affects the shape of the whole work. The first seven
tales concern miraculous events that took place at the very peak of the Holy
Mountain. This prominent placement, as André Binggeli noted, suggests 'that
the holy place itself contributed to the holiness of the Fathers who lived in the
surrounding deserts'.[60] It is therefore a different case from the earlier collections, where the ascetics turn the desert, originally the utmost hostile place,
inhabited by demons, into a miraculous heterotopia.[61] Furthermore, the choice
to open the whole collection with a passage dedicated to a specific location
indicates not only the importance of this location, but also the importance of
space as such and urges the recipient to pay special attention to space also in
the following parts.

Moreover, in the first seven tales space functions as a metaphor for spiritual ascent, as a sort of 'ladder to heaven'[62] (to allude Anastasios' fellow monk
John Klimax): the higher the characters ascend, the closer they come to the
holy. The first seven tales narrate various visions and miracles happening to the
monks ascending to the top, with the holy fire as a frequent coulisse:

> As they approached the shrine [of prophet Elijah on Mount Horeb],
> behold! They saw it blazing inside like a fiery furnace, with fire flickering
> out of all of its windows. When the disciple saw the vision it made him
> shudder, but the old man reassured him, saying, 'What are you afraid of,
> my child? They are angelic powers, our fellow slaves. Don't be a coward.
> In heaven, they venerate our nature, not we theirs.' And so, as into a fur-
> nace, they fearlessly entered the shrine and prayed.[63]

> Πλησιάσαντες οὖν τῷ ναῷ ἰδοὺ θεωροῦσιν αὐτὸν ἔνδον ὡς κάμινον πυρὸς και-
> όμενον, καὶ τὸ πῦρ γλωσσίζον καὶ ἐξερχόμενον δι᾽ ὅλων τῶν θυρίδων αὐτοῦ. Ὁ
> γοῦν μαθητὴς θεασάμενος ἔφριξε τὴν ὀπτασίαν, ὁ δὲ ἐπιστάτης ἐθαρσοποίει

---

59   For a recent thorough study of these topoi, see Della Dora, *Landscape, Nature and
     the Sacred*.
60   Binggeli, "Collections of Edifying Stories" 150.
61   Cf. Della Dora, *Landscape, Nature and the Sacred* 126–129.
62   Ibidem, 165–166.
63   Trans. Caner, *History and Hagiography* 174. The holy fire acts also in 1.4 and 6.

αὐτὸν λέγων· Τί φοβεῖ ὦ τέκνον; Ἀγγελικαὶ δυνάμεις εἰσί, σύνδουλοι ἡμῶν εἰσι. Μὴ δειλιάσῃς αὐτοὶ τὴν ἡμετέραν φύσιν προσκυνοῦσιν ἐν οὐρανοῖς, οὐχ ἡμεῖς τὴν αὐτῶν. Οὕτως οὖν ὡς ἐν καμίνῳ ἄφοβοι εἰσελθόντες ἐν τῷ ναῷ ηὔξαντο.[64]

The tales of this group present the intimate experiences of one or two monks (with one exception of a group experience in tale 1.4) which were testified unwittingly and unintentionally through the monks' shining faces:

> When the custodian saw them, he observed that their faces were gloriously shining as the face of Moses once shined. He said to them, 'What was it that you saw on your ascent?' Since they wanted to keep it secret, they said, 'Nothing, Father.' Then the custodian, who was himself a slave of the Lord, spoke to them once more: 'Believe me, you saw a vision, for behold! Your faces are beaming with the glory of the Holy Spirit.' They made obeisance before him and begged him not to tell anyone.

> Ἰδὼν οὖν αὐτοὺς ὁ παραμονάριος εἶδε τὰ πρόσωπα αὐτῶν δεδοξασμένα καὶ λάμποντα καθά ποτε τὸ πρόσωπον Μωυσέως, καὶ λέγει πρὸς αὐτούς· Τίποτε ἐθεάσασθε ἀνερχόμενοι; Οἱ δὲ διαλαθεῖν βουλόμενοι λέγουσιν· Οὐχί, πάτερ. Τότε λέγει πάλιν πρὸς αὐτοὺς ὁ παραμονάριος καὶ αὐτὸς δοῦλος Κυρίου ὑπάρχων· Πίστευσον, ὀπτασίαν τινὰ ἐθεάσασθε, καὶ ἰδοὺ τὰ πρόσωπα ὑμῶν ἐκλάμπουσι τὴν δόξαν τοῦ ἁγίου Πνεύματος. Βαλόντες οὖν αὐτῷ μετάνοιαν παρακάλεσαν μηδενὶ θαρρῆσαι.[65]

Toward the end of the collection, there is another group of seven tales connected by the main spatial motif: a place appearing and disappearing amid the desert, or a place where characters appear, disappear, or are transformed (tales 30–36). These places are found at remote spots, often in deep ravines,[66] having the shape of a garden.[67] The heroes of this group are anchorites, both living and dead, who exceed the average monks in spirituality. The garden is as powerful a topos of monastic literature as the mountain. When used together with the third topos, the desert, gardening the wilderness becomes a metaphor for spiritual transformation.[68] In one of these tales an elder takes his disciple into the desert in search of anchorites. At the bottom of a valley, they see a cell

---

64   Ansastasios, *Edifying Tales*, 1.1.7–13.

65   Ansastasios, *Edifying Tales*, 1.15–22; trans. Caner, *History and Hagiography* 174–175.

66   Ibidem, 1.30, 32, 35.

67   Ibidem, 1.31, 34, 35.

68   See Della Dora, *Landscape, Nature and the Sacred* 133–137.

SPACE IN EDIFYING STORIES   233

with various fruit-bearing trees surrounding it. As they are descending toward
the place, they hear voices welcoming them, but when they arrive, the whole
place disappears.[69] The narrator of another tale is luckier and finds himself
within such a garden:

> Once when I was shepherding my goats in winter, I suddenly found
> myself by a garden with fruits of all sorts and a small spring of water.
> I saw an elderly man sitting at the spring and a great number of wild goats
> coming to drink. As I stood there astonished by the things that I saw, the
> old man told me, 'Take as much fruit as you can carry in your sack'.

> Ποιμαίνοντός μού ποτε αἰγίδια τῷ χειμῶνι, ἐξαίφνης, ηὑρέθην πλησίον κηπίου
> παντοίους καρποὺς ἔχοντος καὶ πηγάδιν ὕδατος, καὶ ὁρῶ ἄνδρα γηραλέον
> ἐν τῷ πηγαδίῳ καθήμενον καὶ πλῆθος αἰγαγρίων ἐρχομένων καὶ πινόντων.
> Θαμβουμένου μου οὖν, φησίν, ἐπὶ τοῖς ὁρωμένοις λέγει πρός με ὁ γέρων·
> Ἔπαρον καρποὺς εἰς τὸ μαζάθιν σου ὅσους βαστάσαι δύνασαι.[70]

When the narrator comes back the next day, he only finds the herd of goats.
The next tale narrates a story about a place where three (probably dead)
anchorites disappear until the second day. The tale concludes with the following commentary: 'For it is the custom of the holy anchorites, both in life
and after death, to reveal themselves and to conceal themselves whenever
they want, by power of God' ("Εθος γὰρ τοῦτο τοῖς ἁγίοις ἀναχωρηταῖς καὶ ἐν ζωῇ
καὶ μετὰ θάνατον, ὅτε θέλουσιν φαίνεσθαι, καὶ ὅτε θέλουσιν κρύπτεσθαι τῇ δυνάμει
τοῦ Θεοῦ).[71]

Between these two longer sections of a sacred heterotopia located at the top
of the mountain and several heterotopias of the remote desert, there are more
than twenty tales which are set in different places in the desert around Mount
Sinai, the καθ' ἡμᾶς ἔρημος, named as Tourba, Goudda, Arselau, or Malocha.[72]
These combine inhospitality and inaccessibility with everyday miracles taking place in in-between spaces. The most frequent spatial frame is a place by
a grave, where communication between the living and the dead occurs and
where God's signs are manifested.[73] For instance, a virtuous deceased ascetic
repetitively throws out of the tomb a neglectful brother who died after him and

---

69   Anastasios, *Edifying Tales*, 1.30.
70   Anastasios, *Edifying Tales*, 1.34.5–10; trans. Caner, *History and Hagiography* 192.
71   Anastasios, *Edifying Tales*, 1.31.12–14; trans. Caner, *History and Hagiography* 191.
72   For probable identifications of these places see Dahari U., *Monastic Settlements in South
      Sinai in the Byzantine Period: The Archaeological Remains* (Jerusalem: 2000).
73   Anastasios, *Edifying Tales*, 1.8–10.

was buried with him, until the monastery's hegumen arrives to have a word with him.[74] Another frequent type of space is an open location where the desert Fathers perform miracles involving various animals, such as goats, coneys, snakes, and leopards. In these cases, the human and animal worlds meet in an in-between space where natural rules are inverted through the miraculous powers of the Fathers, who tame the wild animals. When, for example, a Father laments because his modest garden is repeatedly devastated by coneys, a leopard comes to his feet. After the Father's plea, the beast stays by him for several years protecting his garden.[75]

Many of the examined stories take place in the open space of nature. In other tales, the exact spatial frames are not specified. The enclosed space is foregrounded and thematized only in the first collection's last three tales. For the heroes of tales 37 and 38, it is necessary to undergo an examination of the closed space in order to gain salvation. The former tale narrates the story of a monk who is tested during Lent fasting while he finds himself in a cave.[76] The latter tale thematizes the closed space of a human body: it narrates the story of a monk whose body trembled uncontrollably for many days before his death. The very last tale returns to one of the collection's most frequent themes: a holy Father's death.

> He departed to the Lord and was buried in the tomb of the Fathers. The next day another of the fathers died. When we opened the tomb to bury him, we did not find the body of the brother who had previously been buried. He had been transported by God to the land of the living.

> ἀπῆλθε πρὸς Κύριον· καὶ ταφέντος αὐτοῦ ἐν τῷ μνημείῳ τῶν πατέρων, μετὰ μίαν ἡμέραν ἐτελεύτησεν ἄλλος τῶν πατέρων. καὶ ἀνοίξαντες τὸ μνῆμα ὅπως θάψωμεν αὐτόν, οὐχ ηὕρομεν τὸ σῶμα τοῦ προταφέντος ἀδελφοῦ, μετενεχθέντος αὐτοῦ ὑπὸ τοῦ Θεοῦ ἐν τῇ χώρᾳ τῶν ζώντων.[77]

In this case, the enclosed space and the corpse's miraculous disappearance are emphasized.

---

74 Ibidem, I.8.

75 Ibidem, I.21.

76 For the liminal character of caves in Christian literature, and in the Mediterranean world more generally, see Della Dora, *Landscape, Nature and the Sacred* 179–202.

77 Anastasios, *Edifying Tales*, I.39.8–12; trans. Caner, *History and Hagiography* 194–195.

SPACE IN EDIFYING STORIES   235

6   Conclusions

What have we learned about Anastasios' first collection by examining his treatment of space? As the preceding discussion has hopefully shown, space in the examined collection is deeply rooted in contemporary cultural reality, while at the same time it is based on generic conventions. Yet it offers a set of interesting divergences and variations. Most importantly, the dichotomy of earthly sacred and secular story space, so important in the earlier collections of edifying stories (or even contemporary ones, including Anastasios' second collection), does not exist, since the author chose to limit story space to the sacred desert of Mount Sinai.[78] The most characteristic feature of this space is liminality. The recipient explores a series of particular heterotopias throughout the collection (the places at and around the Holy Peak, the gardens in the middle of the desert, and the closed spaces), while the whole Sinai area is itself a heterotopia, an in-between space. Thus, it is more the space that affects the people than the other way around. Moreover, Anastasios not only maximally exploited the three main topoi of monastic geography, the mountain, the desert, and the garden, but also used space as an organizing principle for the whole collection: it starts high on the Holy Peak, then it broadens into the desert surrounding the mountain, and subsequently it reaches the very boundaries of the factual world in a series of tales with emerging and disappearing spaces. Finally, the collection concludes with three stories thematizing the enclosed space. These stories simultaneously repeat in a sort of summary three important motifs that emerge throughout the collection: the monk in a cave, the end of the earthly life, and the tomb as a heterotopia of reinforced closeness to the divine.

At the same time, we have observed yet another function of space in this collection, namely characterology. It means that the spatial frames contribute to the construction of characters, being used as the metaphor of spiritual ascent in the case of the Holy Peak, of spiritual transformation in the case of gardens, or just underscoring the ascetic qualities of the heroes in the case of remote, inaccessible locations. Mirroring the psychical state or the virtues of the characters, space provides the recipient with additional information about normally flat and stereotypical figures, typical representatives of characters in medieval literature.[79]

---

78   Cf. Kulhánková, "Zwischen Wüste und Welt"; Della Dora, *Landscape, Nature and the Sacred* 132–134.

79   For the 'flatness' of the typical medieval character, serving rather as a vehicle of the plot than a psychologized being, see e.g. Schulz A., *Erzähltheorie in mediävistischer Perspektive* (Berlin – Munich – Boston: 2015) 12.

With Anastasios' tales, the recipient experiences the paradoxical nature of space: the high peak and the deep ravines, the gardens appearing in the midst of the desert can be seen as an innovative exploitation of the paradoxical concept of the biblical wilderness, which was both a site of trial and punishment and a potential paradise.[80] The liminal space links together life, death, and afterlife and at the same time adds plasticity to the heroes.

Bibliography

Primary Sources

Anastasios of Sinai, *Edifying Tales*. In ed. F. Nau, "Le texte grec du moine Anastase sur les saints pères du Sinaï", *Oriens Christianus* 2 (1902) 58–89 [first collection]; F. Nau, "Le texte grec des récits utiles à l'âme d'Anastase (le Sinaïte)", *Oriens Christianus* 3 (1903) 56–75, and S. Heid, "Die C-Reihe erbaulicher Erzählungen des Anastasios vom Sinai im Codex Vaticanus Graecus 2592", *Orientalia Christiana periodica* 74 (2008) 71–114 [second collection]; A. Binggeli, *Anastase le Sinaite: Récits sur le Sinaï et Récits utiles à l'âme* (Ph.D. dissertation, University of Paris IV: 2001) 170–261 [both collections].

Daniel of Sketis, *Narrations* (BHG 2099z–2102f, 79–80, 121–122, 618, 2255, 2453). In ed. B. Dahlman, *Saint Daniel of Sketis: A Group of Hagiographic Texts*, Studia Byzantina Upsaliensia 10 (Uppsala: 2007).

History of the Monks in Egypt (BHG 1333–1334). In ed. A.-J. Festugière, *Historia monachorum in Aegypto*, Subsidia hagiographica 34 (Brussels: 1971).

John Moschos, *Spiritual Meadow* (BHG 1440f–1442z). In *Patrologia Graeca* 87.3:2852–3112.

Secondary Works

Binggeli A., "Collections of Edifying Stories", in Efthymiadis S. (ed.), *The Ashgate Research Companion to Byzantine Hagiography*, vol. 2: *Genres and Contexts* (Farnham: 2014) 143–159.

Brooks Hedstrom D.L., "The Geography of the Monastic Cell in Early Egyptian Monastic Literature", *Church History* 78 (2009) 756–791.

Brown P., *The Body and Society* (New York: 1988).

Brown P., *The World of Late Antiquity: AD 150–750* (London: 1971).

Caner D.F. (trans.), *History and Hagiography from the Late Antique Sinai* (Liverpool: 2010).

Chitty D., *The Desert a City* (Oxford: 1966).

Dahari U., *Monastic Settlements in South Sinai in the Byzantine Period: The Archaeological Remains* (Jerusalem: 2000).

---

80   Cf. Della Dora, *Landscape, Nature and the Sacred* 124.

de Jong I.J.F., *Narratology and Classics: A Practical Guide* (Oxford: 2014).

Della Dora V., *Landscape, Nature and the Sacred in Byzantium* (Cambridge: 2016).

Detoraki M., "Récits édifiants et hagiographie: À propos du Pré spiritual", in Rigo A. (ed.), *Byzantine Hagiography: Texts, Themes and Projects* (Turnhout: 2017) 167–178.

Flusin B., "Démons et Sarrasins: L'auteur et le propos des *Diègèmata stèriktika* d'Anastase le Sinaïte", *Travaux et mémoires* 11 (1991) 380–409.

Flusin B., "Palestinian Hagiography (Fourth–Eighth Centuries)", in Efthymiadis S. (ed.), *The Ashgate Research Companion to Byzantine Hagiography*, vol. 1: *Periods and Places* (Farnham: 2011) 199–226.

Foucault M., "Of Other Spaces: Utopias and Heterotopias", in Leach N. (ed.), *Rethinking Architecture: A Reader in Cultural Theory* (New York: 1997 [1967]) 330–336.

Frank G., *The Memory of the Eyes: Pilgrims to Living Saints in Christian Late Antiquity* (Berkeley – Los Angeles – London: 2000).

Galatariotou C., "Travel and Perception in Byzantium", *Dumbarton Oaks Papers* 47 (1993) 221–241.

Genette G., *Narrative Discourse: An Essay in Method*, trans. J.E. Levin (Ithaca, NY: 1980 [1972]).

Haldon J., "The Works of Anastasius of Sinai: A Key Source for the History of Seventh-Century East Mediterranean Society and Belief", in Cameron A. – Conrad L.I. (eds.), *The Byzantine and Early Islamic Near East*, vol. 1: *Problems in the Literary Source Material* (Princeton: 1992) 107–147.

Harmless W., *Desert Christians: An Introduction to the Literature of Early Monasticism* (Oxford – New York: 2004).

Kulhánková M., *Das gottgefällige Abenteuer: Eine narratologische Analyse der Byzantinischen erbaulichen Erzählungen* (Červený Kostelec: 2015).

Kulhánková M., "'I Went Aboard a Ship and Reached Byzantium': The Motif of Travel in Edifying Stories" in Mitrea M. (ed.), *Holiness on the Move: Mobility and Space in Byzantine Hagiography* (London – New York: 2023) 90–101.

Kulhánková M., "Zwischen Wüste und Welt: Die Konstruktion des Raumes in den byzantinischen erbaulichen Erzählungen", *Byzantinische Zeitschrift* 108 (2015) 715–733.

Lidov A., "Hierotopy: The Creation of Sacred Spaces as a Form of Creativity and Subject of Cultural History", in Lidov. A. (ed.), *Hierotopy: Creation of Sacred Spaces in Byzantium and Medieval Russia* (Moscow: 2006) 32–58.

Mantova Y., "Space Representation in the Life of St. Gregentios and the Life of St. Nikon the Metanoite", in Rigo A. (ed.), *Byzantine Hagiography: Texts, Themes and Projects* (Turnhout: 2017) 157–165.

Messis C., "Fiction and/or Novelisation in Byzantine Hagiography", in Efthymiadis S. (ed.), *The Ashgate Research Companion to Byzantine Hagiography*, vol. 2: *Genres and Contexts* (Farnham: 2014) 313–341.

Messis C. – Mullett M. – Nilsson I. (eds.), *Storytelling in Byzantium: Narratological Approaches to Byzantine Texts and Images* (Uppsala: 2018).

Minets J., "Palladius of Helenopolis: One Author, Two Ways to Write", *Journal of Early Christian Studies* 25 (2017) 411–440.

Mullett M., "In Peril on the Sea: Travel Genres and the Unexpected", in Macrides R. (ed.), *Travel in the Byzantine World* (Aldershot: 2002) 259–284.

Papaioannou S., "Theory of Literature", in Papaioannou S. (ed.), *The Oxford Handbook of Byzantine Literature* (Oxford: 2021) 76–109.

Roilos P. (ed.), *Medieval Greek Storytelling* (Wiesbaden: 2014).

Ryan M.-L., "Space", in Hühn P. – Pier J. – Schmid W. – Schönert J. (eds.), *The Living Handbook of Narratology* (Hamburg: 2014) 420–433.

Saradi H.G., "The City in Byzantine Hagiography", in Efthymiadis S. (ed.), *The Ashgate Research Companion to Byzantine Hagiography*, vol. 2: *Genres and Contexts* (Farnham: 2014) 412–452.

Schulz A., *Erzähltheorie in mediävistischer Perspektive* (Berlin – Munich – Boston: 2015).

Turner V.W. – Turner E., *Image and Pilgrimage in Christian Culture: Anthropological Perspectives* (New York: 1978).

Uthemann K.-H., *Anastasios Sinaites* (Berlin – Boston: 2015).

Uthemann K.-H., *Studien zu Anastasios Sinaites* (Berlin – Boston: 2017).

Van Gennep A., *The Rites of Passage* (Chicago: 1960 [1909]).

Veikou M., "Space in Texts and Space as Text: A New Approach to Byzantine Spatial Notions", *Scandinavian Journal of Byzantine and Modern Greek Studies* 2 (2016) 143–175.

Veikou M., *Spatial Paths to Holiness: Literary 'Lived Spaces' in Eleventh-Century Byzantine Saints' Lives*, Studia Byzantina Upsaliensia 22 (Uppsala: 2023).

Veikou M. "'Telling Spaces' in Byzantium: Ekphraseis, Place-Making and 'Thick Description'", in Messis C. – Mullett M. – Nilsson I. (eds.), *Storytelling in Byzantium: Narratological Approaches to Byzantine Texts and Images* (Uppsala: 2018) 15–32.

Veikou M. – Nilsson I., "Ports and Harbours as Heterotopic Entities in Byzantine Literary Texts", in Carnap-von Bornheim C. – Daim F. – Ettel P. – Warnke U. (eds.), *Harbours as Objects of Interdisciplinary Research: Archaeology, History, Geosciences* (Mainz: 2018) 265–277.

Wortley J., "The Genre of the Spiritually Beneficial Tale", *Scripta & e-Scripta* 8/9 (2010) 71–91.

Wortley J., "The Repertoire of Byzantine 'Spiritually Beneficial Tales'", *Scripta & e-Scripta* 8/9 (2010) 93–306.

General Index

Achilles Tatius, author, 2nd century AD 59,
62, 77
Leukippe and Kleitophon 59, 74
Aelios Aristides, author, AD 117–180 18, 26,
28
Sacred Tales 18
Agatharchides of Cnidus, author,
b. 208 BC 132
On the Erythraean Sea 132
agent 5, 7, 41–42, 56, 192, 203–204, 218
biographical agent 218
human agent 7, 192
marvelous agent 7, 192, 218
supernatural agent 7, 192, 218
Alexandria 29, 56n28, 57, 109, 122, 131, 138,
148, 152
allegory 14, 21–22, 63, 69, 200, 209
Amnianus Marcellinus, historian, *c.* AD
330–*c.*391/400 59
Anastasios of Sinai, author, *c.* AD 630–701
7, 30, 196, 206, 221–222, 224–236
Edifying Tales 30, 196, 198–199, 206,
221–222, 224–236
Anastasios the Persian, saint
*Miracles of Anastasios the
Persian* 164n17, 168, 170, 173, 176
anecdote 83, 99
Anthemios of Tralles, geographer, architect
and writer, *c.* AD 474–533/538 61, 63
anthology 6–7, 108
Antigonos of Karystos, author,
3rd century BC 45–46, 53–55, 162
Collection of Paradoxical Stories 45,
53–55, 162
Anton Chekhov, author, 1860–1904 4, 21
Antonius Liberalis, grammarian and author,
c. AD 100–300 70
Metamorphoses 70
Apophthegmata Patrum 2, 20, 108, 192, 196
alphabetical collection 33–34
anonymous collection 16, 33n63, 197
Arabian Nights 2, 67, 152
Aratos, poet, 315–240 BC 166
Phaenomena 166n31
Archimedes, mathematitian and pysicist,
*c.*287–*c.*212 BC 61

Aristippos of Cyrene, philosopher,
*c.*435–*c.*356 BC 90
Aristotle, philosopher and polymath,
384–322 BC 61, 68
Arkady Martin (pseudonym of AnnaLinden
Weller), author, 1985– 65
Arnold van Gennep, ethnographer and
folklorist 1873–1957 229
Artemios, saint 177, 203
Miracles of Artemios 164n17, 168, 170,
173–174, 176–177, 202
Athanasios of Alexandria, *c.* AD
296/98–373 48
Life of Anthony the Great 48
Athenaeus of Attalia, physician, fl. end of the
first century BC 92
audience 211, 217, 225
embedded audience 28
fictional audience 35
implied audience 28, 35
intended audience 28, 35
real audience 28, 35
Aulus Gellius, author, *c.* AD 125–
after 180 62, 171
Attic Nights 62, 171n53

bestiary 159
biography 4
Boccaccio
Decameron 3, 67

C.S. Lewis, author, 1898–1963 13
Canterbury Tales 67
catalogue 7, 21, 159–189
epic catalogue 160, 165–170
paradoxographical catalogue 161–164
Charles May, literary theorist, 1941– 21
chronicle 61, 196
Chrysippos of Jerusalem, author, d. AD
479 164n17, 170
Encomium of Theodore Teron. See
Theodore Teron, saint
Miracles of Theodore Teron. See Theodore
Teron, saint
Claude Bremond, literary
theorist 1929–2021 4

240   GENERAL INDEX

Clysma, Egyptian city at the head of the Gulf
    of Suez   198–199
collection
    collection of beneficial tales. *See*
        collection of edifying tales
    collection of edifying tales   2, 121–128,
        192, 221–222, 224–236
    collective biography   20, 108–109, 115,
        192, 218
    miracle collection   2, 20, 27, 108–109,
        159–188, 192, 195–196, 202, 218
conversational storytelling   16, 19
Cornelius Gallus, poet and orator,
    *c.*70–26 BC   73
Crates of Thebes, philosopher,
    *c.*365–*c.*285 BC   90

Damaskios, philosopher and author,
    AD 458–550   62
    Logoi paradoxoi   62
Daniel of Sketis, ascetic, 6th century AD   30,
    121–128, 148, 151, 196
    Narrations   30, 121–128, 196, 228
Dante   152
    Divine Comedy   152
Demetrios, saint   187
    Miracles of Demetrios   30, 164*n*17, 168
        anonymous miracles   164*n*17
        by John of Thessalonike   164*n*17, 169,
            173, 177, 186–188
dichotomy   228–230
Diogenes, philosopher,
    *c.*412/404–323 BC   90
dream   22, 26–27, 83, 108, 111, 116–121,
    123–127, 148, 185, 203, 209–210, 216, 225

Edgar Allan Poe, author, 1809–1849   8
ekphrasis   224
enumeration   177, 179, 182, 184–186, 188
epic   50, 72, 159, 166
epiphany   14, 22, 26, 118, 177, 203, 209
    demonophany   22, 26
    hagiophany   22, 24–26
    theophany   22, 26
episode   7, 192, 203, 209–210, 216, 218
    multiple-episode tale   7, 116, 192, 203–211,
        215, 218
        monothematic tale   204, 210, 216
        polythematic tale   204, 206, 210, 216

single-episode tale   7, 110, 192–203, 216,
    218
Eric Hayot, literary critic 1972–   65–66
ethical case history   101
Eumathios Makrembolites, author, *c.* AD
    1150–1200   59
Eustathios of Thessaloniki, bishop and
    author, AD 1115–1198   63, 71, 77

fable   83
folklore   4, 132

Galen of Pergamum, medical author and
    physician, AD 129–*c.*216   6, 83–102
    Elements According to
        Hippocrates   92–96
    Exhortation to the Study of
        Medicine   89–90
    On Avoiding Distress   90–91
    On My Own Opinions   87–89
    On the Affections and Errors of the
        Soul   96–103
    The Different Kinds of Pulse   95–96
geography   42, 230
George Garrett, author, 1929–2008   3
George the Great, saint   148
Gérard Genette, literary theorist,
    1930–2018   211
Great Fire of AD 192   90
Greek Anthology   171
Gregory of Nyssa, *c.* AD 335–395   48, 134
    Life of Gregory Thaumatourgos   46
grotesque   22, 27, 199–200, 201

hagiography   5, 7, 40–56, 133, 196, 230
    See also hagiographical tale
Hanna Meretoja, literary critic 1977–
    134*n*11, 149
Herakleitos the Paradoxographer, author,
    1st/2nd century AD   63–64, 67, 69–76
    On Unbelievable Tales   70
Hermas, author, 2nd century AD   18, 22*n*30,
    26
    Shepherd   18
Herodotus, historian, *c.*484–*c.*425 BC   59,
    61, 165
    Histories   165
Hesiod, poet, 8th century BC   166, 184
    Catalogue of Women   184
    Theogony   166

GENERAL INDEX

Hesychios of Jerusalem,
  5th century AD   134, 139
  homily on Longinos. *See* Longinos, saint
hetero-diegetic narrator   48
heterotopia   228–231, 233, 235
historiography   42–43, 67, 226
History of the Monks in Egypt   19–20, 30–32,
  109–115, 194–196, 212–217, 222, 228
humor   15, 54, 95

Iliad   159–160
imagery   21, 27, 217
Incense Route   6, 131–153
inexpressibility topos   165–170, 178, 180
irony   95, 98, 108

J.R.R. Tolkien, author, 1892–1973   151
James Joyce, author, 1882–1941   3
John Chrysostom, AD 347–407   134
John Klimax, saint   227, 231
John Moschos, author, d. AD 619   17, 28, 30,
  34–35, 171, 196–197, 222
  Hexaemeron   222
  Questiones et responsiones   222
  Spiritual Meadow   17, 28–29, 30, 34–35,
    107n3, 171, 196–197, 222, 228
  Viae dux   222
John of Thessalonike, bishop, end of
  6th–7th century AD   169
  Miracles of Demetrios. See Demetrios,
    saint
John Tzetzes, writer and intellectual, 12th
  century AD   60–61, 63
Jorge Luis Borges, author, 1899–1986   3

Kalīla wa Dimna   2
Kosmas and Damian, saints
  Miracles of Kosmas and Damian   30,
    164n17, 168, 170, 172–173, 175–176
Kosmas Indicopleustes, author,
  6th century AD   132
  Christian Geography   132
Kyrillos of Skythopolis, *c.* AD 525–*c.*559   48,
  52
Kyros and John, saints
  Encomium of Kyros and John   168–169
  Miracles of Kyros and John   15, 30, 164n17,
    170, 173, 175

liminality   228–230, 235
list
  genealogical list   159
  paradoxographical list. *See* catalogue
Longinos, saint
  Arabic Syaxarion   134–147
  Ethiopic Synaxarion   134–147
  homily on Longinos by Pseudo-
    Hesychios   134–147
  Inventio Capitis   134–147
  Symeon the Metaphrast   134–147
  tale of Longinos   131–153
Longus, author, 2nd century AD   74
  Daphnis and Chloe   74
Lucian of Samosata, *c.* AD 125–after 180   62
  True Histories   62
Lydda, ancient city in Israel   6, 148, 151

magical   1
Marie-Laure Ryan, literary critic 1946–   67,
  75–76, 225
marvel, marvelous   1, 5, 7, 36, 61, 162–164, 177
  See also marvelous tale
Meleager of Gadara, poet, 1st century BC
  171
  Garland   171
Menas, saint
  Arabic *Synaxarion*   134–147
  Coptic Encomium. *See Encomium of Apa
    Mena*
  Encomium of Apa Mena   134–147
  *Encomium to the Great Martyr
    Menas*   136
  Ethiopic *Synaxarion*   134–147
  Miracles of Menas   136, 164n17
  Passion of Menas   136
  shrine of Menas   6, 151–152
  Synaxarion of Constantinople   134–147
  tale of Menas   131–153
metaphor   21, 170–171, 180, 231
Michael Toolan, literary critic 1953–   107, 128
Michel Foucault, historian, philosopher, and
  literary critic, 1926–1984   228–229
Miguel de Cervantes, author, 1547–1616   3
Mikhail Bakhtin, philosopher, literary
  critic 1895–1975   27
mirabilia   1, 36, 159–160, 163, 188

GENERAL INDEX

miracle, miraculous   1, 5, 7, 36, 40–44,
    49–50, 53, 55, 56, 60–61, 107, 111, 121,
    146, 148, 152, 160, 164–165, 170, 174, 209,
    225, 227, 229, 231
  See also miracle tale   1
miscellany   19, 32–34, 192
Monica Fludernik, literary theorist
    1957–   16, 19
monstrous   22, 27
Mount Sinai   56, 227, 233, 236
Muriel Rukeyser, poet and
    esssayist 1913–1980   103
myth   70, 71–73, 75, 83
mythology   63, 69–70, 72, 74

narrative
  frame narrative   1, 20
  narrative climax   53–56
  narrative device   6, 21–22, 26–27, 116, 221
  narrative genre   4
  narrative universe   225
  narrative world   225, 229
narratological theory   4–5, 13
narratology   4, 65, 224
Niketas Eugenianos, author,
    12th century AD   59
Nonnos of Panopolis, poet,
    5th century AD   166
  Dionysiaca   167n31
Northop Frye, literary theorist, 1912–1991   4
novel   3–4, 13, 16, 59–62, 67, 74–75, 221
  ancient novel   3

Oppian, poet, 2nd century AD   166
  Halieutica   166n31
Oxia, ancient location in
    Constantinople   196
    Church of John the Forerunner   203

Palaephatus, author, 4th century BC   63, 70
  On Unbelievable Tales   63, 70
Palladios, author, AD 363–431   16, 29–30,
    196, 204–206, 215, 222
  Lausiac History   16, 29, 108n6, 196,
    204–206, 215, 222
paradoxography   1, 5, 7, 19, 40–56, 59–77,
    159–189
Parthenios of Nicaea, 1st century
    BC–AD 14   67, 70, 73–76, 87–89

Sufferings in Love   70, 73–75
Pascale Casanova, literary critic,
    1959–2018   64, 66
*Passion of Akindynos, Pegasios and
    Anempodistos*   49
Passion of Catherine   55–56
Periplus of the Erythraean Sea   131
Peter Brooks, literary theorist, 1938–   13
Philostratos, philosopher, *c*. AD 170–240   59
Phlegon of Tralles, author,
    2nd century AD   27, 63, 162, 165
  Mirabilia   27, 162
Photios, Patriarch, AD 801–891   1n4, 62
  Library   1n4
Phrygia, ancient city in Turkey   148
Plato
  Euthydemus   92
  Phaedo   92
  Symposium   92
Pliny the Elder, author and philosopher, AD
    23/24–79   59, 77, 132
  Natural History   77, 132
Plutarch of Chaeronea, historian and
    philosopher, *c*. AD 45–*c*.120   84–86, 98
  Moralia   85
  On Talkativeness   84
possible worlds   64–68
Pseudo-Alexander of Aphrodisias, author,
    b. 2nd century–d. 3rd century AD   67–
    69, 74–75
  Allegories   69
  *Medical Puzzles and Natural
    Problems*   68–69
Pseudo-Aristotle   51
Pseudo-Eratosthenes, author,
    1st century AD   70
  Constellations   70

repetition   6, 15, 21–22, 55, 98, 107–128, 172,
    194, 217
  narrative repetition   108
  stylistic repetition   107
rhetorical device   6, 95, 98, 108, 177
rhetorical technique. *See* rhetorical device
Roland Barthes, literary theorist, 1915–
    1980   3, 83n1
Roman Jakobson, linguist, literary
    theorist 1896–1982   14

GENERAL INDEX

243

romance
  medieval romance   3

saint's Life   52, 61
Seleukeia, ancient city in Turkey   181, 196
sermon   196
setting   225
Shapur II, Persian king, AD 309–379   49
short fiction   3–5, 8, 13, 16, 20–21
Silk Road   131
Sophronios of Jerusalem, bishop, *c.* AD
  560–638   15, 30, 164*n*17, 168–170, 173
  Encomium of Kyros and John. See Kyros
    and John, saints
  Miracles of Kyros and John. See Kyros and
    John, saints
source   5, 41–42, 44–49, 56
  acting source   49–53
space   7, 221–222, 224–236
spatial frames   225
story
  short story   3–4, 13
  story space   225, 228–230, 235
story-effect   5, 14, 28–36, 91, 94–97
storyness   5–6, 13–15, 20–28, 35, 91–93,
  95–96
storyteller   5–6, 14–20, 23, 25, 40, 48, 85, 91,
  93, 95, 194–195, 196, 198, 200, 205–206,
  210–212, 215–217, 227
  chosen storyteller   6, 18, 115–121
  combined storytelling   19–20
  holy storyteller   6, 109–115
  repentant storyteller   6, 121–127
  single omnipresent storyteller   19–20,
    48*n*17, 115
  storyteller's profile   107–128
  storytelling chain   19–20, 28, 48*n*17, 109,
    115, 192–193
storyworld   5, 59–77
Strabo, philosopher, geographer, and
  historian, b. 63/64 BC–d. *c.* AD 24   132
  Geography   132
stylistic device   7, 21
suddeness   53–56
Susan Lohafer, literary theorist, 1942–   13,
  20–21
Symeon the Metaphrast, author,
  AD 900–987   135, 138

tale
  (auto)biographical tale   7, 15, 115–119, 122,
    128, 192–218
  beneficial tale   43–44, 108, 221, 226, 228
  didactic tale   6, 83–103
  edifying tale   43, 221
  fairy tale   1, 4, 67
  frame tale   7, 110–112, 122–124, 192, 203,
    211–218
  hagiographical tale   192–218
  macro-tale   96–103
  marvelous tale   7, 22, 70, 192–218
  miracle tale   25, 28, 62, 108, 119, 140,
    147–149, 172
  stand-alone tale   92–96
  supernatural tale   7, 22, 192–218
  tale theory   5, 14, 21, 91
  thauma tale   44–53
technology of enchantment   6, 147–152
thauma   5, 40–56, 162, 165, 188
Thekla, saint   23–25, 32–33, 167, 179–180, 183,
  185–186
  Life of Thekla   115
  Miracles of Thekla   15, 18, 22, 32, 115–121,
    164–165, 167–168, 171–175, 177–186, 188,
    206–211
Theodore Teron, saint
  Encomium of Theodore Teron   164*n*17
  Miracles of Theodore Teron   164*n*17, 168,
    170, 173, 176
Theodoret of Cyrrhus, *c.* AD 393–466   48
  Life of Symeon Stylites   48
Thucidides, historian, 460–*c.*400 BC   61
Tilmann Habermas, psychoanalyst and
  author 1956–   103
Timothy of Alexandria, bishop and author,
  d. AD 384   164*n*17
  Miracles of Menas. See Menas, saint
transfictionality   75–76
treasury   159
Tzvetan Todorov, literary critic, sociologist
  1939–2017   3, 192, 195, 201

Umberto Eco, author, historian, philosopher
  1932–2016   7, 159–160, 163, 165
  La vertigine della lista   7, 159

GENERAL INDEX

Virgil, poet 70–19 BC 166
  Aeneid 166
  Georgics 166
vision 22, 26, 121, 225
Vladimir Propp, literary theorist,
  1895–1970 4

Walter Benjamin, philosopher 1892–1940
  17, 19
Walter Scott, author, 1771–1832 3
wonder, wondrous 5, 36, 41–42, 46, 48–53,
  196–197, 200

Printed in the United States
by Baker & Taylor Publisher Services